The
Portable
English
Handbook

**Third Edition**

# The Portable English Handbook

## An Index to Grammar, Usage, and the Research Paper

**William Herman**
The City College of
The City University of New York

**Holt, Rinehart and Winston**
New York   Chicago   San Francisco
Philadelphia   Montreal   Toronto
London   Sydney   Tokyo   Mexico City
Rio de Janeiro   Madrid

*For my darling daughter Lisa Jane Herman:*
*Some day you too will be a grammar!*

Library of Congress Cataloging in Publication Data

Herman, William, 1926 –
    The portable English handbook.

    Bibliography: p.
    Includes index.
    1. English language — Rhetoric.    2. English language —
Grammar — 1950 –    .    3. English language — Usage.
4. Report writing.    I. Title.
PE1408.H464    1986    808′.042    85-17548

ISBN 0-03-002137-5

CBS COLLEGE PUBLISHING
Holt, Rinehart and Winston
The Dryden Press
Saunders College Publishing

# Preface

The third edition of *The Portable English Handbook* has been revised in response to the experience of users of the second. Thus in Part 2, there are new entries on prewriting and proofreading, revising and editing, and an expanded entry on paragraph development. The Basic Grammar has been simplified and Part 3, The Research Paper, has a new sample research paper whose thesis is argumentative. This section has been brought up to date with the inclusion of the new MLA documentation style, outlined in the 1984 edition of the *MLA Handbook for Writers of Research Papers*. In addition, Part 3 emphasizes the possibilities for student research outside the library in the form of direct investigation by interview, questionnaire, and survey. Still, the book is no longer than previous editions.

As with those previous editions, the overriding purpose guiding the organization of this one has been to make it not only a book that is useful in the classroom but also one that students will be able to use on their own. To achieve this end, the book has five key features: (1) Its index organization makes it *easy* to use. (2) It is complete. (3) It contains many exercises. (4) Its coverage of the research paper is thorough, including an entire model paper. (5) It opens with a thorough and yet concise review of basic grammar.

1. Students will find this book easy to use. For one thing, there is no complicated letter-and-number coding system. Instead, the principal reference section, Part 2 on usage and effective writing, is arranged alphabetically. The Glossary of Usage is also, of course, alphabetical. In addition, Parts 1 and 3 on grammar and the research paper consist of units that progress in a logical teaching and learning order. Also, there are many cross-references throughout the book, and the index and the organizational chart on the inside front and back covers offer further aids to easy access by students.

2. The book is complete. The alphabetical Part 2, "An Index to Usage and the Principles of Effective Writing," contains entries ranging from Abbreviations to Verbs; it concentrates on errors in usage and such important rhetorical matters as Unity, Diction, Coherence, Paragraph Development, and Thesis Statement. This section is conveniently thumb-indexed.

3. The book offers many exercises—"Test Yourself" sections by means of which students can consolidate the gains they make through understanding the text. Virtually every entry in Part 2 contains exercises, and they also appear at critical points in Parts 1 and 3. For immediate student feedback, answers to the first five questions in objective exercises appear in an answer key preceding the index.

4. The book is comprehensive in its treatment of the research paper in Part 3. This section takes the student through a step-by-step approach to writing a research paper. Sample note cards and reference materials are reproduced at the appropriate stages, and the section ends with a *complete* sample research paper.

5. Part I, "A Basic Grammar," gives students a basic grounding in the fundamentals they need to know before they start writing. This opening section is intended to be useful both for teaching in the classroom and for independent student study and review. The section clearly explains words, sentences, clauses, and phrases, in that order, with many examples and exercises along the way.

The book is, as its title denotes, portable—it is no burden to carry around and have handy; this feature is especially important. Finally, I should add that the basic approach to grammar here lays before students only what is essential for their grasp of the writing problems in their own work; I have avoided a top-heavy burden of fine exegesis which could only confuse students and take their attention away from their own writing. I hope, too, that I have written with plain diction and a lively style, so that students will not be led astray by *my* writing.

An *Instructor's Manual* to the text is available. Primarily an answer key to virtually all the exercises, it also includes a list of possible research paper topics. The *Manual* may be obtained through a local Holt representative or by writing to English Editor, College Department, Holt, Rinehart and Winston, 383 Madison Avenue, New York, N.Y. 10017.

For the instructor who wants more exercise material in any particular area of student need, I have prepared and Holt has published *The Portable English Workbook*. Its table of contents is conveniently keyed to *The Portable English Handbook*.

I wish to thank my colleagues in the English Department of the City College, CUNY, for their generous responses to my queries. Special thanks are due Professors Edward Quinn and Arthur Zeiger for reading the manuscript. In addition, the following reviewed the manuscript of the third edition and made constructive comments: Jane Colville Betts, University of Wisconsin — Eau Claire; Commodore Craft, Thornton Community College; Barbara Haxby, Triton College; Robert Noreen, California State University — Northridge; Douglas Pearson, Jr., University of Wisconsin — Eau Claire.

My editors, Charlotte Smith and Charlyce Jones Owen, have done what all good editors do: everything in their power to help me get my work done. As for my wife, Joanna, I could never have done without her mind and heart.

W.H.

# Contents

The
Portable
English
Handbook

PART 1

# A Basic Grammar

# Why Study Grammar?

Grammar need not frighten you.

Grammar is simply a set of rules that describes how we all speak and write. The frightening word here is *rules*, because it makes us think of penalties for doing something wrong. But it need not. There are all kinds of rules, some of which we don't know are operating, and most of which we fall easily into obeying. For example, you understand what these words you are now reading are saying. The reason for this is that you are obeying the grammatical rules *you* already know.

For all of us, this understanding of some grammatical rules is unconscious, long ago learned and incorporated into our mental processes. The purpose of studying grammar here is to make more of these rules conscious and to do so for a number of very good reasons.

For one thing, grammar is interesting. Language is fascinating when you come to understand that its grammar is a remarkably coherent piece of human knowledge and that most human activities would be impossible without the subtle riches of linguistic communication. More important, however, the study of basic grammar can help you to improve your writing by reminding you of how it works. For example, if you know that a verb must agree with its subject, you are less likely to write "The humor and personal concern of Mr. Jones, my sociology professor, *is* what I like best about the course." Moreover, knowing grammatical terms can help you discuss your writing with instructors trying to make it more effective. If an instructor suggests that you *use subordinate clauses for subordinate ideas*, the suggestion will not get through to you if you do not know a clause from a hammock.

In Part 2 of this book, "An Index to Usage and the Principles of Effective Writing," you will find many suggestions for improving your writing. In order to use that index intelligently, you will need to understand the basic grammar we are about to discuss. We begin here with words and sentences, then go on to clauses and phrases.

# Words

Words have been traditionally placed into classes called *parts of speech* according to their forms and the ways in which they communicate meaning in sentences.

Before we begin to study the characteristic features of these classes, it is important to point out that some words can fall into more than one class, depending on how they are used in the sentence. For example, consider this group of sentences:

> The *light* is hurting my eyes.
>
> Let's *light* the Christmas tree.
>
> Kathy has a *light* complexion.
>
> She wore a *light* brown dress.

If your native language is English, you can make out the different meanings of these sentences quite easily. The fact that you *can* make out the different meanings is partly due to your ability to understand the word *light* in a different way in each sentence. In other words, in each sentence you are identifying *light* as a member of a different class, because in each sentence *light* has a different function.

You should be aware that hundreds of words can behave the way *light* does in those four sentences. Good dictionaries always define such words according to each of the various ways in which they can be used, and as we go along you will be able to see the logical processes governing the classification of these words. But you need to know the characteristic features of the various classes.

## Nouns

A noun is a word used to name something: a person, a place, an object, an idea. Words like *apple, car, table,* and *freedom* are nouns. The following features of nouns will help you identify them:

**1** Nouns can be made into plurals, usually by adding *-s* or *-es*.

cars    peaches    taxes

**2** Nouns can be made into possessives, usually by adding an apostrophe and *-s*.

*Danny's* shoes

*Democracy's* advantages

a *car's* engine

**3** Nouns can be preceded by words like *a, an, the, my, each, this, that,* or even another possessive noun. When you see such a word, you know a noun is coming.

*a* horse

*this* chicken

*Saul's* computer

**4** Nouns fit into the noun position in a sentence.

The _____ is beautiful.        The *house* is beautiful.
I bought a _____.        I bought a *car*.
I fought with my _____.        I fought with my *brother*.

**5** Some nouns are formed by adding suffixes (characteristic word endings) either to other nouns or to other parts of speech.

mile + *age* = mileage

deny + *al* = denial

young + *ster* = youngster

## TEST YOURSELF ON
## Identifying Nouns

Circle the nouns in each of the following word groups.

1. An American elephant.

2. The blue notebook.

3. I saw the light.

4. Cheese is available in Wisconsin.

5. The Trail Blazers are a good team.

6. Alligators are fond of dating crocodiles.

7. I have a boat on the lake.

8. A message from my nose to my brain tells me it's spring.

9. I am going to invite Republicans to my party.

10. The fire is blazing in the fireplace.

## Verbs

A verb is used to describe an action or a state of being.

> Karl *plays* basketball. (describes action)
>
> Karl *is* tall. (describes a state of being)

To be a sentence, a group of words must include at least one verb. Here are the features of verbs that will help you identify them and understand their functions:

**1** Verbs can be single words *(sings, touched)* or they can consist of several words in a *verb phrase (has gone, will be working, might have been murdered)*. *Has, will, might, have, be,* and *been* are called *auxiliary* or *helping verbs*. See pages 10–11 for more information about auxiliaries.

**2** Verbs can change form to indicate a change of time. When verbs change form this way we say that they have changed *tense*.

> Alice *is walking* to the movies.
>
> Alice *walked* to the movies.

The word in the sentence that can be changed to indicate a change of time — that's the verb.

**3** Verbs have certain persistent forms. Nearly all have an *-ing* form (runn*ing*, jump*ing*). All third-person-singular present-tense verbs in the indicative mood end in the letter *-s* (pushe*s*, live*s*, grow*s*). Many verbs form their past tenses by adding *-d* or *-ed*.

**4** Verbs in ordinary use always follow the subject in the sentence.

George *drives* a car. (George is the subject.)

Spring *came* early this year. (Spring is the subject.)

## Identifying Verbs

Circle the verbs in the following sentences. Keep in mind the features of verbs you have just read about.

1. Betsy plays the piano.

2. A civil engineer earns a good salary.

3. My sister is jumping rope.

4. Sally waited in the rain for an hour.

5. She trusted Jean to show up.

6. I called at her apartment, but she had left.

7. The mail will be late today.

8. Mom has given Dad perfect instructions on how to use the camera.

9. The Dean told her that she would graduate with the rest of her class.

10. I am curious about the history of slavery in this country.

## Identifying Verbs by Changing Tenses

Identify the verbs in the following sentences by changing their tenses.

*Example:* Tom *played* basketball for his college team.
Tom *plays* basketball for his college team.
*Verb: played.*

1. Tom played basketball for his college team.

2. George passes his examination easily.

3. The apples were delicious.

4. Your help makes a lot of difference to me.

5. He seemed unhappy.

6. In fact, Arthur works for his father.

7. She will be happy with his birthday present.

8. Frank understood the lesson.

9. The piano piece will end the program.

10. She has taken her father's car to school.

11. We will sit at different tables.

12. He has taken a vacation.

---

**5**  Verbs can be either *linking verbs* or *action verbs*. All forms of the verb *be* and such other verbs as *seem, appear, become,* and *feel* are *linking* verbs. They link together the subject of a sentence with another word describing the state of being of that subject.

Frank *felt* anxious.

You *are* beautiful.

Uncle Al *seemed* quiet.

Fred *is* a dancer.

*Action* verbs, on the other hand, describe action. They are either *transitive* or *intransitive*, depending on whether they act on something or not. When a verb is transitive, it acts on something, which is called the *direct object* of the verb.

Gravity *moves* the *planets*. (*Planets* is acted on by *moves*.)

Women *date men*. (*Men* is acted on by *women*.)

*An intransitive* verb also describes action, but it does not act upon an object. It describes an action performed *by* the subject that also applies *to* the subject and to nothing else.

Lila *dresses* stylishly.

Patricia *sat* down.

Some verbs can be used transitively in one sentence and intransitively in another.

> Charley *works* hard. *(intransitive)*
>
> Charley *works* the tractor. *(transitive)*

**6** Verbs have a property called *voice.* When the verb is in the *active* voice, the subject performs the action. When the verb is in the *passive* voice, the subject receives the action.

> John *ate* a rabbit. (The rabbit went into John's stomach.)
>
> John *was eaten* by a rabbit. (John went into the rabbit's stomach.)

**7** Verbs also have a feature called *mood,* to indicate the manner or mode in which they are used. The *indicative* mood is used for ordinary statements of fact and questions, the *imperative* for issuing commands or giving directions, and the *subjunctive* for statements that are contrary to fact or that express potential or possibility.

> I *gave* him five dollars. (indicative — statement of fact)
>
> Can you *give* me a lift? (indicative — ordinary question)
>
> *Give* me five dollars. (imperative — a command)
>
> *Turn* left at the overpass. (imperative — a direction)
>
> If I *were* a millionaire, I'd be happy. (subjunctive — contrary to fact)

## TEST YOURSELF ON
## Identifying Types of Verbs

Circle all the verbs you can find in the following sentences. Above each circle, write T if the verb is transitive, I if the verb is intransitive, and L if the verb is a linking verb.

1. I feel wealthy.

2. Charley smokes too much.

3. He is riding his motorcycle.

4. My father plays golf every Sunday.

5. The bomb exploded.

6. Willie loves hats.

7. My brother needs a job.

8. Lawyers are officers of the court.

9. Judges make rulings.

10. My wife is very slender.

11. Jane played the piano.

12. Students read all day long.

## Auxiliaries

An *auxiliary* verb is also called a *helping* verb. Frequently, auxiliaries signal a reader that a verb is coming. *Is, did, have, was, can, may, would*, and *had* are all examples of auxiliaries.

The following features of auxiliaries will help you understand their form and functions:

**1** Auxiliaries have different meanings and change the meanings of the verbs they couple with in various ways. For example, they indicate time and therefore change tense.

He *is* playing.      He *was* playing.

A subgroup of auxiliaries called *modals (should, would, could, can, may, might, must, ought to, have to, shall, will)* add meanings that suggest possibility, ability, obligation, and so forth.

He *can* play.      He *should* play.      He *must* play.

Notice that this group of auxiliaries is always used with the present tense stem of the verb.

**2** Auxiliaries are widely used in asking questions.

*Did* you go?

*Must* you go?

*Can* you go?

**3** The auxiliary that always appears with verbs ending in *-ing* is the verb *be*, in any of its forms:

He *is* playing.

I *was* playing.

He *has been* playing.

They *will be* playing.

**4** Only two auxiliaries, *be* and *have*, are used with past verb forms such as *known, played, gone, remembered*.

I *am remembered*.     She *has gone*.     It *has been known*.

## TEST YOURSELF ON
## Identifying Auxiliaries

Place the proper auxiliary into each of the blank spaces in the following sentences.

1. You _____ visit your sick friend.

2. We _____ need some milk for our coffee.

3. He _____ planning to take a course in physics.

4. He says they _____ trying to climb the rocks.

5. When _____ you take the exam?

6. She _____ gone to the hairdresser's.

7. _____ you continue playing the piano?

8. _____ he see what we _____ doing with the fish?

9. He _____ decided to find out if they _____ taken.

10. He _____ laughing and we _____ crying but nobody

_____ paying attention.

## Adjectives

Adjectives modify nouns, making them more specific. A hamburger is good, but if we call it a *juicy* hamburger, we have said more about it. The following important features of adjectives will help you identify them and understand their functions:

**1** Adjectives can be changed in form to compare two or more objects. The *comparative* form can be made by adding the ending *-er* to the basic adjective (called the *positive* form). The *superlative* can be formed by adding the ending *-est* to the positive form.

| Positive | Comparative | Superlative |
|----------|-------------|-------------|
| happy | happier | happiest |
| young | younger | youngest |

However, some adjectives form the comparative and superlative by adding the words *more* and *most*.

| Positive | Comparative | Superlative |
|----------|-------------|-------------|
| beautiful | more beautiful | most beautiful |
| honest | more honest | most honest |
| recent | more recent | most recent |

Also, some adjectives form the comparative and superlative irregularly.

| Positive | Comparative | Superlative |
|----------|-------------|-------------|
| good | better | best |
| bad | worse | worst |
| many | more | most |

The comparative form is used to compare two objects.

He is *happier* than I am.

Her cat is *more beautiful* than mine.

My cold is *worse* today. (i.e., "than it was yesterday")

The superlative form is used to compare more than two objects.

I am the *happiest* man in the whole world.

Here is the *most beautiful* hat I've seen.

He is the *best* player on the team.

**2**   Adjectives in a sentence appear after a linking verb or before a noun.

He was *happy.*     A very *happy* girl arrived.

**3**   Many adjectives have characteristic endings that can help you identify them. Here are a few:

-al (international)

-ant, -ent (resistant, excellent)

-able, -ible (affable, irresistible)
-ar, -ary (solar, ordinary)
-ive (attentive)
-ous (generous)
-y (funny)
-ish (foolish)

For more information on adjectives, see **Modifiers** and **Dangling Modifiers** in Part 2.

## TEST YOURSELF ON
## Identifying Adjectives

Identify all the adjectives you find in the following sentences.

1. My computer has a better memory than yours.

2. She seems courageous.

3. My father was kind to my mother.

4. He made her happier than she had ever been.

5. It is childish to be greedy.

6. The engine on this car is lively, but the body looks old.

7. She was athletic, girlish, and sensitive.

8. The greatest football player I ever saw was Eric Dickerson.

9. That's a funny costume!

10. I get nervous when I have to take an exam.

## Adverbs

Adverbs modify verbs, adjectives, other adverbs, and whole sentences.

Old people *often* sit. (modifies the verb *sit*)
She was *rarely* unhappy. (modifies the adjective *unhappy*)

I ate *too* quickly. (modifies the adverb *quickly*)

*Unfortunately*, we can't have a vacation this year. (modifies the whole sentence)

The following important features of adverbs will help you identify them and understand their functions:

**1**    A few adverbs, like adjectives, can change form to compare degrees or qualities by adding the endings *-er* and *-est*.

| *Positive* | *Comparative* | *Superlative* |
|---|---|---|
| soon | sooner | soonest |
| quick | quicker | quickest |

However, most adverbs form the comparative and superlative by adding the words *more* and *most*.

| *Positive* | *Comparative* | *Superlative* |
|---|---|---|
| often | more often | most often |
| rapidly | more rapidly | most rapidly |

A few adverbs form the comparative and superlative irregularly.

| *Positive* | *Comparative* | *Superlative* |
|---|---|---|
| badly | worse | worst |
| well | better | best |

**2**    Adverbs can often be moved from one position in the sentence to another without changing the meaning of the sentence. This is in contrast to adjectives, which must remain relatively fixed if the sentence is to make sense.

| *Adverbs* | *Adjectives* |
|---|---|
| *Often* she was lucky. | *Lucky* she was often. |
| She *often* was lucky. | She *lucky* was often. |
| She was *often* lucky. | She was *lucky* often. |
| She was lucky *often*. | She was often *lucky*. |

You can see that all the sentences under *Adverbs* make sense even though in each the word *often* is in a different position. On the other hand, only the last two sentences under *Adjectives* make sense.

However, not all adverbs are as movable as *often*. For more on how to control the placement of adverbs, see **Misplaced Modifiers** and **Dangling Modifiers** in Part 2.

**3**  Adverbs frequently end in the suffix *-ly*, and many adverbs are formed by adding this suffix to an adjective.

**Adjective + -ly = Adverb**

| | |
|---|---|
| rapid | rapidly |
| sweet | sweetly |
| brave | bravely |

The difficulty is that not all words ending in *-ly* are adverbs. Some nouns add *-ly* to form *adjectives*.* There are not many of these, but they are important. Here are a few:

**Noun + -ly = Adjective**

| | |
|---|---|
| beast | beastly |
| father | fatherly |
| love | lovely |
| saint | saintly |

## TEST YOURSELF ON
## Identifying Adverbs

Take this test by changing the conditions indicated in each of the sentences below. That is, change the manner *(rapidly* to *slowly)*, the time *(now* to *then)*, or the place or direction *(here* to *there*, *up* to *down)*. The word you change is the adverb.

*Example:*  Gilda walked *slowly* into the lion's cage.
     Gilda walked *quickly* into the lion's cage.

1. Gilda walked slowly into the lion's cage.

2. She drove in.

3. He went up.

4. He put the apple here.

5. He answered the question sweetly.

6. She is often absent.

7. He did his homework sloppily.

8. She lived upstairs.

---

* Some adjectives ending in *-ly* are *not* formed from nouns, e.g., *unsightly* and *unlikely*.

9. He is never happy.

10. She walked over.

## Prepositions

A preposition connects a noun or a pronoun with other parts of the sentence.

> The man *in* the truck drove away. (connects *man* and *truck*)
>
> She passed him *by*. (connects *passed* and *him*)

A preposition forms a prepositional phrase when it is followed by a noun, with or without a small word (such as *the*) in between.

> *in* the truck    *to* California    *at* the movies

In these phrases, we would call the word *truck* or *California* or *movies* the *object of the preposition* — the word that the preposition connects to the rest of the sentence. (More on the prepositional phrase will be found on pages 33–37.)

Prepositions usually denote direction or position, as you can see from this list:

| | | | |
|---|---|---|---|
| aboard | behind | from | through |
| about | below | in | throughout |
| above | beneath | inside | till |
| across | beside | into | to |
| after | besides | like | toward |
| against | between | near | under |
| along | beyond | of | until |
| alongside | by | off | up |
| amid | concerning | on | upon |
| among | despite | onto | with |
| around | down | over | within |
| at | during | since | without |
| before | for | | |

In addition to these, there are a number of prepositions in English that consist of more than one word. Here are some:

| | | |
|---|---|---|
| according to | by way of | in spite of |
| ahead of | contrary to | in view of |
| apart from | due to | instead of |

| as for | in addition to | on account of |
| as well as | in back of | out of |
| away from | in case of | up to |
| because of | in front of | |
| by means of | in place of | |

All the words in the first list *may* be used as prepositions. Some words on the list — *during, among, with,* and others — are regularly prepositions, but most of the words are also used as other parts of speech. For example, you may recall that the words *in, over,* and *by* were adverbs when used in the following ways:

He drove *in.*

He drove *over.*

He drove *by.*

But the same words are prepositions when used in these ways:

He drove *in* the truck.

He drove *over* the bridge.

He drove *by* the house.

Prepositions occupy certain typical positions in sentences. Notice the positions occupied by the prepositions italicized in the following sentences:

The house *across* the road is mine.

The name *on* the door is my father's.

He wrote an essay *on* Shakespeare.

He was carrying a bag *of* potatoes.

He went *to* his class.

He lived *in* my building.

Notice that there is nearly always a small word *(the, his, my)* between the preposition and the following noun to form what we call a prepositional phrase (see p. 33 for more on this structure).

## TEST YOURSELF ON
## Using Prepositions

Using the following list of nouns, select twenty of the prepositions listed above and make prepositional phrases by using a small word *(the, a, my, his, her, your,* and the like) where appropriate.

**Nouns**

| | | |
|---|---|---|
| farm | tomato | day |
| apple | pizza | camp |
| newspaper | chopsticks | lake |
| automobile | burglary | room |
| ferry | television set | cage |
| chair | stadium | planet |
| horse | football field | |

*Example:* beyond our lake

## Conjunctions

Conjunctions are words that act to join together words, groups of words, or whole sentences. Different conjunctions do different jobs, and there are three different classes of them to consider.

### 1   Coordinating Conjunctions

This group consists of the seven words *and, or, but, yet, for, nor,* and *so.* All are commonly used to join together two independent clauses (see pp. 29 – 31), while suggesting a relationship between them.

> He was poor, *but* he felt rich in spirit. (suggests an unexpected contrast)

> He was happy, *for* he had passed his exams. (suggests cause)

*Note:* The punctuation of such sentences is important. You will find more on the subject in Part 2 under **Comma Rules.**

*But* and *yet* are frequently used to join pairs of adjectives in suggesting unexpected contrast.

> He was angry *yet* calm.

> He was aggressive *but* gentle.

In addition to the coordinating conjunctions, there are four pairs of *correlatives: both . . . and, not only . . . but also, either . . . or,* and *neither . . . nor.*

> *Both* apples *and* peaches are delicious.

> *Not only* apples *but also* peaches are delicious.

> He was *either* young *or* inexperienced.

> He was *neither* young *nor* inexperienced.

## 2   Conjunctive Adverbs

Conjunctive adverbs are a group of words used to connect sentences; they act in a sentence like the word *therefore*.

> The school year was over; *therefore*, he decided to take a long vacation.
>
> The children were playing in the yard; *therefore*, he took a nap.

The following words are commonly used as conjunctive adverbs:

| | | | |
|---|---|---|---|
| besides | hence | indeed | subsequently |
| consequently | however | moreover | therefore |
| furthermore | in fact | nevertheless | thus |

> He ate the whole pie himself; *furthermore*, he was not sorry.
>
> He ate the whole pie himself; *moreover*, he was not sorry.
>
> He ate the whole pie himself; *nevertheless*, he was not sorry.

Note that conjunctive adverbs can change position in the sentence and still act as connectors.

> The clock struck twelve; *therefore*, Eddie got ready to leave.
>
> The clock struck twelve; Eddie, *therefore*, got ready to leave.
>
> The clock struck twelve; Eddie got ready to leave, *therefore*.

Note too that when words like *and* join two sentences together, they are preceded by a comma; when words like *therefore* join two sentences together, they are preceded by a semicolon or a period and followed by a comma. (For more detailed information on punctuating with conjunctive adverbs, see **Comma Rules, Fragments,** and **Semicolon** in Part 2.)

## 3   Subordinating Conjunctions

Subordinating conjunctions are words used to join a word or a word group to a sentence by subordinating that word or word group — by making it less important.

> Writer A says: *Although John doesn't sing well,* he is a member of the church choir.
>
> Writer B says: *Although he is a member of the church choir,* John doesn't sing well.

Writer A is emphasizing one kind of disparity and Writer B another. Each is modifying his main declaration — the part of each writer's sentence that follows the comma—in a different way. Each has therefore *subordinated* a different idea by introducing it with a subordinating conjunction.

It's important to note that the subordinated portion can begin or end the sentence.

> John doesn't sing well *although he is a member of the church choir.*
>
> *Although he is a member of the church choir,* John doesn't sing well.

Subordinating conjunctions generally act like the word *although*. Depending on the meaning you want to convey, you can use any of the following words as subordinating conjunctions:

| | | |
|---|---|---|
| after | provided | whatever |
| although | since | when |
| as | that | whenever |
| because | though | where |
| before | unless | wherever |
| if | until | whether |
| lest | what | while |

## TEST YOURSELF ON
## Using Conjunctions

1. Write ten sentences in which a coordinating conjunction joins two sentences. Try to use each of the seven coordinating conjunctions at least once.
2. Write eight sentences in which you use each pair of correlatives at least once.
3. Write a dozen sentences in which you use each of the conjunctive adverbs on page 19 at least once.
4. Take the sentences you just wrote and change the position of the conjunctive adverb in each sentence.
5. In how many of the sentences that you have written in response to exercise 3 can you substitute a coordinating conjunction for a conjunctive adverb? Try the substitution and find out.

## Pronouns

Pronouns are words that can replace nouns. Such words as *he, she, him, them, somebody, mine,* and *this* are all pronouns. An important word associated with pronouns is *antecedent.* Consider these examples:

> I just saw *Alice. She* seems fine.
>
> *Richard* put *his* money into real estate.

In the first example we say that the word *Alice* is the antecedent of the pronoun *she.* In the second example we say that the word *Richard* is the antecedent of the pronoun *his.*

Not all pronouns have antecedents in all cases, but you will want to keep the term in mind and be sure that pronouns agree with their antecedents in your writing. For more details on this subject, see **Pronoun References** in Part 2.

All pronouns can occupy some of the typical noun positions in sentences, although not all can occupy every noun position.

### Sentence with a Noun
The *man* is over there.

### Pronouns Substituted for the Noun
*He* is over there.

*Mine* is over there.

*Somebody* is over there.

*Neither* is over there.

### Sentence with a Noun
I know the *man.*

### Pronouns Substituted for the Noun
I know *him.*

I know *hers.*

I know *somebody.*

I know *neither.*

Here are the chief kinds of pronouns and the names they are known by:

### 1 Personal Pronouns

| | | |
|-----|-----|-------------|
| I   | me  | my, mine    |
| you | you | your, yours |
| he  | him | his         |
| she | her | her, hers   |
| it  | it  | its         |

| we | us | our, ours |
| they | them | their, theirs |

### 2 Reflexive Pronouns

| myself | ourselves |
| yourself | yourselves |
| himself | themselves |
| herself | |
| itself | |

### 3 Relative Pronouns

| who | which |
| whose | that |
| whom | |

Relative pronouns are used to connect a subordinate word group to another part of the sentence.

> John, *who* sings well, is a member of the church choir.

> The foreign country *that* I like best is Italy.

The antecedent of *who* in the first example is *John,* and the antecedent of *that* in the second example is *country.*

Sometimes a relative pronoun is omitted but understood in a sentence.

> The car [that] I liked was a Toyota.

### 4 Interrogative Pronouns

| who | which |
| whom | what |

Interrogative pronouns are used to ask questions.

> *Who* is your friend?

> *Which* would you like?

> *What* did you say?

### 5 Demonstrative Pronouns

| this | these |
| that | those |

Demonstrative pronouns act to *point* to a noun, but they may also be used by themselves.

> *This* hat is mine. (pointing to a noun)
>
> *This* is mine. (as a pronoun)

### 6   Indefinite Pronouns

Common indefinite pronouns are the following:

| | | |
|---|---|---|
| one | somebody | all |
| no one | other | few |
| anyone | another | either |
| everyone | anything | neither |
| someone | everything | none |
| anybody | something | most |
| everybody | nothing | more |
| nobody | | |

### 7   Reciprocal Pronouns

each other
one another

## TEST YOURSELF ON
## Using Pronouns

**A**   Use each of the following words in two sentences.

| | | | |
|---|---|---|---|
| 1. many | 3. that | 5. either | 7. all |
| 2. his | 4. few | 6. several | 8. three |

**B**   Replace each of the italicized words in the sentences below with a pronoun. In some cases you will have to drop a few words from the sentence.

*Example:* My old *grandmother* needs false teeth.
    *She* needs false teeth.

1. My old *grandmother* needs false teeth.

2. My old grandmother needs false *teeth*.

3. My *boss* complained to me.

4. *People* are funny.

5. *Congressmen* are politicians.

6. No *lakes* can ever be emptied.

**C**   Underline all the pronouns you can find in the following sentences. Some sentences have more than one.

1. His shoes are brown.

2. Mine are black.

3. Everybody knows something.

4. You should be honest with yourself.

5. My brother wanted him to be nice to everyone.

6. Anyone can tell that you have a sunburn.

7. Students are friendly to one another.

8. Nothing bothers me when I myself am driving.

9. She put herself in his position.

10. Much will be gained and nothing lost if you go swimming with us this afternoon.

11. Neither will be enough.

12. Several will be fine.

## Sentences

Now that we have discussed words, we must begin to consider sentences. Sentences can be commands or directions on how to do something or go somewhere (imperative sentences):

> Turn on the lights. Make a left turn.

Or they can be questions (interrogative sentences):

> Who are you?

Or they can be statements (declarative sentences):

I saw Uncle Bud this morning.

In this section, we will be concerned mainly with sentences that are statements.

## Basic Sentence Facts

**1** Every sentence can be divided into two parts because every sentence accomplishes two things: (1) It names something (an object, an idea, a person, a place), and (2) it says something about what it has just named.

| *Part 1* *(What Is Named)* | *Part 2* *(What Is Said About It)* |
|---|---|
| Dogs | bark. |
| Birds | are beautiful. |
| Babies | drink milk. |

The thing named we call the *subject* of the sentence; what is said about the subject we call the *predicate*.

In a sentence like *The large, tropical birds are beautiful* we say that the *complete subject* is *the large, tropical birds* but that the *simple subject* is *birds*. The simple subject *birds* is the thing about which something is being said. The complete subject, *the large, tropical birds, includes* the simple subject and other words that describe it more exactly. A complete subject can also look like this: *the birds in the trees,* where *birds* is the simple subject.

**2** Every predicate contains at least one verb. A single verb may contain several words, also called a *verb phrase* (examples: *has been married, should be married* ). A sentence can never have only an *-ing* verb.

**3** To find the subject of a sentence, first find the verb. You can do this by locating the word in the sentence that denotes action or a state of being, the word that can change tense.

George *feels* good.     George *felt* good.

Clearly, *feel* is the verb because it changes tense. Now if we ask the question *who* (or in some sentences *what*) *feels,* and refer to the sentence for our answer, we must reply *George*. And *George* is the subject.

In the sentence *George and Frank traveled to Europe together*, the verb is *traveled*. When we ask *who traveled*, we get the answer *George and Frank*. Sentences like this one, therefore, are said to have a *compound subject*. A compound subject has more than one part.

## TEST YOURSELF ON
## Locating Subjects of Sentences

**A**   In each of the following sentences, underline the subject. To find the subject, first locate the verb — the word that denotes action or a state of being and that can change tense. Then ask the question *who* or *what* (of the verb). The answer will be the subject.

1. Whiskey burns my tongue.

2. She is beautiful.

3. My father is a policeman.

4. Hot dogs taste good sometimes.

5. Parents sometimes scold their children.

6. The truckdriver and his helper quit early.

7. Misery loves company.

8. You and your brother look happy.

9. The pipe blows bubbles.

10. Everybody seemed sad.

**B**   In the following sentences, underline the complete subject, and circle the simple subject.

*Example:*  Big, friendly (bears) live in the woods.

1. The charming English teacher gave us an assignment.

2. The man in the blue suit looked sinister.

3. The beautiful old woman was fascinating.

4. Sensible young people think ideals are as important as material wealth.

5. My mother's old college roommate came to town.

## Basic Sentence Parts

Depending upon the kind of verb in the sentence — transitive verb or linking verb — we can conveniently identify the following basic parts:

### 1   Predicate Noun and Predicate Adjective

A predicate noun or predicate adjective completes the sense of a linking verb, suggesting an equivalence between the subject and the predicate noun or predicate adjective.

> My mother is a *police officer.* (subject + linking verb + *predicate noun*)
>
> Allan is *friendly.* (subject + linking verb + *predicate adjective*)

*My mother is* what*?* and *Allan is* what*?* are the questions to ask to locate the predicate adjective or predicate noun.

### 2   Direct Object and Indirect Object

Direct and indirect objects occur with action verbs. The direct object is the part of the sentence that *receives* the action of the verb. Consider this sentence:

> George threw the ball.

*Threw* is the verb (it denotes action and can change tense). Who threw? *George,* the subject. George threw what? The ball — so *ball* is the direct object of the verb.

The italicized portions of the following sentences are all direct objects:

> Mechanics repair *automobiles.* (Automobiles are repaired.)
>
> My uncle lent me his *car.* (The car was lent.)
>
> The professor taught his students *biology.* (Biology was taught.)

Now for the sake of keeping in practice, locate the verb and the subject of each of these sentences. Using the who-what method we've been discussing.

The indirect object is the person or thing in the sentence *to* or *for whom* the action is performed.

My brother gave his friend a camera.

The action performed in the sentence is the brother giving the camera. *Camera* is the direct object. It was *given*. *To whom?* to his friend. *Friend* is the indirect object.

**3** **Object Complement (Noun or Adjective)**

The object complement completes the meaning of the direct object by identifying it more exactly. A noun can do this; so can an adjective.

subj.    verb     dir. obj.    obj. comp., noun
We considered the cowboy a hero.

subj.    verb     dir. obj.    obj. comp., adj.
We considered the cowboy foolish.

## TEST YOURSELF ON
# Identifying Basic Sentence Parts

**A** Underline the simple subjects of the following sentences once and the predicates twice.

1. My mother is a good cook.

2. We elected Jim our spokesman.

3. He had an idea.

4. Everybody likes ice cream.

5. Some do not.

6. Sally taught her sons arithmetic.

7. All Washington politicians are the same.

8. Your friendly local shopkeeper is really a small businessman.

9. Unknown composers often write famous songs.

10. He gave me his heart for Christmas.

11. That movie made my friends angry.

12. The big grey clouds are drifting slowly.

13. Summers are too long.

14. The boys considered the girls intelligent.

**B** Describe each word of the predicates you underlined in A by writing above each word VL (for linking verb), VT (for transitive verb), VI (for intransitive verb), PA (for predicate adjective), PN (for predicate noun), DO (for direct object), IO (for indirect object), OCN (for an object complement that is a noun) and OCA (for an object complement that is an adjective).

# Clauses and Phrases

Clauses and phrases are groups of words. Sentences are frequently made up of phrases and clauses.

## Clauses

A clause is a group of words having both a subject and a verb. A clause can be either *independent* or *dependent*. Another word for *dependent* is *subordinate*. Another word for an *independent clause* is a *sentence*.

Independent Clause/Sentence = Subject + Verb = Can Stand
Alone

Dependent/Subordinate Clause = Subject + Verb = Cannot Stand
Alone

Dependent clauses can act as parts of sentences, as adjectives, adverbs, and nouns.

### 1  Adjective Clauses

Cats are animals *that can scratch.*

The italicized portion of the sentence is an adjective clause. It is a clause because it has a subject, *that*, and a verb, *can scratch*. It is dependent because it cannot stand alone. The word *that* makes it dependent on being hooked to something else — a noun (in this case *animals*), which it modifies. It is, therefore, an adjective clause.

An adjective clause can modify a noun regardless of where the noun appears in the sentence.

> Chairs *that are covered in velvet* look elegant. (modifies *chairs*)

Three points about adjective clauses are worth noting here:

**A**   We usually make this distinction in using *who* and *which:* When the noun being modified refers to a person, we use *who;* when it does not, we use *which.* But we often use *that* instead of either one.

> The doctor *who* (or *that*) treats me is a graduate of Mount Sinai Medical School.

> The law *which* (or *that*) was passed in 1964 prohibits discrimination in housing.

**B**   Frequently, in both speech and writing, we use adjective clauses but omit the subordinating conjunction.

> The girl ~~that~~ I'm dating lives in Mill Valley.

**C**   Sometimes a *which* clause can modify a whole sentence —not just a single noun in it.

> It was a great party, *which everyone agreed was a pleasant change for a Saturday night at Harry's.*

### 2   Adverb Clauses

> Babies drink milk *when they are hungry.*

The italicized group of words is an adverb clause. It modifies the word *drink* by answering the question, *When* do babies drink milk? They don't drink it all the time, only *when they are hungry.* The adverb clause differs from the adjective clause in two ways: (1) Its connecting word (*when,* in this case) is not part of the clause but stands at the beginning of it; (2) it can be moved around in the sentence and still do its job.

> Babies drink milk *when they are hungry.*
>
> *When they are hungry,* babies drink milk.

Adverb clauses begin with one of the subordinating conjunctions listed on page 20 (words like *whenever, although, if, until, unless,* and so forth).

**3** Noun Clauses

*What I am eating* tastes good.

The italicized group of words is a noun clause. Occupying the place of a noun, it is the subject of the sentence. You can test to see if this is true by asking the question: *What* tastes good? The only satisfactory answer is *what I am eating*. Therefore, the clause is the subject. But the noun clause can also occur in most of the other positions typically occupied by nouns (that is, as predicate noun, as direct object, or in the position of a noun in a prepositional phrase).

That is *what I am eating.* (predicate noun)

I love *what I am eating.* (direct object)

I am satisfied *with what I am eating.* (object of a preposition)

Noun clauses are very commonly signaled by words like *whoever*, *whatever*, and *what*.

I can supply *what you need.*

*Whoever runs* will be short of breath.

*Whatever needs fixing* can go to the repair shop.

## TEST YOURSELF ON
# Clauses

**A** Using the word *who, whom, which,* or *that,* construct a clause that modifies each word or group of words below.

*Example:* money
money *that I spent yesterday*

1. money

2. people

3. little boys

4. apples

5. laws

6. women

**B** Using a word such as *although, unless, because,* or any of those listed on p. 20, construct a clause to go with each of the following simple sentences.

*Example:* The Scholarship Fund gave me what I asked for.
*Although my grades weren't as good this year as they were in
1985,* the Scholarship Fund gave me what I asked for.

1. The Scholarship Fund gave me what I asked for.

2. It has hair on it.

3. Onions give me indigestion.

4. I can see my brother.

5. Parades make me nervous.

6. The office was empty.

**C**   Underline the clause in each of the following sentences and
above each write ADV if the clause is acting as an adverb, N if it is
acting as a noun, or ADJ if it is acting as an adjective.

1. What I want for supper is fish.

2. Until you come home, I have to babysit for our little brother.

3. The car that pleases me most gives good gas mileage.

4. Whatever you do is all right.

5. The man whom I pointed out is my uncle.

6. I don't know what will happen next.

7. Although I came early, the show was sold out.

8. I am disappointed because my grades were not higher this
term.

9. The basketball court that is in the gym is occupied day and
night.

10. The thing that hurts most is indifference.

**D**   Below are printed ten sentences. Part of each sentence is in
*italics.* Place an I over the part that is independent, a D over the part
that is dependent. After that, decide whether the clauses marked
with a D are adjective, adverb, or noun clauses; label each as ADJ,
ADV, or N.

1. *The man* that was here yesterday *was Judy's father.*

2. *Although I never went past the tenth grade,* I can write pretty well.

3. Whenever you cross the yellow line at the center of the road, *you're in danger.*

4. *Whoever asks* should be directed to the Administration Building.

5. I can guess *what you're thinking.*

6. The doctor *whom I saw* said I'd recover in a week.

7. *The tractor,* which I bought last year, *is in terrible shape.*

8. You'd better look *before you leap.*

9. I'll wait for you *until nine o'clock.*

10. Because he was late getting up, *he missed the bus.*

---

## Phrases

A phrase is a group of words having neither a subject nor a verb. Phrases can be used as adjectives, adverbs, and nouns.

### 1  Phrases Used as Adjectives

The man *in the blue suit* spoke quietly.

The birds *flying toward the barn* are beautiful.

My father was a man *known for his kindness.*

I need shoes *to wear to the wedding.*

The italicized part of each example is a phrase being used as an adjective. By function, each is an adjective phrase in the sentence. However, it is convenient to learn to recognize adjective phrases by what they look like — that is, by the first word (or headword) of the group.

The italicized phrase in the first sentence is a *prepositional phrase* because its headword *in* is a preposition and it looks like the prepositional phrases we spoke of on pages 16–17. The second phrase is a *participial phrase* because it begins with a present participle, *flying*. The third is also a participial phrase because it begins with the past participle *known*. The fourth is an *infinitive phrase* because it begins with the infinitive form of a verb, *to wear*. Each of the names we gave the phrases in this paragraph is a name given by form, by what the phrases look like. But each phrase is the same in function: Each acts as an adjective.

### 2   Phrases Used as Adverbs

He spoke *in the afternoon.*

The italicized group of words has the form of a prepositional phrase (preposition + the + noun), but it answers the question *when* and functions as an adverb modifying the verb *spoke*.

*To avoid fatigue,* he rested.

Here we see another kind of phrase that can be used as an adverb — an infinitive phrase *(to avoid fatigue)*, modifying *rested*.

### 3   Phrases Used as Nouns

*Riding a motorcycle* can be dangerous.

The italicized group is a phrase used as a noun — the subject of the sentence. (Test this by asking *what* can be dangerous. The only satisfactory answer is *riding a motorcycle* because the sentence does not say that *riding can be dangerous* or that *a motorcycle can be dangerous.*)

In form, this is called a *gerund phrase*. It is named after the *gerund*, the *-ing* form of the verb that acts as a noun (for example, as the word *swimming* does in the sentence *Swimming is fun*). In function, it is a noun phrase.

A gerund phrase can go in other noun positions in the sentence. Here it is the direct object of the verb *like*.

I like *riding a motorcycle.*

An infinitive phrase can also be used as a noun.

*To ride a motorcycle* can be dangerous.

I like *to ride a motorcycle.*

Occasionally, a prepositional phrase is used as a noun in the position of the subject of the sentence.

*Over the fence* is out.

*After supper* is all right.

## TEST YOURSELF ON
# Phrases

**A**   Underline each phrase you find in the sentences below, and above each write ADJ if the phrase is being used as an adjective, ADV if it is being used as an adverb, or N if it is being used as a noun. Some sentences have more than one phrase.

1. He traveled in the afternoons.

2. The cameras carried in stock were all cheap.

3. After a few minutes, he saw the sun set over the trees.

4. Known for his pure tenor voice, he often gave concerts in the park.

5. To love deeply is my goal in life.

6. I saw him riding a bicycle.

7. Come up to my house for an hour.

8. He wants to study chemistry.

9. I saw the shoplifter running down the street.

10. She stood next to my brother.

**B**   For each of the sentences or parts of sentences given below, construct the type of phrase that is called for to serve the given function.

*Example:* The man (participial phrase: adjective) looked sinister.
The man *walking alone* looked sinister. (The phrase acts as an adjective modifying *man*.)

1. The man (participial phrase: adjective) looked sinister.

2. Charley traveled (prepositional phrase: adverb).

3. (Participial phrase: noun) should be a pleasure.

4. She looked like a lady (participial phrase: adjective).

5. He talked (prepositional phrase: adverb).

6. (Infinitive phrase: adverb), he broke up with his girl.

7. He typed (prepositional phrase: adverb).

8. He loved (participial phrase: noun).

9. She begged me (infinitive phrase: noun).

10. She was a woman (participial phrase: adjective).

**C**   First, go through the passage printed below and underline all the phrases you can find. Then answer the questions that follow the passage.

> In the morning, James is at his best. He snorts out of bed with a whoop and a shout and beams a smile at everyone in the house. Flying through the air with the greatest of ease, his first stop is usually his trapeze. There he gets the kinks out of his kinkless muscles and beats a tattoo on the ceiling with his straining toes as he soars higher and higher. After this, to make sure that nobody in the household is still sleeping, he puts a hot tempered rock and roll tape into his portable stereo player, turns the volume up loud and aims it up the stairs. Now he'd like to tell a few jokes. Determined to find a willing listener, he jumps on a few adult shoulders and shouts directly in their ears "Wanna hear a joke?" Each of James's maneuvers lights up the house with the sights and sounds of vitality and confirms us in our perception that a new day has arrived and all's right with the world.

1. Can you point to a participial phrase that functions as an adjective?
2. Point out two examples of a prepositional phrase.
3. How many infinitive phrases are there in the passage? How does each one function in the sentence?
4. Is there a phrase in the passage acting as a noun?
5. Point out two examples of phrases acting as adverbs and specify whether each is prepositional, participial, or infinitive.

## TEST YOURSELF ON
## Recognizing Parts of Speech

From the following passage, find at least two examples of the parts of speech named below and write them in the spaces provided.

> Sometimes I think that I'm the world's sloppiest person. I can't seem to keep my little office in any kind of reasonable order. Papers accumulate on my desk, overflow onto the floor into great piles, get put on shelves but fall out of them down onto the floor again, and, finally, force me out of my office and into the nearest empty one. My inclination is to spread out, I guess. A woman who knows me pretty well says I'm determined to fill up empty space; however, she doesn't quite understand that filling up empty space is painful to me. When the papers start to pile up, I agonize over them. And when I have filled up several offices, I go into a real tailspin. For that's when I must go back to my own place and start cleaning up, filing some things, throwing other things out, and generally restoring order. It's no use, because no sooner do I succeed in that restoration than the whole cycle starts again.

Nouns _____

Adjectives _____

Adverbs _____

Verbs _____

Auxiliaries _____

Pronouns _____

Prepositions _____

Conjunctions _____

If you have worked your way carefully through this part of the book, you should now be ready to tackle any of the entries in Part 2. These entries all focus on specific writing problems or principles of effective writing. Many of them cannot be understood without reference to some of the ideas discussed in Part 1. Thus you should continue to use this part as a reference. The improvement it can make in your writing is worth the effort.

PART 2

An Index to Usage
and the Principles of
Effective Writing

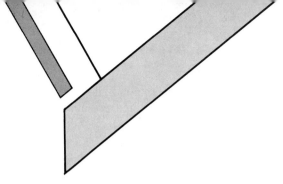

# Abbreviations

Over the years there has developed a set of conventions that tell us when we may and when we may not use abbreviations in essay writing. Here they are divided into the appropriate and the inappropriate.

## Appropriate

### Forms of Address and Titles

It is permissible to use such abbreviations as *Mr., Mrs., Ms., Messrs.* (plural of *Mr.*), *Mmes.* (plural of *Mrs.*), *St., Jr., Sr., M.D.* (Doctor of Medicine), *D.D.S.* (Doctor of Dental Surgery), *B.A.* (or *A.B.*, Bachelor of Arts), *M.A.* (Master of Arts), *Ph.D.* (Doctor of Philosophy), and *Esq.* (Esquire, a title appropriately used only by attorneys).

### Conventional Foreign Words and Phrases

The following abbreviations of certain useful foreign words and phrases may be used:

| | |
|---|---|
| c *or* ca. (about) | i.e. (that is) |
| cf. (compare) | v. (see) |
| e.g. (for example) | viz. (namely) |

### Technical Terms

The following technical terms may be abbreviated:

| | |
|---|---|
| BTU (British Thermal Unit) | kph (kilometers per hour) |
| cc (cubic centimeter)* | mpg (miles per gallon) |

* cm³ is preferable in technical writing.

**A**

cm (centimeter)                    mph (miles per hour)
g (gram)                           rpm (revolutions per minute)
km (kilometer)

### Organizations, Institutions, Government Agencies, Trade Unions

It is common practice to abbreviate the names of institutions. Occasionally, an abbreviation forms an *acronym,* that is, a pronounceable word, such as WHO for World Health Organization. In an essay, first write out the whole name of the organization; subsequent references to it may be abbreviated.

> The Committee on Dental Education (CODE) issued a stern warning about the use of kangaroo flakes in toothpaste. CODE officials noted that very few kangaroos have had good checkups this year. CODE stated that fluorides are the most effective additives for toothpaste.

Here is a brief list of some common abbreviations for well-known groups; some of them are acronyms, as you can see:

CARE (Cooperative for American Relief to Everywhere)
CBS (Columbia Broadcasting System)
FBI (Federal Bureau of Investigation)
GSA (General Services Administration)
UN (United Nations)
UNESCO (United Nations Educational, Scientific, and Cultural Organization)

### Expressions of Time

These may be abbreviated:

1434 B.C. (before Christ)
A.D. 953 (anno domini; in the year of Our Lord)
8 A.M. *or* 8 a.m.
7:29 P.M. *or* 7:29 p.m.
EST (Eastern Standard Time)
DST (Daylight Saving Time)
MST (Mountain Standard Time)
CST (Central Standard Time)
PST (Pacific Standard Time)

## Inappropriate

It is inappropriate to abbreviate in the following ways in a written text. (Many of these abbreviations are acceptable in addresses and certain short references.)

### Titles

***Wrong***   *Prof.* Smith and *Sen.* Smith are brothers.
***Right***   *Professor* Smith and *Senator* Smith are brothers.

### Given Names

***Wrong***   Geo., Wm., Thos., Ed., Jas., Theo.
***Right***   George, William, Thomas, Edward, James, Theodore

### Places

***Wrong***   I plan to spend my vacation in *N.M.*
***Right***   I plan to spend my vacation in *New Mexico*.

***Wrong***   Of all the underdeveloped areas, *S.A.* has the highest economic growth rate.
***Right***   Of all the underdeveloped areas, *South America* has the highest economic growth rate.

***Wrong***   To get to Sarah's, take County *Rd.* to Closter.
***Right***   To get to Sarah's, take County *Road* to Closter.

***Wrong***   Jerry lives at Elm *St.* and Carson *Ave.*
***Right***   Jerry lives at Elm *Street* and Carson *Avenue*.

### Days of the Week, Names of the Months, and Holidays

***Wrong***   The King died on *Tues.*
***Right***   The King died on *Tuesday*.

***Wrong***   The academic calendar runs from *Oct.* to May.
***Right***   The academic calendar runs from *October* to May.

***Wrong***   For *Xmas*, I'd like a new bathrobe.
***Right***   For *Christmas*. I'd like a new bathrobe.

### Units of Measurement

***Wrong***   ins., ft., yds., mi., lbs., oz.
***Right***   inches, feet, yards, mile, pounds, ounces

**A**

### Academic Courses

**Wrong**  Richard is failing *eco.* and *psych.* this term.
**Right**  Richard is failing *economics* and *psychology* this term.

### Miscellaneous Items

Do not use an ampersand (&) unless it is part of an official company name, for example, *Earl H. Rovit & Son, Inc.* In ordinary circumstances, use *and* in place of *&*.

Do not abbreviate ordinary words through laziness or because you are uncertain about their spellings. Do not, for example, substitute *thru* for *through, tho* for *though, yrs* for *yours,* or *mtns* for *mountains.*

## TEST YOURSELF ON
# Abbreviations

By using abbreviations where appropriate, correct the errors in the following sentences. Place the letter C next to the sentences that you think are correct.

1. _____ Mister Tuten took the stand and stated that at 8 ay em, when the accident took place, he was traveling at 55 miles per hour.

2. _____ The physician on duty administered 100 cubic centimeters of insulin.

3. _____ He said he was able to get through the winter by taking a short vacation in Florida at Christmastime.

4. _____ By using the Panama Canal, ships can avoid going around the tip of S. A.

5. _____ The Council to Rehabilitate Urban Military Back Yards announced a fund-raising drive today. Officials of the Council to Rehabilitate Urban Military Back

Yards set their goal at $3,000,000 and said they hoped to reach it by St. Pat's day.

6. _____ Many species of fish inhabit this lake, e.g., pike, perch, and catfish; some specimens have measured as much as twenty inches and weighed as much as fourteen pounds.

7. _____ On Mon., Wed., and Fri. I go from eco to philo and then on to gym.

8. _____ Driving west toward California, you can pass through Ill. and Kan.

9. _____ Before I started my diet on Thurs., I weighed 242 lbs.

10. _____ The mtns look toward Penn. on one side and W.Va. on the other.

11. _____ Gail & Grace have both broken up with their boyfriends.

12. _____ His parents hope that Joseph Young, Junior, will grow up to be like Joseph Young, Senior.

# Active Voice

See **Voice.**

# Adjectivals

An adjectival is any word, phrase, or clause that can act as an adjective in a sentence. See **Modifiers.**

## Adverbials

An adverbial is any word, phrase, or clause that can act as an adverb in a sentence. See **Modifiers.**

## Ambiguity

When something can be read in two or more ways, then we say it is ambiguous, that is, it has ambiguity. *Mail leaves tomorrow* could mean that *the mail will leave tomorrow* or that the writer of the message wants *his leaves* mailed tomorrow. See **Modifiers, Pronoun References, Shifts.**

## Antecedents

An antecedent is what a pronoun may sometimes refer to and must always agree with. See **Pronoun References, Shifts;** Pronouns.

## Apostrophe

The apostrophe is a mark used by convention (agreement) to signal contractions, possessives, and certain special plurals.

### Contractions

The rule for contracting two words into one is to use the apostrophe in place of the missing letter or letters.

are not = aren't
Bud is = Bud's (see also Possessives, below)
cannot = can't
it is = it's (but *its*, without the apostrophe, is possessive)
let us = let's

we have = we've
would not = wouldn't
you will = you'll

## Possessives

In English, there are two ways to express possession, ownership, and similar relationships when using nouns.

> The *office of the manager* is located at the top of the stairs.
>
> The *manager's office* is located at the top of the stairs.

Both ways are correct. In general, we would use the first method (using the word *of* ) for nouns that stand for something inanimate and the second (using an apostrophe and -s) for nouns representing something animate.

> ***Animate***   Judy's room; Mark's office; Franny's eyes; Colin's book
> ***Inanimate***   the light of the moon; the color of the paint; the score of the game

Nevertheless, it is valuable to know that both forms mean the same thing: possession. If you are having trouble with the apostrophe -s ( *'s*) form, you can determine whether or not the *'s* is needed by using the fact we've just noted. For example, suppose that one of your essays contained the following phrases, and that you were unsure whether an apostrophe were needed in any of them.

1. Charlies horse
2. Clarences cross
3. Janeys boss
4. Marks loss
5. the Smiths went

Using the fact previously noted — that the *of* form and the *'s* form both mean the same thing — we can try to see whether any of the five phrases can be turned into the alternative *of* form.

1. Charlies horse = the horse of Charlie
2. Clarences cross = the cross of Clarence
3. Janeys boss = the boss of Janey
4. Marks loss = the loss of Mark
5. the Smiths went ≠ the went of Smith

**A**

We can see clearly that the first four examples *can* be changed into the alternative form and therefore need an apostrophe in the original form — as follows:

1. Charlie's horse
2. Clarence's cross
3. Janey's boss
4. Mark's loss

Example 5 needs no apostrophe because it contains no possessive.

### TEST YOURSELF ON
## Changing from One Form of Possession to the Other

Using the rule you learned, change the following into the alternative possessive form:

1. the outcome of the game

2. the tirade of Lenny

3. the argument of the Mayor

4. the future of the boy

5. the impatience of my father

6. the wit of Eddie

7. the engine of Phil

8. the winged chariot of time

9. the ale of Gail

10. the acting of Colin

### Forming the Possessive of Singular Nouns and Indefinite Pronouns

In order to form the possessive of singular nouns and indefinite pronouns* that do not end in -s simply add *'s.*

| | |
|---|---|
| my father's cigarette | a doctor's appointment |
| my mother's comb | anybody's game |

\* *Note:* Never use an apostrophe for any of the possessive personal pronouns. That is, *his, hers, its, yours, ours, theirs, mine* already indicate possession and need no additional marks to indicate that fact.

*TV Guide's* features     teacher's pet
everybody's future     nobody's fault

## Forming the Possessive of Plural Nouns

To form the possessive of plural nouns, add 's to nouns with an irregular plural (e.g., *children, men, women*); but add *only* an apostrophe to plurals ending in -s.

| *Irregular Plurals* | *Regular Plurals* |
|---|---|
| *men's* clothing | the *boys'* hats (the hats belong to more than one boy) |
| *women's* liberation | |
| *children's* growth | his *parents'* devotion (the devotion of two people: mother and father) |
| | *students'* grades (the grades of more than one student) |

## Forming the Possessive of Nouns Ending in -s, -x, and -z

The rule here is the same as the previous one for plurals ending in -s.

Marx' philosophy     the Joneses' garage
Lefty Gomez' career     Ulysses' voyage
the boss' daughter     Venus' orbit

However, you have a spelling option based on how you pronounce these possessives. For example, if you actually say *boss-es* in pronouncing *boss'* then you may spell it to conform with the pronunciation. Thus the following alternative spellings would also be correct:

Marx's philosophy

Lefty Gomez's career

the boss's daughter

## Forming the Possessive of Two or More Nouns

Place the 's after the last item in a series of nouns if you want to indicate joint ownership; place the 's after each item if you want to show individual possession but talk about both items in the same sentence.

I stayed at *Fred and Ed's* house. (They own the house together.)

I have sympathy for *Fred's and Ed's* troubles. (Each man's troubles are his own; the speaker declares sympathy for that which belongs to each man — and does so in the same sentence.)

**A**

**Forming the Possessive of Compound Nouns**

In a compound noun, the last word takes *'s*:

my mother-in-law's generosity

the Attorney General's order

my brother-in-law's book

## Special Plurals

The apostrophe is used to form the plurals of certain signs, numbers, letters, and words.*

Count up all the +'s and −'s.

On her quizzes, she had all *8*'s and *9*'s.

He had trouble pronouncing his *s*'s and his *th*'s.

Don't use too many *which*'s in your writing.

## TEST YOURSELF ON
## The Correct Use of the Apostrophe

Each of the sentences below has an apostrophe problem for you to correct. Except for a few that are placed correctly, the apostrophe is either misplaced, superfluous, or missing and badly needed.

1. The womens' liberation movement grows stronger every day because of it's militant posture.

2. During the 50s, the outspoken would'nt speak; their's was the silent age.

3. Charleys horse had a Charley horse before Tuesday's race's.

4. The Attorney Generals office is flooded with work; federal crime's seem to be taking place at a record rate.

5. If you get 90s and 100s on your exams, your grade index this term will be higher than Max'.

---

* The apostrophe is sometimes also used for plural dates: "The 1800's were a time of change." However, it is preferable to write *1800s* for this kind of date.

A

6. If she wont give you her book's, thats all right; Grandmas grammars are hers to give.

7. Its in your pant's pocket.

8. My mother-in-laws kindness to others has made her famous in Waterbury.

9. Harry's and Frank's book is likely to be published this year.

10. Mrs. Gonzalez's fathers sister was the first member of his family to arrive in the United States.

11. My father-in-laws' storytelling is always fascinating.

12. I'm tired of Michael Jacksons; play someone elses records.

13. Anybody's troubles are my trouble's.

14. Ham and egg's is my favorite dish.

15. Peoples interests are determined by the complicated fact's of their lives.

## Appositives

An appositive is a noun, or some structure that can take the place of a noun, that is set right next to another noun to further explain or define it. It is set in *apposition* — in the next position in the sentence — to the noun which it will expand on. An appositive can be a single word or a group of words. In the following examples, the first noun is in italics and the appositive is in boldface.

> The *teacher*, **Davis,** spoke slowly. (word)
>
> Magic Johnson's *skill,* **stuffing a basketball through a hoop,** earns him a large salary. (phrase)
>
> The *teacher*, **a physics professor,** spoke slowly. (noun phrase)

An appositive can occur in a sentence in various positions where nouns occur.

> That was *Eddie*, **my friend.**
> He liked my *car*, **a '57 Chevy.**

A useful fact to understand about the appositive is that this structure is really an abbreviated clause.

> The *teacher*, **Davis,** spoke slowly. (The appositive *Davis* is really a part of the clause *whose name is Davis.*)
>
> Magic Johnson's *skill*, **stuffing a basketball through a hoop,** earns him a large salary. (The appositive, *stuffing a basketball through a hoop,* is really a part of the clause *which is stuffing a basketball through a hoop.*)

There is another important fact about appositives that you should understand. Some are not essential to complete the meaning of the sentence; these are therefore called *nonrestrictive.* They are set off by commas. The appositives are italicized in the examples:

> The doctor, *Allan Peters,* treated me for the flu. (The essential meaning is "The doctor treated me for the flu.")
>
> For Christmas, I got a camera, *a Kodak Instamatic.* (The essential meaning is "For Christmas, I got a camera.")

However, some appositives *are* essential to the meaning of the sentence; these are called *restrictive.* They are *not* set off by commas because they *belong* to the noun they are set beside.

> The mechanic *John* gave my car a lube job. (The essential meaning here is not that *the* mechanic gave my car a lube job, but that the mechanic named John did the job—there were several mechanics and *John* identifies the correct one.)
>
> I was helped through college by my Aunt *Martha.* (If the speaker had had only one aunt, then the word *Martha* would have been nonessential; as it is, *Martha* identifies one of the aunts and is an essential word.)

(See also **Comma Rules,** 5, for more on restrictives and nonrestrictives.)

## TEST YOURSELF ON
# Appositives

The following sentences all contain appositives, but they are all improperly punctuated. First, underline the appositive; then decide whether or not to set it off by a comma or commas. *Remember:* If the appositive is essential to the sentence (restrictive), do not use the comma or commas; if the appositive is nonessential (nonrestrictive), do use the comma or commas.

1. We slept that night in the tent an old piece of canvas with a dozen holes in it.

2. The Colonel Thomas Jones commanded the regiment as if he were a drill sergeant.

3. The police arrested two people a pickpocket and a burglar.

4. My aunt who lives in California Rebecca Rose is a movie producer.

5. We had to read *War and Peace* a book by someone named Tolstoy.

6. The cop we liked best O'Reilly treated us like human beings.

7. We were in the hands of the mediator the one who would decide.

8. Arthur Hopkins was a law professor a status he had achieved at a very young age.

9. The fighter we were eager to see Jackson was up against a tough opponent.

10. The author of the book Grace Paley will be autographing copies at Macy's today.

# Auxiliaries

Auxiliaries, or helping verbs, are the following: forms of the verb *be (am, is, are, was, were); has, have, had; do, did; can, could; be able to; may, might; would; should; must; ought to; shall* and *will*. For detailed information on how auxiliaries are used, see Part 1, Auxiliaries.

# Capitalization

The use of capital and lowercase (small) letters follows a number of clear rules. We can number these for convenience as follows:

**1   Beginning a Sentence**
Capitalize the first words of sentences.

*L*asagna and pizza are Italian delicacies.

*Travel* agents are now offering charter flights to Mars.

**2   The Pronoun *I* and the Interjection *O* (or *Oh*)**
Capitalize these no matter where they occur in the sentence.

Doug says *I* am an astronaut.

He had *O* such an elegant jacket!

**3   Days of the Week, Months, Holidays**
Capitalize all of these no matter where they occur in the sentence.

| Tuesday | April | Memorial Day |
| Friday | August | Easter |
| Sunday | January | Christmas |

**4   Titles of Books, Plays, Movies, Television Shows, Short Stories, Poems**
Capitalize all of these no matter where they occur in the sentence. Articles and conjunctions are not capitalized unless they begin the title.

*The Sun Also Rises* (book)

*Caesar and Cleopatra* (play)

*Dune* (movie)

*Dynasty* (TV show)

"Asparagus Soup" (short story)

"Lycidas" (poem)

*Important note:* These titles should also be either italicized or enclosed in quotation marks, as they are above. See **Italics** and **Quotation Marks** for further information.

**5  Proper Names, Proper Adjectives, and Titles**

Capitalize the names of persons or geographical entities. Capitalize an official title when (a) it is used in place of a name to refer to the titleholder or (b) when it is used with the titleholder's name. *Do not* capitalize when the title refers to the office but not the person.

Kathy Roe            Oneonta, New York

Middle East          Mars

Italian                 New Englander

*Justice Holmes* is presiding. The *Justice* is late today.

We are electing a *senator* today. (Refers to office, not person.)

**6  Historical Events, Historical Terms, Historical Artifacts**

Use a capital letter for items such as the following:

the Civil War                               the Enlightenment

the Declaration of Independence      the Augustan Age

the Magna Carta                          the Battle of the Marne

**7  Terms Associated with Colleges and Universities**

Use a capital letter for courses that are specifically designated by number. Use a lowercase letter for those that are not so designated (except languages, which are always capitalized). Use a capital letter for academic titles or where the title alone is used to refer to the person holding it.

Biology 137

Math 11

French

anthropology (as in, "I am taking anthropology this term.")

Dean Theodore L. Gross

C

The Dean (referring to Dean Gross)

Professor Blanche Skurnick

Dr. Dennis Turner

**8** **Miscellaneous Items**

Use a capital letter for the names of public or private buildings.

| | |
|---|---|
| the White House | the Gardner Mansion |
| the Flatiron Building | the Kennedy Center |
| the World Trade Center | the Renaissance Center |

Use a capital letter for the names of both private and public organizations.

the Agriculture Department

the United Nations

the New York Yankees

Hadassah

the Modern Language Association

the Missouri Historical Society

Use a capital letter for virtually all references to things religious: deities, churches, adjectives based on these.

| | |
|---|---|
| God | the United Methodist Church |
| the Lord | Christian |
| Anglican | the Bible |
| Christ | Genesis |
| Moses | |

Use a capital letter for products referred to by brand name.

| | | |
|---|---|---|
| Xerox | Rice Krispies | Chevrolet |
| Scotch tape | Kleenex | Sony |

## TEST YOURSELF ON
## Capitalization

Read carefully each of the following sentences. Where there is an error in capitalization, indicate the error by writing CAP in the space provided. Then correct the error. If the sentence is correct, write C in the space.

1. _____ On friday we are taking the venus Special to Mars.

2. _____ Senator D'Amato made his maiden speech in congress today; the senator spoke on rock'n'roll.

3. _____ To be mayor of New York is a little crazy.

4. _____ He didn't say i was a graduate of City college — he said I was a prisoner.

5. _____ An arabian knight is oil right.

6. _____ President Reagan favors a policy of lasting peace in the Middle East.

7. _____ The level of pollution in lake Erie is superseded only by the level of pollution in the Passaic river, according to measurements conducted by the Environmental protection administration, made last january.

8. _____ The work of a college president would be no challenge to the Dean.

9. _____ Next semester, I plan to take chemistry, Biology 101, mathematics, History 98, and Physics.

10. _____ The junior colleges in this state are suffering great decreases in student enrollment.

## Case

Case refers to the function of a noun or pronoun in a sentence. In the sentence *He lent me his father's car*, the nominative case form *he* shows it is being used as the subject; the objective case form *me* indicates that the pronoun is an object; the possessive case form *father's* shows that the noun is possessive.

**C**

Case endings of nouns were once important in English but have now all but disappeared. Nouns have just two case forms: (1) the common form, for example, *doctor,* and (2) the possessive form, *doctor's.* It is the case of pronouns — where there are three cases: nominative, objective, and possessive — that requires the writer's attention.

| | | | | | | | | |
|---|---|---|---|---|---|---|---|---|
| **Nom.** | I | we | you | he | she | it | they | who |
| **Poss.** | my, | our, | your, | his | her, | its | their, | whose |
| | mine | ours | yours | | hers | | theirs | |
| **Obj.** | me | us | you* | him | her | it* | them | whom |

Following are the rules for the proper use of each case.

## Nominative

**1**   Use the nominative case for the word in the subject position in the sentence. We need hardly say more about this rule, since few of us are likely to write sentences like "*Us* have a date tomorrow" or "*Me* want an apple."

**2**   Use the nominative case *who* in a clause where it is clearly the subject of the verb; do not be tempted into using *whom* by the words that intervene between *who* and its verb.

> clause
> There is a professor *who I know works hard to make contact with students.* (*Who* is here the subject of *works;* you should not make the error of thinking that *whom* should replace it because of the words *I know.*)
> clause
> He saw some men in uniform *who he thought were Marines.* (*Who* is the subject of *were;* do not think that *whom* should replace *who* because of the words *he thought.*)

**3**   In formal writing, use the nominative case after forms of the verb *be* (*is, are, was, were,* and so forth). Many good writers and speakers use the objective case, but formal writing requires the nominative.

> **Formal**   It is *I.* It might be *they.*
> **Informal**   It's *me.* It might be *them.*

**4**   Use the nominative case, in formal writing, after the conjunctions *as* and *than.* In these constructions, the pronoun is the

---

* As you can see, *it* and *you* do not change in the objective case, only in the possessive.

C

subject of an omitted verb. In informal writing and in speech the objective case is frequently used.

> **Formal**  He is hungrier *than I* [am]. (*Am* in this sentence is omitted but understood by the reader, and *I* is the subject of *am;* therefore, *I* must be in the nominative case.)
>
> **Informal**  He is hungrier *than me.* (Here the conjunction *than* is made into a preposition, with *me* as its object.)
>
> **Formal**  We are as intelligent as *they* [are]. (*Are* is omitted but understood by the reader; *they* is the subject of *are* and is therefore in the nominative case.)
>
> **Informal**  We are as intelligent as *them.* (*As* is made into a preposition, with *them* as its object.)

**5**  Use the nominative case when the pronoun appears as part of a compound subject.

> Jack and *he* played cards last night. (The compound subject of this sentence is the words *Jack* and *he;* the whole sentence really combines two sentences: "*Jack* played cards last night" and "*He* played cards last night.")

**6**  Use the nominative case of a pronoun in an appositive where that pronoun explains or further identifies a noun that is either the subject or the predicate noun.

> appositive
> It was the *coach, he alone,* who held the team together. (*Coach* is the predicate noun; therefore, *he,* the appositive pronoun, is in the nominative case.)
>
> appositive
> Those *two*—the policeman and *he*—prevented a robbery. (*Two* is the subject; therefore, *he,* the pronoun in the appositive, is in the nominative case.)

*Note:* Not all pronouns in appositives are in the nominative case. See **Objective** for examples of appositive pronouns in the objective case.

## Possessive

**1**  Use pronouns in the possessive case to indicate possession, source, authorship, and similar relationships.

> I liked *his* speech very much.
>
> I know *whose* house that is.
>
> The legislature has *its* power limited by the judiciary.

C

**2** In formal writing, use the possessive case of a noun or a pronoun before a *gerund*. A gerund is the *-ing* form of a verb that is used as a noun; for example, *swimming* is a gerund when used in the sentence "Swimming is fun." In informal writing, you will sometimes see the objective case used instead of the possessive.

**Formal** There was a good reason for *his* working hard.
**Informal** There was a good reason for *him* working hard.

**Formal** She was glad about *Charley's* organizing the concert.
**Informal** She was glad about *Charley* organizing the concert.

Notice the subtle difference in meaning in the last pair of examples. In the first, the emphasis is on the organizing of the concert. In the second, the emphasis is on Charley.

## Objective

**1** Use the objective case where the pronoun is the object of a verb.

The weird noise troubled *him*. (*Him* is the object of *troubled*.)

*Whom* did you invite? (*Whom* is the object of the verb.)

It is important to understand that where the object is a compound construction containing, say, a proper name and a pronoun, the pronoun must be in the objective case.

The club elected Paul and *me* co-chairmen. (*Paul* and *me* are the objects of the verb *elected;* therefore, *me* is in the objective case; do not say "Paul and *I*" in a construction like this. You would not say, "The club elected *I* chairman.")

**2** Use the objective case when the pronoun is the object of a verbal. A verbal is either a verb ending in *-ing* or an infinitive, that is, a verb with the word *to* preceding it (*to work, to play,* and so forth).

Knowing *him* was a pleasure. (*Him* is the object of *knowing*.)

Whenever I see babies, I want to kiss *them*. (*Them* is the object of *to kiss*.)

*Note:* An exception to this rule occurs when the infinitive is *to be* and its subject is unexpressed; then formal usage requires that the nominative case be used after the infinitive. The subject of the infinitive is the italicized word: I wouldn't want *him* to kiss her. An

C

unexpressed subject of the infinitive is the word in parentheses: I wouldn't want (me) to be he.

> ***Formal*** I wouldn't want *to be he*.
> ***Informal*** I wouldn't want *to be him*.

**3** Use the objective case for a pronoun that is the object of a preposition.

> Three of *us* went to the movies last night. (*Us* is the object of the preposition *of*.)
>
> He is the professor for *whom* I worked hardest. (*Whom* is the object of the preposition *for*.)

It is important to note that on occasion two pronouns will be objects of the same preposition. Both must then be in the objective case.

> Bob and I both wanted the job; the boss would have to choose between *him* and *me*. (Both *him* and *me* are objects of the preposition *between*.)

**4** In formal writing, use the objective case *whom* in a clause where it is clearly the object of the verb. In informal writing, *who* is widely used instead of *whom*.

> ***Formal*** She is the visitor *whom* we expected. (*Whom* is the object of *expected*.)
> ***Informal*** She is the visitor *who* we expected.
>
> ***Formal*** *Whom* are you criticizing? (*Whom* is the object of *are criticizing*.)
> ***Informal*** *Who* are you criticizing?

The word *whom* is now used less and less, even among well-educated writers and speakers. Still, in certain cases, *whom* is the much-to-be-preferred formal choice.

> *Whom* do you want to see?
>
> *Whom* are you waiting for?

*Note: Whom* is *always* used when the pronoun directly follows a preposition.

> *For whom* are you waiting?
>
> *To whom* do I pay my dues?

**5** Use the objective case of a pronoun following the conjunctions *as* and *than* if that pronoun is the object of a verb that has been omitted from the sentence.

> He likes her more *than* [he likes] *me*. (*Me* is the object of *likes*.)
>
> I treated her as fairly as [I treated] *him*. (*Him* is the object of *treated*.)

**6** Use the objective case of a pronoun that appears in an appositive when that pronoun explains or further identifies a noun that is an object.

appositive

> The coach fired two players, *Colin and me*. (*Me* is in the objective case because it further identifies the noun *players*, the object of *fired*.)

*Note:* Do not use the reflexive pronoun *myself* in place of the objective pronoun *me*.

> ***Wrong*** My aunt willed her estate to my brother and *myself*.
> ***Right*** My aunt willed her estate to my brother and *me*.

## TEST YOURSELF ON
## Using the Correct Case of Pronouns

Select the proper case of the pronoun from the choices in parentheses in each of the following sentences. Make your choices in accordance with correct formal usage.

1. She talked to Ed and (I, me) for a long time.

2. I can't imagine (his, him) accepting the job.

3. He didn't look it, but Paul was as tired as (I, me).

4. The Mayor, (he, him) alone, was responsible for slum conditions in our city.

5. The blue jeans fitted Bob as well as (I, me).

6. Somehow, Richard thought he was better than (I, me).

7. When Betty ran to answer the phone, she knew it was (he, him).

8. They never found out the names of the vandals (who, whom) they believed were destroying the highway signs.

9. Chris and (he, him) got drunk together last night.

10. The two of them — Irv and (he, him) — drove to California in three days.

11. I can do the job without (his, him) instructing me every minute.

12. The girls considered Jim and (I, me) the most attractive bachelors they knew.

13. (Who, Whom) are you waiting for?

14. They gave medals to two swimmers, Janet and (me, I).

15. After the party, the host was as tired as (I, me).

# Coherence

The word *coherence* means "a sticking together." When we use it to refer to writing, we mean (1) that the parts of a sentence stick together to form a correct and logical utterance; (2) that the sentences in a paragraph are in logical and smoothly connected order; and (3) that each paragraph in a piece of writing is logically and smoothly connected to the ones that precede and follow it.

## Achieving Coherence in Sentences

Many different kinds of errors contribute to the lack of coherence in sentences. Some of these are discussed in separate entries (**Dangling Modifiers; Diction,** especially the section on idioms, p. 107; **Misplaced Modifiers; Parallel Construction; Pronoun References; Shifts**). In order to achieve coherence in a sentence, it is necessary to avoid the following kinds of errors as well.

### 1 Avoid Split Constructions

**A** Do not needlessly separate the subject of the sentence and the verb.

**C**

*Poor*  *Lisa,* after gathering together her clothes, books, and papers, *packed.*

*Better*  After gathering together her clothes, books, and papers, Lisa packed.

**B**  Do not needlessly separate the verb and its complement.

*Poor*  The truck driver delivered, after driving all night in a terrible rainstorm, the new boiler we had ordered.

*Better*  After driving all night in a terrible rainstorm, the truck driver delivered the new boiler we had ordered.

**C**  Do not needlessly split an infinitive. To do so may destroy the coherence of the sentence. A split infinitive, however, does not always lead to incoherence; sometimes it cannot be avoided and produces perfect clarity.

*Awkward*  He asked me *to as quickly as possible drop over* to his house.

*Correct*  He asked me *to drop over* to his house as quickly as possible.

*Awkward*  I promised *to immediately try out* for the football team.

*Correct*  I promised *to try out* for the football team immediately.

*Appropriate*  IBM expects *to more than double* its business this year.

*Appropriate*  *To just miss* the train is a bad start for anybody's day.

## 2  Avoid Illogical Subjects and Complements

**A**  Do not carelessly use a modifying phrase or clause as the subject of a sentence.

*Wrong*  *Because he drove too slowly* made him miss the first inning of the game. (The adverb clause cannot be the subject of *made.*)

*Right*  Because he drove too slowly, he missed the first inning of the game.

*Right*  Driving too slowly made him miss the first inning of the game.

*Wrong*  *By using power tools* will save a lot of hard work. (The italicized phrase cannot be used as the subject of *will save.)*

*Right*  Using power tools will save a lot of hard work.

*Right*  The use of power tools will save a lot of hard work.

**B**  Do not use *when* or *where* as part of the complement of the verb *is.*

*Wrong*  The thing I like to do most at parties *is when* I'm dancing.
*Right*  The thing I like to do most at parties *is dance.*

*Wrong*  A vacation *is where* you relax.
*Right*  A vacation is *a period of relaxation.*

**3  Avoid Using Mixed or Incomplete Comparisons**

**A**  Do not use comparisons that mix two comparative constructions.

*Mixed*  My biology course is as interesting, *if not more interesting* than, my chemistry course. (The italicized modifying phrase is misplaced, making the main clause read: "My biology course is as interesting than my chemistry course.")
*Unmixed*  My biology course is as interesting as my chemistry course, if not more interesting.
*Correct (but stilted)*  My biology course is as interesting as, if not more interesting than, my chemistry course.

*Mixed*  Willie Mays was one of the greatest, if not the greatest, players in all of baseball history.
*Correct*  Willie Mays was one of the greatest players in all of baseball history. He may even have been *the* greatest.

**B**  Do not use inexact or incomplete comparisons.

*Inexact*  New York City is farther from Albany than Newark. (Confusion: which place is farther from which?)
*Exact*  New York City is farther from Albany than Newark *is.* (Both terms of the comparison are filled in here.)
*Exact*  New York City is farther from Albany than *it is from* Newark. (Again, the comparison is now exact.)

*Inexact*  I like to watch television because it has more varied entertainment. (More varied than what?)
*Exact*  I like to watch television because it has more varied entertainment *than other media.*
*Incomplete*  Her prospects for a job after graduation looked lower than a laborer. (Is a laborer *low?*)
*Complete*  Her prospects for a job after graduation looked lower than a *laborer's.*
*Complete*  Her prospects for a job after graduation looked lower than *those of a laborer.*

**C**

### 4   Avoid Omitting Necessary Words

**A**   Do not omit words that are necessary to maintain parallel structure in the sentence. (See **Parallel Construction** for a complete explanation of the term.)

> *Wrong*   He told her that she was intelligent but she lacked confidence. (The omission of *that* between *but* and *she* makes it uncertain whether she was told she lacked confidence or whether she thought so herself.)
>
> *Right*   He told her *that* she was intelligent but *that* she lacked confidence.

**B**   Do not omit necessary parts of verbs. When the two parts of a compound construction are in different tenses or there is a change of number between them, be sure to include all the parts of *both* verbs.

> *Wrong*   Freedom *has* and always *will be* the most cherished American ideal. (*Be* goes properly with *will* to form the future tense; but *has* needs *been* to form the present perfect.)
>
> *Right*   Freedom *has been* and always *will be* the most cherished American ideal.
>
> *Wrong*   Jack *was fishing* and the other men *sleeping*. (*Jack* is singular and properly takes the singular auxiliary *was; men* is plural and needs the plural *were*.)
>
> *Right*   Jack *was fishing* and the other men *were sleeping*.

*Note:* It is permissible to omit parts of compound verbs when both parts of the construction are in the same tense.

> She *had read* the assigned books and *[had] done* the required term paper. (The tenses are the same, so the bracketed *had* may be omitted.)

**C**   Do not omit words through sheer carelessness; careful proofreading can usually pick up these errors. But notice how careless omissions give a special incoherence to sentences.

> *Omission*   He took a five-mile walk the pool. (A reader might think that the letter *p* in *pool* should be an *f*; what was actually omitted was the word *to*.)
>
> *Complete*   He took a five-mile walk to the pool.
>
> *Omission*   The moon gave him the *feeling wonder* and *romance*. (Did the moon give him three separate things, the italicized words? No. The word *of* has been omitted.)
>
> *Complete*   The moon gave him the feeling of wonder and romance.

## TEST YOURSELF ON
# Revising Incoherent Sentences

Each of the following sentences is plagued by one of the problems we have been discussing in this section. Analyze each problem, and then write out what you consider to be a good revision of the sentence; be prepared to explain why you think your version is superior.

1. In the basket is where I put the apples.
2. Because cheating the consumer is so widespread that we need a permanent Department of Consumer Affairs.
3. Jack, after the heat, the crowds, and the excitement, fainted.
4. The doctor wanted, because he suspected a kidney problem and needed to be sure, a urine sample.
5. The invitation said that I was to only reply if I couldn't make it.
6. A good disco is where they play music for dancing.
7. Professor Gould is one of the best, if not the best, teachers in the department.
8. A Toyota is built better and gets better gas mileage.
9. The actor's makeup looked like a clown.
10. Northerners are just as friendly as the South or West.
11. Loneliness is when you are starved for intimacy.
12. The bookcase I built myself cost far less than a carpenter.
13. The music instructor told her that she had talent but she needed to improve her technique.
14. In lower Manhattan are a pair of skyscrapers reaching toward the clouds and which provide great sightseeing for millions of visitors.
15. He was working and still does at the packing plant.

## Achieving Coherence in Paragraphs

Most kinds of writing require that sentences be written one after another to form coherent paragraphs. A coherent paragraph is one in which (1) there is a logical order to the sentences; some principle governs why each sentence in the paragraph occupies its particular place there; and (2) there are clear connections — smooth bridges — between these sentences.

**1** To assure that your paragraphs have coherence, choose the appropriate logical plan with which to govern the order of your sentences. Usually, the subject of your paragraph will suggest the right plan to follow. If you are telling a story, a common plan is the chronological one; you order your sentences according to time. If your paragraph is describing something, say a house, then a common plan of organization would have you describe the house from the inside out or vice versa: We call this a spatial plan. Here are examples showing the difference a plan can make in the coherence of your paragraphs.

### Incoherent (sentences without order)

Last night, my father discovered that our car had been stolen. The detectives didn't hold out much hope for its return, but they said they would be in touch if there were any news. They took down all the information about the car and were very polite. My father asked my mother if she thought I had taken it without permission, but she assured him I hadn't. He just couldn't believe it wasn't parked in the usual place, and ran down the hill to see if maybe the brakes had given out and it had rolled down. When he was finally convinced that the car had been stolen, he phoned the police. After they left, my father was depressed.

### Coherent (chronological order imposed)

Last night, my father discovered that our car had been stolen. He asked my mother if she thought I had taken it without permission, but she assured him I hadn't. He just couldn't believe it wasn't parked in the usual place and ran down the hill to see if maybe the brakes had given out and it had rolled down. When he was finally convinced that the car had been stolen, he phoned the police. The detectives took down all the information about the car and were very polite. They didn't hold out much hope for its return, but they said they would be in touch if there were any news. After they left, my father was depressed.

### Incoherent (sentences without order)

A spiral ramp hugging the wall goes whirling up as far as the eye can see, leaving a huge cone of space in the center. The entrance hall is also very dramatic. When you first approach the museum, you notice that it's very different from the buildings around it — ordinary high-rise apartment houses. It is low, first of all, almost squat in appearance. The squat impression made by the outside is lost on the inside. The building is made of massive geometric forms: cones, tubes, rectangles, and squares, all solidly connected to form a unitary, dramatic mass of concrete, with here and there a strange vertical slit in the façade. Everything inside is airy and light, turning and curving. From the top of the ramp, what you see is so slender and spacious you can hardly believe it's the same building you saw from the outside.

**C**

### Coherent (spatial order imposed)

When you first approach the museum, you notice that it's very different from the buildings around it — ordinary high-rise apartment houses. The museum is low, first of all, almost squat in appearance. It is made of massive geometric forms: cones, tubes, rectangles, and squares, all solidly connected to form a unitary, dramatic mass of concrete, with here and there a strange vertical slit in the façade. The entrance hall is also very dramatic. A spiral ramp hugging the wall goes whirling up as far as the eye can see, leaving a huge cone of space in the center. Everything inside is airy and light, turning and curving. From the top of the ramp, what you see is so slender and spacious you can hardly believe it's the same building you saw from the outside.

## TEST YOURSELF ON
## Making Coherent Paragraphs

**A**  Write a coherent paragraph that incorporates all the following information about Ralph Ellison. Begin your paragraph with sentence 1.

1. Ralph Ellison, the distinguished American novelist, was born in Oklahoma in 1914.
2. Afterward, he became interested in sculpture, and finally, of course, in writing.
3. While attending school in Oklahoma City, he had a decisive experience when he heard Lester Young play the saxophone.
4. Probably the whole experience helped orient him toward art in general.
5. In 1965, *Invisible Man* was voted the most distinguished novel to have been published in the previous twenty years.
6. Hearing the great jazz player prompted him to go to Tuskegee Institute, in 1933, with the intention of studying music.
7. Since 1952, he has also published a collection of essays, *Shadow and Act;* from 1958 onward, he has taught literature at various colleges.
8. Ellison started publishing in 1937, but it wasn't until 1945, after service in the Merchant Marine in World War II, that he began his famous *Invisible Man.*

**B**  Both of the following paragraphs are incoherent because the sentences are poorly arranged. Impose some orderly plan on each and make coherent paragraphs of them.

C

1. Most Americans have become increasingly interested in leisure activities these days. There is so much intensity invested in these activities that we can fairly say Americans now have two jobs: One is real work, the other real play. Jobholders work fewer hours and thus have more leisure. Besides, Americans have always been sociable and sociability goes hand in hand with leisure. The reasons have to do with changes that have taken place in American life in the last twenty-five years. Interest in health has grown, and this has led many to take an active role in sports. Moreover, the idea has gained prominence that self-fulfillment means gaining skills in pleasurable leisure activities like photography, sailing, woodwork, painting, and many others.

2. The outside of the building is typical of old farmhouses in this part of the country. So is the blackened tin funnel that was once used to lead cooking fumes to the outside. Inside, the house has been modernized — a new stove, a refrigerator, wall heaters — but the old wood stove is still there. A chimney squirts into the air from the top of each addition. Even a faded print on the living room wall, showing the original house without the additions, testifies that what used to be is not entirely gone. The furniture also reflects the original identity of the house. It is a white frame square, with two little additions — afterthoughts — sloping off either side of the square.

---

**2**   To assure that there are clear connections between your sentences, you must keep in mind the following four considerations.

**A**   Present your ideas from a consistent point of view. This means that you must speak, in each sentence, from the same position or vantage point. You must not needlessly shift tense, number, or person within a paragraph.

### Shift in Tense
In the story, Tom *went* to Canada to make a life as a hunter and trapper. Then he *goes* to Alaska to search for gold. His restlessness *was* emphasized repeatedly. Thus by the end of the story, he *is* a sad man.

### Shift in Number
Young *people* who look for security in their jobs rather than satisfaction are likely to be disappointed. A young *person* needs to choose a career that will stimulate his imagination while it is

young and responsive. *They* can always gain security later on, at the appropriate age. *He* must be wary of experiencing the worst possible regret: looking back on life and knowing *he* hasn't lived.

### Shift in Person

Now more than ever, *parents* need to pay close attention to children's gaining basic skills like reading, writing, and mathematics. *You* need to do more than help them with their homework. *You* cannot expect children to honor those skills if *you* don't. Therefore, a *parent* must set an example for *children*.

**B**  For the purpose of presenting parallel or coordinate ideas, use parallel construction in sentences that follow each other.

> My mother has passed along to me certain rules for getting along with others. Don't argue with parents; they'll think you don't love them. Don't argue with children; they'll think themselves victimized. Don't argue with husbands and wives; they'll think you're a tiresome mate. Don't argue with strangers; they'll not want to be friends. My mother's rules can be summed up in two words: don't argue.

> Most of us feel the troubles we encounter are not of our own making. We think that the system has failed us. We think that our loved ones have failed us. We think that circumstances have failed us. It rarely occurs to us that the failure has been our own and that it might be temporary and perhaps even reparable.

(See **Parallel Construction** for more information.)

**C**  Repeat key words and phrases to keep the flow of your thought before the reader. If you fail to do this, gaps in your thought are created. Pronouns referring precisely to their antecedents can also serve this bridging function.

> A *magic show* works by carefully directing our *attention*. But the *show directs* our *attention* where the *magician wants* it to be. *He wants* us to look away from the *place* where his transformations go on. For that *place* has no *magic;* it's a *work place.* The *magical* quality of the *show* depends on our not seeing the *work*. When we do not look at that *work,* we see the *magic,* and our *attention*—focused on the right *place*—is well rewarded.

**D**  Use transitional devices where they are necessary to further this bridging function between sentences. A transitional device is a word or a phrase that can serve as a point of reference *(finally, at last )* or that can actually indicate the relationship between one sentence and the next *(consequently, as a result )*.

C

Soon, he was able to walk. *Afterward,* he was even able to swim a little and he managed a few minutes in the pool every day. *Consequently,* when spring came, his physical condition had improved considerably. He was stronger, could walk without tiring, and was able to swim as long as he wanted to. *However,* he was still depressed by the ordeal of the accident and the recuperation period during which he was unable to work. *On the whole, though,* he had much to be thankful for.

Here is a list of some of these transitional devices, classified according to meaning:

**Time**    after a while, afterward, at last, at the same time, in the meantime, immediately, later, soon

**Place**    here, there, nearby, close by

**Addition**    again, also, besides, further, furthermore, in addition, likewise, moreover, next

**Result**    as a result, accordingly, consequently, hence, therefore, thus

**Comparison**    likewise, similarly, in such a manner

**Contrast**    after all, and yet, however, in contrast, in spite of, nevertheless, on the contrary, on the other hand, otherwise

**Concession**    It may be true, I admit, naturally, of course

**Summary**    in brief, in short, on the whole, to conclude, to sum up, finally, to summarize

**Illustration and Example**    for example, for instance, to be specific, in particular, indeed, in fact, that is, to illustrate

See also **Transitions.**

## TEST YOURSELF ON
## Revising Incoherent Paragraphs

The following paragraphs contain confusing shifts in person, tense, or number, or lack smooth transitions. Eliminate the shifts wherever they appear and add transitions where necessary to make them all coherent.

1. My parents always argue with me about my wanting a moped. They said the machines were dangerous, but I believed they were not. Mopeds go only twenty miles an hour. It ran cheaply

and had no license or insurance requirements. They have been sold cheaply too.

2. Cooking is both easy and fun if one observes certain basic rules. First, you should have the right utensils. As the saying goes, "a cook is only as good as his pots." A cook should buy only fresh ingredients. You ought to learn how much heat to apply to particular foods. Save good recipes.

3. A professor I know who is older than I am says that rock and roll is terrible music. I said it's just a form of what he used to think was popular music when he was young. He says rock and roll lyrics can't be heard because the music is too loud. He said the lyrics are foolish. I pointed out that though he may be right about the lyrics, they have not been more foolish than *his* kind of pop music. The degree of loudness is a matter of taste.

## Achieving Coherence Between Paragraphs

As you might have expected, the rules for achieving coherence between paragraphs are identical with those that apply to achieving coherence *within* paragraphs. For example:

[1] Strong faith, no matter where it is directed, can also erase anxiety, fear, and doubt from the human soul. These are often direct causes of many modern illnesses both real and imaginary. Faith seems to have a calming and soothing effect on a troubled mind. Thus in a sense the patient often cures himself by his own strong *faith, faith* which is stimulated by the efforts of the *healer* and reinforced by the *group traditions* surrounding the *healing* ceremony.

[2] Nonmedical *healing,* whether it be on the *folk or mass culture* level, contains many more components than power and *faith.* There are always rudimentary elements of auto-suggestion, crowd hysteria, thought transference, and subtle forms of hypnotism lurking in these rituals, but the healing ceremony always centers on these two key ingredients. When the balance between the two is right, when the patient and audience exhibit deep, sometimes emotional, faith, then this strange power called healing begins to flow. What this force really is, modern science, psychology, and technology have not as yet determined. Perhaps it is a creation of man's imagination. Perhaps it is a substantial

C

> and measurable force. But whatever it is, it should be considered an intrinsic part of both popular and folk medical belief.
> Greg Johnson, "A Classification of Faith Healing Practices," *New York Folklore Quarterly*, Summer 1975

Notice in the example that the words *faith, healer, healing* constitute a bridge from paragraph 1 to paragraph 2 and that the idea "group traditions" acts as a bridge to the idea "folk or mass culture level."

# Colloquial

See **Diction.**

# Colon

The colon is a mark of internal punctuation that can be used according to the following rules:

**1** Use the colon to introduce a series of items explained in the main clause of the sentence.

> In order to enjoy camping, you need the right supplies: a tent, a sleeping bag, good walking shoes, foul weather gear, waterproof matches, and the right kind of food.
>
> He had a bad group of symptoms: headache, nausea, fever, and an itchy rash.

**2** Use the colon to direct the reader's attention to a final fact or explanation.

> You lack the one thing that rich people have: money.
>
> One quality is essential for the good teacher: patience.

**3** Use the colon to introduce a direct quotation of some length and formality.

> The problem was clearly outlined by the Mayor, who put it this way: "The cities are in a state of decay. Our lives, our children's lives, and the future of cities everywhere depend upon how we

C

choose to confront the renewal of the urban environment. Either we undertake rebuilding our cities with enthusiasm or we suffer the consequences with shame.''

Longer direct quotations can of course be introduced by a comma, too, but a comma *should* be used when the material is more informal and shorter:

John smiled and answered softly, "You can do as you please.''

**4** Use a colon for the purposes of mechanical separation.

Matthew 8:10 (separating chapter and verse in Biblical citation)
Dear Mr. Kojak: (after the salutation in a formal letter, to separate it from the body)
2:32 a.m. (separating numbers in a time designation)

*Note:* Do not use a colon interchangeably with a semicolon.
Do not use a colon after a verb or a preposition in a sentence to introduce a series.

**Wrong** My priorities *are:* home, country, and God.
**Right** My priorities are as follows: home, country, and God.
**Right** My priorities are home, country, and God.

**Wrong** This summer I am planning *to*: study French, get a part-time job, and swim a half-mile every day.
**Right** This summer I am planning to do the following: study French, get a part-time job, and swim a half-mile every day.
**Right** This summer I am planning to study French, get a part-time job, and swim a half-mile every day.

## TEST YOURSELF ON
## the Use of the Colon

In each of the sentences below, insert colons where they are needed or change their position after inserting another word.

1. It is now 245 p.m.

2. Whatever he wanted from Sarah, he got love, affection, kindness, money, or food.

C

3. The things that need repairing around the house are: the rain gutters, the front steps, the upstairs storm windows, and the leaks in the attic.

4. What do I spend my money on? I spend my money on: food, clothing, shelter, movies, medicine, skateboards, lobsters — a lot of things!

5. You need only one thing for a perfect golf swing, control.

## Comma Fault

Another term for **Comma Splice.** See also **Run-on Sentences.**

## Comma Rules

The comma is used to separate sentence elements. It is the most frequently used of all the punctuation marks. Its appearance signals the reader that something is interrupting the flow of the main statement (main clause), that something is being added or subtracted, usually something that is not so closely related to that main flow of thought. The specific rules given below are aimed at ensuring that a writer's flow of thought is presented with clarity; they should be applied with that aim in mind. When there is a conflict between applying these rules and your own sense of the fitness of a comma placement, consult your instructor.

**1** Use a comma to separate independent clauses joined by the coordinating conjunctions *and, but, or, nor, for, so, yet.*

> Greene has washed and cleaned his old car, *and* he hopes that it will attract a buyer.

> The plan was to leave on Sunday morning, *but* we found that we couldn't get ready on time.

> We can stay home and have leg of lamb for dinner, *or* we can eat out and have pizza.

C

Jones could not name any of the original thirteen states, *nor* could he identify any of the original signers of the Declaration of Independence.

*Note:* A comma may be omitted between short independent clauses.

I laughed and he cried.

I asked but he didn't answer.

**2** Use a comma to separate items in a series. These items may consist of words, phrases, or clauses.

**Series of Words** I'd like a big bowl of fruit with *apples, pears, peaches,* and *plums.*

**Series of Phrases** He liked *going to the movies, eating at fancy restaurants,* and *visiting museums.*

**Series of Clauses** She liked him *when he was thoughtful, when he was kind,* and *when he was relaxed.*

Note that in each of these examples, there is a comma as well as the word *and* between the last two items in the series. In the case of items in a series, you have the option of following the practice in the above examples or of omitting the comma just before the *and* preceding the final item. Both procedures are correct; probably the retention of the comma is more formal than its omission. But whatever you choose to do, *be consistent.* Do not use one system with one series and another with a second series.

The words separated by commas in the first of the above examples are nouns. A series of adjectives can present a slightly different problem in punctuation. For example, consider the following sentences:

They were *energetic, pretty, intelligent,* and *sensitive* girls.

They had an *interesting European summer* vacation.

In the first example, we could substitute the word *and* for each of the commas — energetic *and* pretty *and* intelligent. We could also alter the order of these adjectives; it would make little difference to the sense of the sentence if we wrote "sensitive, pretty, energetic, and intelligent." Therefore, the adjectives in this example are *coordinate adjectives* and are properly separated by commas.

**C**

By contrast, the adjectives in the second example are not coordinate. We could not logically join them by the word *and* (interesting *and* European *and* summer is illogical). And we could not alter the order of these adjectives: We could not say "summer European interesting vacation." In fact, the word *interesting* really modifies *European summer vacation;* the word *European* then modifies *summer vacation* and the word *summer* modifies *vacation*—there are layers of modification, so to speak. Where we have such a series of adjectives that are not coordinate we do not use commas to separate them.

> **Coordinate** It was a *happy, productive,* and *prosperous* season in his life.
> **Not Coordinate** He was wearing a *light green* belt.
>
> **Coordinate** His remark was *foolish, rude,* and *embarrassing.*
> **Not Coordinate** Last night we went to a *lively little faculty* party.

**3** Use a comma to separate introductory elements from the rest of the sentence. These elements can be words, phrases, adverb clauses, or transitional expressions.

> **Introductory Word** *Usually,* he took a nap after lunch.
> **Introductory Phrase** *Coming through the alley,* the car swerved to avoid a garbage can.
>
> **Introductory Clause** *Although he had already eaten dinner,* he sat down to have a sandwich.
>
> **Transitional Expressions** *In other words,* I'm in love. *On the other hand,* meat loaf is fattening.

*Note:* Certain introductory elements do not need to be followed by a comma, if they are short and if omitting the comma does not cause a lack of clarity in the sentence.

> *Probably* he won't win.
>
> *Naturally* he found what he was looking for.

But note too how confusion can enter a sentence when a comma that *should* come after an introductory element is omitted:

> After he ate the horse took a romp in the fields.
>
> Because he needed to hit the catcher choked up on the bat handle.

As we have shown, introductory adverb clauses should be set off from the rest of the sentence by a comma. The need for a comma when the adverb clause comes at the end of a sentence depends on the relationship of the adverb clause to the main clause of the sentence. When the information contained in the adverb clause is essential to the meaning of the sentence, no comma is needed.

> I will keep knocking *until they* open the door.

The speaker here tells us that *until they open the door,* the speaker will keep on knocking; therefore, that information is essential — it gives the motive for the information in the main clause — and no comma is needed.

> I came to this school *because the engineering courses are so good.*

This states the essential reason that the speaker came, and so the clauses need not be separated by a comma.

However, when the adverb clause merely gives nonessential explanatory material, a comma should be used between it and the main clause.

> Our seats were in the last row of the balcony, *although we had ordered a pair in the orchestra.*

Here the italicized clause has no *essential* relationship to the main clause: It gives no *reason* that the seats were in the balcony (far from it, in fact; it suggests a contrast) nor any motive for the seats' being where they were. Therefore, it needs a comma, as if to emphasize the separateness of its information from that in the main clause.

**4**   Use a comma to set off a parenthetical element at the beginning of a sentence; use one comma before and one after a parenthetical or appositive element that occurs in the middle of a sentence. A parenthetical element is one which is not essential to complete the meaning of the sentence but which supplements a part or parts of the sentence.

### Parenthetical Element at Beginning of Sentence
*To be frank,* I'm completely broke.
*Certainly,* he has a right to do what he wishes.

### Parenthetical Element in Midsentence
The car, *you see,* is in the garage.

**Appositive**   Mr. Morris, *the patient in room 950,* has been wheeled down to occupational therapy.

**Appositive**   My uncle, *Harry Jackson,* was a stingy millionaire.

**C**

It should be clear from the above examples that appositives and parenthetical elements do not affect the meaning being delivered by the sentence; they can be omitted without loss of meaning.

Notice that if only one comma is used in each of the last two examples, some confusion in meaning results.

> Mr. Morris, the patient in room 950 has been wheeled down to occupational therapy. (Meaning, possibly, that the speaker is addressing a Mr. Morris and advising him that the patient in room 950 has been wheeled down.)

> My uncle, Harry Jackson was a stingy millionaire. (Again, it is not clear that *my uncle* and *Harry Jackson* are the same person.)

**5**   Use commas to set off nonrestrictive elements in a sentence. Another way of talking about a parenthetical or appositive element is to say that it is *nonrestrictive:* it does not *restrict* or essentially modify what it refers to; therefore, it *must* be set off by commas. On the other hand, if the element in question is *restrictive* or is essential to what it modifies, it must *not* be set off by commas.

> ***Restrictive Element***   The audience *that gave him the most applause* pleased him the most. (No commas necessary.)

> ***Nonrestrictive Element***   The audience, *which paid a fortune for its seats,* applauded for five minutes.

The first sentence is not about the *audience*—it is about *the audience that gave him the most applause*. Therefore, the clause must not be separated by commas from the subject word *audience;* the clause is part of the complete subject (italicized in this paragraph), and if it were separated the sentence would lose its essential meaning. On the other hand, the second sentence *is* about the *audience;* it is only incidental, not essential, information that this audience paid a fortune for its seats. Therefore, the clause in that sentence must be separated from *audience* by commas.

Try to figure out which of the following sentences contain restrictive elements and which ones contain nonrestrictive elements that should be set off by commas. Answers follow immediately below.

1. People *who live in glass houses* shouldn't throw stones.
2. Students *who take this film course* are guaranteed an exciting experience.
3. My doctor *who is on vacation this month* leads a busy professional life.

C

4. The foreman at the factory *who was a conscientious worker* was taking evening courses in business administration.
5. The man *leaning over the edge of the balcony* is being reckless.

*Answers:* 1, 2, and 5 all contain *restrictives*. In these, no commas should be used. But commas *are* needed in 3 and 4 because they contain *nonrestrictive* elements.

3. My doctor, who is on vacation this month, leads a busy professional life.
4. The foreman at the factory, who was a conscientious worker, was taking evening courses in business administration.

The reason that we need commas in these examples is that, in each, the material between the commas is not essential to the writer's message. In 3, it is only incidental that the doctor is on vacation, not essential. Similarly, in 4, the material between the commas is also incidental; it has nothing to do with the main message of the sentence — that the foreman was taking evening courses in business administration.

On the other hand, the reason we do not use commas in 1, 2, and 5 is that, in each, the italicized material is essential to what is being said about the subject.

1. People *who live in glass houses* shouldn't throw stones.

This writer doesn't mean that "people shouldn't throw stones" and that incidentally those people live in glass houses — although "People shouldn't throw stones" is a grammatical sentence and may even be a pretty good rule to live by. The writer means that *only people who live in glass houses* shouldn't throw stones; therefore, we must have *people* and all the words that follow it as one single unit, unbroken by commas.

2. Students *who take this film course* are guaranteed an exciting experience.

The writer of this sentence doesn't mean that "students are guaranteed an exciting experience," and incidentally, that those students are taking this film course. "Students are guaranteed an exciting experience" is a grammatical sentence and may even be true, but the writer of 2 really means that *only students who take this film course* receive the guarantee. Therefore, we must take these words as a single unit, unbroken by commas.

Try analyzing 5 as we have just analyzed 1 and 2.

**C**

**6** Use a comma to separate a contrasting element from the rest of the sentence; a comma emphasizes the contrast.

He came to the dance with me, *and not with you.*

She says she loves exercise, *but doesn't do it.*

**7** Use a comma to achieve clarity, even in places where you ordinarily might omit it.

In brief, dresses will be longer this year.

People who like to see wild birds, walk through the woods.

Whatever he did, did no good.

The soldier dropped, a bullet in his leg.

**8** Use a comma in dates, addresses, and letter forms.

***Dates***   August 4, 1986 (or 4 August 1986) Friday, November 30, 1988

***Address***   Waterbury, Connecticut

***Letter Forms***   Dear Mary Lea,
Yours sincerely,

## TEST YOURSELF ON
## the Use of the Comma

**A**   Write your own sentences to test your ability to use commas correctly.

1. Construct five compound sentences, each with two independent clauses; use the coordinating conjunctions *and, but, or, nor,* and *so* once each — and place commas in the correct position.
2. Construct five sentences, each beginning with an adverb clause and followed by a simple main clause. Place the comma in the correct position.

**B**   Some of the following sentences use the comma correctly; next to these, place the letter C. In the others, either there is a comma missing or too many commas are used. Supply those that are needed; cross out those that are superfluous.

1. _____ The boys in the back of the room are noisy.

2. _____ Women, who are very poor drivers should have their

   licenses revoked.

C

3. _____ During the summer days are long.

4. _____ Above all the rooftops are filled with TV antennas.

5. _____ I saw you talking to a pretty slim girl.

6. _____ I'd like to be rich married secure and famous.

7. _____ The ship, which docked yesterday is the *Queen Elizabeth II*.

8. _____ People, who live beyond their incomes, shouldn't complain about money.

9. _____ I will keep taking the test, until I pass it.

10. _____ I need to buy a gray, summer suit and a pair of white seersucker pants.

11. _____ Wherever you're going to get there requires planning and purpose.

12. _____ On Friday, November 30, 1973, I met my wife, and my life, has not been the same, since.

13. _____ In fact I stole the books.

14. _____ George, who is very nearly my age, is much further along in his career than I am in mine.

15. _____ The revolution in education which so many educators talk about has yet to take place.

16. _____ A college really consists of a group of students who want to learn, a group of teachers who want to teach, and a good collection of books.

17. _____ I paused but he went on.

18. _____ Either he goes or I go.

19. _____ He eats drinks and talks too much.

20. _____ Usually living alone is a matter of personal choice.

## Comma Splice

When two independent clauses are joined only by a comma, and *not* by a comma and a coordinating conjunction, we call the error a comma splice or comma fault.

For a detailed discussion of this problem, see **Run-on Sentences.**

## Contractions

When two words are joined together with one or more letters omitted and an apostrophe in its place, we have a contraction.

do not = don't     is not = isn't     we will = we'll

See **Apostrophe** for more detailed information.

## Dangling Modifiers

A dangling modifier is a phrase or a clause that either modifies no word in the sentence or refers to the wrong word.

> ***Dangling Participial Phrase***   *Walking home from school,* the fire engine came screeching around the corner.

The thing to notice about this example is that it *says* one thing but *intends* to say another. Because *walking home from school* modifies *fire engine,* it *says* that the fire engine, as it was walking home from school, came screeching around the corner. Clearly this is ridiculous.

It *intends* to say that as *someone* was walking home from school, the fire engine came screeching around the corner, or that walking home from school, *someone saw* the fire engine come screeching around the corner.

Therefore, to correct the dangling phrase, we must get *someone* into the action. We can accomplish this by giving the phrase something to modify in the main clause *(the fire engine came screeching around the corner):*

> Walking home from school, *I saw* the fire engine come screeching around the corner. (Now the phrase modifies the word *I* in the main clause.)

Alternatively, we can turn the phrase into a dependent clause and get the *someone* into the action that way:

> *As I was walking home from school,* the fire engine came screeching around the corner. (Now someone — *I* — has been gotten into the action by appearing in the italicized clause.)

How you decide to correct this dangling modifier depends on where you want to place the emphasis. Since emphasis naturally falls on the subject of the main clause, you would use the first revision if you wanted to emphasize the speaker, I, and the second if you wanted to emphasize the fire engine.

You can avoid dangling modifiers if you proofread carefully. Learn to recognize and correct the various kinds of dangling modifiers likely to appear in your work.

### 1 Recognize and Correct Dangling Participial Phrases.

These are similar to the example just discussed.

**Dangling** *Smoking a cigar,* the horse stood on its hind legs. (The phrase seems to modify *horse* — the wrong word.)
**Revised** *As I was smoking a cigar,* the horse stood on its hind legs. (Phrase turned into a clause — a person getting into the action.)
**Revised** Smoking a cigar, *I saw* the horse stand on its hind legs. (Now the phrase clearly modifies the new subject of the main clause: *I.*)
**Dangling** Our summer passed happily, *swimming and playing baseball.* (Note that the dangler can come at the end, not just at the beginning of the sentence; the summer did not swim and play baseball — *we* did; therefore, the phrase modifies the wrong word.)
**Revised** We passed our summer happily, swimming and playing baseball. (Note that the addition of the word *we* as the new subject does the correcting job nicely.)

**D**

*Revised*    *Because we were swimming and playing baseball,* our summer passed happily. (The phrase has been converted into a clause.)

*Dangling*    *Lying on my back on the raft,* the stars burned brightly in the sky. (It is not the *stars* that are lying on the speaker's back, but the speaker; the phrase is modifying *stars,* the wrong word.)

*Revised*    *As I was lying on my back on the raft,* the stars burned brightly in the sky. (The phrase is turned into a clause.)

*Revised*    *Lying on my back on the raft,* I could see the stars burning brightly in the sky. (Adding the words *I could see* to the main clause gives the phrase the correct word to modify: *I.*)

**2**    **Recognize and Correct Dangling Gerund Phrases.**
A gerund is an *-ing* word that functions as a noun. A gerund implies the presence of a *someone.*

*Dangling*    *After filling my cavity,* my tooth stopped aching. (The *tooth* did not do the *filling.*)

*Revised*    *After the dentist filled my cavity,* my tooth stopped aching. (The phrase is now a clause.)

*Revised*    *After filling my cavity,* the dentist stopped my tooth from aching. (Now the phrase refers clearly to the new subject of the main clause: *dentist.*)

*Dangling*    *In planning a college education,* careful preparations are needed. (*Careful preparations* cannot do the *planning;* a *someone* is needed.)

*Revised*    *In planning a college education,* a student needs to make careful preparations. (The *someone,* in the form of *a student,* has been added to the main clause; now the phrase correctly modifies *student.*)

**3**    **Recognize and Correct Dangling Infinitive Phrases.**
An infinitive phrase has for its headwords the *to* form of a verb: *to play, to work, to love,* and so forth.

*Dangling*    *To become a movie star,* talent and luck are needed. (*To become a movie star* does not logically refer to *talent and luck,* the subject of the main clause; people become movie stars.)

*Revised*    *To become a movie star,* one [or *a person*] needs talent and luck. (Now the phrase refers logically to *one*—or *a person.*)

*Revised*    *If you want to become a movie star,* you need talent and luck. (The phrase has been converted into a clause.)

**D**

**Dangling**   *To make a delicious stew,* fresh ingredients must be used. (The *ingredients* do not cook the stew; people do.)
**Revised**   *To make a delicious stew,* you must use fresh ingredients. (We have supplied the subject in the main clause, *you,* to which the phrase can logically refer.)
**Revised**   *If you want to make a delicious stew,* you must use fresh ingredients. (The phrase has been converted into a clause.)

**4**   Recognize and Correct Dangling Elliptical Clauses.
An *elliptical* expression has words missing. An *elliptical clause* is missing either a subject or a verb; these are understood instead of being stated. You can correct dangling elliptical clauses either by making the subject of the elliptical clause agree with the subject of the main clause or by supplying the missing subject and verb.

**Dangling**   *When driving,* my seat belt is always fastened. (The *seat belt* is not *driving;* the italicized clause is missing the words *I am,* so the implied subject, *I,* does not agree with the *seat belt* of the main clause.)
**Revised**   *When driving,* I always fasten my seat belt. (Now the implied subject, *I,* is the same as the new subject of the main clause.)
**Revised**   *When I am driving,* my seat belt is always fastened. (With the missing words supplied, the clause is expanded and refers, properly, to *is fastened.*)
**Dangling**   *When at the age of six,* my Uncle Fred gave me my first haircut. (*Uncle Fred* was not *at the age of six* when the haircut was given — the speaker was: *I was* are the missing words.)
**Revised**   *When at the age of six,* I was given my first haircut by my Uncle Fred. (The implied subject of the clause now matches the new subject — *I* — of the main clause.)
**Revised**   *When I was at the age of six,* my Uncle Fred gave me my first haircut. (The missing words supplied expand the clause and make it modify, properly, the verb *gave.*)

*Note:* Some verbal phrases do not intend to modify any single portion of the main clause. Rather, they make statements about the whole sentence. These are called *absolute constructions;* using them puts the writer in no danger of creating a dangling modifier.

*Considering the time,* we're not doing badly.

*Parking regulations having been suspended,* we decided to leave the car on 12th Street.

*The air being nippy,* we brought along our parkas.

*Winning being impossible,* we figured we'd just have fun playing.

**D**

## TEST YOURSELF ON
## Recognizing and Correcting Dangling Modifiers

Some of the following sentences are correct; place a C next to them. For those that have dangling modifiers, underline the dangling modifier; then correct it according to the methods just discussed.

1. _____ Before leaving for California, hotel reservations must be made.

2. _____ Being an American, his knowledge of Italy was limited.

3. _____ Arriving in Chicago, his suitcase was in California.

4. _____ To understand one's spouse, good communications should exist.

5. _____ After putting my son to sleep, I settled down with a good book.

6. _____ After changing my shoes, my girlfriend took me out to dinner.

7. _____ To understand true happiness, you need to know true love.

8. _____ Although planning to get married, my girl's parents didn't know it.

9. _____ His eyes caught the glint of a strange seashell walking barefoot on the beach.

10. _____ Listening to the concert, the Rolling Stones seemed like the funkiest group in the world.

11. _____ My examinations were passed, sweating and praying.

12. _____ To travel in grand style, money is essential.

13. _____ Driving through Ohio, I decided to stop in Akron.

14. _____ If sleepy, your car can be very dangerous.

15. _____ Before going up for a parachute jump, the airplane was thoroughly inspected.

# Dash

The dash is a mark of internal punctuation that has the separating effect of the comma or parentheses but that confers emphasis on what follows it. (See **Parentheses** for a brief discussion of the differences in the use of the three marks.)

If you use a typewriter, the dash is made by striking the hyphen key twice: --. If you write by hand, make the dash twice as long as the hyphen. In either case, do not leave a space before or after the dash — run it directly up against the letters of the preceding and following words. The dash may appropriately be used in the following circumstances.

**1**  Use the dash to set off a final appositive that is short and would benefit from emphasis.

What was in the package was what he feared and desired — poison.

After he read the thesis, one word came to mind — nonsense.

**2**  Use the dash to set off nonrestrictive appositives that would benefit from emphasis or that need dashes for clarity.

My doctor — my friend for thirty years — always told me the truth.

Three girls — Jackie, Leslie, and Margo — came to my birthday party.

Note that we could replace the dashes in the last example with commas, but see what confusion might result if we did:

Three girls, Jackie, Leslie, and Margo, came to my birthday party.

In this sentence, we cannot be sure that the names given are those of the three girls; it is possible, in this case, that six people came and that Jackie and Leslie are men. The dashes, however, clear up any possible confusion.

**D**

**3**   Use a dash to set off a series of items, occurring either at the beginning or the end of a sentence, where the items are separated by commas.

> ***Beginning of Sentence***   Love, friendship, caring for children, personal fulfillment, protecting nature's bounties, concern for others — these are the values that free men strive for.
> ***End of Sentence***   We look for the same qualities in an athlete that we find in a soldier — agility, stamina, strength, courage, and competitiveness.

**4**   Use a dash to set off parenthetical elements that abruptly interrupt the sense of the sentence.

> In the blackness of the mine shaft, we started climbing slowly — what else could we do? — until at last we saw a pinpoint of light.
>
> The character of the voting population — 8,500 registered Democrats — makes it impossible to elect a Republican to office.

## TEST YOURSELF ON
## the Use of the Dash

Use the dash to improve the clarity, emphasis, and meaning of the following sentences.

1. You owe me one thing, loyalty.

2. There is a possibility that we who have paid our rent will be evicted from our apartment.

3. The pilgrims went devoutly to Rome Catholicism's holy city.

4. That's what I would call it a crying shame!

5. The crises in his life, divorce, separation from his children, the loss of his job, the attack of pneumonia, these were all too much for him.

6. I notified the Dean of my decision, resignation.

7. Job training programs, increased educational opportunities in the professions, federally sponsored housing, improved day-care facilities, all these are necessary to begin the attack on poverty.

8. The defeat of communicable diseases and the increase in the food supply these have been partly responsible for the rise in world population.

9. One of the world's great religions Islam was begun by an Arab merchant, Mohammed.

10. He drove in a cold fury not for one minute taking his eye off the prisoner beside him.

# Diagramming

Diagramming a sentence is a way to represent graphically how its parts go together — to enable the student to *see* what he or she is trying to grasp as an abstraction.

## Standard Method of Diagramming

Here is how the standard method works:

**1   The Basic Sentence**

Line is perpendicular
to base line

| Subj. | Verb | Dir. Obj. |
|-------|------|-----------|
| He | threw | baseballs |

Base line

Perpendicular line
bisects base line

Slant line

| Subj. | Linking verb | Pred. Adj. |
|-------|--------------|------------|
| Cats | are | independent |

### 2   Modifiers

Modifiers of all types are placed below the base line.

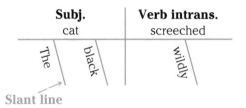

*Words that modify modifiers* are attached with a right angle struc-ture to the words they modify.

The pale blue flower wilted very suddenly.

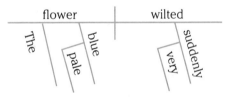

An *indirect object is treated as a modifier*— equivalent to a phrase beginning with *to* or *for*— and placed in the diagram as follows:

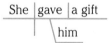

### 3   Word Groups Substituting for Basic Parts and Modifiers

A word group substituted for a subject, object, or comple-ment is pictured parallel to and above the base line joined by a figure that looks like this:

### Example of a Gerund Phrase as Subject

*Making a glass bottle* is skilled work.

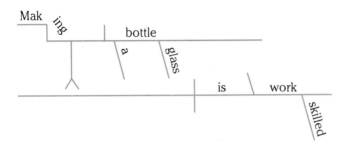

### Example of a Noun Clause as Complement

Her idea was *that she needed some advice.*

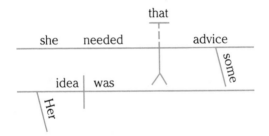

### Example of an Infinitive Phrase as Object

My Uncle Fred has decided *to live in France.*

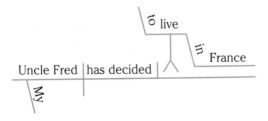

**4   Word Groups Substituting for Single-Word Modifiers**

A word group substituted for a single-word modifier follows the procedure for modifiers and is *placed below the base line.*

**Example of a Prepositional Phrase Used as an Adverb**

The police came *in a hurry.*

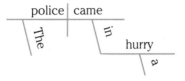

**Example of a Clause Used as an Adverb**

*After the plane takes off,* we can relax.

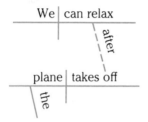

**Example of a Prepositional Phrase Used as an Adjective**

Louis is the man *in the window.*

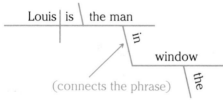

**Example of a Clause Used as an Adjective**

The student *who needs help* goes to his adviser.

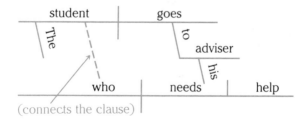

### Example of a Participial Phrase Used as an Adjective

Having ordered his breakfast, he sat quietly.

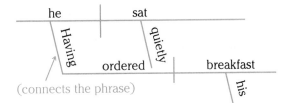

(connects the phrase)

### 5 Compound Constructions

Compound constructions are placed in parallel, as follows:

#### Compound Subject

*Donuts and coffee* taste good.

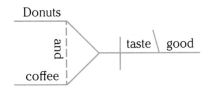

#### Compound Verb

Cats *scratch and claw*.

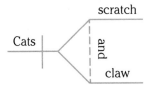

### Compound Sentence

He wanted to go home for Christmas, but he couldn't afford the fare.

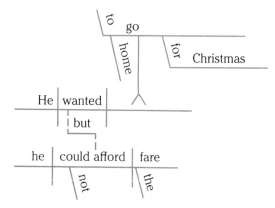

## Alternative Method of Diagramming

Some authorities prefer an alternative method of diagramming which proceeds as follows:

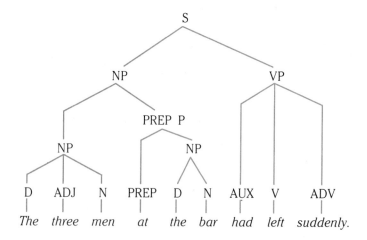

Key to abbreviations: ADJ (adjective); ADV (adverb); AUX (auxiliary); D (determiner); N (noun); NP (noun phrase); PREP (preposition); PREP P (Prepositional phrase); S (sentence); V (verb); VP (verb phrase).

## TEST YOURSELF ON
## Diagramming Sentences

**A**   Use the standard method to diagram these sentences.

1. Eggs are oval.
2. Fordham defeated Columbia.
3. John loves Mary.
4. The dark clouds covered the far horizon.
5. In the morning, he shaved.
6. He decided to give his mother a ring.
7. When you eat spaghetti, you get indigestion.
8. A man who lives on my block is the owner of a new car.
9. Cats and mice love to play.
10. They swam, fished, and played tennis.

**B**   Try diagramming the following by using the alternative method.

1. The silver fish floating in the lake are feeding slowly.
2. The new secretary in our office is typing furiously.

**C**   Go back to the standard method for the following:

1. Although he considered himself a workhorse, he could not maintain the pace set by his sister.
2. Myra's basic principle was that language was the most important element in a short story.
3. He had a tractor for which he had paid a thousand dollars, and a car for which he had paid much more.
4. Television is not only entertaining, but it is also educational.
5. His great ambition, which he had told no one, was to make money soon and retire early.

# Diction

Diction means "the use of words." The use of words always involves choice, and in this entry we will discuss the considerations that govern a writer's choice of words. Before we do so, however, we must consider two preliminary matters: (1) the sources where

**D**

writers can find words and (2) the standards commonly applied to the use of language.

## Sources

### 1 Dictionaries

The dictionary is an invaluable source of words. It is not just an alphabetical list of definitions; for each word, a good dictionary will also give such information as the part of speech the entry belongs to (i.e., noun, verb, preposition, etc.), its level of usage (archaic/obsolete, informal/colloquial, nonstandard, dialect, slang, etc.), plural spelling, pronunciation, synonyms and antonyms, and more. You should become familiar with the dictionary and take advantage of what it has to offer. The following are recommended in the event that your instructor does not suggest a particular dictionary:

*The American College Dictionary*
*The Random House Dictionary*
*Webster's New Collegiate Dictionary*
*Webster's New World Dictionary*
*The American Heritage Dictionary*

A specimen entry from *The American Heritage Dictionary of the English Language* (The American Heritage Publishing Company, Inc., and Houghton Mifflin Company, Boston, 1973 rpt.) is reproduced at the top of page 99.

Here we find a main boldface entry followed by a pronunciation guide in parentheses and in italics the designation *n.* for noun. Within this entry, following the seven numbered definitions of the sense of the noun *worm*, there follows a smaller boldface line, *wormed, worming, worms,* following the designation — *v.* for verb. These three smaller boldface words tell us that the verb form is regular, that is, has an *-ed* ending. Directly following the main entry for the noun are parentheses enclosing *wûrm*, which indicates pronunciation. Referring to the pronunciation key at the front of the dictionary, we find that the *û* is pronounced like the *-ere* in the word *were*.

The definitions that follow that first entry are divided into the

D

**worm** (wûrm) *n.* **1.** Any of various invertebrates, as those of the phyla Annelida, Nematoda, or Platyhelminthes, having a long, flexible rounded or flattened body, often without obvious appendages. **2.** Any of various insect larvae having a soft, elongated body. **3.** Any of various unrelated animals resembling a worm in habit or appearance, as the shipworm or the slowworm. **4.** An object or device that is like a worm in appearance or action, as a threaded screw or a zigzag road. **5.** An insidiously tormenting or devouring force: *"The worm of conscience still begnaw thy soul!"* (Shakespeare). **6.** A pitiable or contemptible creature; poor wretch. **7.** *Plural. Pathology.* Intestinal infestation with worms or wormlike parasites. In this sense, also called "helminthiasis." —*v.* **wormed, worming, worms.** —*tr.* **1.** To make (one's way) with or as if with the sinuous crawling motion of a worm. **2.** To elicit by artful or devious means. Used with *out of.* **3.** To cure of intestinal worms. **4.** *Nautical.* To wrap yarn or twine around (rope). —*intr.* **1.** To move in a sinuous manner suggestive of a worm. **2.** To make one's way by artful or devious means. Used with *into* or *out of.* [Middle English *worm,* Old English *wyrm,* worm, serpent. See **wer-³** in Appendix.*]

senses of the word by boldface numerals and proceed from the most common and exact senses (entries 1, 2, and 3) to later accretions (4, 5, 6) which show how the word has come into other than exact, scientific uses. The numeral 7 gives the sense — when used in the plural — of a special usage, a term in the field of pathology.

In a similar way, definitions are given for the verb form, following first the designation — *tr.* which stands for *transitive*, that is, a verb taking an object. As in the series of definitions given for the noun, the last numeral here — 4 — carries the special sense, the technical sense of the verb in nautical use. After this portion of the entry come two further definitions following the designation — *intr.* meaning *intransitive*, that is, taking no object.

At the end of the whole entry, within square brackets, is the etymology, or derivation of the word. We see that the word derives from the Middle English word *worm*, from Old English *wyrm*, whose original sense was *worm* or *serpent*. The reader is then referred to a useful entry in the Appendix (which follows the main vocabulary), where Indo-European roots are discussed. The entry noted is the third (see superscript 3) given under *-wer*. There we would find that one of the original meanings of the root was "to turn or wind."

## 2  Dictionaries of Synonyms and Antonyms

Dictionaries of synonyms and antonyms are especially valuable in helping you to expand and enliven your vocabulary and to choose the exact and accurate word — a crucial aspect of good diction. Two kinds of synonym dictionaries are available. One simply lists under the word you are looking up a whole group of words having similar meanings. A second type discriminates between synonyms by way of a discussion of shades of meaning. The following are recommended:

Norman Lewis, *The New Roget's Thesaurus of the English Language in Dictionary Form* (hardcover; lists synonyms)
*Webster's New Dictionary of Synonyms* (hardcover; makes discriminations)
*Roget's II: The New Thesaurus* (hardcover; lists synonyms)
*The Merriam-Webster Thesaurus* (softcover; lists synonyms)
*The Merriam-Webster Dictionary of Synonyms* (softcover; makes discriminations)

**3   Other People's Writing**

An important source for fresh and lively words is your reading. When you read, do so with a sharp eye for what is well said. It is not only permissible, it is desirable, to use — in your own way — words and expressions that other writers have used well. This does not mean that you should, in response to a writing assignment, *lift* (plagiarize) a whole essay or even a couple of sentences from someone else's writing and try to pass them off as your own; rather it means that you should feel free to incorporate into your own work the best words and expressions that other writers have used and that seem to you especially eloquent.

## Standards

Good English is a relative term. Linguists define it as the level useful to the particular situation in which it is spoken and written. Thus good English varies from one social or regional group to another and from one particular kind of writing and speaking to another. What is *good* for speakers and writers in southern Australia differs from what is good for users of the language in western Ireland — or middle America. Many kinds of variations have been described for speakers of our language; but the most important for our purposes are the distinctions made between *standard* and *nonstandard* English, and, within standard English, the distinction between *formal* and *informal.*

Standard English is the spoken and written language used by well-educated people when they wish to communicate as effectively as they can. People who use standard English enjoy a certain measure of social prestige; their language is used routinely in business, law, science, the humanities, and whenever an occupation or a profession requires written communication. Journalism, literature, and the great bulk of printed matter also use standard English. On the other hand, *nonstandard* English is the term given to the speaking and writing characteristics of the relatively uneducated. Writers and speakers of nonstandard English have usually had little opportunity to use written communication, and, more often than not, they have had little formal education.

### Standard

Most people today feel politically powerless. A relatively small group participates in nominating candidates for office, and not many more go to the polls to elect these candidates. More important, few citizens have access to government at any level. Thus politicians are not in touch with the real needs of their constituencies. The people know it, and this is the source of the feeling of powerlessness. Unfortunately, that feeling leads to apathy.

### Nonstandard

We was asking ourselfs the other day what we would be doing if we was rich. Charlie didn have no idea, he say it couldnt never happen anyway, so whats the difference. Herbie said he buy himself a car — a Cadillac — a house, a boat, and so many pair of shoes he couldn't never wear them out, cause he couldn't never wear em at all. Me, I say if I was rich, I just keeps on *buying.* I don't care *what.*

The advice given in this book is directed toward helping you to achieve competence in standard English. Since most students using this book will be seeking to enter the world where standard English is considered the appropriate level of spoken and written communication, we adhere to this standard. What we mean by good diction, then, will refer to standard English.

Within standard English, good diction depends on three basic considerations: the use of language that takes into account both your subject matter and your audience — in other words, the levels of usage called *formal* and *informal* and the appropriate uses of the *colloquial* and *slang;* the use of the *exact* word that will convey your *exact* meaning; and the use of words that are fresh, clear, and concrete.

**D**

## Levels of Usage: Subject Matter and Audience

### 1  Formal

The formal level is appropriate whenever you want to establish an impersonal relation to your subject and your audience. It is a useful level for conveying serious information to an audience wanting exact information, because formal writing strives for clarity and precision. Serious books and articles in science, social science, technology, law, and the humanities employ the formal level. Characteristically, the formal is found mainly in writing, but it is also used in speeches, lectures, and discussions — such as those commonly held at formal meetings. Formal writing is characterized by seriousness of tone, complexity of sentence structure, and elaborate vocabulary — all in the interest of conveying exact, serious, and clear information.

> Ginseng is the perennial herb *Panax* native to North America and Asia. Asiatic ginseng *(Panax schinseng)* has been known in Asia for centuries and particularly prized by the Chinese as an important item in their herbal formulary. They have used ginseng as a virtual panacea, prescribing it for conditions ranging from flatulence to pneumonia. The demand for ginseng in America is a recent development. For the purpose of export, China and Korea have developed the North American *Panax quinquefolius*. Here ginseng root is also virtually a panacea, but most users employ it to enhance natural vitality.

### 2  Informal

In recent years, it has become increasingly difficult to separate the formal from the informal. Still, there are distinct differences. The informal is the everyday language employed by well-educated people. It is the language used in private letter-writing, ordinary conversation, and even books and articles that aim to catch the attention of an audience that feels at home with a familiar tone.

> Policemen make friends with other policemen. It isn't that they're not friendly; they're just busy. In fact, they spend so much time on the job, they don't have much time for socializing. So they just naturally tend to be friendly with the people they see most: other policemen. Most policemen enjoy each other's company, but most wish they had a wider range of acquaintants.

Note that this sample of the informal is conversational in tone; that it has a speaker's vocabulary, uses contractions, and has a less complicated sentence structure than the formal sample. All but the most sternly academic, scientific, or legal writing has some informal cadences in it.

D

An important thing to bear in mind — regardless of whether your writing is formal or informal — is to maintain consistency of tone, except when you are so well in control of your material that you are able to mix tones purposefully.

### Unintentionally Mixed Tones
The beauty of the uninhabited desert regions *doesn't do a thing for me.*

### Revised to Maintain Formality
The beauty of the uninhabited desert regions *does not impress me.*

### Intentionally Mixed Tones
The President's tour of European capitals must be described as a *bust* — considering that he failed to negotiate any of the trade agreements he had hoped for.

Some discussions (and some dictionaries) regard the *colloquial* level as synonymous with informal or nonstandard or both. But the word *colloquial* really means *spoken* and can be used to describe a wide range of language that appears in standard, nonstandard, formal, or informal writing.

Here is a small list of words and expressions that are considered colloquial, along with their more formal counterparts:

| Colloquial | More Formal |
|---|---|
| boss | superior, supervisor |
| bug | germ |
| brainy | intelligent |
| flunk | fail |
| hunch | premonition |
| job | position |
| kid | child |
| snooze | nap |
| splurge | spend lavishly |
| stump | puzzle |
| alibi | excuse |
| funny | strange |
| phone | telephone |
| guy | man |
| slob | unkempt person |

**D**

### 3  Slang

Slang is highly informal language, mostly spoken, rarely used in written standard English — but not absolutely forbidden there. Slang consists of both newly coined words and expressions and new and extended meanings attached to older words. It develops from attempts to find fresh and colorful language — funny, pungent, surprising. It also develops as a kind of shorthand, and that is frequently at the root of its downfall. As shorthand, slang comes to be so overused that it falls into disuse. For example, *heavy*, a "heavy" expression of the late sixties and early seventies, is no longer in frequent use by those who habitually use slang. *Groovy* has also been banished by many slang users, and *let's tip*, meaning *let's leave* (on the analogy of "let's tiptoe out"), is so short a piece of shorthand that it never really caught on.

Nevertheless, slang has its place in both formal and informal writing and it is unwise to suppose that slang is "bad" English. In fact, many words and expressions that began as slang have passed into general (formal) usage, and our language is richer for having them. The use of slang, like the use of other words, should be determined by audience and subject matter. Some purists would object to a slang expression like the following:

The new Woody Allen movie is *a real kick in the head.*

although, conceivably, it might prove a highly effective concluding sentence for a first paragraph reviewing that movie, especially if the review were addressed to a suitable audience (the subject matter is certainly suitable for slang expression).

Woody Allen is a comic on his way up; Diane Keaton is a lovely, scatterbrained, painfully shy Midwestern singer-model; *Annie Hall* is a hilarious and touching film that depicts the bittersweet progress of an on-again, off-again romance between a New York ethnic and a middle American. Conclusion: *the new Woody Allen movie is a real kick in the head.*

Examine carefully the following three examples. Are these effective uses of slang? Can you think of a way to improve the one or ones you think are ineffective? Can you think of contexts in which one or more of them might be effective?

I didn't want to get hung up on a 9–5 trip but I needed the money that this gig had to offer, so I rapped about it with my old lady and got a good handle on the whole shebang. Then I said okay.

D

To me his apartment was pure raunch. It looked like he had pigged out there over the weekend.

Man, don't get all bent out of shape!

## Identifying Slang and Colloquial or Informal Language

Using your own sensitivity to language, put a C or an I next to those words or expressions below that strike you as colloquial or informal, and an S next to the ones that seem to be slang. After you have marked all of them, look each of them up in a good dictionary and check the dictionary labels against your answers. How many did you get?

1. bitch (verb)
2. freak (fan, enthusiast)
3. up-tight
4. jazz (verb)
5. bust (verb)
6. cool it
7. beef (verb)
8. cop (noun)
9. scat
10. funky
11. slob
12. buggy (crazy)

## Selecting the Proper Level of Usage for a Specific Piece of Writing

Think about each of the specific pieces of writing given below and for each one choose the proper level of usage. Prepare to defend your choice with a logical argument.

1. A report to the Board of Directors of IBM Corporation on the sales prospects of a new product: a tiny, portable minicomputer.
2. A review of the movie *The Empire Strikes Back* written for an underground newspaper.
3. An introduction to the form of popular music called punk rock, written for *Time* magazine.
4. The same — written for the Sunday magazine section of your hometown newspaper.
5. An article for the campus newspaper on a recent budget crisis at your college.

6. An account of your football (or basketball or baseball) team's fortieth consecutive loss — written for your school newspaper.
7. An essay written for a course in sociology giving an account of how your family (including aunts, uncles, and cousins) celebrates weddings.
8. A speech at a fraternity or club dance announcing the dissolution of the club or fraternity.
9. A basic explanation of enzymes for a scientific journal.
10. A review of children's literature published in the past year — for a journal of psychology.

## Using Exact Words to Convey Exact Meaning

Writers who care about their work — which is another way of saying writers who care about their readers — will expend the time and energy necessary to write with precision; that is, they will go over what they have written to make sure that the words they have used convey their exact meaning.

### 1   Precise Expression

Writers who want to increase the precision of their word choices must be prepared to acquire the habit of rereading and then revising their written work. They must develop the habit of *seeing* and changing constructions like the following:

> ***Inexact***   Americans are *totally* interested in sex.

It's hard to say exactly *what* this sentence intends to express; it may mean something like "Americans are *completely* interested in sex" but more likely a word like *exclusively* or *solely* or *only* was intended, instead of either *totally* or *completely*. The writer may have meant to say that "Americans have an *absorbing* interest in sex" — but the failure to be exact asks the reader to consider many possibilities.

> ***Inexact***   Lisa was asked to testify as an *uninterested* observer of the burglary.

Here the writer simply confuses two words: *uninterested*, which means "without interest," and *disinterested*, which means "free of bias; impartial." Obviously, then, the exact expression would be

"Lisa was asked to testify as a *disinterested* observer of the burglary."

> **Inexact**  We swam until we were tired, played volleyball on the sand, ate too much seafood, and got bad sunburns. We had a *nice* time.

Here the offending word is *nice;* it's simply too vague and doesn't in the least describe what has gone before. Better would be "we had an *exhausting but exhilarating day*."

## TEST YOURSELF ON
## Using Exact Expressions

In each of the following examples, the italicized word or phrase is not as exact as it should be. Supply a better expression in each case.

1. Corruption in the District Attorney's office was *first known* in the *Times*.
2. He *fulfilled* the court orders.
3. By the time the summer was over, he *knew* his desires.
4. Summer jobs for students were *not easy*.
5. Unemployment was an important *fact* in our economy.
6. Many of those who were flower children have *lost their appeal* for working on the land.
7. Her *immaturity* may improve as she gets older.
8. The rural atmosphere *subjects* a person to the beauties of nature.
9. He decided to *expect* the job.
10. After the meal, he felt *nice*.

### 2  Idioms

An idiom is an expression whose meaning cannot be determined by the ordinary meanings of the words used in it. Native speakers of English have no trouble recognizing the idiom in the sentence "A gunman *held up* the supermarket." They would not think that the gunman *lifted high*, but rather that he *robbed*, the supermarket. Thus we could not literally translate *held up* into, say, French, and expect a Frenchman to understand it to mean *robbed*. Logic also offers no help in understanding idioms. Because it is *customary* in English to say "He was acquitted *of* the charges" rather than "he was acquitted *from* the charges," we say that the use of certain prepositions after certain words is idiomatic — that is, not logical but just peculiar to our language.

Although most native speakers of English automatically use idiomatic expressions, some writers have difficulty with verbs or adjectives that must be followed by particular prepositions in order to deliver their intended meaning. Here is a brief list of some troublesome combinations:

**absolved by, from**   I was *absolved by* the court. I was *absolved from* blame.

**accompany by, on**   I was *accompanied by* Tom. I was *accompanied on* my trip by Tom.

**acquitted of**   He was *acquitted of* all charges.

**adapted to, from, by**   The gasoline engine can be *adapted to* air-conditioners. The movie script was *adapted from* a novel; it was *adapted by* William Goldman.

**agree to, on, with**   *We agree to* the terms. We *agree on* a course of action. He *agreed with* me.

**angry with, at, about**   Terry was *angry with* me, *angry at* her mother, and *angry about* her situation.

**argue with, for, against, about**   I *argued with* Harry *about* air pollution; he *argued for* and I *argued against* government controls.

**capable of**   He was *capable of* being deceitful.

**compare to, with**   *Compared to* me, he's a saint. He *compared* a Volkswagen *with* a Toyota.

**communicate with, about**   I asked him to *communicate with* me soon. The two countries *communicated about* agriculture.

**confide in, to**   Can I *confide in* you? Then I want to *confide to* you that I broke the law once.

**conform to, with**   You must *conform to* (or *with*) this standard.

**conformity with**   You must act in *conformity with* prevailing customs.

**connect by, with**   The hose is *connected by* a coupling. I am *connected with* the English Department.

**correspond to, with**   I *correspond with* my colleagues regularly. A French province *corresponds* roughly *to* an American state.

**describe as, to**   It was *described as* a blessing. I *described to* him my latest project.

**despair of**   He *despaired of* ever understanding algebra.

**differ about, from, with**   We *differ about* the best wine to drink with fish. My ideas *differ from* his. I beg to *differ with* you.

**different from**\* My plans are very *different from* yours.

**enter into, on, upon** We *entered into* an agreement. The United States *entered on* (or *upon*) a new era in foreign relations.

**free from, of** We were *free of* him at last. I need to be *freed from* my obligations.

**identical with** Your hat is *identical with* mine.

**independent of** He is *independent of* his family.

**interest in** He *interested* himself *in* politics.

**live at, in, on** He *lives at* 525 East 89th Street. He *lives in* an elegant mansion. He *lives on* his independent income.

**listen to, at** He *listened to* nobody. She *listened at* the door.

**necessity for, of** The *necessity for* vitamins has been proven. There is no *necessity of* your catching cold.

**object to** I don't *object to* your statement.

**overcome by, with** Sarah was *overcome by* sadness. Arthur was *overcome with* admiration.

**parallel between, with** There is a *parallel between* his attitudes and his behavior. The course of his career ran *parallel with* mine.

**persuade of, to** I was *persuaded of* the rightness of his argument. I was *persuaded to* accompany him on the trip.

**preferable to** Hawaii is *preferable to* Alaska for a vacation.

**superior to** His stereo set is *superior to* mine.

**vary from, in, with** Ideas *vary from* one another just as shoe sizes *vary in* width. My mood *varies with* changes of weather.

**worthy of** He is *worthy of* my sympathy.

Idiomatic expression also requires that some verbs be followed by a gerund and some by an infinitive.

| *Infinitive* | *Gerund* |
|---|---|
| able to go | capable of going |
| like to go | enjoy going |
| eager to go | cannot help going |
| hesitate to go | privilege of going |
| need to go | purpose of going |
| ask to go | consider going |
| consent to go | deny going |
| want to go | put off going |

---

\* *Different than* is the colloquial usage when a clause is the object of the prepositional phrase. *Formal:* The farm looks different *from what* I had expected. *Colloquial:* The farm looks *different than* I had expected.

**D**

## TEST YOURSELF ON
## Using Correct Idiomatic Expressions

In each of the blank spaces, write the correct idiomatic expression needed for the sentence. The expression required may be a preposition, an infinitive, or a gerund.

1. With fish dinners, drinking white wine is preferable _____ drinking red.

2. I hesitate _____ him what I think of him. (Use a form of *tell*.)

3. He lives comfortably _____ his pension.

4. They argued _____ who would do a better job as major.

5. He was described _____ me as a liberal, which was quite different _____ what I had been led to believe.

6. She was capable _____ making her feelings known.

7. Because she was angry _____ me, I was overcome _____ guilt.

8. I was not eager _____ (use a form of *leave*) school, but there was a necessity _____ doing so.

9. We entered _____ a contract; therefore, we were legally connected _____ each other.

10. George confided _____ his friends that he

    was breaking up with Kathy.

D

## Fresh, Specific, and Concrete Language

A writer's language should be fresh, specific, and concrete; it should avoid clichés and try to make a vivid impression on the reader. Plain language can do this if it strives for a proper balance between the abstract and the concrete, the general and the specific.

### 1 Clichés

The word *cliché* (pronounced *clee-shay*) comes from the French word for stereotype plate or printing block. Hence any word or expression whose freshness or clarity has been lost through constant usage is called a cliché, a stereotype. Such words or phrases are also called tired, stale, trite, or worn out. Writers who habitually use clichés not only use tired words but also present the reader with tired ideas.

Nevertheless, we all use clichés in ordinary conversation. In those circumstances, they are frequently forgiven — perhaps because we make up for the tired expression with a lively presence. In any case, whether your writing is formal or informal, you should develop an ear for clichés and avoid using such expressions as the following:

| | |
|---|---|
| the beginning of the end | the last straw |
| better late than never | mother nature |
| bigger and better | neat as a pin |
| cool as a cucumber | on balance |
| a crying shame | pretty as a picture |
| deep, dark secret | right on |
| do justice to | rotten to the core |
| free as a bird | sadder but wiser |
| hard as nails | tell it like it is |
| hot under the colar | variety is the spice of life |
| last but not least | viable options |

Writers who persistently use clichés are not in control of their material. Writers who are in control of their material can *use* clichés to make fresh points.

**D**

The fact that Harry was so often late for appointments made it obvious that he would never be known as *a regular guy*.

My response to what you've just proposed is *wrong on*.

*The bigger the better* simply does not apply to things like budget deficits and the headaches they invariably bring on.

## TEST YOURSELF ON
## Identifying Clichés

Circle any words or expressions you find in the following passages that you think are clichés; then supply better — fresher — words or expressions to replace them.

1. Although I was financially embarrassed, I decided to eat out anyway. I didn't care that I was getting to be fatter than a pig; I wanted to do justice to a great meal — and the bigger the better. I settled on McDonald's and started eating like there was no tomorrow. I had six Big Macs, four large orders of fries, and three large shakes. Last but not least, I topped the whole thing off with four apple turnovers. That, however, was the last straw. My stomach really started to growl, and later on that evening I realized that I had eaten myself sick. The next morning I was, believe it or not, sadder but wiser.

2. In this day and age, the American way of life demands that college students get on the ball and learn more than just the stuff taught in classes. Students should get out and mingle. This is the only way to develop a well-rounded personality and the ability to get along with others. There are all kinds of things students can do to become more interesting personalities. They can join a club, attend dances, or just start being friendly — straight from

the shoulder—with their fellow students in class. Hitting the books isn't the only way to go in college. If you want to get what you pay for, you have to pass the acid test. Beyond a shadow of a doubt, if you want to get more out of life, you have to put more into it.

## 2 Concrete and Abstract Language

Writers should use the concrete wherever possible. A concrete word is one that appeals directly to the senses—it points to something that exists. Thus *engine* is a concrete word: We can see, hear, and feel an engine when we lift the hood of a car. But what the engine supplies, *power* (or *energy*), is abstract: Power cannot be directly perceived; but many concrete things deliver power: an engine, a turbine, a locomotive, a football fullback, and so forth. We would not say, giving the reason for not buying a specific car, "The Ford had no power" if we meant that it had no engine—but we might say "The Ford had no power" if we meant that its engine wasn't efficient. So both abstract and concrete language have their uses. But the advice still holds: Writers should use the concrete word whenever they can, because the mind's ability to picture a concrete word makes the writing more vivid. This policy also applies to sentences. Sentences with abstract ideas can be made clearer by supporting them with concrete illustrations.

> ### *Sentence Containing Needlessly Abstract Words*
> The *grounds* were *sloppy* and the *planks* on the porch were *bad*.
> ### *Revised to Supply Concrete Words*
> The *front yard* was *littered with broken furniture and rusted tools* and the *steps* of the porch were *rotted and splintered*.

Frequently, the pattern of abstract-concrete shows up in good writing as the form of a paragraph; that is, the first sentence is an abstraction that following sentences seek to make concrete.

> ### Abstract First Sentence of a Paragraph
> When dealing with institutions, people are made to feel small.
> ### Concrete Follow-up Sentence
> They are made to fill out needlessly complicated forms, to spend long hours waiting on line, and frequently to visit an office several times in order to get what they came for.

**D**

### 3  Specific and General Language

The terms *specific* and *general,* applied to words or expressions, mean much the same as is meant by the labels *concrete* and *abstract*—with this difference: *Specific* and *general* attest to the relative degrees of concreteness of a particular set of words.

```
meat—poultry—chicken
animals—primates—gorillas
military—soldier—Pvt. Mudd
foliage—trees—oak
clothing—trousers—blue jeans
```

Note that as you read from left to right, the words become more specific; the reader is better able to *picture* the concrete object. Though we would not say that the words in the left-hand column are abstract, they are *more general* terms than those in the other two columns. Good writing requires that the writer use the more specific term whenever possible. Although it is true that good writers use general terms as well as specific ones, more often than not there is a loss of freshness and clarity in writing when writers abandon control of their work and use constructions like the following:

**General**  Shade was provided by a big *tree* on the *grass*.
**Specific**  Shade was provided by a *spreading maple* on the *lawn*.

**General**  College students are forced to waste a lot of time.
**Specific**  A college student must often waste time waiting on registration lines, filling out forms, and making more than one trip to a professor's office to obtain a grade. (Notice how this idea is expanded when it is made more specific.)

## TEST YOURSELF ON
## Using Specific, Concrete Language

**A**  For each of the italicized words in the sentences below, find at least two other words that convey a more specific meaning.

1. He *slept* for half an hour.
2. He *ate* his food as if it were his last meal.
3. He decided not to *tell* that he'd had an accident.
4. She *called* for help.
5. Al didn't want to *show* his feelings.
6. He *ran* all the way home.
7. He *worked on* his essay for an hour; then he gave up.

8. Out of the corner of his eye, he *noticed* someone approaching.
9. He *walked* lazily down to the corner market.
10. They *wrote* their compositions in class.

**B** Follow each of the general statements in the sentences below with two more sentences, giving concrete details to illustrate them.

*Example:* When I woke up this morning, I felt as if I'd been drugged.
*Follow-up with concrete details:* My head ached dully, and my vision was blurred. When I tried to move, it felt as if I were walking through water.

1. When I woke up this morning, I felt as if I'd been drugged.
2. My garden is growing beautifully.
3. I don't think my parents understand that I'm an adult.
4. Most college freshmen have special problems.
5. Registering for classes at this college takes its toll on a student.

# Double Negative

The use of an additional negative to reinforce an already negative statement is called a double negative and is not acceptable in standard English. Usually, the writer of a double (or even a triple) negative is intent on being emphatic in his no saying, and several hundred years ago this usage was acceptable, but not now.

> **Double Negative** Nobody loves me no more.
> **Revised** Nobody loves me *anymore.*
>
> **Double Negative** He can't hardly walk anymore.
> **Revised** He *can* hardly walk anymore. (*Hardly* is the negative.)
>
> **Double Negative** Scarcely none of my friends likes rock music.
> **Revised** Scarcely *any* of my friends like rock music. (*Scarcely* is the negative.)
>
> **Triple Negative** He never had no faith in nobody.
> **Revised** He never had faith in *anybody.*

One form of the double negative *is* acceptable, however, and its use is a form of stylistic choice. For example, we could say, "He was frequently late to my classes," or to achieve a slightly different emphasis, "He was *not in*frequently late to my classes." Another example: "She said she was willing to go out on dates with Tom," or "She said she was *not un*willing to go out on dates with Tom." The slightly different emphasis in the two sentences using the acceptable double negative is one of qualification.

**TEST YOURSELF ON**
## Eliminating Unacceptable Double or Triple Negatives

**E-H**

Each of the sentences given below contains an unacceptable double or triple negative. Correct them in the spaces provided.

1. I don't want nothing to do with you.

_____

2. There was never nobody like him.

_____

3. He never had no reason to give nobody a present.

_____

4. He didn't hardly have any friends.

_____

5. There wasn't scarcely a soul in the library when I was there on
   Saturday night.

_____

# Ellipsis

The omission of a portion of quoted text is called ellipsis. Spaced dots (ellipsis points) are used to indicate where text has been omitted.

### The Full Text Being Quoted
Mr. Ross Alexander's play moves across the stage like a dream of yesterday, stinging us with its wit and wisdom, arguing our case

before an ethical court, lifting our spirits as we contemplate our
battered selves.
Edward Quinn

***A Portion Quoted from This Text with Some Words Omitted***
Quinn says "Alexander's play moves . . . like a dream . . .
arguing our case . . . lifting our spirits. . . . "

The spaced dots in this quoted portion are ellipsis points. When the
ellipsis comes at the end of a sentence, use a period followed by
three spaced dots to indicate omitted material.

Ellipsis points are also used to indicate a pause or an unfin-
ished statement, especially in dialogue.

"Be careful, John. If you're not . . ."

"I don't know . . . I just don't know."

# End Punctuation

The punctuation marks that end sentences — periods, exclamation
points, and question marks — suggest how a reader is to understand
the whole sentence. Internal punctuation (colons, commas,
dashes, parentheses, and semicolons) indicates relations of the
parts of the sentence. See **Colon, Comma, Rules, Dash, Exclamation Point, Parentheses, Period, Question Mark, Semicolon.**

# Examination Skills

See **Study and Examination-Taking Skills.**

# Exclamation Point

The exclamation point (!), which always signifies strong emphasis,
should be used as follows.

**1**   Use the exclamation point to mark the end of an exclamatory sentence, phrase, or clause. An exclamatory expression is an abrupt, forceful outcry — very emphatic.

How he must be suffering! (sentence)

What a tragedy! (elliptical clause, i.e., one with words missing: full clause is "What a tragedy this is!")

No kidding! (phrase)

A single exclamation point does the job. Don't use more than one for extra emphasis.

**2**   Use the exclamation point to emphasize a form of direct address or an interjection when there is strong feeling being conveyed.

George! I need help!

Hurray! We won!

**3**   Use an exclamation point to add emphasis to an imperative sentence (a command) where strong feeling is being conveyed.

Shut your mouth!

Stay away from me!

Give me an answer now!

**4**   Do not use an exclamation point for (a) statements that are not exclamatory, (b) ordinary forms of address, (c) unemphatic interjections, or (d) mild commands.

*Wrong*   That's too bad!

*Wrong*   George! I'd like to speak to you.

*Wrong*   Well! we've arrived.

*Wrong*   Turn left at the corner!

*Note:* When the exclamation point is overused, it gives your writing an air of phony excitement — almost hysteria — and robs you of the opportunity to provide real emphasis where it is needed. So use the exclamation point sparingly.

## TEST YOURSELF ON
## Using the Exclamation Point Appropriately

Some of the sentences below use the exclamation point appropriately; next to these, place the letter C. In the rest, strike out the exclamation points that are unnecessary.

1. _____ War is hell!

2. _____ How the mighty have fallen!

3. _____ College courses ask too much of a student!

4. _____ Get your hands off me!

5. _____ How he must have suffered!

6. _____ This coffee is terrible!

7. _____ I need aspirin!

8. _____ What a crazy man!

9. _____ Turn the car around!

10. _____ What big teeth you have, Grandma!

F

# Fragments

The word *fragment* means a piece or a part; therefore, a sentence fragment is a piece of a sentence. Beginning writers frequently write pieces of sentences because they distrust the *length* of what they are writing, and they think that if they insert a period after they have written a certain number of words their writing will "look" better. This is an error. Length is not the main factor in determining when to end one sentence and begin another.

> [A] Whenever I try to hold a long and serious conversation with my parents about my career. [B] They get me angry by raising irrelevant issues and arguments.

The writer of this material decided to place a period after the word *career* because the string of words looked long. In fact, however, the portion that is marked A is an incorrect *sentence fragment*. The reason it's a fragment is that it is a *dependent clause;* that is, it has a subject (*I*) and a finite verb (*try*) — which all sentences need — but it also has a subordinating conjunction, *whenever.* The whole structure hangs from this conjunction — which signals us that the structure must be connected to an independent clause — and therefore it cannot stand alone.

**F**

We can make A independent and therefore able to stand alone by eliminating *whenever;* this detaches the clause from what it depends on and makes it a whole sentence — an independent clause.

The second method of correcting the fragment error is to take the fragment, A, and hook it onto an independent clause. This we can do by substituting a comma for the period after *career* and making the capital letter in *they* into a lowercase letter, for the B portion of the example *is* an independent clause. (If you have forgotten the meaning of dependent and independent clauses, go back to Part 1, pp. 29–33, and study the subject.)

### Original Example
Whenever I try to hold a long and serious conversation with my parents about my career. They get me angry by raising irrelevant issues and arguments.

### Example Corrected by the First Method
I try to hold a long and serious conversation with my parents about my career. They get me angry by raising irrelevant issues and arguments.

### Example Corrected by the Second Method
Whenever I try to hold a long and serious conversation with my parents about my career, they get me angry by raising irrelevant issues and arguments.

Which of the corrections do you think is better?

In this case, the second method is better because retaining the word *whenever* establishes a clear relation between the two parts.

### Fragment
While I was listening to some punk rock on the stereo the other night. Someone came along and stole my car.

### Corrected by First Method
I was listening to some punk rock on the stereo the other night. Someone came along and stole my car. (Grammatically correct, but gives no sense of how the two parts are related.)

### Corrected by Second Method
While I was listening to some punk rock on the stereo the other night, someone came along and stole my car. (Also grammatically correct, but a better correction because the two parts are better related.)

## TEST YOURSELF ON
## Correcting Sentence Fragments

The following are all incorrect. Rewrite each as a complete sentence.

1. They wouldn't let Agnes on the basketball court. Because she wasn't wearing sneakers.
2. I'm worried about my final exams. Which come in about three weeks.
3. Professor Urban took me out for an expensive dinner. Although he had mentioned to me that he was short of money.
4. Unless I'm given the salary I want. I won't take the job.
5. Whenever he hears the Beatles sing "Yesterday." He's reminded of the sixties.

Another kind of sentence fragment is made when beginning writers mistake verbals for verbs and think that the structure containing a verbal can stand alone. (See Phrases.)

> *Incorrect*  Joey has an overwhelming desire. *To leave town.*

> *Incorrect*  Arthur believes he has one purpose in life. *To teach.*

> *Incorrect*  Uncle Bud is happy doing only one thing. *Running.*

Even if you haven't written much, you would not be likely to make the errors in these examples, because in each case the verbal is limited to just a few words. The problem remains the same, however, when these verbals are extended into long verbal phrases.

> *Incorrect*  Joey has an overwhelming desire. *To leave town in order to start a new career.*

> *Incorrect*  Arthur believes he has one purpose in life. *To teach youngsters the fundamentals of mathematics.*

> *Incorrect*  Uncle Bud is happy doing only one thing. *Running ten miles a day to prepare himself to compete in marathon races.*

The italicized phrase in each of these examples is dependent and cannot stand alone. Each must be connected, with or without a comma, to the sentence that precedes it. Besides having no subjects, these phrases have no finite verbs — only verbals — and a sentence must have a subject and a finite verb.

A third type of fragment appears when you punctuate prepositional phrases as if they were complete sentences (see Phrases). Only complete sentences should be punctuated as such.

prepositional phrase
*Incorrect*   Financial aid at this college is given. *To students*.

prepositional phrase
*Incorrect*   Financial aid at this college is given. *To students who show need*.

prepositional phrase
*Incorrect*   Financial aid at this college is given. *To students who show need and whose records are outstanding.*

Once again, it is unlikely that beginning writers will make the error shown in the first example, because the prepositional phrase there consists of only two words. But in the other two examples, the possibility is greater because the number of words is greater. In all three examples, of course, the period after the word *given* is incorrect and creates the fragment that follows it.

A fourth type of fragment is created when you fail to recognize that a portion of what you are writing is really a final appositive and not a sentence.

*Incorrect*   This summer, I'm spending my vacation with George.
appositive
*A friend.*

*Incorrect*   This summer I'm spending my vacation with George.
appositive
*A friend, a sportsman, a very funny guy.*

The first example contains an error that a beginning writer probably won't make, because the appositive consists of only two words. But the error in the second example is more likely to be made because the appositive has more words. In fact, appositives can be quite long and complicated, but no matter how long they are, they cannot stand as sentences. To correct the fragments above, change the period to either a comma or a colon.

## TEST YOURSELF ON
## Recognizing and Correcting Sentence Fragments

**A**   Turn the following sentence fragments into sentences by crossing out a word in the fragment.

1. Until I reached home.
2. Although he seemed like a nice enough man.

3. Whenever I have gone to the movies.
4. Unless the college gives me some financial support.
5. Because you have dry skin.
6. If I saw her at a party.
7. After the doctor changed my bandage.
8. Since he wasn't a practicing Christian.
9. While the cows were being milked.
10. As my uncle walked through the door.

**B** Correct the following fragments by adding an independent clause to the beginning or the end of each.

*Example*

> *Fragment:* Which cost me twelve dollars.
> *Fragment connected: His birthday present was a shirt,* which cost me twelve dollars.

1. Which cost me twelve dollars.
2. Although I rarely eat at a restaurant.
3. If I never buy another automobile again.
4. Running along the side of the road.
5. To understand auto mechanics.
6. In the woods behind my house.
7. A friend, a teacher, an adviser.
8. To students who are able to undertake advanced studies.
9. Unless I hear from you tonight.
10. To people who are interested in art.
11. Traveling all over the world.
12. Enough time, enough equipment, enough spirit.

**C** Read carefully each of the following examples. Underline a sentence fragment wherever you see one, and correct it. Some of the examples are complete sentences, containing no fragments; next to these, write C.

1. _____ Horses racing together through the surf.

2. _____ When Americans celebrate a holiday, they usually have a picnic and a parade.

3. _____ The Founding Fathers had a wish. To leave to us a good model for democratic living.

4. _____ She cooked a large and elaborate dinner. To impress her husband's parents.

5. _____ Last summer we visited Niagara Falls and then crossed over into Canada. Which is what I had always wanted to do.

**F**

6. _____ Although I am not at all sure what I will do after graduation. I am very sure that I want to spend four years studying ecology.

7. _____ They drove 3,000 miles across the country to see their son's graduation. An event that they had yearned to see for four long years.

8. _____ The black experience in America has been a frightful one. Which accounts for the revolutionary tone of recent black writing.

9. _____ Although television programming seems innocuous, its effects are not.

10. _____ I'm not leaving here. Until I get my money back.

## TEST YOURSELF ON
## Correcting Fragments by Proofreading

The following passage contains eight sentence fragments. By careful proofreading, find and correct each one.

My father was a farmer. Although he'd gone to college, where he studied engineering. Life on the farm was hard, but my father was ingenious, probably because of his training as an engineer, and he took delight in solving mechanical problems. Problems that would come up with the tractors or the milking machines or even the plumbing in our house. He never had time for long vacations. Which doesn't mean he ever in any way felt "burnt out." The way so many of us feel today when we work for long periods without appropriate rest. My father's secrets were two: He was a champion at resting whenever rest periods came—at night, for example. When he'd settle down with the weekly paper by the fire after a good supper. The other secret was the real sense of joy he took in his work. No aspect of the work on the land or with the livestock ever seemed to bore him. Although some of the tasks required constant repetition. In fact, whenever he needed to leave the farm to be present at ceremonious occasions. He'd be nervous and irritable for all the time he was away. It would be fine if all of us could live a work life like my father's. Loving the labor we performed.

## Free-writing

See **Prewriting.**

## Homophone

A homophone is a word identical in sound with another word, but different in spelling, origin, and meaning. Examples are *sun* and *son*, *bear* and *bare*, and so on. See **Spelling.**

# Hyphen

The hyphen is used between words or between prefixes and words to indicate that the hyphenated structure should be taken as a unit (*un-American, twenty-two, low-level*); to separate prefixes from words when the combination is spelled like a word with another meaning (e.g., *re-creation,* "a creation again," and *recreation,* "leisure"); and to divide a word at the end of a line of text to show that it continues on to the next line. This last use is a matter of convention; we will begin with it.

**1**   Use a hyphen when you must divide a word at the end of a line of text and continue it on the next line. When you must do this, place the hyphen between syllables. A syllable is a unit of spoken language consisting usually of a vowel alone or a vowel with one or more consonants. Good dictionaries give the proper syllables of a word in each entry. Here is the proper syllabication of a few multi-syllable words. Notice that each syllable is pronounceable.

| | | |
|---|---|---|
| a-bove | con-ver-sa-tion | pa-tience |
| ac-tor | dis-trib-ute | pic-ture |
| bap-tism | hy-dro-gen | rev-er-end |
| bi-cy-cle | op-po-nent | sep-a-ra-tion |
| bur-y | | |

Here are examples of proper word divisions at the end of a line.

It turned out on Friday that our *conversa-tion* had been unnecessary. We were really agreed on everything.

After graduating from college, Henry became an *ac-tor,* something I had not thought possible when I knew him.

If you are unsure of the proper syllabication of a word, consult a good dictionary. But never leave a single letter on one line even if it *is* the proper syllabication. And never divide a word of one syllable, such as *France* or *trout*.

***Wrong***   There was a line of low, threatening clouds *a-bove* the mountains.
***Right***   There was a line of low, threatening clouds *above* the mountains.

***Wrong***   We decided it would be in our best interest to *bur-y* the hatchet and be friends again.

**Right**  We decided it would be in our best interest to *bury* the hatchet and be friends again.

**Wrong**  In the fall, when we finally left for *France*, we were very excited.

**Right**  In the fall, when we finally left for *France*, we were very excited.

**2**  Use a hyphen to join words or words and prefixes together. The hyphen used in this way is, in most cases, a transitional mark. For example, usually (but not always), when words are first linked to each other, they are written separately — as in *basket ball*. Later, this word became *basket-ball,* and it is now, of course, always written *basketball*. Thus, just how to use the hyphen for any compound word at any particular moment is difficult to determine, because usage is continually changing and even good, recently published dictionaries are likely to be behind the times. Still, the dictionary is the soundest authority and should be consulted when the writer is doubtful about some case of hyphenation.

The following rules were accurate when this book was written.

**A**  Words beginning with *all, self,* and *ex* (meaning *former*) are always hyphenated.

He is a *self-made* man.

In Washington, the President's staff is *all-powerful*.

The *ex-President* has hardly any influence on national policy.

**B**  When the root word is a proper noun or proper adjective, use a hyphen to separate prefixes.

anti-Nixon      un-American      pro-Reagan

**C**  Prefixes ending in a vowel are frequently hyphenated, especially if the root word begins with the same vowel.

| | | |
|---|---|---|
| anti-intellectual | semi-invalid | pre-election |
| re-educate | de-escalate | re-evaluate |
| co-ordinate | | |

*Note:* Some constructions with a double vowel are acceptable without hyphenation.

cooperate      preeminent      preexisting.

**H**

**D** Certain prefixes are hyphenated to avoid confusing a word with another whose spelling is identical.

> A work of art is a *re-creation* of experience. (to avoid confusion with *recreation,* "leisure")

> Since the math teacher couldn't follow his logic, the student had to *re-prove* the theorem. (to avoid confusion with *reprove,* "rebuke")

> Now that my wife has emptied our closets, we have to *re-store* all our things. (to avoid confusion with *restore,* "return to a former condition")

**3** A good many compound nouns are hyphenated; a good many others are not; and some are written as single words. (A compound noun is one that consists of more than one word.)

| *Hyphenated* | *Unhyphenated* | *Single Words* |
|---|---|---|
| air-brake | dream life | blackbird |
| bee-sting | diving board | headache |
| bull's-eye | first cousin | highway |
| cave-in | high school | landslide |
| free-for-all | ice cream | madman |
| merry-go-round | oil spill | newsstand |

*Remember:* If you are unsure about a particular case, consult a good dictionary.

**4** Compound adjectives — groups of words that when taken together act like a single-word adjective — are usually joined together by hyphens.

| | |
|---|---|
| *able-bodied* seaman | *low-level* official |
| *devil-may-care* attitude | *middle-of-the-road* politician |
| *double-parked* car | *out-of-work* actor |
| *fence-busting* outfielder | *two-tiered* stadium |

*Note:* When these adjectives are in the predicate adjective position, following a linking verb, the hyphen is omitted.

> The actor is *out of work.*

> His car was *double parked.*

**5** Hyphens are used between parts of compound numbers — twenty-one to ninety-nine — and in specifying fractions. Hyphens are also frequently used to connect numbers in specifying dates.

This is my *twenty-second* birthday.

My professor is only *thirty-one* years old.

He is taxed *two-fifths* of his income.

The meetings will take place September *4-11.*

My vacation runs *July 31-August 14.*

*Note:* Do not use a hyphen in noncompound numbers.

one hundred twelve

H

## TEST YOURSELF ON
## the Appropriate Use of the Hyphen

Some of the sentences below contain uses of the hyphen that are correct; next to these, write C. Some sentences, however, contain word groups that need a hyphen. Insert a hyphen wherever you think one is missing.

1. _____ Sarah is a well trained teacher, but she would rather be a well paid researcher.

2. _____ Resort the laundry so that we can get all the white things together.

3. _____ Everything Jeffrey does is self-serving.

4. _____ Call in a carpenter; those bookshelves are not a doityourself job.

5. _____ Ed's colorblindness is due to a genetic defect.

6. _____ If you don't like spaghetti and meat balls, you're unItalian.

7. _____ Coal mine caveins are preventable.

8. _____ The actor used to be an able bodied seaman.

9. _____ Ex naval officers frequently become business executives.

10. _____ The all-powerful Internal Revenue Service takes two-fifths of my income in taxes.

11. _____ My friend was a semiinvalid and a proKennedy pseudoliberal.

12. _____ He scored a bull'seye in target shooting, but she was uninterested.

## Idiom

See **Diction.**

## Internal Punctuation

See **End Punctuation.**

## Italics

*Italics is the name given to the typeface in which these words are printed.* On the other hand, the typeface in which these words are printed is called roman. In hand-written manuscripts or typescripts, underlining is the equivalent of italics. Italics are conventionally used in the following special cases.

**1** Use italics for the names of books, plays, movies, television shows, newspapers, magazines, ships, aircraft, long musical compositions.

Shakespeare's *Hamlet*

Melville's *Moby Dick*

*The New Yorker* (magazine)

The Los Angeles *Times* (Note that the name of the city is not in italics here.)

*S.S. Rotterdam, Queen Elizabeth II*
*The City of Birmingham* (name of aircraft)
Beethoven's *Ninth Symphony*
*Star Wars* (movie)
*Dallas* (TV show)

**2** Use italics for foreign words and phrases that have not become part of the English language.

He lived in Peekskill but kept a small *pied-à-terre* in New York. (*pied-à-terre* = temporary or secondary lodging place)

Writing poems was his whole *raison d'être*. (*raison d'être* = reason for being)

Dave is known as a *bon vivant*. (a person who enjoys good food and other pleasant things)

*Note:* Some foreign words and phrases *have* become part of the English language and should not be italicized. Here is a small list of them:

| cliché | gamin | guru | genre | lacuna |
|--------|-------|------|-------|--------|
| café | bona fide | ensemble | elite | Gesundheit |

**3** Use italics for words and phrases considered for themselves.

The word *elegant* is derived from Old French.

The term *end of the line* is a cliché.

**4** Use italics for scientific terms in Latin.

The constellation Great Bear (*Ursa major*) is in the northern hemisphere.

For genetic research, the species of mosquito known as *anopheles* is most useful.

**5** Use italics for giving special emphasis to ordinary words. You should achieve emphasis by placing the important word or words in an emphatic position in the sentence — not by carelessly using italics. Italics should be reserved for words that cannot be emphasized enough by ordinary work on structure.

**Weak**   I'm talking about *love*, as an emotion.
**Revised**   Love is what I'm talking about. (Here the position of *love* as the subject gives it enough emphasis without italics.)

**Weak**   He said he would *never* marry.

**Revised**   To the question of when he would marry, he replied with one word: never. (The final position of the word in the rewritten sentence is very emphatic; note, too, that the sentence has been designed to emphasize *never.*)

**Proper Use of Italics**   What's important is not what she *was,* but what she has *become.* (Italics point up the contrast between *was* and *become.*)

Charley is henpecked not because he has a wife but because *his wife has him.* (Italics call attention to the reversal.)

## TEST YOURSELF ON
## the Use of Italics

Some of the following sentences show the correct use of italics. Next to each of these, write C. Some sentences, however, need to have italics added or removed; in these, make the appropriate corrections.

1. _____ The current craze for *nostalgia* knows no limits.

2. _____ The expression freaked out is slang.

3. _____ The New York Daily News has only one competitor.

4. _____ Great books like Moby-Dick and Anna Karenina occupy the mind long after we've read them.

5. _____ My Uncle Ted is on the cover of *Time* this week.

6. _____ The program includes Beethoven's Sixth Symphony and his Fidelio Overture.

7. _____ I felt much better after I spoke to my *guru.*

8. _____ The porcupine anteater belongs to the family *echidna.*

9. _____ The Transatlantic Review published Myra's first story.

10. _____ We're sailing on the *S.S. Rotterdam.*

11. _____ She worked as a *fille de chambre* [lady's maid].

12. _____ It was his last performance as Hamlet.

# Logic

Clear and forceful writing always involves clear thinking and the presentation of honest evidence. Therefore, in this brief treatment of a complex subject, we shall deal with aspects of logic useful to writers who wish to impart to their work the rigor and strength of solid thought. The topics to be covered are these: (1) fairness in argument, (2) the careful use of evidence, (3) methods of clear reasoning, and (4) errors in thinking.

## Fairness in Argument

To be sure that your arguments or generalizations (or thesis statements) are fair and not prejudiced, you should avoid the errors discussed here.

**1** Avoid basing your argument on belief rather than knowledge.

*Prejudice* is prejudgment, before the facts are known. We may *wish* to believe something is true and argue a case using that something as a generalization. But we would only be displaying prejudice.

> Sally doesn't know how to drive a car. I always see her sitting in the back seat of her parents' automobile. (How does the speaker know that Sally isn't just following family custom by sitting in back?)

> She must have a sugar daddy somewhere. Every time I see her, she's wearing a new outfit. (The speaker is merely *assuming.* Sally may have money that is *not* the gift of an "admirer" but that she has earned or been given as a gift by a relative.)

These leaps in logic are frequent in ordinary conversation or in careless discourse elsewhere. They are prejudicial and lead to serious distortions. Consider the way that racial prejudice follows the same model of slack thought; for example, all Italians are loud, blacks on welfare, Jews rich and stingy, and so forth.

L

**2** Avoid arguing by discrediting an opponent or his idea.

This is known as *argumentum ad hominem,* or "arguing to the man." It is a form of nonevidence that fails to notice a person might be wrong about one thing and right about another.

> Don't believe Quinn when he says our college isn't doing right by its students. He never went to school himself. (Quinn may have been wrong in avoiding a formal education — although we can't tell from what the speaker says — and right in his analysis of the way the college functions.)

> Tuten is wrong about the town's need for more roads. He's a contractor and naturally he wants the money. (Tuten doesn't *know* he'll get the contract; besides, he could be right about the need for roads.)

The examples given show that the speaker in both cases is arguing to the man rather than to the issues involved.

**3** Avoid making capital by associating your idea or argument with a great name.

This is called the *argumentum ad verecundiam,* where it is hoped that the association of one's position or thought with a great name will transfer the authority or prestige of that name onto one's own thought. It also works in reverse. By associating an opponent's ideas with some person or movement of low prestige, one discredits one's opponent.

> If John Kennedy were alive today, he'd be fighting to put this bill through Congress.

> Like all radicals, he believes in sharing the wealth.

## TEST YOURSELF ON
## Judging the Fairness of Generalizations

Read carefully each set of statements printed below. Then prepare for each a discussion of its fairness or unfairness according to the discussion you've just read.

1. The Bible says "honor thy father and thy mother," so I never disobey mine.
2. College students don't work as hard as they did in my day. Nowadays all they do is listen to rock music.
3. Business is nothing but thievery. How else could they make so much money?

4. Black people make terrific athletes.
5. I would never hire an ex-convict to work for me. Once a thief, always a thief. That's what I say.

## The Careful Use of Evidence

Instead of using prejudice and low blows, the logical writer employs evidence that appeals not to passion but to reason.

Good evidence is the proper use of facts, opinion, or statistics. Evidence honestly and carefully used supports a generalization (a thesis statement) in such a way as to persuade a reader that the case being presented is solid to the point of being unassailable.

Failure to be careful leads to errors in handling evidence, and these usually fall into the following categories:

### 1 Biased Evidence

This is a form of evidence so unreliable that it is sure to do the arguer more harm than good. If you were to argue that the American people are in favor of the economy going on a war footing on the basis of a poll taken among aircraft workers in Seattle who favor stepped-up production, your evidence would be biased. Those workers would not necessarily favor making warplanes alone — though surely they are saying they want more work. Similarly, if you were to argue that Europe has a weak capacity to defend itself from aggression, citing its weak defensive capacity compared to the offensive might of the Russians, you would also be arguing from biased evidence. Europe's defense is not only in its own but in American hands as well.

Biased evidence is frequently the mainstay of advertising and other forms of commercial presentation. There the evidence is made biased by taking things out of context. Soft drinks advertised as sugar-free (good) do not, in the same ad, acknowledge that they contain saccharin (bad).

The testimony of character witnesses at trials can also be seen as a form of biased evidence, for such witnesses are always prepared to say only good things about a defendant.

Advertising blurbs and character witnesses are, among others, notoriously deliberate employers of biased evidence. But writers need to be careful that they do not inadvertently use such material. The way to make sure is to use only the most rigorously impartial and respectable sources.

### 2 Insufficient Evidence

It is December in northern Minnesota. For three days, the temperature hovers around 55 degrees. A native exclaims, "We're having a mild winter." This is a clear case of insufficient evidence. What about the other days between December and March?

Another case: If after your first week at the college you attend you have failed to make a friend, are you justified in thinking, "This school is a drag; everybody's unfriendly"? Not really. You have insufficient evidence because it has only been a week and you haven't been exposed to *all* the possible friends you might make.

Thus insufficient evidence most frequently involves having too few cases on which to build a generalization. Writers must be sure to make their evidence plentiful enough to be convincing.

### 3 Poorly Evaluated Statistics

Faulty evidence in the form of poorly evaluated statistics is easy to present if the writer is not wary. For example, the U.S. Department of Labor, Bureau of Labor Statistics, issues a statistic on unemployment for a particular month: 8.7 percent. Before citing this figure in support of an argument that the U.S. economy is performing about as well as expected, you had better consider this question: as well as expected with regard to whom? For buried in that single 8.7 percent statistic there may be others — for example, that teenagers suffer an unemployment rate of 26.7 percent and black teenagers an even higher one. The economy does not perform for all the people all the time.

Another example, closer to home, will make this issue even clearer. Suppose you've been working during all of 1986 at your usual part-time job for the salary of $100 a week. Then in 1987, your boss recognizes your true value (at last) and starts paying you at the new rate of $200 a week. Can we assume that you now have twice as much money? Would that be a fair way to make inferences from the statistics? Not at all. It should be fairly obvious that you've jumped into a new tax bracket and more taxes are withheld from your paycheck and that more Social Security payments are being deducted as well.

The point is that all of us need help with statistics. For this reason, although statistics are very useful in an argument, we need to be wary about how we use them.

## TEST YOURSELF ON
## Recognizing Biased, Insufficient, and Statistically Unreliable Evidence

Each of the following groups of statements is a case of evidence poorly conceived. Given a name to each error in each case.

1. Twelve percent of the American people earn 50 thousand or more dollars a year. Let's look for the rich ones on this campus: there are 3,000 of us, so there must be 360 who earn that much.
2. Everybody I know is buying a motorcycle. They must be terrific.
3. If you live in Alaska, you must have warm blood.
4. I read that the lumberjacks in Oregon want to cut down more trees. That must mean nobody in the state is interested in ecology.
5. My sister's not doing well in math. Women can't handle math and sciences.
6. The price of cars has doubled in the past ten years. Detroit must really be raking in the money.
7. A cigarette ad showing two lean and leathery horsemen riding in a beautiful range of western American mountains.
8. I can't hire that ex-convict; he might steal something.
9. Now that I've bought a car, I need a bigger allowance.
10. Inflation last year was 8 percent; this year it's 16 percent; next year, it'll be 24 percent.

## Methods of Clear Reasoning

Logic refers to clear reasoning, and reasoning involves two basic processes called *induction* and *deduction*.

*Induction* is the name we give to a process involving rational movement from particular facts to general statements. Scientists and the scientific method rely on induction. For example, when a number of cases of influenza are diagnosed in the same part of the country (particular facts), we can say (make the generalization) that there is a flu epidemic there. Similarly, when a physicist determines, after a number of experiments, that metal $A$ is a more ready conductor of electricity than metal $B$, the determination (the generalization) is made possible by the many experiments (particular facts). Induction can also be thought of as an ordinary mental process — the way we are influenced by experience: If a number of attempts to make friends with Jack come to nought and we think to ourselves that Jack is unfriendly, we are only making use of the inductive process. Similarly, one important way in which the thesis statement comes into being is induction: We examine the facts and make a generalization from them.

However, a warning must be given here about induction. First, we can never be as sure about a conclusion based on a certain number of facts as we can about a conclusion based on all of them. When a scientist says that water freezes at 32 degrees Fahrenheit, he means that having observed it to do so on a number of occasions, he predicts that it will always do so. Similarly, if you should conclude, having met seven bright graduates of Stanford University, that *all* Stanford graduates are bright, your certainty will still be limited by the principle involved: it is never an absolute certainty when one leaps from *some* to *all*. Still, we can be more sure that physical nature is uniform than we can that human nature is.

Thus in inducing a generalization, the writer must bear this warning in mind; that is, he must at least be sure that he has a sufficient number of cases (facts) on which to base his conclusion (generalization), that these are typical cases (e.g., that the Stanford graduates were not all honors people who graduated *summa cum laude* but just ordinary graduates), and that exceptions can be explained (e.g., one of the Stanford graduates seems not so bright when you ask her a tough question; is it true that she is not bright or is it that when you asked, she had been without sleep for a few days and wasn't performing well on that one occasion).

*Deduction,* on the other hand, is a kind of thinking that proceeds from a generalization to a particular fact. From the generalization that people who are overweight tend to die earlier than those who are not, you can deduce that it is best to watch one's diet carefully. Or if you know that a particular restaurant serves wonderful food (generalization), you can deduce (particular fact) that it would be a good place to take a friend to dinner.

You may now understand that there is a relationship between induction and deduction, and so there is. For example, sound conclusions reached through scientific induction may be just the useful generalizations from which to make particular deductions — about health for instance. The National Institutes of Health has records showing causes of death in millions of cases; it has concluded (induced) that death by heart attack is hastened by the intake of cholesterol-rich foods. From that generalization, you can deduce that it is bad for your health to eat too many eggs or too much cheese or red meat.

In order for the inductive process to yield a true generalization, the facts must be true; similarly, in order for the particular fact deduced to be true, the premises from which it was made must be true.

In the case of deduction, there is a process for testing the validity of conclusions; for in its most familiar form, the deductive form is exemplified by the *syllogism*. A *syllogism* is nothing but a little argument in the form of two premises and a conclusion drawn from them.

> ***Major premise***   All citizens pay income taxes.
> ***Minor premise***   All Americans are citizens.
> ***Conclusion***   All Americans pay income taxes.

To understand why the conclusion in this syllogism is valid, we can think of those mentioned as belonging to classes and begin to represent these classes visually.

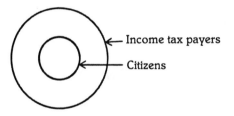

This is a visual representation of the major premise. Within the outer circle are all those who belong to the class of income tax payers. The inner circle encloses the class of citizens. Now let us represent the minor premise in the diagram.

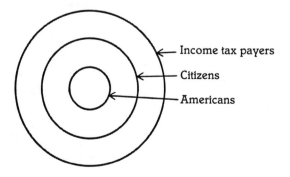

Now the innermost circle encloses the class of Americans. That circle is enclosed not only within the circle of citizens but also in the circle of those who pay income tax. Hence it is clear visually that all Americans pay income tax (are a class included within the class of income tax payers). But notice that if we had started with a major premise stating that "*some* citizens pay income tax," our conclusion could not be so straightforward.

Now we would need to conclude that *some Americans pay income taxes*.

Some Americans pay income taxes.

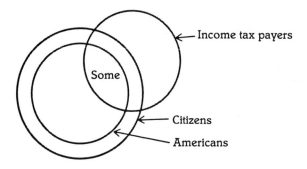

You will rarely if ever encounter a syllogism either in written work or in conversation. More likely in conversation there is the appearance of part of a syllogism: Either one of the premises or the conclusion is missing.

> *The Electric Horseman* is playing at the movies. I hate Westerns. (Conclusion missing: I won't go to the movies.)
>
> It's Tuesday, so I'd better go to work. (Missing premise: Tuesday is payday.)

But a syllogism is not useful unless our premises are true, because a syllogism can validate an untruth. For example, here's a syllogism that provides a perfectly valid conclusion:

> All cats are gray.
> All gray things are stupid.
> All cats are stupid.

It certainly follows from the premises that all cats are stupid, but it's not true because the premises are not. This is an obvious example,

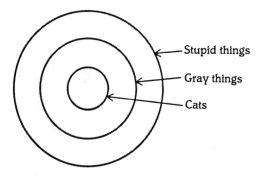

and you are not likely to make this kind of error. But take another syllogism:

> Conservative doctors oppose national health plans.
> Dr. Greene opposes national health plans.
> Dr. Greene is a conservative doctor.

Here is a visual representation:

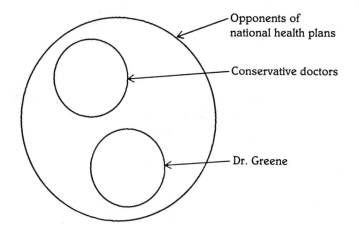

Notice that Dr. Greene is not included in the class of conservative doctors. He doesn't have to be. If the major premise had been that *only* conservative doctors oppose national health plans, the conservative doctors' circle would lie virtually on top of the one enclosing those who oppose national health plans, and Dr. Greene would have to be included. But common sense will confirm what the diagram indicates, for many others oppose national health plans for many reasons: they don't like the plans so far proposed; they don't like government interference in all avenues of our lives; and so on. But Dr. Greene need not be conservative either; that is, his objections to the plans may not lie in the area of venality presumably ascribed to the conservative doctors. Perhaps he's a young physician just starting out and honestly feels he's entitled to a large financial reward for the many years he spent preparing for an exacting profession. Perhaps he believes that a national health plan will deliver poorer health care than private plans. In any case, it is clear that although the premises here are true — conservative doctors *do* oppose national health plans as does Dr. Greene — the conclusion is clearly false.

Thus in addition to using the diagram method of checking syllogistic deduction, the writer needs to check carefully the truth of his premises. Another way of putting it is to say that the writer must check his evidence, the facts from which he draws his conclusions. The writer needs to check the support that underlies his evidence, and this involves induction.

# TEST YOURSELF ON
## Applying Induction or Deduction

**A**    *Induction:* Below are five sets of factual statements, each followed by a conclusion induced from them. Consider the value of the conclusion in the light of the foregoing discussions. Is the conclusion a reasonable one? Why? Why not?

1. Richard was a colonel in the army. He is used to taking responsibility, engaging in long-range planning, dealing effectively with large numbers of subordinates, executing policy. Therefore, he would make a good business executive.
2. The last three times America suffered from terrific inflation, we had a Democratic president. It's obvious that the Democrats don't know how to run the domestic economy.
3. Margie's family is always calling on her for help, and I'll be involved in it. Look what happened to Fred after he married Miss Dooley! I'm not going to marry Margie.
4. I heard that Professor Brody always springs surprises when he gives exams. I'm not going to study for them.

5. The average temperature in Athens in the summer is 85 degrees. So I think I'd better take light cotton clothing on my trip.

**B** *Deduction:* Below are five syllogisms. Make a visual representation of each and check the conclusions. Are they valid? After you have checked on the valid conclusions, ask yourself whether these valid conclusions are also true.

1. All cats are independent.
No independent animal likes humans.
Cats don't like humans. *(conclusion)*

2. Most Americans are friendly.
Most friendly people are hospitable.
Most Americans are hospitable. *(conclusion)*

3. All Irishmen like to drink whiskey.
Ed Quinn likes to drink whiskey.
Ed Quinn is an Irishman. *(conclusion)*

4. Violence is wrong.
War is violence.
War is wrong. *(conclusion)*

5. Some actors are out of work.
Out-of-work people are usually a little desperate.
Some actors are a little desperate. *(conclusion)*

L

## Errors in Thinking

Even reasonable people make errors when they think, so we must take the time to deal with some common forms of thinking errors called *fallacies*.

### 1 Post Hoc Ergo Propter Hoc

This fallacy is known by its Latin name, meaning "after this, therefore because of this." Do not think that because event *B* follows or comes after event *A*, event *A* was the cause of event *B*. The conclusion that Phyllis started to be unhappy after she married Norman is not necessarily a criticism of her marriage to Norman. Her unhappiness may have nothing to do with Norman *or* the marriage. It might be that her career has taken a critical turn and she is under great pressure at her job. Or it is possible that her health is deteriorating, something entirely unrelated to the marriage.

The need to avoid this fallacy becomes even clearer when we consider public questions.

> This town started to deteriorate rapidly after Mayor Buckley was elected.

This conclusion is especially pernicious because the so-called evidence (the deterioration) is visible and on that account may seem convincing. But a moment's thought will show that the conclusion is false. Deterioration, especially in an urban setting, is not an instantaneous process; it takes time. Ignoring the general nature of the accusation, we can extrapolate from what we know that deterioration takes place in a number of separate areas — housing, transportation, an increase in crime, and so on — a complex of events that cannot be attributed to the mayoral term of one man; its seeds were no doubt planted long before Buckley's nomination. If anything, Buckley arrived in the middle of all this. He did not cause it.

### 2   Non Sequitur

This Latin term means "it does not follow." This fallacy occurs when the writer either leaves out steps in the thought process or draws conclusions that do not follow from the premises.

> He's the best teacher I've ever seen and he should be made Dean.

The conclusion doesn't follow. Is it a fact that very good teachers make very good deans? How so? And even if this were true, how many teachers has the speaker seen?

> Kennedy's an aristocrat; that's why he's for the common man.

The conclusion doesn't follow because steps have been omitted in the writer's reasoning process; that is, he hasn't let the reader in on these steps:

1. Kennedy is an aristocrat.
2. His family owns a considerable fortune.
3. Among people of his class, it is an important value to do public service to the underprivileged.
4. His brothers carried on in this tradition.
5. That's why he's for the common man.

To avoid non sequitur, you should be sure that, in your papers, all steps in the thinking process are included.

### 3 Hasty Generalization

This fallacy is a form of using insufficient evidence. For example, if you know a seventeen-year-old who refused to get a job when his father asked him to and an eighteen-year-old who wouldn't observe his mother's 2 A.M. curfew, you do not have enough evidence to conclude that young people today are a bad lot because they don't obey their parents. Such a conclusion makes a statement about millions of individuals on the basis of a couple of cases — a bad business. If your main proposition is based on such evidence, you would do well to reconsider the whole thing.

### 4 False Analogy

Analogies are useful in clarifying certain points under discussion, but they are seldom enough to win an argument because *alike* does not mean *identical.* But they are useful. For instance, we call a vehicle that travels over interplanetary distances a *spaceship,* thus making an analogy between the craft and a seagoing vessel and between space and water. But these two likenesses have the power to explain space travel in only a limited way. For example, both a spaceship and an oceangoing vessel travel far distances through a uniform medium, and both must be built in such a way as to protect against that medium's leaking into the ship; both must carry sufficient supplies; and so forth. But the analogy doesn't hold up entirely: Spacecraft need to be entirely enclosed, carry their own oxygen, and begin their journeys with an enormously powerful rocket thrust.

Analogies are useful, then, in clarifying certain points under discussion, but they are seldom enough to win an argument. Be careful in your use of analogy not to make false ones.

### 5 Begging the Question

In this fallacy, the writer or speaker assumes in his thesis the validity of something that really needs to be proven. To say *He's an idiot because he says stupid things* is neither explanation nor proof. The word *idiot* in this context means *someone who says stupid things.* Thus the original utterance means *He's someone who says stupid things because he says stupid things.* We should have to hear these so-called stupid things before we accept the declaration of idiocy. On the level of formal argument, a statement like *The crucially important hospital should be built* is a similar type of statement. That is because *crucially important* here simply means *should be built*. Thus the statement means *The hospital which should be built should be built.* We need to know why it should be built. Otherwise, the statement begs the question.

**TEST YOURSELF ON**
## Recognizing Logical Fallacies

Examine each set of statements below and point out the logical errors in the thinking behind each.

1. Ever since those Hispanics moved into the neighborhood, the crime rate has gone up. They must be responsible.
2. Nowadays, it's a crime to waste food.
3. It's a vital necessity that everyone get out and vote on Election Day.
4. He'd make a great Secretary of Defense. He's spent all his life in the army.
5. My two little cousins don't like candy. I guess children don't like sweets.
6. It's Tuesday. I'd better not skip work today.
7. All I can say is, he wasn't an alcoholic *before* he married Gail!
8. Professors are like tiny pieces of toast: They should be buttered up and swallowed whole.
9. My aunt and uncle love to visit Russia. They must be Communists.
10. The movie I saw last night was wonderful. It should easily win an Oscar.

**M**

# Misplaced Modifiers

A misplaced modifier is a word, phrase, or clause that does not point clearly and directly to what it is supposed to modify. When using modifiers, be sure to place the word, phrase, or clause close to the word or words it actually modifies, for meaning changes with the placement of the modifier.

> He *almost* had a heart attack every time he looked at his bank statement. (He almost had the attack—but not quite—every time he looked.)

He had a heart attack *almost* every time he looked at his bank statement. (He actually had the attack—sometimes, but not every time he looked.)

**1** Be careful to place the adverbs *almost, even, hardly, just, merely, only, nearly,* and *scarcely* close to the words they modify. Misplacing words like *almost* and *only* occurs quite often in informal writing, but you should learn to be careful about their placement because misplacing them can often confuse the reader badly.

> ***Misplaced Word*** I *only* told the jury what I had seen. (The choices here are three: *I only*—and nobody else—told the jury; *I told only* the jury—and nobody else; or I told the jury *only what I had seen.*)
> ***Revised*** I told the jury *only* what I had seen.
> ***Revised*** I told *only* the jury what I had seen.
> ***Revised*** *Only* I told the jury what I had seen.
>
> ***Misplaced*** I *nearly* went halfway to Canada.
> ***Revised*** I went *nearly* halfway to Canada.
>
> ***Misplaced*** I *almost* ate half the pie.
> ***Revised*** I ate *almost* half the pie.

**2** Be careful to place modifying phrases close to the word or words they modify.

> ***Misplaced Phrase*** My history professor made it clear why wars take place *on Tuesday.* (The *wars* take place on Tuesday?)
> ***Revised*** *On Tuesday,* my history professor made it clear why wars take place.
>
> ***Misplaced Phrase*** Airlines serve martinis to passengers *in little bottles.* (The *passengers* are in little bottles?)
> ***Revised*** Airlines serve passengers martinis *in little bottles.*
>
> ***Misplaced Phrase*** Environmental groups protested the oil leaks *all over the country.* (Were there *oil leaks* all over the country?)
> ***Revised*** Environmental groups *all over the country* protested the oil leaks.

**3** Be careful to place modifying clauses close to the word or words which they modify.

> ***Misplaced Clause*** Sid bought books for his library *that cost $19.04.* (Did his *library* or his *books* cost that much?)
> ***Revised*** Sid bought books *that cost $19.04* for his library. For his library, Sid bought books *that cost $19.04.*

**M**

A special case of the misplaced modifier is called a *squinting modifier* because it looks in two directions at the same time; that is, it "squints."

> **Squinting Modifier** To be beautifully dressed *often* pleases my wife. (Is she *often pleased* or *often beautifully dressed?*)
> **Revised** It *often* pleases my wife to be beautifully dressed. It pleases my wife to be beautifully dressed *often*.

> **Squinting Modifier** Lucia said *when she was on her way* home she would stop and buy the vegetables. (Did she say it while traveling home? Or did she say that sometime on her way home she would stop?)
> **Revised** When she was on her way home, Lucia said that she would stop and buy the vegetables. (*Said* while on her way home.) Lucia said that on her way home she would stop and buy the vegetables. (She will *stop* on her way home.)

**M**

## TEST YOURSELF ON
## Revising Misplaced and Squinting Modifiers

Some of the following sentences contain well-placed modifiers; next to these, write C. Others, however, have misplaced or squinting modifiers; correct these, even if it means recasting the sentence.

1. _____ With this calculator, I can show you how to make a million dollars in twenty seconds.

2. _____ The sick patient wanted to live happily.

3. _____ The sunset that we loved completely stunned us.

4. _____ We made plans to leave over the weekend.

5. _____ Professors who teach rarely get rich.

6. _____ Subconsciously, Kathy wanted to become famous.

7. _____ Caesar was stabbed in the heyday of his glory.

8. _____ He just left for a minute.

9. _____ For Christopher's sake, I decided to go to California.

10. _____ The state penalizes those who commit murder for good reason.

11. _____ Robert DeNiro just arrived here last week.

12. _____ The father heard the news that his son had been born with joy.

13. _____ *True Confessions* appeals to readers with scandalous stories.

14. _____ Those who jog slowly develop heart trouble.

15. _____ The ugly face scared him that looked through the window.

---

# Modifiers

**M**

In Part 1, we noted that adjectives and adverbs act to modify or further describe members of other word classes: nouns and verbs. Adjectives and adverbs are called modifiers. But the question of modification is a bit more complicated than you may have imagined from reading about it in Part 1. Here we shall discuss the complications by discussing other words that can act as adjectives and adverbs. These other words are called *adjectivals* and *adverbials*.

## Other Words Used as Adjectives: Adjectivals

Some words are nearly always used as adjectives: *old, young, happy, proud,* and so forth. But other words, ordinarily belonging to other parts of speech, can also act as adjectives. So, of course, can phrases. All are entitled to be called adjectivals.

### 1  Nouns Used as Adjectives

We looked into the *bear* cage. (modifies *cage*)

She was wearing her *party* dress. (modifies *dress*)

We went to the *baseball* game. (modifies *game*)

### 2  Verbs Used as Adjectives

A whole class of verbs are commonly used as adjectives. These are the participles: the *-ing* forms ( present participles), the *-d* or *-ed* forms (past participles), and the irregular past participles (*gone, broken, kept,* and so forth).

> The *fleeing* suspect was caught by the police. (modifies *suspect,* the subject)
>
> The *broken* arrow was useless. (modifies *arrow,* the subject)
>
> He seemed *defeated.* (acts as predicate adjective)
>
> The job was *finished.* (acts as predicate adjective)

### 3  Adverbs Used as Adjectives

> The apartment *below* is mine. (modifies *apartment*)
>
> The road *ahead* is closed. (modifies *road*)

### 4  Phrases and Clauses Used as Adjectives

*Phrase*  The men *in the truck* were tired. (modifies *men*)
*Phrase*  The planes *flying overhead* are bound for Europe. (modifies *planes*)

*Clause*  The people *who rented my house* will stay until August. (modifies *people*)
*Clause*  I bought a Toyota, *which runs like a top.* (modifies *Toyota*)

## Other Words Used as Adverbs: Adverbials

Some words are nearly always used as adverbs: *often, soon, rarely,* and so forth. But other words, ordinarily belonging to other parts of speech, can also act as adverbs, as can phrases and clauses. All these are entitled to be called adverbials.

### 1  Nouns Used as Adverbs

> I went *home.* (modifies *went*)
>
> She arrived *yesterday.* (modifies *arrived*)

### 2  Verbs Used as Adverbs

> Because he was in a hurry, he decided to eat *standing.* (modifies *to eat.*)
>
> Peter played *to win.* (modifies *played*)

**3** Phrases and Clauses Used as Adverbs

***Phrase*** We are staying *at a hotel.* (modifies *are staying*)
***Phrase*** We were impatient *to leave for the theater.* (modifies *impatient*)

***Clause*** *Although we were tired,* we couldn't fall asleep. (modifies the whole of the main clause)
***Clause*** *When they saw the shark,* they were frightened. (modifies *were frightened*)

## TEST YOURSELF ON
## Recognizing Modifiers: Adjectivals and Adverbials

Identify each of the italicized words or word groups as either an adjectival or an adverbial.

1. We were going on a *holiday* trip.
2. We would arrive *in the afternoon.*
3. He went *home.*
4. *When he spoke softly,* we had to strain to listen.
5. He gave the apples to the man *in the raincoat.*
6. He was promoted to *plant* manager.
7. The books, *which cost $18,* were overpriced.
8. The man *who sent her the flowers* was in love with her.
9. He was a *broken* man.
10. They were a *defeated* team.
11. The *purring* cat likes his milk.
12. The man *in the gray flannel suit* looks like my brother.

**N-P**

# Number

See **Shifts.**

# Numerals

Whether your writing is formal or informal, the basic guideline in handling numerals is to be consistent in your usage: Either use numerals or spell the numbers out in words — do not mix the two. There are several basic rules for handling numerals in formal writing.

**1**   Spell out numbers that require no more than two words. In other cases, use numerals.

> There were *seventy-five* cases of swine flu reported.
>
> The population of New York City is less than *eight million.*
> *but*
> My federal tax refund amounted to *$88.37.*

*Note:* In business and technical writing, numbers from 10 up are often written as numerals.

**2**   In writing dates, addresses, percentages followed by %, page numbers, or the time of day followed by *a.m.* or *p.m.*, use numerals.

> **Date**   October 19, 1926 *or* 19 October 1926
>
> **Address**   55 East 9th Street, Apartment 7K
>
> **Percentages**   Sales at IBM declined 27.3% during the last quarter of 1986.
> *but*
> This bank pays five percent interest.
>
> **Page Numbers**   See Chapter 3, page 112.
>
> **Time of Day**   11:30 p.m. *or* 11:30 P.M., *but* three o'clock

**3**   Use numerals for quantities in scientific and technical writing.

> The barometric pressure is *29.31.*
>
> The specimen was *.37* centimeter in length.

**4**   It is appropriate to use in the same sentence a combination of words and numerals where such a combination will make your writing clear.

> You may take only *six* 6-inch trout from this stream.
>
> The cashier counted out *70* one-dollar bills.

**5**   Do not begin a sentence with a numeral that is not spelled out.

> **Wrong**   *250,000,000* is the approximate population of the U.S.S.R.
> **Right**   The population of the U.S.S.R. is approximately 250,000,000.

***Wrong*** *6* miles from here there is a gas station.
***Right*** *Six* miles from here there is a gas station.

*Note:* If your text includes a great many numbers or a mixture of whole numbers and decimals, it is preferable to use numerals for all the numbers.

## TEST YOURSELF ON
### Using Numerals Correctly

Each of the following sentences contains errors in handling numerals. Correct them.

1. 2,000 years ago, an important event took place in Palestine.

2. Including finance charges, this new car would cost you five thousand six hundred and thirty-eight dollars.

3. They live at nine-0-eight President Street, apartment three E.

4. Dennis drinks about 36 cases of wine every year.

5. The father is 40, the mother is 37, and their children are 12 and ten.

6. 3 years ago I owned a Volkswagen.

7. The average annual rainfall in the Mato Grosso district of Brazil is one hundred twelve point seven three centimeters.

8. On February second, nineteen twenty-two, he managed to publish a book of some seven hundred pages.

9. On page five, there is a good description of a corrupt man.

10. His author's royalties amounted to twelve percent of the price of the book.

O

# Organization and Planning

Organization and planning are essential to good writing. An essay that is disorganized is incoherent, but achieving proper organization takes planning. This entry is devoted to both.

## Organization

An essay is commonly organized into three parts: an introduction, a main body, and a conclusion. The main body is the most important of these parts, for in it the writer treats the main ideas of the essay. The organization of the body of the essay is treated under **Unity, Paragraph Development,** and **Coherence.**

Here we are interested in introductions and conclusions, but before we take up these important items, let us consider a whole essay — including introduction, main body, and conclusion:

### *My Disaster at Freshman Registration*

[1] If you've ever wondered why you see so many prematurely gray-haired freshmen on this campus, this little story will answer your question.

[2] Bright and early on the first day of registration, I showed up at the Bursar's Office at 8 a.m. to pay my fees. The line at Window 1 snaked halfway around two corners to the lobby of the Administration Building. But I was patient (not to say in shock). After a half-hour, I was at the promised land — the grilled window. I paid. They stamped my receipt. I was pushed out of the way.

[3] Suddenly, it dawned on me that I didn't know what to do next. I looked around, stupidly, I'm afraid. A passerby took pity on me. "Window 2 for your days and hours booklet," he snapped.

[4] So there I was, back in line. Another half-hour passed. There I was, back at the grill. I showed my receipt. They gave me — a *torn* booklet. I was shoved out of the way again. But the booklet might have been ripped into shreds for all I cared; the crazy abbreviations and symbols were nearly unreadable. How would I ever figure out how to register?

[5] This problem seemed small when I arrived at the main registration area in the gymnasium, because there it was literally a matter of survival. The physical contact here made the shoving at the Bursar's Office seem like love pats. Again, a friendly person intervened; that is, I found an adviser who explained that I needed to go to each departmental desk and register for courses one by one according to the days and hours I preferred.

[6] By this time, afternoon was crawling toward late afternoon. As I pondered my choice, I decided I'd better get cracking before dying of starvation (I'd missed lunch by now). So I ran to the English Department desk to register for Composition 101. But I was twenty yards away from that desk — without having registered — before I realized I didn't understand what they'd meant when they told me I'd been "closed out."

[7] I'll spare you the catalog of further horrors I endured that long day. You will learn whatever else you need to know about the registration experience by looking for me on campus. I'm the stooped, graying male freshman you see arriving for an 8 a.m. math class, the same one you see leaving after his 5 p.m. biology lecture.

The *introduction,* paragraph 1, opens the essay by proposing a challenge to the readers, and it does so in a humorous vein. It also tunes the readers in to the nature of what they are about to read: a little story. Further, it gives the tone of the piece and its main idea in brief.

The *main body* consists of paragraphs 2 to 6 and includes everything that actually happened; this portion of the paper is the centrally important part of what the writer has to say.

The *conclusion,* paragraph 7, ends the piece by returning to an idea presented in the introduction. It also gives a climactic end to the story by telling the reader the kind of schedule the poor freshman managed for himself — a long, ten-hour day.

The main body here is a little story — a piece of narration. Under **Paragraph Development,** other types of development are explained. See that entry to study more about how to handle a main body according to your specific purpose in writing a particular paper. For now, we will continue with more on introductions and conclusions and go on to planning an outline.

### Introductions

Introductions are important because they are the first words of yours that readers will see. Effective introductions perform a number of different tasks. Perhaps the most important is to catch the readers' interest and attention; right behind this come the tasks of identifying the subject and setting some sort of limit on it. A good introduction also sets the tone for the rest of the piece — it advises the readers how you, the writer, intend to treat the subject.

Here are a number of introductions, each identified by the method the writer employs:

#### *Using the Writer's Personal Experience*
There was, I think, only a brief period in my life when I actually turned heads. It was the summer of my seventeenth year when, newly graduated from a private girls' school, I was in that transition stage between being an old child and a young woman,

a state of half and half that men of all ages apparently find
disarmingly erotic.
Anne Taylor Fleming, "In Defense of Flirting"

### Making an Unusual Statement
There are certain things an American is not permitted to hate.
Americans may, without social ostracism or penalty of law, hate
their partisan or ideological opposites. They may hate someone
because of race or religion or class so long as they show selective
decorum and speak in coded euphemisms.
Larry L. King, "Un-American Peeves"

### Offering a Strong Opinion
The current terrorist epidemic has mystified a great many people,
and various explanations have been offered — most of them quite
wrong.
Walter Laqueur, "Terrorist Myths"

### Stating and Illustrating the Main Idea
The dedicated baseball fan is a man who likes to kid himself.
He'll get to a World Series game early, see a ballplayer yawning
and take it as a sign of nervousness. He'll see a nervelessly
relaxed body leaning against a batting cage and consider it merely
feigned indifference. He'll watch an outfielder casually scratching
his nose and count it as a tic. He's wrong. In fact, what looks like
boredom on behalf of the people involved in the World Series is
most often just that.
Jim Bouton, "A Few World Series Sinkers"

### Opening with a Challenge to the Reader
If you want your mate to stop guessing about your feelings and
motives, you have to be prepared to reveal yourself.
Nena and George O'Neill, "Communicating with Yourself"

## Conclusions
A good conclusion to an essay leaves readers feeling that they
have enjoyed a satisfying, rounded-off reading experience. It does
this in one of the following ways:

**1** By concluding with a reiteration, often in some varied
form, of your thesis statement or main idea. A paper called "Abolish
Big-Time Collegiate Sports" might end like this:

> If big-time sports on campus were abolished, as I have suggested
> they should be, then perhaps some real sports enthusiasts could
> begin to engage in sports — myself, for example.

**2**   By concluding with a summary of your main points, thus reinforcing in the readers' minds the effective things you have said. A possible ending for "Nuclear Energy Versus Solar Power" might go as follows:

> Nuclear energy presents us with the prospect of dangerous operation, deadly waste products, and sinister accidents, but the sun — as we have known all along — is an endless source of pleasure, enduring and powerful.

**3**   By making a climatic point. This type of conclusion is effective when you present a series of points in ascending dramatic order and finish with a particularly high note.

## Planning

Planning an essay — or even a five-hundred-word theme — begins with note-taking, jotting down ideas as you ask questions about your subject. Say it's "freshman registration." What time did I get there? *Awful. Arrived at eight in the morning.* Then what happened? *Got on line at Bursar's Office to pay fees.* Next? *Didn't know what to do — had to get on line again to ask!* Ask enough questions, and you may wind up with a list that looks something like this:

1. Awful. Arrived at 8 in the morning.
2. Got on line at Bursar's Office Window 1 to pay fees.
3. Had to line up again — find out what to do next!
4. Closed out of English.
5. Had to ask what "closed out" means.
6. Found out I needed to go to Window 2 for days and hours booklet.
7. Days and hours booklet torn.
8. Couldn't read it, anyway.
9. Entered registration area and was shoved and pushed for five minutes before I found an adviser.
10. Lost my pack of computer cards.
11. Finally got classes that begin at 8 and end at 6, four days a week.

### Outlines

The ultimate tool for planning an essay is an outline, and although the notes above do not exactly constitute an outline, you couldn't start to make an outline without them, and very little effort will enable you to make an outline from the notes. They have, embedded within them, just what you need for *controlling* and *directing* the way your theme will proceed.

For one thing, a quick glance at the notes tells you that there is a main point here — registration is a shocking, traumatic experience for an uninformed and inexperienced freshman. Furthermore, the fact that two areas are mentioned — The Bursar's Office and the registration area — provides a way of dividing the essay and beginning to organize an outline:

**I. The Bursar's Office**
   A. Got on line to pay fees
   B. Got on line again for booklet
      1. Booklet torn
      2. Couldn't read it
**II. The registration area**
   A. Got pushed and shoved before finding adviser
   B. Got closed out of English
      1. Found out what "closed out" means
      2. Missed lunch
   C. Got laborer's 8–6 schedule

This outline would help you to control your writing. It is an aid in keeping your plan in mind, indicates the order in which you discuss things, and manages to suggest the relative importance of the two places on the day of registration, by assigning a greater proportion of space to one (registration area) than to the other.

In order to become competent at making useful outlines, you should know something about the formal principles of outlining and the different types of outlines that can be used.

### Types of Outlines

The three types of outlines most commonly employed are the topic outline, the sentence outline, and the paragraph outline. In a *topic outline,* each entry is a word or a small group of words. In a *sentence outline,* which has the same basic structural pattern as the topic outline, the words are replaced by complete sentences. In a *paragraph outline,* there are no divisions, headings, and subheadings, as in the others, but only a list of paragraph topic sentences. Some writers feel that the paragraph outline is most suitable for short papers, and the others for longer papers. A writer using a sentence outline is likely to keep in closer touch with the points because of the fuller information contained in sentences.

Whatever you do, decide beforehand which kind of outline

you plan to use, and then follow its requirements systematically: Use *only* sentences in the sentence outline; be sure you have topic sentences for the paragraph outline. And check your outline to be sure that it is consistent with the principles that apply to all outlines.

Here are samples of each kind of outline, for a paper on "The Energy Crisis on Oil and Two Alternate Sources of Power":

### Topic Outline
I. **The Arab oil embargo of 1973**
   - A. Shortage of oil
   - B. Dwindling of resources
II. **Alternative of nuclear power**
   - A. Expensive
   - B. Dangerous
   - C. Likely to run out
III. **Solar power**
   - A. Inexpensive
   - B. Not dangerous
   - C. Limitless supply
   - D. Needs technology

### Sentence Outline
I. **The Arab oil embargo of 1973 pointed up the need for America to find alternate sources of fuel.**
   - A. The embargo produced a shortage of oil.
   - B. It reminded us that all our fossil fuel resources are limited.
II. **Nuclear power as an alternative, though widely favored, is not likely to be the answer.**
   - A. It's very expensive — both for new plants and fuel processing.
   - B. It's very dangerous.
   - C. It's also likely to prove a limited resource.
III. **Solar power is probably a more attractive alternative.**
   - A. It's relatively inexpensive except for start-up costs.
   - B. It's easy to handle and not dangerous.
   - C. The supply is limitless.
   - D. The technology is expensive and not yet in place, however.

### Paragraph Outline
1. The Arab oil embargo of 1973 pointed up the need for America to find alternate sources of fuel, by creating a shortage of oil and reminding us that oil was in any case in very limited supply — a dwindling resource.
2. Nuclear energy is widely favored as an alternative source of power, but it has many serious drawbacks.

3. Solar power is probably a more attractive alternative because it is cheap, limitless in supply, and relatively inexpensive.
4. It may be that solar energy will not be adopted because of industry's reluctance to provide the expensive technology.

### Testing the Outline

Use the following criteria to be sure that your outline is logical and consistent:

**1** Use a conventional form of notation. The following example is a useful one; it is rarely necessary to subdivide more than is shown:

```
I. . . . . . . . . . . . . . . .
    A. . . . . . . . . . . . . . . .
        1. . . . . . . . . . . . . . . .
            a. . . . . . . . . . . . . . . .
            b. . . . . . . . . . . . . . . .
        2. . . . . . . . . . . . . . . .
    B. . . . . . . . . . . . . . . .
II. . . . . . . . . . . . . . . .
```

**2** Be sure that your outline covers your subject adequately. The major headings in your outline should include enough material to satisfy the expectations provoked by your subject. For example, consider these two outlines:

### The Federal Government

| *Inadequate Material* | *Adequate Material* |
| --- | --- |
| I. Congress | I. Congress |
| II. The Executive Branch | II. The Executive Branch |
| | III. The Judiciary |

Obviously, the outline on the left shows the writer's failure to consider the entire subject; of course this is a simple example, but checking your outline against this criterion of completeness can save you a great deal of trouble.

**3** Be sure that your outline is in logical order. All the heads and subheads in your outline indicate parts. No category of head or subhead, therefore, can have only one part — if the essay or part is brief enough to be considered one part, it doesn't need to be outlined. Every outline must have at least two main headings, and wherever you divide one of these (I, II), you must divide it into at least two parts. If a I has an A, it must have a B. If an A has a 1, it must have a 2, and so forth.

Moreover, the order of your parts (the progression from I to II to III) must follow some consistent principle: chronology is one, cause and effect another. Do not mix your principles.

### Consistent Time Order
   I. Selecting the date
   II. Inviting the guests
   III. Preparing the menu
   IV. Cooking the food
   V. Setting the table

### Mixed Order
Crime
   I. Its increase since Vietnam (time order)
   II. Its causes (cause-and-effect order)
   III. Robbery versus rape (order by classification)

If your outline fails to meet this criterion, you are probably uncertain of your whole approach and need to reexamine your central idea or thesis statement.

**4**   Be sure to cast groups of headings and subheadings in parallel grammatical form. This will ensure that the parts of the outline are clearly related to one another. Notice in the sentence outline on page 159 that I A and I B are parallel (in B, the pronoun *it* stands for *the embargo*), but that they are not parallel with II A, II B, and II C — which are parallel with one another. (*Note:* It is only due to the nature of the subject that III A, III B, and III C are parallel with the same group under II; in most cases, they need not be and will not be parallel.)

## TEST YOURSELF ON
## the Principles of Outlining

**A**   Using one of the manageable titles given at the end of **Subjects for Essays** (p. 245, exercise A), construct three outlines for it: a topic, a sentence, and a paragraph outline.

**B**   Choose one of the topics in exercise B on page 247, give it a manageable title, and construct a sentence outline for it.

# Paragraph Development

Adequate development is one of the three criteria for an effectively written paragraph. (For the other two, see **Unity** and **Coherence.** Also discussed under **Unity** is the important idea of the *topic sentence:* if you are not familiar with the topic sentence, read **Unity** before reading further here.)

A paragraph that is adequately developed is one that gives reasons, details, illustrations, or examples to fully support its topic sentence. The failure to give full development to every topic sentence leads to a series of short, choppy statements — not paragraphs — and leaves readers with the impression of a hasty and ill-thought-out composition.

> The United Nations, which was established to maintain peace, does not do so. Since 1945, there have been many wars — Korea, the Middle East, and Vietnam, to name just a few.
>
> Besides, the United Nations is an instrument for propaganda. The Russians use it constantly for this purpose.

Obviously, this writer opposes the United Nations, but the first "paragraph" gives inadequate development to the topic sentence because not enough examples of the U.N.'s failure are given. Similarly, the second "paragraph" fails to be specific enough; it doesn't give examples of *how* the Russians use the U.N. for propaganda.

> With nuclear energy, there is still the possibility of accidents. One big one in Iowa in 1962 caused three deaths and a permanent shutdown.
>
> Moreover, there is also the problem of waste materials. Some of those waste materials have toxic effects for as long as 150,000 years!

The one example given in the first fragment is unpersuasive. Has there been only one? If not, how many? The emphatic exclamation point in the second fragment does not hide the fact that the fragment is undeveloped. What is being done now with waste materials? Why is it inadequate? The fragment is badly in need of development.

## TEST YOURSELF ON
## Developing Fragmentary Paragraphs

Each of the following sets of sentences is badly in need of further development. Develop each.

1. The more money you make, the more money you spend. When your income is low, you yearn for more — but learn to be restrained. As soon as your salary rises, however, you begin to give in to your desires.
2. Television tends to make us passive. The reason for this is that we have nothing to *do* as television viewers. It's all done for us.
3. Woodworking is not as difficult as it appears. The first thing you need is a reliable set of tools.

Development is not a haphazard process, but one that depends upon your topic sentence; that is, it depends on the nature of the subject you are dealing with in your paragraph. Therefore, it is important to be clear about what you're writing and to try to determine the best way to express and develop your thought. Most well-constructed paragraphs follow one or another of the following basic developmental plans: chronological, spatial, or logical (also called expository).

## Chronological Order

Use chronological order wherever time and sequence are important. In the example that follows, the author achieves clarity by constant reference to time, date, and season in an orderly manner.

The *Terra Nova* sailed from London 15th June 1910 and from New Zealand 26th November. She was fearfully overloaded; on deck, as well as the motor-sledges in their huge crates, there were 30 tons of coal in sacks, $2\frac{1}{2}$ tons of petrol in drums, 33 dogs, and 19 ponies. She rode out a bad storm by a miracle. "Bowers and Campbell were standing upon the bridge and the ship rolled sluggishly over until the lee combings of the main hatch were under the sea . . . as a rule, if a ship goes that far over she goes down." It took her thirty-eight days to get to McMurdo Sound, by which time the men were in poor shape. They had slept in their clothes, lucky if they got five hours a night, and had had no proper meals. As soon as they dropped anchor they began to unload the ship. This entailed dragging its cargo over ice floes which were in constant danger of being tipped up by killer whales, a very tricky business, specially when it came to moving ponies, motor-sledges and a pianola. Then they built the Hut which was henceforward to be their home. Scott, tireless himself, always drove his men hard and these things were accomplished in a fortnight. The *Terra Nova* sailed away; she was to return the following summer, when it was hoped that the Polar party would be back in time to be taken off before the freezing up of the sea forced her to leave again. If not, they would be obliged to spend a second winter on McMurdo Sound. Winter, of course, in those latitudes, happens during our summer months and is perpetual night, as the summer is perpetual day. The stunning beauty of the scenery affected the men deeply. When the sun shone the snow was never white, but brilliant shades of pink, blue and lilac; in winter the aurora australis flamed across the sky and the summit of Mount Erebus glowed.

Nancy Mitford, ''A Bad Time,'' from *The Water Beetle**

## Spatial Order

Use spatial order when it is necessary to describe physical reality and the spatial relationships between persons, things, or parts of things. A spatial ordering can proceed from inside to outside, top to bottom, up to down, and so forth. This description of a turtle crossing a road is a classic one.

The sun lay on the grass and warmed it, and in the shade under the grass the insects moved, ants and ant lions to set traps for them, grasshoppers to jump into the air and flick their yellow wings for a second, sow bugs like little armadillos, plodding restlessly on many tender feet. And over the grass at the roadside a land turtle crawled, turning aside for nothing, dragging his high-domed shell over the grass. His hard legs and yellow-nailed feet threshed slowly through the grass, not really walking but boosting and dragging his shell along. The barley beards slid off his shell, and the clover burrs fell on him and rolled to the ground. His horny beak was partly open, and his fierce, humorous eyes, under brows like fingernails, stared straight ahead. He came over the grass leaving a beaten trail behind him, and the hill, which was the highway embankment, reared up ahead of him. For a moment he stopped, his head held high. He blinked and looked up and down. At last he started to climb the embankment. Front clawed feet reached forward but did not touch. The hind feet kicked his shell along, and it scraped on the grass, and on the gravel. As the embankment grew steeper and steeper, the more frantic were the efforts of the land turtle. Pushing hind legs strained and slipped, boosting the shell along, and the horny head

*P*

* Reprinted by permission of A. D. Peters & Co., Ltd.

protruded as far as the neck could stretch. Little by little the shell slid up the embankment until at last a parapet cut straight across its line of march, the shoulder of the road, a concrete wall four inches high. As though they worked independently the hind legs pushed the shell against the wall. The head upraised and peered over the wall to the broad smooth plane of cement. Now the hands, braced on top of the wall, strained and lifted, and the shell came slowly up and rested its front end on the wall. For a moment the turtle rested. A red ant ran into the shell, into the soft skin inside the shell, and suddenly head and legs snapped in, and the armored tail clamped in sideways. The red ant was crushed between body and legs. And one head of wild oats was clamped into the shell by a front leg. For a long moment the turtle lay still, and then the neck crept out and the old humorous frowning eyes looked about and the legs and tail came out. The back legs went to work, straining like elephant legs, and the shell tipped to an angle so that the front legs could not reach the level cement plain. But higher and higher the hind legs boosted it, until at last the center of balance was reached, the front tipped down, the front legs scratched at the pavement, and it was up. But the head of wild oats was held by its stem around the front legs.
John Steinback, *The Grapes of Wrath**

## Logical or Expository Order

**P**

Use logical or expository order to present illustrative details, examples, or reasons in supporting a topic sentence. There are a number of methods of expository order. They are the methods by which paragraphs and whole essays are organized for their specific purposes. One of these methods will be suitable for your particular paragraph or your particular purposes. The chief methods are (1) illustrative details and examples, (2) comparison and contrast, (3) definition, (4) classification, (5) process analysis, and (6) causal analysis.

### 1 Illustrative Details and Examples

A common and sturdy way of explaining and making vivid a generalization is to offer concrete details or examples to support the topic sentence. Most of the other methods also include use of this one at one point or another.

As things now stand, the office is a slightly meaner battleground than the home. Male bosses seem to dominate their women underlings as they would never dominate their wives, as if women's lib has sent them a gift to make up for what they've lost at home, while women bosses must practice either a paper-thin toughness that fools nobody or a sort of crisp femininity that must be terribly hard to sustain. The male prejudice against working for women may be the last to go, and even the best women executives must sometimes feel that the men under and around them are toying with them, helping the little woman out, carrying her and tolerating her. She is there at their pleasure and could be snuffed out in an instant if they weren't such nice, well-adjusted guys with such super-secure self-images.
Wilfrid Sheed, "Now That Men Can Cry . . ." *New York Times Magazine,* October 30, 1977

The world becomes narrower as friends and family die or move away. To climb stairs, to ride in a car, to walk to the corner, to talk on the telephone; each action seems to take away from the energy needed to stay alive. Everything is limited by the strength you hoard greedily. Your needs decrease, you require less food, less sleep, and finally less human contact; yet this little bit becomes more and more difficult. You fear that one day you will be reduced to the simple acts of breathing and taking nourishment. This is the ultimate stage you dread, the period of helplessness and hopelessness, when independence will be over.
Sharon Curtin, "Aging in the Land of the Young," *Atlantic,* July 1972

To illustrate a general concept, the writer can name a specific member of the general class: a **herring** is a **fish.** A **Toyota** is a *car.* He can also specify how something operates: **Hitler was a mad dictator;** *during World War II, he ordered the deaths of 6 million Jews.* The specification of parts is another technique for giving details, illustrations, and examples. Narrating one's story in detail illustrates very well one's conclusion about the kind of a day one had, and there are a number of other approaches as well.

## 2  Comparison and Contrast
Where your need is to set two items alongside each other for the purpose of noticing their similarities or differences, comparison and contrast are the developmental method of choice. By using this method, you can also isolate one of the items as being the better of the two — thus advancing an argument; or you can isolate for study

the lesser known of the two items (say the British Parliament) by comparing it with the better known (say the U.S. Congress).

Fundamentally Grant was superior to Lee because in a modern total war he had a modern mind, and Lee did not. Lee looked to the past in war as the Confederacy did in spirit. The staffs of the two men illustrate their outlook. It would not be accurate to say that Lee's general staff were glorified clerks, but the statement would not be too wide of the mark. Certainly his staff was not, in the modern sense, a planning staff, which was why Lee was often a tired general. He performed labors that no general can do in a big modern army — work that should have fallen to his staff, but that Lee did because it was traditional for the commanding general to do it in older armies. Most of Lee's staff officers were lieutenant colonels. Some of the men on Grant's general staff, as well as the staffs of other Northern generals, were major and brigadier generals, officers who were capable of leading corps. Grant's staff was an organization of experts in the various phases of strategic planning. The modernity of Grant's mind was most apparent in his grasp of the concept that war was becoming total and that the destruction of the enemy's economic resources was as effective and legitimate a form of warfare as the destruction of his armies. What was realism to Grant was barbarism to Lee. Lee thought of war in the old way as a conflict between armies and refused to view it for what it had become — a struggle between societies. To him, economic war was needless cruelty to civilians. Lee was the last of the great old-fashioned generals, Grant the first of the great moderns.
T. Harry Williams, *Lincoln and His Generals*

A century of association has inevitably acculturated both Hispanos and Anglo-Americans to some extent, but there still persists a number of culture traits that neither group has relinquished altogether. Nothing is more disquieting to an Anglo-American who believes that time is money than the time perspective of His-panos. They usually refer to this attitude as the "*mañana* psychology." Actually, it is more of a "today psychology," because Hispanos cultivate the present to the exclusion of the future; because the latter has not arrived yet, it is not a reality. They are reluctant to relinquish the present, so they hold on to it until it becomes the past. To an Hispano, nine is nine until it is ten, so when he arrives at nine-thirty, he jubilantly exclaims: "¡Justo!" [right on time]. This may be why the clock is slowed down to a walk in Spanish while in English it runs. In the United

States, our future-oriented civilization plans our lives so far in advance that the present loses its meaning. January magazine issues are out in December; 1973 cars have been out since October; cemetery plots and even funeral arrangements are bought on the installment plan. To a person engrossed in living today the very idea of planning his funeral sounds like the tolling of the bells.

Arthur L. Campa, "Anglo vs. Chicano: Why?" *Intellectual Digest,* January 1973

To develop a paragraph or an essay in this method, you would proceed by selecting points of comparison that could be applied to each member of the pair you are working with. For example, if you were comparing an American and a foreign car, you might select as points the initial costs of the cars, subsequent costs of maintenance, convenience of service, economy with respect to energy, and ease of handling. The comparison essay reveals something about one member of the pair (by comparing a known item to an unknown one) or decides which is best by measuring their respective merits.

### 3  Definition

Essays frequently require paragraphs defining important terms or objects. Definition can be an important aid to the reader in understanding complex matters, especially where highly connotative words or terms are being employed.

The *satire* is a verbal caricature which distorts characteristic features of an individual or society by exaggeration and simplification. The features picked out for enlargement by the satirist are, of course, those of which he disapproves: "If Nature's inspiration fails," wrote Juvenal, "indignation will beget the poem." The comic effect of the satire is derived from the simultaneous presence, in the reader's mind, of the social reality with which he is familiar, and of its reflection in the distorting mirror of the satirist. It focusses attention on abuses and deformities in society of which, blunted by habit, we were no longer aware; it makes us suddenly discover the absurdity of the familiar and the familiarity of the absurd.

Arthur Koestler, *The Act of Creation*

One mark of schizophrenia or a schizoid personality according to R. D. Laing, one of the world's experts on the subject, is that a person gets to feeling that at least part of his life and experience is somehow unreal. There's a real self and an unreal self. The real self, his actual core personality, is what he calls me. But it's the me nobody knows. The other part, the unreal, accidental, or artificial self, is the one he projects to the world. The sicker he gets the more he thinks it is the unreal self and not the real self that is acting when he acts. The him that is driving a car, listening to the radio, fighting with his wife, or robbing a bank is not the real him. However, if you have to deal with this individual the real him is the one that's doing these things. What he thinks of as the real him is what is unreal to everybody else. The individual they see walking, acting one way or another, is what that individual really is as far as they are concerned. That inner him that nobody knows, nobody knows—so it is unreal to them.

Charles Osgood, *Profile,* CBS News, November 10, 1971

To define a word like religion, which most of us need to define for ourselves since there is no general agreement on its full implications, the writer would plan to give examples of *religion;* he would also include a logical definition of the term, separating it from other terms that were near it in meaning by giving its distinctive properties and perhaps also say what *religion* is *not.* The wise writer of definitions uses the full range of explanatory resources.

## 4 Classification

The grouping of persons, things, or ideas according to some principle or order frequently sheds new light on those things. Thus the paragraph that classifies also explains.

P

Symbolic immortality is an expression of man's need for an inner sense of continuity with what has gone on before and what will go on after his own limited biological existence. The *sense* of immortality is thus more than mere denial of death, and grows out of compelling, life-enhancing imagery of one's involvement in the historical process. This sense of immortality may be expressed *biologically,* by living on through one's sons and daughters and their sons and daughters, extending out into social dimensions (of tribe, organization, people, nation, or even species); *theologically,* in the idea of a life after death or of other forms of spiritual conquest of death; *creatively,* through "works" and influences persisting beyond biological death; *naturally,* through identification with nature, with its infinite extension into time and space; or *transcendentally,* through a feeling-state so intense that time and death disappear.

Roberty Jay Lifton, "The Struggle for Cultural Rebirth," *Harper's,* April 1973

But who, then, is the desirable man—the patron who will cajole the best out of the writer's brain and bring to birth the most

varied and vigorous progeny of which he is capable? Different ages have answered the question differently. The Elizabethans, to speak roughly, chose the aristocracy to write for and the playhouse public. The eighteenth-century patron was a combination of coffee-house wit and Grub Street bookseller. In the nineteenth century the great writers wrote for the half-crown magazines and the leisured classes. And looking back and applauding the splendid results of these different alliances, it all seems enviably simple, and plain as a pike-staff compared with our own predicament—for whom should we write? For the present supply of patrons is of unexampled and bewildering variety. There is the daily Press, the weekly Press, the monthly Press; the English public and the American public; the best-seller public and the worst-seller public; the high-brow public and the red-blood public; all now organised self-conscious entities capable through their various mouthpieces of making their needs known and their approval or displeasure felt. Thus the writer who has been moved by the sight of the first crocus in Kensington Gardens has, before he sets pen to paper, to choose from a crowd of competitors the particular patron who suits him best. It is futile to say, "Dismiss them all; think only of your crocus," because writing is a method of communication; and the crocus is an imperfect crocus until it has been shared. The first man or the last may write for himself alone, but he is an exception and an unenviable one at that, and the gulls are welcome to his works if the gulls can read them.
Virginia Woolf, "The Patron and the Crocus," from *The Common Reader*

The writer selects a principle of order according to his interest, bearing in mind the need to arrive at logical categories that are informative for a reader. Using the principle of gender to divide your English class into men and women is not very useful, but interest in writing or previous grades in English composition or reading habits would all yield significant categories and significant information. A writer's purpose in classification essays is usually to inform, but it can also be to entertain: classifying the kinds of bores you know can be fun.

### 5  Process Analysis

Process analysis is a method of separating some complex whole into its component parts—usually a mechanical process. A paragraph that explains in detail how something functions or how a machine is put together is filled with explanatory power. Process analysis is also useful in giving directions on how to do something, and paragraphs using this method of development frequently employ chronological or spatial order.

> These solitary wasps are beautiful and formidable creatures. Most species are either a deep shiny blue all over, or deep blue with rusty wings. The largest have a wing span of about four inches. They live on nectar. When excited, they give off a pungent odor — a warning that they are ready to attack. The sting is much worse than that of a bee or common wasp, and the pain and swelling last longer. In the adult stage the wasp lives only a few months. The female produces but a few eggs, one at a time at intervals of two or three days. For each egg the mother must provide one adult tarantula, alive but paralyzed. The mother wasp attaches the egg to the paralyzed spider's abdomen. Upon hatching from the egg, the larva is many hundreds of times smaller than its living but helpless victim. It eats no other food and drinks no water. By the time it has finished its single Gargantuan meal and become ready for wasphood, nothing remains of the tarantula but its indigestible chitinous skeleton.
> Alexander Petrunkevich, "The Spider and the Wasp," *Scientific American*, August 1952

> The three absolute acts of the tragedy are first the entry of the bull when the picadors receive the shock of his attacks and attempt to protect their horses with their lances. Then the horses go out and the second act is the planting of the banderillos. This is one of the most interesting and difficult parts but among the easiest for a new bull fight fan to appreciate in technique. The banderillos are three-foot, gaily colored darts with a small fish hook prong in the end. The man who is going to plant them walks out into the arena alone with the bull. He lifts the banderillos at arm's length and points them toward the bull. Then he calls "Toro! Toro!" The bull charges and the banderillero rises to his toes, bends in a curve forward and just as the bull is about to hit him drops the darts into the bull's hump just back of his horns.
> *By-Line: Ernest Hemingway,* ed. William White

Those who write to tell others how to do something are usually very careful about several things. First, they are careful to demarcate the stages in the process. Second, they take into account how much the reader knows or doesn't know; so that they are quick to define terms that may not be familiar to the reader. Finally, though their essays are heavily factual, they make sure that a thesis statement controls what they write.

### 6  Causal Analysis

This method too separates something into its component parts, but here the something is some specific event or other human situation, and the aim of the writer is to suggest the causes that produced some particular result.

> We are the first society in which parents expect to learn from their children. Such a topsy-turvy situation has come about at least in part because, unlike the rest of the world, ours is an immigrant society, and for immigrants the *only* hope is in the kids. In the Old Country, hope was in the father, and how much family wealth he could accumulate and pass along to his children. In the growth pattern of America and its ever-expanding frontier, the young man was ever advised to Go West; the father was ever inheriting from his son: the topsy-turviness was built-in from the beginning. In short, a melting pot needs a spoon. Kids' Country may be the inevitable result.
> Shana Alexander, "Kids' Country," *Newsweek*, December 1972

> Now, failure to uphold the law is no less corrupt than violation of the law. And the continuing shame of this country now is the growing number of Americans who fail to uphold and assist enforcement of the law, simply — and ignominiously — out of fear. Fear of "involvement," fear of reprisal, fear of "trouble." A man is beaten by hoodlums in plain daylight and in view of bystanders. These people not only fail to help the victim, but, like the hoodlums, flee before the police can question them. A city official knows of a colleague's bribe but does not report it. A pedestrian watches a car hit a woman but leaves the scene, to avoid giving testimony. It happens every day. And if the police get cynical at this irresponsibility, they are hardly to blame. Morale is a matter of giving support and having faith in one another; where both are lacking, "law" has become a worthless word.
> Marya Mannes, "The Thin Gray Line," *McCall's*, January 1964

To enter into a discussion of why some complex human event took place, the writer must generate his materials by asking a great many questions of his subject, thus arriving at an essay that declares the multiplicity of cause and effect in the world of affairs. The writer must also be wary of simplistic thinking in other ways; for example, because event A happened *before* event B it is not necessarily the cause of it. Writing the cause-and-effect essay also requires that you use a solid chain of reasoning. (See **Logic,** pp. 123–146.)

## TEST YOURSELF ON
## Understanding Methods of Paragraph Development

**A** Which method of development would be most suitable for making a paragraph out of each of the following topic sentences? Give reasons. Then select one topic sentence and develop it into a paragraph.

1. Marijuana is not more harmful than alcohol, though my parents seem to think so.
2. The Guggenheim Museum, from the outside, looks like a bomb shelter.
3. Unexpected things happen to freshmen on this campus.
4. Television commercials don't care what they do as long as they sell, sell, sell.
5. Intelligence is the capacity to face what you do not know how to handle.
6. There are three kinds of English teacher on this campus.
7. Lung cancer is a result of certain environmental pressures on the respiratory system.
8. My troubles with mathematics began in 1985.
9. The secret to treating raw wood to look like fine furniture finishing is patience.
10. Foreign cars and American cars differ in crucial ways.

**B** Write three separate paragraphs using the following topic sentence:

*My attitudes toward teachers have changed since I came to college.*

In the first paragraph, explain *why* this change has taken place. In the second, explain *how* these attitudes have changed. Finally, in the third, compare and contrast two sets of attitudes toward teachers: the ones you had in high school and the ones you have now.

# Parallel Construction

Wherever grammatical structures — words, phrases, or clauses — are repeated, we have a parallel construction.

> **Words**   Jenny *whispered* in David's ear, *touched* his arm, *winked* at him, then *walked* away. (parallel verbs)
> *Impetuously, bravely, daringly,* Colin drove to the hoop and stuffed the ball through. (parallel adverbs)
>
> **Phrases**   *To think clearly, to act ethically, to love completely* — these were Dierdre's goals. (parallel infinitive phrases)
>
> **Clauses**   *When you have learned who you are, when you have experienced the world, when you have come to respect others* — then you are entitled to be called an adult. (parallel adverbial clauses)

The advantage of parallel construction is that it binds ideas together and allows the reader to grasp each point because he or she has been prepared for the second and third points by the *form of the first.* You may not want to use parallel construction to the extent that it is used in the above examples, but ineffective writing results when you *begin* to use parallel construction and then abandon it. You must be sure either to use it or avoid it — and not use it partly, as in the following examples:

> **Partly Parallel**   Melissa was *bright, beautiful,* and *a person who had great consideration for others.* (1. single-word adjective; 2. single-word adjective; 3. noun + adjective clause)
>
> **Revised**   Melissa was *bright, beautiful,* and *considerate.*
>
> **Partly Parallel**   The Governor favored *a revised income tax schedule, simplifying the criminal code,* and *less money for judges of the State Supreme Court.* (1. adjective + compound noun phrase; 2. gerund phrase; 3. adjective + noun + prepositional phrase)
>
> **Revised**   The Governor favored *a revised income tax schedule, a simplified criminal code,* and *a lowered salary for State Supreme Court judges.*

The problem with the partly parallel examples above is that they set up an expectation in the mind of the reader and then don't fulfill that expectation. The result is confusion.

In order to avoid incomplete parallels, you should make sure that whatever grammatical construction follows the word *and* (or any of the other coordinating conjunctions) in your sentence construction also precedes it. If you have a construction like . . . *and a policeman,* you would need a noun to parallel *a policeman* before the word *and (a doctor and a policeman).* Similarly, if one of your sentences contained . . . *and which always haunted him,* you would need the same kind of construction *before* the word *and (which always followed him and which always haunted him).*

**TEST YOURSELF ON**
## Filling in the Other Side of *and, but, or* Constructions

What could go on the other side of the words *and, or,* and *but* in each of the following examples?

1. . . . and snake oil.
2. . . . and whose mother came from Italy.
3. . . . and that hasn't been seen since.
4. . . . but who thinks of himself as a gentleman.
5. . . . and lovely.
6. . . . or to live longer.
7. . . . but never wanted to live there.
8. . . . but hates whiskey.
9. . . . and tries everything.
10. . . . or went alone.

**P**

**TEST YOURSELF ON**
## Making Constructions Parallel

Now that you have had some practice in making the sides of coordinating conjunctions parallel, try your skill at whole sentences. First locate the coordinating conjunction in each of the following examples. Then, if the constructions on either side of the conjunctions are not parallel, revise the sentences to make them parallel. If the sentence is correct, write C beside it. Make sure you underline all parallel constructions, whether or not the sentence is correct.

1. _____ The purpose of this meeting is to review past procedures, recognize what we have to do in the future, and so that we can get to know each other better.

2. _____ This term I learned math, biology, and how to write a term paper.

3. _____ My mother is neat, patient, and a person who is filled with pride.

4. _____ Bob liked falling in love and to write poetry.

5. _____ She was happy but nervous.

6. _____ Whenever I visit my relatives, I'm nervous, exhausted, and I feel like I am disoriented.

7. _____ Traveling in Italy makes you aware of art and the food is wonderful for your taste buds when you eat there.

8. _____ Having a sprained ankle and then to try to walk is murder.

9. _____ Joking with my friends, swimming in the lake, and horseback riding in the woods — those are the things I like to do on my vacation.

10. _____ At the party, I spoke to a sociologist, a detective, a stockbroker, and this man who repaired television sets.

**P**

## Parentheses

*Parentheses* is the plural of the word *parenthesis*. *Parentheses* signifies *both* curved marks: ( ). Parentheses are used to set off material that is not absolutely essential to complete the meaning of the sentence pattern but that supplements or further explains a part or parts of that sentence. We call such material *parenthetical elements;* these elements can be appositives or other nonrestrictive phrases or clauses.

But since parentheses, commas, and dashes can all be used to set off parenthetical material, you should first note the difference between these marks when they are used for this purpose.

*Dashes* are used either to set off material that is emphatic or to set off material you decide to emphasize. In other words, using dashes gives emphasis; your material should match the emphasis given.

> My friend Lewis — *who drove his pickup into the lake last night* — is a complete madman.
>
> What happened last night — *if you believe him* — was an accident.

*Commas* are used to signal that the parenthetical material is more nearly a part of the sentence than material set off by dashes or parentheses — that the material interrupts the flow of thought only slightly.

> The signs of the storm, *lightning and thunder,* frightened him.
>
> You can, *if you wish,* rent a cheaper model.

*Parentheses* signal that the enclosed material is not emphatic and that its nature is supplemental.

> Channel 4 is owned by the National Broadcasting Company *(a subsidiary of the Radio Corporation of America).*
>
> Most students pay heavy tuition charges *(though there are a few exceptions).*

As you can see, the choice of which marks to use can be a matter of taste. Nevertheless, the following general rules are good guidelines.

**1**   Use parentheses to set off material that is not essential to complete the meaning of the sentence and that is unemphatic and supplemental. Such material may include words, phrases, whole sentences, or even several sentences.

1. At that time, the vice-president (Garner) had very little power.
2. At that time, the vice-president (Garner, a gruff old man from Texas) had very little power.

P

   3. At that time, the vice-president had very little power. (Garner,
      a gruff old man from Texas, understood this well.)
   4. At that time, the vice-president had very little power. (Garner,
      a gruff old man from Texas, understood this well. It was,
      perhaps, Garner's understanding of the situation that later
      prompted Lyndon Johnson, his fellow Texan, to try to raise the
      status of the office.) He presided over the Senate, a largely
      ceremonial post, and greeted visiting dignitaries from abroad.

Note that in the third example, a full sentence is enclosed within the
parentheses. In such cases, *the period comes before the closing
parenthesis.* Note that there *is* a space before the opening parenthesis, but there *is no* space between the opening parenthesis and
the first word or between the period and closing parenthesis.

   Another point about punctuation with parentheses: *where the
parenthetical material is a part of the sentence, the period goes
outside the closing parenthesis.*

   At that time, the vice-president was Garner (a gruff old man from
   Texas).

*Note:* Do not use parentheses for essential material.

   **Wrong**   The men were dog tired; the lieutenant *(therefore)*
   called a halt to the march.
   **Wrong**   I'm going to keep on taking that examination *(until I
   pass it).*

**2**   Use parentheses to set off cross-references and figures
denoting lifespan.

   It will become clear later *(in Chapter 7)* that James Joyce
   *(1882–1941)* was not exactly kind to his brother.

## TEST YOURSELF ON
## Using Parentheses Correctly

Some of the sentences below have parenthetic material correctly
set off by dashes and commas; next to these sentences, write C.
However, some of the sentences should have parentheses *instead*
of the commas or dashes; change these. In addition, where you see
essential material enclosed within parentheses, eliminate those parentheses and, if necessary, substitute other punctuation.

1. _____ I think, if you don't mind, I'll take my nap now.

2. _____ Charley — a good friend of mine — left for California yesterday.

3. _____ The power of the media — with their enormous audience — is hard to overestimate.

4. _____ We whizzed along the highway, all of us on our bicycles, enjoying the breezes and the sunshine.

5. _____ The author — authors? — of Genesis spoke the stories with reverence.

6. _____ I won't go to the party (unless you come with me).

7. _____ He had (probably) a logical mind.

8. _____ The magician — a most amazing sleight-of-hand artist — had us all on the edges of our seats.

9. _____ Then it rolled through the grating, my last coin, and I was flat broke.

10. _____ He was born in 1235, or somewhat earlier, and died about forty-five years later.

**P**

## Passive Voice

See **Voice**

## Period

The period, which is sometimes (especially in British usage) called the *full stop*, is a mark of end punctuation. It signals the end of a *declarative* or mildly *imperative* sentence and is used in most abbreviations. (Spaced periods (. . .) also have special uses; see **Ellipsis.**)

**1**   Use a period to end declarative and imperative sentences. A declarative sentence makes an assertion; an imperative sentence issues a command.

I am going to the movies tonight. (declarative)

Go to the movies tonight. (imperative — this one a very mild command)

*Note:* For strongly imperative sentences, consider using the exclamation point. Example: *Get out of my sight!*

**2**   Use a period after an abbreviation.

| | |
|---|---|
| Mr. Buckley | Ms. |
| Dr. Brody | U.S. |
| Ph.D. | a.m. |

## Person

See **Verbs** and **Shifts.**

## Possessives

See Nouns, Pronouns; **Apostrophe, Case,** and **Pronoun References.**

## Prewriting (including Free-writing)

*Prewriting* is what we call the initial stage of the writing process. This stage begins when you find out you will be required to write an essay, and it ends when you're ready to write a first draft. Some disagree on exactly when prewriting ends, but this is a good approximation.

## The Prewriting Process

What you do first during prewriting depends on what your instructor has asked you to do.

Few instructors will simply ask you to "write something." If one does, however, your first task in the prewriting stage will be to choose something to write about. More often than not, instructors will be more specific in their writing assignments and will ask you to write in a general subject area or ask you to write using a specific form of organization (see **Paragraph Development**, pp. 162–173). In other words, in prewriting you must either choose a subject or explore one that you more or less have in hand.

In either case, prewriting is the stage at which you get started. If you are choosing your own subject, you need to explore possibilities — either from the fund of experience you already have or from the experience you can arrange for yourself for the specific purposes of this writing assignment.

You can search your past experience and look over the incidents, the people, and the places that have figured in your life. Think specifically about individuals — lists of friends, relatives, acquaintances, fellow workers. These lists will produce specific memories that might be fruitful. You can also take the chronological approach. Do a year-by-year survey of what you did and whom you met, the jobs you held, the trips you made, the milestones in your life, the high notes and the low.

Reviewing this lode of experience will lead you to possibilities for your subject.

A second source of possible paper subjects is the experience you can arrange. That is, you can undertake to observe something — to examine the physical world, for example, landscapes, buildings, works of art, man-made things. Or you can study communities, peoples, situations, events, or issues. You can, in fact, observe items of the latter group more systematically by doing formal research (see Part 3 for a discussion of research methods).

The prewriting we have discussed so far involves your using a pen and paper to make lists or scratch notes. Another way to use pen and paper for invention, that is, for the purpose of generating

P

ideas for papers — and more — is called free-writing, and it involves something other than lists and notes. Peter Elbow, who has written extensively on the subject, suggests that free-writing is one of the most efficient techniques available in the prewriting stage.

## Free-writing

In free-writing, you put your pen to paper for a specified period of time — say ten minutes — and you don't stop until the ten minutes are up. Move the pen along at a brisk pace without actually hurrying. The main rule is, *don't stop.* If you go absolutely blank, it's perfectly all right to write "I'm absolutely blank" and to keep on writing that or similar things until you begin to produce something else. It is very important to continue to write without stopping, without thinking, and especially without going back to correct mistakes — or what you think of as mistakes in spelling, grammar, or syntax. It is also important that you do not try to "stick to the subject." If you wander onto another topic, so be it. Eventually, you can get back to the original subject easily enough.

Most of us are inhibited by the need to explore a subject area and to keep a watchful eye on grammar and spelling — *all at the same time.* Through the hand-mind connection, free-writing helps you to loosen your capacity to think. By relieving you of the necessity of being grammatically and syntactically correct *as you write,* free-writing enhances your capacity to explore the corners of your mind. Thus free-writing is a primary aid to invention.

### Free-writing to Explore a Subject

To explore a specific subject, begin with the word or words that characterize your subject and take off from there. Work for ten minutes by the clock. After you've finished, set the pages aside for a few hours. Then examine what you've written for ideas and for directions you might take with your subject. (See also Choosing a Topic and Limiting a Topic in **Subjects for Essays,** pp. 244 – 247.)

Free-writing is not meant to be read by your instructor, or by anyone else for the purpose of evaluating it or criticizing it. You may, if you wish, ask your instructor or a friend to read it, without comment, just so you'll know that someone out there has read it. The free-writing that you do is for *your* benefit. It is a resource that you can examine for possible topics for your paper, directions you might want to take with your paper, useful ideas to support what you want to say, or, in fact, indications of *what* you want to say.

### Free-writing to Keep the Instrument Sharp

Free-writing is also worth using as a form of prewriting that generates fresh, usable words, phrases, and sentences. Every piece of free-writing can be *mined* for the fresh language this exercise often produces. In other words, free-writing is a useful habit for keeping sharp your writing instrument — the instrument that is alive and well in the unexplored corners of your mind. Since you are a college student whose courses often demand writing in one form or another, you might find regular free-writing sessions helpful, say three or four times a week, just to keep your instrument alive. In a writing course, you should consider free-writing a useful technique whenever (a) you are given a subject for a writing assignment, (b) you are blocked at a stage in the writing process, or (c) you need a way to stimulate the free flow of ideas you never quite realized you had.

P

## TEST YOURSELF ON
# Free-writing

Do **one** of the following free-writing exercises, using either pen and paper, a typewriter, or a word processor.

**A**  Simply take out your notebook, turn to a fresh page and, without further ado, start writing. Continue for ten minutes, by your watch, without stopping and without taking the trouble to correct misspelling or errors in punctuation or grammar. Don't lift your pen from the page or your fingers from the keyboard. Just write.

**B**  Start writing — as directed in "A" above — but begin with these words: "Free-writing is like playing basketball without a hoop."

**C**  Start writing — again as directed in "A" above — only this time begin with these words: "Apples are good for your complexion."

# Pronoun References

A pronoun sometimes does its work by referring back to another word or group of words. What the pronoun refers back to is called its *antecedent.*

The following guidelines will be useful to you in making sure that your pronoun references are clear and consistent.

**1** Pronouns must *agree* in person and number with their antecedents.

**A** In referring to persons, places, and things, use pronouns that agree in person and number.

> I saw *John* yesterday; *he* seemed depressed.
>
> The *dog* wagged *its* tail.
>
> When I saw the *Smiths* yesterday, *they* were on *their* way to the movies.

**B** Use a singular pronoun in referring to antecedents like the following: *any, anybody, anyone, each, every, everybody, everyone, either, neither, man, woman, person, nobody, none, someone, somebody.* In informal writing, we frequently find plural pronouns referring to some of these, but formal usage requires the singular.

> ***Formal*** *Everybody* has *his* dreams.
> ***Informal*** *Everybody* has *their* dreams.
>
> ***Formal*** Mathematics requires *each* of us to use *his* intellect.
> ***Informal*** Mathematics requires *each* of us to use *our* intellect.

**C** In the case of a collective noun used as an antecedent, use a singular pronoun if you are thinking of the group as a unit; use a plural pronoun if you are thinking of the members separately.

> The *team* raised *its* batting average by ten points.
>
> The *team* came through when *their* fans began urging *them* on.

**D** When two or more antecedents are joined by *and, or,* or *nor,* the following rules apply: (1) When two or more singular antecedents are joined by *and,* use a plural pronoun; (2) when two or more singular antecedents are joined by *or* or *nor,* use a singular pronoun; (3) when one of the antecedents joined by *or* or *nor* is singular and one plural, use a pronoun that agrees with the nearer of the two.

1. *Tom* and *Lisa* did *their* work together.
2. Neither *Lisa* nor *April* has *her* hat on.
3. Neither the *conductor* nor the *musicians have* held *their* rehearsal.

## TEST YOURSELF ON
## Pronoun Agreement

Make all the pronouns in the following sentences agree with their antecedents according to the principles of formal usage.

1. Anybody who knows their music would know the Rolling Stones.

2. The committee did their work in private.

3. Neither the new professor nor the first-year students knew his way around the campus.

4. Anybody who likes their morning coffee cold is peculiar.

5. When the team scored a touchdown, the band raised its instruments to play.

6. Everybody has a right to their own opinion in politics.

7. If a drugstore or a supermarket opened in our neighborhood, they would do well.

8. Neither of them could do their homework in the middle of all that noise.

9. Every cook thinks their recipes are best.

10. None of the students in biology could identify the specimens under their microscope.

P

**2**   Do not use pronouns ambiguously. *Ambiguous* means "able to be understood in more than one way." Therefore, an ambiguous pronoun reference occurs whenever the pronoun you use can refer back to more than one antecedent.

> ***Ambiguous***   My father told my brother that *he* had to go to Boston. (Who had to go? the father or the brother?)
> ***Clear***   My father said to my brother, "I have to go to Boston." My father said to my brother, "You have to go to Boston."
>
> ***Ambiguous***   When Donna looked at Lisa, *she* blushed. (Who blushed? Donna or Lisa?)
> ***Clear***   When she looked at Lisa, Donna blushed.
> ***Clear***   Donna blushed when she looked at Lisa.
> ***Clear***   Lisa blushed when Donna looked at her.
> ***Clear***   When Donna looked at Lisa, Lisa blushed.

**3**   Do not use pronouns with remote references. A pronoun that is too far away from what it refers to is said to have a remote reference (or antecedent).

> ***Remote***   As for the Concorde, we did everything we could to stop the plane from landing at Kennedy Airport, including sending people out to picket the field and writing letters to our congressmen. *It* is obscene. (The *it*, referring to the airplane, is too far away, too remote, from its antecedent, *Concorde*.)
> ***Revised***   As for the Concorde, *it* is obscene, and we did everything we could to stop the plane from landing at Kennedy Airport, including sending people out to picket the field and writing letters to our congressmen.
>
> ***Remote***   Billy gave up smoking and, as a result, temporarily gained a lot of weight. *It* was very bad for his health.
> ***Revised***   Billy gave up smoking because *it* was very bad for his health and, as a result, temporarily gained a lot of weight.

**4**   Do not use pronouns with faulty broad reference. A pronoun with broad reference is one that refers back to a whole idea rather than a single noun. When the pronoun refers back to more than one idea, it has a faulty broad reference. The vague use of *this*, *that*, and *which* most frequently results in faulty broad references.

> ***Faulty Broad Reference***   He planted a line of tall shrubbery to stop people from looking into his garden. *That* is not easy. (What is not easy? the planting or stopping the people?)

Sometimes, adding a noun can make the loose reference clear.

***Revised*** He planted a line of tall shrubbery to stop people from looking into his garden. *That job* is not easy. (Now the *job* refers clearly to the *planting*.)

***Faulty Broad Reference*** He spent his time getting help with his income tax forms, *which* his wife considered unfair. (What does she consider unfair? that he spends his time that way? that he gets help? Or does she consider the forms unfair?)

In faulty references involving a *which* clause, it is sometimes necessary to recast the sentence, getting rid of *which*.

***Revised*** His wife considered it unfair that he spent his time getting help with his income tax forms.

Now we can see that what the wife considers unfair is the way in which he spends his time.

Despite the fact that writers are prone to errors of broad pronoun reference, the use of the broad pronoun reference is not prohibited. Frequently, such references are perfectly appropriate — where they are perfectly clear.

I'll take the cash to the bank. *That's* the safest thing.

We need to save money. *This* is the only way to stay solvent.

**5** Do not use pronouns with implied antecedents; that is, do not let the pronoun refer to a noun or a whole idea that is absent from the sentence. The vague use of *it, you, they,* and *them* most frequently causes this error.

***Implied Antecedent*** *It* says in my notebook that China has the biggest population in the world.
***Revised*** My notebook says that China has the biggest population in the world.

***Implied Antecedent*** I could have supplied the answer if I had thought about *it*.
***Revised*** I could have supplied the answer if I had thought about the question.

***Implied Antecedent*** In some colleges, *you're* not permitted to live off campus.
***Revised*** In some colleges, students are not permitted to live off campus.

***Implied Antecedent*** *They* have mostly an agricultural economy in Southeast Asia.
***Revised*** The economy in Southeast Asia is mostly agricultural.

> ***Implied Antecedent***   I go to Yankee Stadium because I like to watch *them* play.
>
> ***Revised***   I go to Yankee Stadium because I like to watch the Yankees play.

## TEST YOURSELF ON
## Pronoun References

Some of the sentences below have perfectly clear pronoun references; next to these, write C. Others, however, have faulty pronoun references; correct these, even if you have to recast the sentence.

1. _____ The Montreal Canadiens were soundly beaten by the Boston Bruins on their home ice last night.

2. _____ He carried a briefcase, which looked as if it had cost him a hundred dollars.

3. _____ During the Civil War, they struggled over the question of slavery.

4. _____ The idea that Fred broached to Eddie was one that he had thought of some years earlier.

5. _____ For the first time in months, we went up to the farm last weekend; we cleaned out the barn, pruned the apple trees, and swam in the creek. It was wonderful.

6. _____ Driving through Yellowstone, you are likely to see a bear.

7. _____ Alice's mother died when she was twenty-three.

8. _____ Arthur and Hilda came to the wedding in a horse-drawn carriage, which somewhat amused the other guests.

9. _____ Bill and Joanna are broke, but Arthur is rolling in it.

P

10. _____ Stuart started out to study medicine because society needed them.

11. _____ A great many service professionals do not offer their clients a touch of humanity but only a rule for efficient living. It is a great necessity.

12. _____ Lee stole things because he had no other way of earning a living, and he went to jail for it. It was a shame.

13. _____ I dropped a pebble in the gas tank and heard no splash. That proved we were out of gas.

14. _____ I never buy clothes at Barney's because they are expensive.

15. _____ Petit balanced himself 1,200 feet above the ground, which is a hard thing to do.

# Proofreading

Proofreading is the stage in the writing process during which the writer goes over his pages with painstaking care for the purpose of making final, detailed improvements. The physical act of proofreading involves using a pen or pencil as a pointer while reading every word on a page and every page of a piece of written work. (Those who work with word processors may proofread on a printout or by using a pointer directed at the screen display.) Experienced writers usually proofread with certain goals in mind: to assure that their sentences flow smoothly from one to the next; to make last minute improvements in the choice of a word or a phrase; and to catch any inadvertent errors in spelling, grammar, or punctuation — there are a number of things to look at. Less experienced writers should make a checklist for themselves. For each item on this checklist, they should proofread their papers once.

The important things to remember about proofreading are that (1) it should always be done with a pen or a pencil pointing directly at each word and that (2) it is essential not to skip this stage. Proofreading assures that all the preceding hard work you've done will amount to something. You will be delivering your work in a state that allows for effective communication.

Below is a checklist which you may use as is, or on which you may want to base one of your own.

## Proofreading Checklist

1. Is the paper legible? If written by hand, does a reader have to strain to decode it? Make it legible — even if you must recopy.
2. Have you, in the heat of composition, omitted necessary words? Supply them.
3. Do your sentences flow smoothly from one to the other? If not, supply transitions (See **Transitions**).
4. Is your spelling correct?
5. Are the grammar and punctuation correct?
6. Are there habitual errors here, ones you tend to make regularly? Catch them.
7. It's not too late to sharpen a phrase with a better word or words.
8. It's not too late to make a more precise point, illustrate an idea in a clearer way.

**P**

## TEST YOURSELF ON
## Proofreading Technique

Make up a proofreading checklist of four or five items that apply especially to the writing you do at this stage of your life. Then proceed to proofread the following paragraphs, going over them once for each item on your personal checklist.

A. Armies of Americans are undertaking to make healthy improvements in the way they live, they are hitting the road, jogging to protect their hearts and blood vessels. Their breaking down the doors of health food stores, looking for tofu and beans and other unprocesed foosd with low sodium and low sugar and low fat contents. They also avoiding smoking like the plage, all over the country there are smokeoputs. These activities are having good affects on the nation's death rates and especially on ther rates of death from heart disease and lung cancer and cancer of the stomach.

B. The best way to stop smoking is to undergo whats called aversion thwerapy, it really works. Its based on the simple idea that we will have an aversion toward anything we associates with pain or displeasure. The psychological theory is called behaviorism. When we are rewarded we are reinforced to continue doing what brought us the reward. When we are punished, we experience the opposiet. It sounds like fascism but smoking is really the pits and we must all give it up. The program involves a series of controlled experiences in which the smoker is made to experience their smoking habit with distasteful things. Eventually, he or she gets so turned off by these things they give it up.

**Q-S**

# Question Mark

The question mark is used to end a sentence that asks a direct question.

> Where is Malcolm going?
> He asked where Malcolm was going. (indirect question)
> *Did he* ask where Malcolm is going? (a direct question, indicated by the italicized phrase)

Question marks can also convert declarative sentences into questions.

Betty went to the football game? (Imagine this sentence spoken with the emphasis on *football*.)

Dinitia loves David? (emphasis on *David*)

Colin and Frances are getting married? (emphasis on *married*)

An imperative sentence may also be converted into a question.

Pass the sugar?

Give you the newspaper?

A question mark is used between parentheses to indicate the writer's uncertainty about some detail.

My mother was born in 1893(?) and died in 1972.

Shakespeare was born in 1564 on April 23(?).

It is also permissible, for emphasis, to place a question mark after each question in a series.

Did you tell him you loved him? get interested in his work? try to work out your differences?

Note that this example constitutes a single sentence and that there is no capital letter following the question marks.

For treatment of the question mark in quotations, see **Quotation Marks.**

## TEST YOURSELF ON
### the Use of the Question Mark

**Q**

**A** Convert each of the following into questions by placing a question mark in the proper place; in some, you may have to change the pronouns.

1. Marshak ran the school.

2. Give me your pen.

3. Take off your coat.

4. George likes apples.

5. Fred likes parties.

**B** Some of the following sentences are properly punctuated and some are not. Next to the correct sentences, write C. Supply question marks in the others where needed.

1. _____ He asked me if I would go to the ball game with him.

2. _____ He asked me, "Would you come with me to the ball game."

3. _____ Did he take you seriously read your paper give you a tutoring session grade you fairly?

4. _____ He mentioned to me—did I understand him correctly—that he was going to Scotland next summer.

# Quotation Marks

Quotation marks always appear twice (" "): once at the beginning of the quoted material, once at the end. *Note:* Don't forget that second use; proofread your paper to make sure you haven't, because confusion always results when you do.

## Uses of Quotation Marks

Quotation marks are used in the following cases:

    **1**  Use quotation marks wherever you quote directly someone's *written or spoken* words.

> Declaring themselves openly in awe of that period, Quinn and Dolan wrote: "In the sixth decade of the twentieth century America entered its middle age, and discovered its youth." They conceived of this discovery as violent, radical, dangerous.

> "Well," Norman said, "I wouldn't be surprised if Nancy took off for California and surprised us all."

The first example offers a quotation of someone's (in this case Quinn and Dolan's) *written* words. In the second example, a writer

quotes what Norman has *said* about Nancy. Take careful note of the position of the quotation marks and the position of the other punctuation marks *in relation to the quotation marks*.

**2** Although you use a pair of regular (double) quotation marks ("  ") to enclose direct quotations, use a pair of single quotation marks (' ') to enclose a quote within a quote.

> "Frankly," Lillian said, "Richard answered my inquiry with 'no comment, I'm busy.' "
>
> Louis said, "The answer Donald gave was 'I don't know.' "

**3** Quoting dialogue—conversation between two or more people—requires certain special conventions: (1) Use a separate paragraph when reporting each person's speech; (2) include in the same paragraph such phrases as *he said, she replied,* or *he answered;* (3) punctuate according to the practice in this sample passage, and note especially that the first word of a quotation is always capitalized if the quoted material itself is a full sentence.

> The policeman came running up to me, and I could tell he was furious.
>
> "Do you own this robot?" he asked.
>
> I was startled. "I never saw him before in my life!"
>
> "Then how come," said the policeman, "he just winked at you?"
>
> Sure enough, the robot's green-lit eye was blinking at me. "I think he's just friendly," I replied.
>
> "He just leaked oil on my shoes," said the policeman, menacingly.
>
> "Am I my robot's keeper?" I pleaded.

**4** Use quotation marks for titles of short stories, essays, short poems, songs, articles from periodicals, book chapters, or other parts of books.

> "The Cask of Amontillado" (short story by Poe)
>
> "Soldiers Home" (short story by Hemingway)
>
> "Politics and the English Language" (essay by Orwell)
>
> "The Heavy Bear" (poem by Delmore Schwartz)
>
> "Yesterday" (song by the Beatles)
>
> "Nefarious Times We Live In" (magazine article)

In Chapter 4, "The Myth of the Poet," the author examines a modern dilemma.

Modern socialism is attacked in Part 2, "The Return."

**5**  Use quotation marks to give special emphasis to a word or a phrase or where you speak of a word *as* a word.

Johnny had a "system" for beating the dealers in Las Vegas.

He had a "hands-off" attitude.

"Bad dude" is slang for "splendid chap." (*Note:* Italics may also be used in cases like this one.)

**6**  Do *not* use quotation marks for indirect quotations. An indirect quotation is one that reports what a speaker said but not necessarily in the speaker's exact words.

David asked Dinitia why she wanted to earn a Ph.D. (indirect)
David asked Dinitia, "Why do you want to earn a Ph.D.?" (direct)

Paul said that he liked my book. (indirect)
Paul said, "I like your book." (direct)

## Quotation Marks with Other Punctuation

Be sure to position quotation marks correctly when they are used with other punctuation marks.

**1**  Place commas and periods *inside* quotation marks.

"I wanted to quit early," he said, "but I couldn't think of an excuse." (The only mark *outside* is the one used to separate *he said* from what follows those words.)

Police work is an example of a "high-risk occupation," and policemen are paid accordingly.

He had "the common touch."

**2**  Place colons and semicolons *outside* quotation marks.

He had "the common touch"; consequently, people in all walks of life responded warmly to him.

Tom said that to have a good time he needed the right "equipment": congenial company, enough leisure, and peace of mind.

**3**  Place question marks and exclamation points inside quotation marks if they are actually part of the quote; place them outside if they are not.

> She leaned out the window and shouted "Fire!"
>
> Did you say "I don't know"?

Note that although the exclamation point in the first example applies to "Fire" and the question mark in the second applies to the whole sentence, neither sentence takes any additional punctuation marks at the end.

## Misuse of Quotation Marks

Quotation marks should not be used for the following purposes:

**1**   Do not make a practice of overusing quotation marks for emphasis.

> ***Inappropriate***   The cowboys in the movie were strong "men."
> ***Inappropriate***   I thought Al was a "wise guy."
> ***Inappropriate***   People like Richard are a "dime a dozen."

The first example needs no quotation marks around *men* (or *strong*) to convey its message; the quotation marks in the third example just point up a tired expression which should not have been used in the first place, and the quotation marks in the second are better left out too — though the expression *wise guy* is also trite by now.

**2**   Do not use quotation marks as an excuse to include an unacceptable slang expression in a piece of formal writing. If the slang expression is appropriate, use it without quotation marks; if it is not, do not use it at all.

> ***Inappropriate***   At that point, President Ford simply "flipped out" and pardoned Nixon.
> ***Inappropriate***   Most of the patients at the clinic are children who have "gone ape."
> ***Appropriate***   He was displaying a common twentieth-century *hang-up:* paranoia.
> ***Appropriate***   The carnival atmosphere can only be described as *raunchy.*

**3**   Do not use quotation marks to excuse using a word that does not say precisely what you mean.

> ***Imprecise***   My sister used to "get" me about the braces on my teeth.

***Precise*** My sister used to *tease* me about the braces on my teeth.

***Imprecise*** The cards in the library are kept in a wooden "box."
***Precise*** The cards in the library are kept in a *card catalog*.

## TEST YOURSELF ON
## the Use of Quotation Marks

**A** Some of the following sentences contain direct and some indirect quotations. Change the direct quotations to indirect ones, and change the indirect quotations to direct ones.

1. The student said that he considered me one of the best professors in the English Department.
2. "Judy's ceramics are elegant," said Mark.
3. Matt said, "In my opinion, Donna's a talented actress."
4. Fred said the policeman asked him why he was speeding.
5. Marian told Jean she wanted to see her over Easter.
6. Henry reminded Mike that they were brothers.

**B** Some of the following sentences have quotation marks correctly placed. Next to them, write C. The others need quotation marks in one place or another. Supply them.

1. _____ We read a short story called "The Killers" and our professor said that Hemingway, the author, had been an adolescent loner.

2. _____ In the poem Sailing to Byzantium, what is the significance of the line The salmon-falls, the mackerel-crowded seas?

3. _____ When we say that a recording has a lot of wet, we mean that it contains many echo effects.

4. _____ In a moment of frenzy, Vito wrote: "Elephants can be housed in a car garage just as well as in a regular cage."

5. _____ That song Silverbird is a winner.

6. _____ Part 2 of his book is called "An Analysis of Urban Problems."

**C** Place quotation marks correctly in each of the following sentences.

1. You made a fool of me, Margaret said, and I won't forgive you for it. The name of my article is not Childhood Reams but Childhood Dreams.

2. She had written, I don't care for the climate in the tropics, but when I saw her in Chicago she said, I'm looking forward to visiting Puerto Rico for the second time.

3. Can you lend me a hundred dollars? she asked timidly. Slapping his hand down hard on the table, he replied, I think not, madam. I never saw you before in my life.

4. Imagine, he said, that you are in a strange environment and you are surrounded by alien creatures. What thoughts go through your mind as you try to integrate yourself into this scene? he went on.

5. She said to me, He smirked, you're a loser, and I was startled, to say the least.

6. Who said so? I asked.

## Revising and Editing

At a certain stage in the writing process, you have produced, let us say, two typewritten pages in response to an assignment, but you are by no means ready to hand these in to your instructor. Ideally, these pages have lain in your desk drawer for a couple of days, a procedure that is useful in detaching you from the work and enabling you to examine it critically. We would call these hypothetical pages a *first draft* and say that you were now ready for *revising* and *editing*.

*Revising* describes the process of making such substantial changes as rewriting or recasting sentences, deleting sentences from a paragraph or adding them to it, moving paragraphs to new positions in the essay, or inserting freshly written ones into your text. *Editing* is a term we usually reserve for smaller changes, such as substituting one word for another, changing mechanical things like capital letters, and adjusting spelling and punctuation.

Revision and editing are most difficult to undertake when your papers are handwritten. Revising and editing handwritten papers always involve a good deal of recopying. The way to make revision and editing less laborious is to make several xerox copies of your first draft and use the cut and paste technique. That is, use scissors to cut pieces of your xerox copies and then Scotch tape to assemble the good pieces into a new draft.

The same technique can be used when you type your essays, although retyping revised and edited drafts is not as laborious as recopying by hand.

The word processor is, of course, the most efficient machine for revising and editing. In using a word processor, we generate a text that we "save" (or record) on a diskette. The text is displayed on a screen where the writer is able to perform the most varied tasks of revision and editing with just a few strokes of the keyboard. For example, the text you are reading is being composed on a word processor and, in a matter of seconds, I can remove the sentence you are reading now and insert it anywhere in the whole of the entry I am writing or — with a bit more time — anywhere within the 150 pages or so of text stored on the particular diskette (or floppy disk) inserted in my machine. I could also, if I wished, delete the sentence entirely. But I don't need to delete a sentence *permanently*.

The word processor has a remarkable capacity that makes revision an especially enriching experience. The word processor allows me the possibility of deleting portions of text *temporarily* — and restoring them instantaneously. Thus I can alternately see my revisions and restore my old text, in a back-and-forth rhythm, on my screen, musing and judging and deciding which version is best by looking at each for as long or as short a time as I wish.

Many word processing programs permit a user to store deleted portions of text under a short code name in such a way that typing on a blank screen, say, the three letters of the code and then pressing one other key, results in the display of a deleted text of any length. Thus keeping a half dozen (or more) portions of deleted material in temporary storage is easy and useful, especially since the machine you work on is probably capable of displaying for your inspection the code names of all these portions of text, allowing you to be reminded of what they are and permitting you the opportunity to choose among them — again with great ease and facility.

Regardless of what mechanical means you use, however, revising and editing is best done with some plan in mind. Individual writers will have their own favored methods of proceeding, but most writers, whether or not they are aware of it, go about reworking their drafts in some methodical fashion or other.

A useful plan might go something like this: you would go over your draft, revising and/or editing, once or more than once on behalf of the items given under each number listed here:

**1** *Considering large matters:* Does the general shape of your essay conform to your original plan? If it doesn't, should it? Or is it better the way it is now? Do you go on too long in any given section? Does a particular section need filling in with more detail? Do your paragraphs follow each other smoothly. Are there good transitions between them? When a transition between paragraphs looks rough, consider whether one or the other paragraph belongs where it is: should it be moved? Does your introduction do its job? How about your conclusion?

**2** *At the paragraph level:* Look at each of your paragraphs, one by one: does each one have unity? Or are there sentences that don't belong?

Delete what doesn't belong. Cut it out if it's handwritten or typewritten; "select" it and delete it if it's displayed on a word processing screen.

**3** *At the paragraph level:* Does each sentence run smoothly into the next? Check the transitions between sentences. Make sure you carry your reader carefully over sturdy verbal bridges.

**4** *Looking at sentences:* Do your sentences say what you want them to say? Are they worded as crisply and as leanly as possible?

R

**5**  *At the level of words:* Are you sure your tone is what you want it to be? That is, is your diction satisfactory for the specific purposes of your essay? Change words and phrases wherever you need to in order to sustain the appropriate tone.

**6**  *Grammar and punctuation:* If you make characteristic errors in grammar, check to be sure that those are not here. Have you put periods in the right places? Commas? Closed quotations? Apostrophes?

## TEST YOURSELF ON
## Revising and Editing

**A**  Consider the following paragraphs in the light of numbers 2 – 7 above. That is, do what you can to revise and edit the paragraphs so that they make their points more sharply and correctly and thus make better reading.

> I think that the transplantation of the baboons heart inside the baby was justified because the Doctors were trying to save the infant's life. Wouldn't you like someone to try to save your life? I would. I'm not sure they had much of a choice. Where were they going to get a tiny little heart from a human so fast as they needed the thing? It might have been cruel to the baboon, we have to think more about what we're saying when we say "cruel to the baboon."

> This thing was also justified because the parents said it was all right and they're really the ones who have the right to say what is right for the baby. Another reason why I think the thing was right is that the transplantation was done for Medical Science. If we're ever going to treat heart disease better we have to have more information and a thing like this obviously gives quite a bit more information than you'd get without it.

R

# Run-on Sentences

A run-on or fused sentence is an error in punctuation in which one or more periods are omitted between sentences (or independent clauses).

> My Aunt Bea is a great cook she always provides the food at big family dinners.

The writer of this sentence has failed to recognize that there are two independent clauses in the construction: *My Aunt Bea is a great cook* and *she always provides the food at big family dinners*.

The run-on sentence is a serious error because it confuses and disorients a reader. Equally serious is the error known as the comma splice or comma fault. This error occurs when the writer separates the two clauses with *only* a comma:

> My Aunt Bea is a great cook, she always provides the food at big family dinners.

In both the run-on sentence and the comma splice there is not enough punctuation to link the sentences. There are four ways to punctuate two independent clauses correctly.

**1**   Use a period:

> My Aunt Bea is a great cook. She always provides the food at big family dinners.

**2**   Use a comma followed by a coordinating conjunction *(and, but, or, for, so, nor, yet):*

> My Aunt Bea is a great cook, *and* she always provides the food at big family dinners.

**3**   Use a semicolon, which would provide enough stopping power to properly separate the clauses but would also indicate that the two clauses are closely related and belong together in the same sentence:

> My Aunt Bea is a great cook; she always provides the food at big family dinners.

**4**   Use a semicolon followed by a conjunctive adverb *(anyway, besides, consequently, finally, furthermore, however, instead, meanwhile, moreover, nevertheless, otherwise, subsequently, therefore, thus,* and so forth). The conjunctive adverb acts to relate the two clauses more precisely:

> My Aunt Bea is a great cook; *therefore,* she always provides the food at big family dinners. (Note how this additional word brings the clauses into closer relation.)

*Note:* There is usually a comma following the conjunctive adverb, but the strong linkage between the clauses is provided by the semi-colon.

## Linking Independent Clauses with a Coordinating Conjunction

Link the pairs of sentences below with a comma followed by one of the coordinating conjunctions: *and, but, or, nor, for, yet, so.*

1. Charles was head of the Honors Committee. He carried out his duties with high purpose.

2. He couldn't increase the speed of the car. There was a state trooper waiting at the exit.

3. Carla couldn't type. The paper was due the next morning.

4. Foreign policy was a pressing issue. The President knew he had to deal with it.

5. He could take the train to Boston. He could stay later and take the air shuttle.

6. He had no money for the bus. He decided to walk.

7. In many ways she annoyed him. He thought he wanted to date her.

8. He thought she was kind. She had done him many favors.

9. The snowmobile was dangerous. He planned to go up the mountain in it.

10. Baseball players work a very long season. They are well paid for it.

R

11. Roller skates are ugly. They are fun to ride.

12. They are getting married. They are very much in love.

---

## TEST YOURSELF ON
## Linking Independent Clauses with a Semicolon and a Conjunctive Adverb

Try linking the pairs of sentences below with a semicolon. After you have done so, look at the list of conjunctive adverbs given above and see if the addition of one of those might create a better relation between parts. *Remember:* A comma follows a conjunctive adverb, but the strong link is made by the semicolon.

1. Lucia Ann had confidence in her ability to write. She sat down and wrote a book.
2. Painters have the urge to arrange form, line, color, and mass. They paint pictures working with these principles.
3. Free speech is a precious part of our heritage. We have a whole tradition of freedom and liberty.
4. He had just changed the spark plugs and the points. The car was in good running condition.
5. Arthur's tax refund came on July 25. On August 1, he began his European vacation.
6. His father wrote that he could no longer pay Tom's tuition. Tom had to get a part-time job.
7. Linsey's first novel was well received. Her second work received even greater recognition.
8. Shut the windows during a heavy rainstorm. Your apartment will be flooded.
9. The muscles in his legs were crying out with pain. He pressed on, walking and limping up the trail.
10. He knew he should stay at home and write his paper. He dressed up and went to the dance.

---

Let us return for a moment to the run-on sentence with which we began this discussion:

My Aunt Bea is a great cook she always provides the food at big family dinners.

A fifth way to correct this run-on sentence is to change one of the independent clauses to a dependent clause — and separate the clauses with a comma.

> *Because my Aunt Bea is a great cook,* she always provides the food at big family dinners.

The addition of the word *because* changes the independent clause to a dependent clause and makes a comma the correct punctuation to separate it from the main (independent) clause.

## TEST YOURSELF ON
## Recognizing and Correcting Run-on Sentences and Comma Splices

Some of the sentences below are run-on sentences or comma splices and some are correct. Next to the correct sentences, write C. Correct the other sentences by one or another of the methods discussed in this entry.

1. _____ I love to swim, there is no better exercise.

2. _____ I had to be in California on the 18th, therefore I decided to leave New York on the 12th.

3. _____ Crime does not result from the inborn tendency of individual criminals; rather, it is a complex social problem, having to do with social environment and economic status.

4. _____ Darryl Strawberry didn't get a base hit, the Mets won the ball game.

5. _____ Because she had always been careful about money in her youth, she could look forward to a secure old age.

6. _____ The term *arson* should apply to a fire that someone

R

has set even if the fire isn't set deliberately the results are the same.

7. _____ Potential students are no longer flocking to colleges the job market no longer requires so many college graduates.

8. _____ America's oil reserves are nearly depleted what we need now is her reserves of goodwill if we are to solve the energy crisis.

9. _____ Marriages are not made in heaven, divorces are not made in courts.

10. _____ He looks like my brother, he talks like my enemy.

**TEST YOURSELF ON**
## Proofreading to Catch Run-on Sentences and Comma Splices

Read carefully the following paragraphs, and wherever you see a run-on sentence or comma splice, correct it.

R

Hospitals can really be depressing, it's depressing seeing all those sick people in beds. Of course, some of them get well and go home with their families, but it's depressing knowing that some of them will die in those beds. It doesn't matter hospitals are still depressing places.

The white walls are gloomy, the beds are small and narrow. Some nurses are snobbish and make your stay impossible with their aloofness some of them are so nice you hate to leave. But doctors are so busy that they have no time for you personally, they treat you like an experiment most of the time. As for the food, it too is depressing it's supposed to make you healthy but it really makes you sick just to look at it, even the way its prepared, the way it looks, causes that depressed feeling.

Some people enter the hospital with a minor illness by the time they have been there a few days, they have a major problem, remember the movie *Hospital* they had it right.

Of course, if you think your stay in the hospital is depressing, you should wait until you leave and get the bill *that's* really depressing!

# Semicolon

The semicolon (;) is a mark of internal punctuation that is equivalent to a period in its power to bring an independent clause to an end.

**1** When the semicolon is used to separate independent clauses, it can be used with or without the conjunctive adverb (words such as *nevertheless, moreover, thus, subsequently, consequently, therefore,* and others; see **Conjunctions** for a longer list of these words).

> The car wouldn't run on regular gas; *therefore,* we filled the tank with unleaded.
>
> Sid never liked home cooking; he preferred to eat out every night.

**2** The semicolon can also be used to set off items in a series if they are very long or contain other kinds of internal punctuation.

> What he objected to in her character was that she was angry, willful and stubborn; that she had no capacity to develop or sustain a professional or vocational interest that would lead to her taking or holding a job; and that she was incapable of having easy relationships with either her peers, her family, or her neighbors.

S

> We were divided into three groups: (1) those who could sing, dance, act, or play a musical instrument; (2) those who had carpentry or other technical skills; and (3) those who had some kind of business experience or advertising and public relations skills.

*Note:* Where you use quotation marks, the semicolon goes outside the closing quotation marks:

> He thinks of himself as ''progressive''; he voted for Nixon.
>
> Tom said, ''Stagecraft is vital to any study of Shakespeare''; he meant it, too.

For more on the semicolon, see also **Fragments** and **Run-on Sentences.**

## TEST YOURSELF ON
## the Correct Use of the Semicolon

Each of the sentences below is poorly punctuated because it needs a semicolon for one reason or other. Some of the sentences consisting of two independent clauses could also use a conjunctive adverb after the semicolon. For each sentence, add one or more semicolons where needed.

1. My father thinks I'm lazy he'll only give me my allowance if I do chores around the house.

2. The news we heard on the radio was bad, we went out and got drunk.

3. We could have insisted they cancel the reservation and give us back our deposit so that we could go to another hotel, we could have stayed there without making a fuss and spent three miserable nights sleeping on lumpy mattresses and listening to the sound of the freight trains, or we could have gone quietly away, taken our sleeping bags out to the trailer park, and camped underneath the beech trees by the lake.

4. The elevator shakes and rumbles as it goes up, the inspector says it's safe.

5. Christmas is only three weeks away, this year I don't care.

6. Professors care only about their own lectures, their students' producing a great deal of work for them, their status, and their vacations, students care only about snap courses, getting high grades however they can, and enjoying midwinter and summer recesses, administrators care only about budgets, reputations, and no emergencies.

7. He was given a long prison sentence, he had never been arrested before.

8. Six men were killed in an accident, the mine owners instituted stringent safety regulations.

9. I have a six-figure income and a house that's all paid for, I have investments in real estate and oil wells.

10. I exercise too hard and long, I get muscle aches.

# Sentence Length and Variety

### Avoiding Monotony

Variation in the length and kinds of sentences you write helps to avoid giving your readers the impression of monotony. There are a number of ways to achieve this variation in sentence structure and length, but let us first consider what to avoid.

**1**  Avoid writing a series of short, simple sentences. Children write this way, but that is because their minds are not yet developed to the point where they can understand the relations between ideas.

> *Weak*   We went to the movies. It was a cowboy picture. We bought popcorn. It made noise. The other people were mad. They told us to stop.
>
> *Revised*   Because there was a cowboy picture playing, we went to the movies. We bought some popcorn, but we made so much noise eating it that the other patrons were angered and asked us to stop.

The series of weak sentences constitutes a simple example — something a child might write — but there are occasions when more mature writers fall into the same pattern.

> *Weak*   The house was dark. We walked up the steps. We went through the door. There was a noise. We paused and listened. We decided it was only the wind.
>
> *Revised*   The house was dark as we walked up the stairs and through the door. There was a noise, and we paused to listen more carefully, but it was only the wind.

(For further information on combining short sentences into more complex structures, see **Subordination.**)

**2**   Avoid writing long, excessively compounded sentences. By this is meant sentences that join together, willy-nilly, a number of independent clauses using *and* or other coordinating conjunctions.

> *Weak*   We drove up to the park, but we saw that the gate had been locked for the night, and so we changed our plans and turned around and headed for Warrensburg.
>
> *Revised*   As we drove up to the park, we saw that the gate had been locked for the night. Changing our plans, we turned around and headed for Warrensburg. (First independent clause is made into a subordinate clause by the use of *as*; third clause is made into a phrase; second and fourth clauses become main clauses of two separate sentences.)

> *Weak*   He was the faculty adviser of the campus newspaper, and he was a professor in the English Department, but he was never too busy with his duties to consult with students.
>
> *Revised*   The faculty adviser of the campus newspaper, who was also a professor in the English Department, was never too busy with his duties to consult with students. (First clause becomes a phrase which is the subject of the new sentence; second clause becomes a subordinate clause; third clause becomes the predicate of the sentence.)

S

The excessively simple pattern and the excessively compounded pattern have one thing in common: They are both monotonous. They present independent clauses in the regular order of subject-verb, and they present only one type of sentence — the declarative. To achieve variety, you must occasionally interrupt these patterns — by beginning or ending sentences with subordinate structures or by interrupting a sentence with an appositive.

## TEST YOURSELF ON
## Revising Sentences of Monotonous Length

**A**   Revise the following groups of short sentences.

1. Television commercials are annoying. They insult the intelligence. They waste one's time. They should be banned from the airways.
2. President Reagan is from California. He was an actor there. He was formerly Governor of California. He has brought many business leaders to Washington.
3. She wanted to be a doctor. She studied chemistry. She studied biology. She worked for good grades. She put in long hours. Her senior year arrived. She applied to medical school. She was accepted.
4. The doctor came. He took my temperature. He checked my heart. He took my blood pressure. He prescribed some medicine. Then he said I'd probably recover in a few days.
5. I needed a job. I looked at the want ads. I went to employment agencies. I even visited a number of factories and offices. I got very tired. But I finally landed a job.

**B**   Revise the following sentences. Eliminate excessive joining together of independent clauses by creating subordinate clauses and phrases.

1. The train entered the station, and I got ready to board but then I found I'd left my bag in the checkroom and I ran back inside the waiting room to get it.
2. *Return of the Jedi* was a very successful movie and broke many box office records and this goes to show that science fiction adventure movies appeal greatly to the American public.

3.  There are more than seven million American college students, and most of them believe that they need this education to get better jobs, but the job market is not encouraging for the hopes of these students, and some of them might do better in vocational training.
4.  Members of the volunteer fire company are really dedicated and they give much of their time in public service, but they are not appreciated enough and often feel bitter because of this.
5.  Soccer is the fastest growing sport in America and now as many as 70,000 fans turn out for one game, but if Pelé hadn't given the sport a boost, things might not have turned out so well for soccer.

## Achieving Sentence Variety

So far we have looked at what to avoid: a series of short, simple sentences, and a sentence composed of many independent clauses strung together with coordinating conjunctions. Both types of sentence tend to produce monotony when used exclusively because both begin with the subject of the sentence. This is not a bad thing to do — more than half of your sentences will probably begin that way — but such a practice produces monotony when followed exclusively. Therefore, variety is achieved by changing the order of words in your sentences. Variety is also achieved by occasionally departing from the declarative sentence and using the question or the command. You should undertake these changes with great care, however, since altering the order of words in a sentence always involves a slight alteration of meaning. Choosing the proper alteration is a matter of carefully considering your subject matter and the meaning you want to convey. Here are the principal means of achieving sentence variety.

**1**   Vary the beginnings of your sentences. Suppose you had one sentence that looked like this:

> The miners worked purposefully in the tunnel and they were unaware of the storm outside.

or two that looked like this:

> The miners worked purposefully in the tunnel. They were unaware of the storm outside.

In either case, you could produce variations looking like these:

> *Working purposefully in a tunnel,* the miners were unaware of the storm outside. (beginning with a verbal phrase)

> *In the tunnel,* the miners worked purposefully, unaware of the storm outside. (beginning with a prepositional phrase)

> *Because the miners were working purposefully in the tunnel,* they were unaware of the storm outside. (beginning with an adverbial clause)

> *There* were miners working purposefully in the tunnel, unaware of the storm outside. (beginning with an expletive)

> *And* the miners worked purposefully in the tunnel, unaware of the storm outside. (Beginning with a coordinating conjunction is perfectly acceptable, but usually the meaning of the sentence depends on something that has gone before.)

**2**  Reverse the usual order of subject-verb or subject-verb-object. But to do this is to create a distinctly emphatic order, and you should do so only where your aim is to achieve such emphasis.

| *Subject-Verb* | *Verb-Subject* |
|---|---|
| The mouse ran up the wall. | Up the wall ran the mouse. |
| Mike's letter rested in the mailbox. | In the mailbox rested Mike's letter. |

| *Subject-Verb-Object* | *Object-Subject-Verb* |
|---|---|
| Joanna loves pizza. | Pizza Joanna loves. |
| I never saw him. | Him I never saw. |

**3**  Occasionally use a question or a command instead of a declarative sentence, but only when it is appropriate to do so.

> **Imperative (command)**   *Imagine a fine tapestry,* interwoven with various attractively colored threads, and you will have a picture of the diversity and beauty in the fabric of American life.

> **Question**   *What is the purpose of an education?* One purpose is to train the mind to perceive fine distinctions.

## TEST YOURSELF ON
## Achieving Sentence Variety

Revise the following sentences by revising their beginnings.

1. The car had broken down the night before, and they had to take the bus to school.

2. The Republican party held a fund-raiser at the Holiday Inn, and it attracted a surprising number of young people.
3. His grades were poor, and his scholarship money was almost gone, and he knew he had to do something.
4. The rescue team worked all night at the site of the cave-in, and they were unable to stop for dinner.
5. Readers with lively imaginations read *The Hobbit* and project themselves into its adventurous moments.
6. Governments are less inclined to give in to hijackers' demands these days, but hijackings continue anyway.
7. He knew he would have to save money regularly for next year's tuition, and he opened a savings account and began to make regular deposits.
8. Nobody knew where the cat had gone, but everybody began searching furiously.
9. Big-time professional sports can accommodate very few athletes, but many American youngsters still dream of a career in the big leagues.
10. Inflation has made money worth less, and it is more expensive to live in the United States than it used to be.
11. The man in black stood against the wall.
12. The mouse ran into my computer.

## Shifts

When you begin a sentence by saying "He *begged* and *pleaded* for the loan and . . ." the reader immediately tunes in to *begged* and *pleaded* as verbs in the past tense. The reader's expectation is that if any other verb appears in the sentence, it too will be in the past tense. So if the sentence is completed with ". . . *asks* the bank officer to have some sympathy" (present tense verb), the reader will be shocked, disappointed, and confused because you have *shifted* gears.

It is not easy, but it is absolutely essential, to maintain the kind of consistency that is missing in the above example. In fact, both beginning and experienced writers shift gears in a number of different ways. A writer should understand that achieving consistency requires consistent proofreading — until they are sure they are incapable of producing the various kinds of shifts.

Reread carefully the sentence you have just read (beginning with "A writer"). Notice that the sentence begins with a *singular* subject, *writer,* but that after the dash the second and fifth words, *they,* are plural pronouns. Here we see another kind of shift, a shift in *number.* We can also see shifts in *tense* (as in the first example given in this entry), *person, mood, voice,* and *point of view.* Below is a discussion of each kind of shift.

## Tense

Perhaps no other shift is so annoying to a reader as this one, because a verb carries not only meaning but a sense of time, and the writer who uses verb tenses inconsistently interferes with the reader's sense of a consistent time pattern.

> **Inconsistent**   In the movie *It's My Turn,* Jill Clayburgh *plays* a mathematics professor. She *went* to her father's wedding and *had met* there Michael Douglas, who *played* a former baseball player. Eventually, after a series of delightful romantic adventures, they *get* together.
> **Consistent**   In the movie *It's My Turn,* Jill Clayburgh *plays* a mathematics professor. She *goes* to her father's wedding and there *meets* Michael Douglas, who *plays* a former baseball player. Eventually, after a series of delightful romantic adventures, they *get* together.

> **Inconsistent**   When I *go* to the seashore for my vacation, I *went* to the beach right away because I *loved* to swim. I *see* the lifeguard and I *asked* him if it *was* all right to swim. *Jaws makes* me frightened to go in the water.
> **Consistent**   When I *went* to the seashore for my vacation, I *went* to the beach right away because I *love* to swim. I *saw* the lifeguard and I *asked* him if it *was* all right to swim. *Jaws made* me frightened to go in the water.

## Person

The English verb system recognizes three *persons:* the first person (*I* refuse, *we* refuse), the second person (*you* refuse [both singular and plural]), and the third person (*he, she,* or *it* refuses; *they* refuse). Most shifts in person occur because writers use the second person (*you*) carelessly.

> **Inconsistent**   *People* shouldn't expect to be dependent all their lives. *You* have to take care of *yourself* in adult life.
> **Consistent**   *People* shouldn't expect to be dependent all their lives. *They* have to take care of *themselves* in adult life.

**Inconsistent** When *you* have a cold, *one* should get plenty of rest and drink fluids.
**Consistent** When *you* have a cold, *you* should get plenty of rest and drink fluids.

## Number

Errors in consistency can happen when writers begin with a singular noun and shift to a plural pronoun — or vice versa.

**Inconsistent** The American *medical student* abroad *has* special problems because *they* have to do *their* work in a foreign language.
**Consistent** American *medical students* abroad *have* special problems because *they* have to do *their* work in a foreign language.

**Inconsistent** Business is so good at the U.S. Time Company that *no* one loses *their* job there.
**Consistent** Business is so good at the U.S. Time Company that *no one* loses *his* job there.

**Inconsistent** *Lawyers* have an easy life, because every time *he* goes into court *he* makes a fat fee.
**Consistent** *Lawyers* have an easy life, because every time *they* go into court *they* make fat fees.

## Voice

Once you have begun to use the active voice in a sentence, do not shift to the passive voice, and vice versa. (See also **Voice.**)

**Inconsistent** We *leave* for the beach at 8 o'clock, *swim* from 9:30 to 11, and lunch *is eaten* at 12.
**Consistent** We *leave* for the beach at 8 o'clock, *swim* from 9:30 to 11, and *eat* lunch at 12.

**Inconsistent** *Dig* a hole for the seeds, *drop* them in and cover them with loose soil, and then the ground is lightly *watered*.
**Consistent** *Dig* a hole for the seeds, *drop* them in and cover them with loose soil, and then *water* the ground lightly.

## Mood

Do not shift from the indicative to the subjunctive mood, or vice versa. Maintain consistency by sticking with one or the other, bearing in mind that in formal writing the subjunctive is preferred where it is called for. The indicative mood is used for statements of fact or other kinds of assertions or questions; the subjunctive mood is used for statements contrary to fact or those expressing possibility or potential.

> **Inconsistent** If I *were* a rock star and I *was* making a lot of money, I'd give a lot of free concerts.
> **Consistent** If I *were* a rock star and I *were* making a lot of money, I'd give a lot of free concerts.

> **Inconsistent** The Red Cross representative prefers that the donations *be* given by check and that the amounts *are* entered on their special form.
> **Consistent** The Red Cross representative prefers that the donations *be* given by check and that the amounts *be* entered on their special form.

## Point of View

A point of view is a position from which an observation is made; it is also the place from which an idea springs. You should be consistent in making your observations from the same place (point of view) and should be sure the reader knows whose ideas belong to whom — that is, that the place the ideas come from is consistently named.

> **Inconsistent Observation**
> Lying facedown on the pavement, I could see the collected debris of the day — cigarette butts, candy wrappers, odd bits of paper — *and then came the sound of the ambulance and I could see it approach.* (Obviously, the writer could not see the ambulance if he were lying facedown on the pavement.)
> **Consistent Observation**
> Lying facedown on the pavement, I could see the collected debris of the day — cigarette butts, candy wrappers, odd bits of paper — *and then came the sound of the ambulance and I knew it was getting closer.*

> **Inconsistent Assignment of Ideas**
> Most people understand that animals need space in which to live. Malin Himes, the anthropologist, says that the acquisition of such space is connected to the amount of power the animal has. How we fight for space — and thus gain the necessary power to get it — is determined by our cultural training. The current conflict be-

tween Russia and the United States over outer space exemplifies this idea. (The reader does not know to whom the ideas in the third and fourth sentences belong.)

**Consistent Assignment of Ideas**

Most people understand that animals need space in which to live. Malin Himes, the anthropologist, says that the acquisition of such space is connected to the amount of power the animal has. *Himes asserts* that how we fight for space — and thus gain the necessary power to get it — is determined by our cultural training. *Himes offers as an example of this notion* the current conflict between Russia and the United States over outer space.

TEST YOURSELF ON
## Correcting Shifts

Correct all the unnecessary shifts you find in the sentences below. Some sentences are correct as they stand; next to these, write C.

1. _____ People need to be praised when we work hard and accomplish our goals.

2. _____ Tommy argued with his counselor about the curfew and asks him to make an exception.

3. _____ He goes up to the cashier's window and asked for three tickets.

4. _____ Anybody who cares about his health can have themselves examined by a doctor twice a year.

5. _____ According to Quinn, Shakespeare is the greatest writer in English. Shakespeare takes in all points of view.

6. _____ My wife said she was thirsty and would I please get her a glass of water.

7. _____ We arrive in London on Tuesday, leave for Paris on

Thursday, and then the rest of the week is spent in Rome.

8. _____ Johnny Carson is known to all because he sparkles on television every night.

9. _____ Every basketball player has their own way of driving to the hoop.

10. _____ He went to the movies, sees *King Kong,* is terribly frightened, and was afraid to go home.

11. _____ Finally, we added the icing, and then it was baked for fifty minutes.

12. _____ Barry said that he liked Lorna and would she care to have dinner with him.

13. _____ From the top of the Empire State Building, the people looked like toy figures, strutting mechanically along, smoking their cigars.

14. _____ I was told that cigarette smoking would ruin my lungs and that you should give it up if you wanted to avoid heart trouble, too.

15. _____ Wagner recommended that admissions standards be raised and students warned about their poor preparation for college.

# Specific/General

See **Diction.**

# Spelling

Most readers think of misspelling as a sure sign of inadequate writing. The impression is well-nigh impossible to dispel, but there is hope for poor spellers. For the way you spell is surely a habit and one that you can change.

## The Spelling Problem

The spelling problem can be divided into two parts: (1) you and (2) English spelling.

### You

The burden of improving your spelling rests squarely on you; a teacher cannot help much in your discarding the old habit and taking on the new. Only an increased consciousness that improvement is possible and a disciplined approach can help. To begin, take note of the following suggestions on how to proceed, and design your program based on them or something similar.

**1**  Be aware when you are in doubt about the spelling of a word. If you are *not* aware of your doubts, you cannot dispel them by consulting a good dictionary and will continue to make the same mistake.

**2**  When you have found the correct spelling of a word, don't try simply to memorize it. Hand-brain practice is necessary. Try to visualize the word before you write it out. Then write it out correctly several times. After you've been able to write the word correctly three times, construct five sentences, using the word in each. This practice will reinforce your new spelling habit.

**3**  Keep tabs on the words you misspell; make a list of them and keep the list handy. Notice if there are types of words that you persistently misspell and work through the rule that applies to the group.

**4**  Don't reserve certain words for writing and others for speaking. Try to use your whole vocabulary in both speaking and writing. This is useful because the correct pronunciation of words often helps you to visualize the correct spelling — but not always.

**5**  Proofread everything you write at least once for spelling errors alone.

**6** Develop your own special methods to help you in this process. Some students use flash cards, others tack lists of troublesome words on the walls of their rooms. Be creative. There are many ways to approach the problem.

### English Spelling

We no doubt misspell a few words because we habitually pronounce them wrong.

| | |
|---|---|
| mathematics | NOT mathmatics |
| height | NOT heighth (by analogy with *eighth*) |
| disastrous | NOT disasterous |

The dictionary often helps by giving the correct pronunciation of such words. However, English pronunciation and spelling are notoriously eccentric. Therefore, you must use pronunciation cautiously. You cannot analogize too much, because in English dozens of words with analogous spellings, *through* and *bough,* for example, are not pronounced the same way. Such spellings must simply be learned.

## Spelling Rules

The first place to begin your disciplined study is with the following rules.

### Rule 1: *ie* and *ei*

Memorize this famous jingle:

*i* before *e*
except after *c*
or when sounded like *a*
as in *neighbor* or *weigh.*

| i *before* e | ei *after* c | ei *as in* neighbor *and* weigh |
|---|---|---|
| achieve | deceit | freight |
| cashier | receive | reign |
| believe | ceiling | sleigh |
| *exceptions* | *exceptions* | *exceptions* |
| either | financier | sleight |
| neither | species | height |
| seizure | | eider |
| sheik | | |
| leisure | | |
| weird | | |

S

## TEST YOURSELF ON
### *ie* and *ei*

Complete the spelling of the following words by using either *ie* or *ei* in the blank spaces.

1. fr_____nd
2. conc_____ve
3. bel_____f
4. ach_____vement
5. exper_____nce
5. rec_____ving
7. th_____r
8. f_____ld
9. effic_____ncy
10. conven_____nce

11. aud_____nce
12. dec_____t
13. misch_____f
14. p_____ce
15. y_____ld
16. sl_____gh
17. w_____ght
18. forf_____t
19. v_____n
20. h_____nous

### Rule 2: Final Silent *-e*

**1**   Final silent *-e* is usually dropped before adding a suffix that begins with a vowel.

> argue — arguing          dare — daring
> baste — basting          give — giving
> charge — charging

**2**   Final silent *-e* is usually retained when adding a suffix that begins with a consonant.

> arrange — arrangements     hate — hateful     like — likeness
> love — lovely              sore — soreness    sure — surely

Note the following exceptions:

**A**   Final silent *-e* is retained after soft *c* (as in *dance; color* has the hard *c*) and soft *g* (as in *rage; glove* has the hard *g*) when adding suffixes beginning with *a* or *o*. Because *c* and *g* are generally hard before *a, o,* and *u,* we keep the silent *-e* in order to keep the consonant soft.

> charge — charging — chargeable
> stage — staging — stageable
> slice — slicing — sliceable

**B** In some words, the final silent -*e* must be retained before the suffix -*ing* in order to prevent mispronunciation or ambiguity of meaning.

> singe — singeing (to scorch; retains *e* to prevent confusion with *sing — singing*.)
>
> dye — dyeing (to tint; retains *e* to prevent confusion with *die — dying*.)

**C** Final silent -*e* is retained when the letters *ye, oe,* or *ee* precede the suffix -*ing*.

> free — freeing     shoe — shoeing
> hoe — hoeing     tree — treeing
> see — seeing     eye — eyeing

## TEST YOURSELF ON
## Final Silent -*e*

Complete the spelling of the following words by using an *e* to fill in the blank space in each. If no *e* is needed, leave the space blank.

1. mov_____ing
2. prov_____ing
3. mov_____ment
4. peac_____able
5. chang_____able
6. liv_____ly
7. manag_____ment
8. sens_____ible
9. realiz_____ation
10. ton_____al
11. receiv_____ing
12. bor_____ing
13. bor_____dom
14. car_____ing
15. car_____ful
16. dy_____ing (to tint)
17. rang_____ing
18. rag_____ing
19. troubl_____some
20. bar_____ness.

### Rule 3: Final -*y*
Followed by a suffix other than one beginning with the letter *i*, final -*y* is usually changed to an *i*.

> marry — marriage     beauty — beautiful     busy — business

When the suffix begins with an *i*, retain final *-y*.

cry — crying        enjoy — enjoying

**Some exceptions**
day — daily        lay — laid
pay — paid        say — said

## TEST YOURSELF ON
## Final *-y*

Complete the spelling of the following words by using either *y* or *i* or *ie* to fill in the blank spaces.

1. occup_____ing          11. theor_____s

2. lonel_____ness        12. stor_____s

3. anno_____ing          13. bur_____ing

4. pl_____s              14. histor_____s

5. turke_____s           15. histor_____'s (belonging

                                          to history)

6. fr_____s              16. accompan_____ing

7. plo_____s             17. opportunit_____s

8. repl_____ing          18. happ_____ness

9. cr_____s              19. modif_____ing

10. pra_____s            20. def_____ance

### Rule 4: Final Consonants and Doubling

When adding a suffix that begins with a vowel, double a final single consonant under either of the following conditions:

a. when it ends a monosyllabic word, as in *bat* or *run*.
b. when it appears after a single vowel at the end of a word that is stressed on the last syllable, as in *preFER*.

| | |
|---|---|
| beg — begging | alLOT — alLOTTing |
| beGIN — beGINNing | forGET — forGETTing |
| comPEL — comPELLed | ship — shipping |

Without these conditions, the consonant is *not* doubled.

BENefit — BENefited       GALlop — GALloping

## Notes on Word Endings

The following notes about noun and verb endings and other suffixes
will supplement the above rules.

### Note 1: Noun Plurals and Third Person Singular, Present Tense Verbs

**A**   When a noun ends in a sound that allows a pronounceable final *-s, add -s* to form its plural. For verbs having this capacity,
add *-s* to form the third person singular, present tense.

| *Nouns* | *Verbs* |
|---|---|
| stone — stones | trust — trusts |
| pill — pills | know — knows |
| drawer — drawers | hope — hopes |

*Some Exceptions*

| | |
|---|---|
| tomato — tomatoes | veto — vetoes |
| buffalo — buffaloes | echo — echoes |

**B**   When a noun ends in a sound that does not allow a
pronounceable final *-s*, add *-es* to form its plural. For verbs without
this capacity, add *-es* to form the third person singular, present
tense.

| *Nouns* | *Verbs* |
|---|---|
| lunch — lunches | pass — passes |
| tax — taxes | wish — wishes |

**C**   To form the plural of a noun ending in *y* preceded by a
consonant, change the *y* to *i* and add *-es*. For a verb with the same
ending, do the same to the third person singular, present tense.

| *Nouns* | *Verbs* |
|---|---|
| company — companies | carry — carries |
| party — parties | fly — flies |

**D** When a noun ending in *y* is preceded by *a, e, o,* or *u,* form the plural by adding *-s.* For a verb with the same ending, do the same to form the third person singular, present tense.

| *Nouns* | *Verbs* |
|---------|---------|
| day — days | buy — buys |
| boy — boys | pay — pays |
| toy — toys | enjoy — enjoys |
| key — keys | |

**E** Certain nouns borrowed from other languages frequently form their plurals by retaining the plural form of the original language.

| | |
|---|---|
| alumna — alumnae | datum — data |
| alumnus — alumni | phenomenon — phenomena |
| basis — bases | |

However, good writers have tended to anglicize some of these, and dictionaries frequently list two plural forms. See what your dictionary says is the acceptable plural form of each of these:

beau    focus    index    radius    stadium

### Note 2: Suffixes to Preserve Hard *c*

To preserve the hard sound of *c,* words ending in that letter add a *k* before a suffix ending in *e, i,* or *y.*

panic — panicked — panicking
mimic — mimicked — mimicking
traffic — trafficked — trafficking

### Note 3: Four Special Words and the *eed* Sound

**A** *Supersede* is the only word in English that ends in *-sede.*

**B** *Exceed, proceed,* and *succeed* are the only words in English ending in *-ceed.*

**C** Thus all other words in English ending in the *-eed* sound are spelled *-cede.*

| | |
|---|---|
| accede | precede |
| concede | recede |
| intercede | secede |

## Spelling Rules 1–4

Complete the spelling of the words with blanks in the exercise below by filling in the blank spaces according to one or another of the rules or notes explained in this section. Some blanks do not need filling in.

1. She is occasional_____y absent.

2. The Sh_____k of Araby

3. A sens_____ible commit_____ment

4. Pro_____ to jail; do not pass go; do not collect 200 dollars.

5. He perc_____ved a sunset.

6. Cake top_____ing

7. I like the ic_____ing.

8. The c_____ling is cracking.

9. The professor counsel_____ed me.

10. The water is boil_____ing.

11. A terrible argu_____ment

12. He stud_____ed hard.

13. He went swim_____ing.

14. He was stop_____ing me from drop_____ing my p_____ce of cake.

15. The lovel_____ness of the flowers

16. It is occur_____ing often.

17. A bus_____ness appoint_____ment

18. Standing around ey_____ing girls

19. Attorn_____s work in courthouses.

20. My brother is dy_____ing

S

## Word Lists

One or both of the following lists of words may be useful to you in working on your spelling problem.

**1** **Words that Sound Alike but Mean Different Things (Homophones)**

The following pairs of words sound alike or look somewhat alike, but are spelled differently. Of course, their meanings are different, too. To master this list, you should write out sentences, using each word correctly in a number of different ways.

After each word is an abbreviation indicating the part of speech to which it belongs (*n.* for *noun; v.* for *verb; adj.* for *adjective; adv.* for *adverb; prep.* for *preposition; conj.* for *conjunction; pro.* for *pronoun; poss.* for *possessive; contr.* for *contraction*). This is followed by a definition.

**accept**   *v.* to receive
**except**   *prep.* not included
**except**   *v.* to leave out

**advice**   *n.* counsel; information offered
**advise**   *v.* to give advice or counsel

**affect**   *v.* to have an effect on; to influence
**effect**   *n.* the result of some action
**effect**   *v.* to accomplish or execute

**all ready**   *pro. + adj.* all are prepared
**already**   *adj.* at or before this time

**all together**   *pro. + adj.* all in the same place
**altogether**   *adv.* entirely

**allusion**   *n.* a reference
**illusion**   *n.* a false impression

**altar**   *n.* a special place for religious ceremony
**alter**   *v.* to change

**always**   *adv.* constantly; at all times
**all ways**   *adj. + n.* in every manner

**ascend**   *v.* to rise or go up
**ascent**   *n.* a movement upward
**assent**   *n.* an agreement
**assent**   *v.* to agree

**assistance**   *n.* help given
**assistants**   *n. pl.* helpers

**beside**   *prep.* by the side of
**besides**   *prep. and adv.* in addition to

**boarder**   *n.* a person paying for subsistence in someone's house
**border**   *n.* a boundary

**born**   *v. (always passive)* given birth to
**borne**   *v.* carried; given birth to

**breath**   *n.* air inhaled or exhaled
**breathe**   *v.* to inhale and exhale

**canvas**   *n.* a heavy, coarse cloth
**canvass**   *v.* to search for, examine, or solicit

**capital**   *n.* a city that is a seat of government; an uppercase letter;
   money
**capital**   *adj.* principal; first-rate; uppercase
**capitol**   *n.* a building used by a legislature

**choose**   *v.* to select
**chose**   *v. (past tense of choose)* selected

**cite**   *v.* to quote; to charge with an offense
**site**   *n.* a place or location
**sight**   *n.* the faculty of seeing

**coarse**   *adj.* rough; not refined
**course**   *n.* school subject; a way or a path

**complement**   *n.* something that completes
**compliment**   *n.* praise

**conscience**   *n.* part of the mind that rules on moral questions
**conscious**   *adj.* awake or alert

**council**   *n.* a deliberative body
**counsel**   *n.* advice given; a lawyer
**counsel**   *v.* to give advice

**descent**   *n.* a downward movement
**dissent**   *n.* disagreement
**dissent**   *v.* to disagree

**desert**   *n.* a dry, barren area of land
**desert**   *v.* to abandon
**dessert**   *n.* final course of a meal

S

**device**　*n.* something contrived
**devise**　*v.* to prepare, originate, or make a contrivance

**do**　*v.* to perform
**due**　*adj.* owing; with *to* specifies the cause of something

**dual**　*adj.* twofold
**duel**　*n.* a formal fight between two people

**eminent**　*adj.* famous
**imminent**　*adj.* about to happen

**envelop**　*v.* to enclose
**envelope**　*n.* a paper container used for mailing

**extant**　*adj.* still existing
**extent**　*n.* the degree of something

**farther**　*adv. and adj.* usually refers to distance
**further**　*adv. and adj.* usually refers to time, quantity, or degree

**formally**　*adv.* in a formal manner
**formerly**　*adv.* at an earlier time

**forth**　*adv.* forward; onward; out
**fourth**　*adj. or adv.* the one following the third

**human**　*adj.* pertaining to people
**humane**　*adj.* compassionate or kindly

**idle**　*adj.* not occupied or employed
**idle**　*v.* to spend time in idleness
**idol**　*n.* a likeness of something, usually a god, for worship

**ingenious**　*adj.* resourceful, clever
**ingenuous**　*adj.* showing innocent or childlike simplicity

**its**　*poss. pro.* belonging to it
**it's**　*contr.* it is

**know**　*v.* to understand, recognize, have experience of
**no**　*adv.* expressing the negative
**now**　*adv.* at the present time

**lead**　*n.* (pronounced *led*) the metal
**lead**　*v.* (pronounced *leed*) to show the way; to conduct
**led**　*v.* (past tense of *lead*) showed the way; conducted

**loose**　*adj.* not tight
**lose**　*v.* to misplace; to be defeated

**maybe**   *adv.* perhaps
**may be**   *v.* possibly may exist or happen

**moral**   *adj.* relating to right or wrong
**morale**   *n.* the mental or emotional condition of a person or group

**passed**   *v.* past tense and past participle of *pass*
**past**   *n.* an earlier time
**past**   *prep.* at the farther side of

**peace**   *n.* not war
**piece**   *n.* a part of

**personal**   *adj.* relating privately
**personnel**   *n. pl.* a group of persons employed

**principal**   *n.* chief; head of a school; capital owned
**principal**   *adj.* most important
**principle**   *n.* rule or doctrine

**prophecy**   *n.* a prediction
**prophesy**   *v.* to predict

**quiet**   *adj.* not noisy
**quit**   *v.* to depart from or out; resign
**quite**   *adv.* rather; almost completely

**respectfully**   *adj.* showing deference
**respectively**   *adv.* each in the order given

**right**   *adj.* correct or suitable
**rite**   *n.* a ceremony or ritual

**stationary**   *adj.* fixed or immobile
**stationery**   *n.* paper for writing or typing

**than**   *conj.* a comparative term
**then**   *n. or adv.* indicates time

**their**   *poss. pro.* belonging to them
**there**   *adv.* a place; also used as expletive at beginning of sentences
**they're**   *contr.* they are

**to**   *prep.* indicates direction
**too**   *adv.* excessively; overly much
**two**   *n.* the number

S

**weather**   *n.* climate
**whether**   *conj.* expresses alternatives

**were**   *v.* past tense plural of *to be;* also subjunctive form
**we're**   *contr.* we are
**where**   *adv. or pro.* indicates place or position

**who's**   *contr.* who is or who has?
**whose**   *poss. pro.* belonging to whom?

**your**   *poss. pro.* belonging to you
**you're**   *contr.* you are

### 2   Words that Are Troublesome to Spell

The following list consists of words that are habitually troublesome to spell. The part or parts of each that are the sources of the trouble are printed in boldface or noted in parentheses, or both. The best way to use this list is to write sentences using each of the words; write as many as five sentences for each word, and in that way embed in your hand, eye, and brain the correct spelling of each word. Proceed gradually. If you do a mere five words a day, you will master the whole list by the end of the semester.

a lot of (three words)
ab**sence**
acad**e**my
**a**ccepta**ble**
**a**cceptance
**a**cce**ss**i**ble**
a**cc**idental
a**cc**ident**all**y
a**cc**laim
acco**mm**odate
accomp**ani**ment
accomp**any**ing
a**cc**om**p**lish
accum**u**late
a**cc**ura**cy**
a**cc**u**r**ate (one *r*)
a**cc**us**tom**
ach**ie**vement
a**c**quaint**a**nce
a**c**qui**r**e

actual**i**ty
actua**ll**y
a**d**mi**tt**ance
adole**scence**
adole**scent**
advertising (no *e* after *s*)
advi**c**e/advi**s**e
**a**ffect/**e**ffect
alle**vi**ate
allo**tt**ed
a**ll**o**t**ment (one *t*)
all right (two words)
all together (two words)
a**l**ready (one *l*)
alt**ar**/alt**er**
a**l**together (one word; one *l*)
am**ateu**r
anal**y**sis
anal**yz**e
a**nn**ual**ly**

apologetically
apology
apparent
applies
appreciate
appreciation
appropriate
arctic
argument (no *e* after *u*)
arguing (no *e*)
arise
arising
arouse
arrangement
article
athlete (no *e* after *h*)
attack (no *t* after *k*)
attempts
attendant
attended
audience
authority
autumn

bargain
basically
beauteous
beauty
becoming (no *e*)
before
beginner
belief
believe
beneficial
benefited (one *t*)
boundary
breath (no final *e*)
breathe
brilliance
burial
business

busing, bussing
busy

calendar
capitalism
career
careful (one *l*)
carried
carrying
category
cemetery
changeable
chief
children
Christian
choice
choose (double *o*)
chose
cigarette
clothes
coming (no *e* after *m*)
commercial
committee
communist
comparative
compatible
concede
conceivable
condemn
connotation
conscience
conscientious
conscious
consequently
continuously
controlled
controversy
convenience
correlate
criticism
criticize

S

cruelly
cruelty
**curio**sity
**curious**
c**urr**iculum

d**ea**lt
dec**ei**ve
defini**te**ly
depend**ent**
de**s**cription
de**s**irability (no *e* after *r*)
desp**air**
det**ri**ment
dev**a**stating
devi**ce**/devi**se**
di**ff**er**ent**
di**le**mm**a**
disas**tro**us (no *e* after *t*)
di**sc**iple
di**sc**ipline
di**s**crimi**n**ation
disi**ll**usioned
di**ss**atisfied
domin**ant**

**e**ffect/a**ff**ect
effi**ci**ency
eigh**th**
**e**limi**n**ate
emba**rra**ss
empha**s**ize
end**eav**or
envi**ron**ment
equi**pm**ent (no *e* after *p*)
e**sc**apade
e**sc**ape (no **x**)
e**sp**eci**a**lly
exa**gg**erate
**exc**ept
ex**erci**se

expl**an**ation
extrem**e**ly

fa**ll**acy
famili**ar**
famil**ies**
fanta**sies**
fant**asy**
fa**s**cinate
ficti**ti**ous
for**ei**gners
**for**ty (no *u* after *o*)
fo**rwa**rd/fo**rewo**rd
fourth
fri**e**ndli**n**ess
fulfi**ll**
furth**er**

g**aie**ty
gover**n**ment
gover**nor**
gr**ou**p
**gua**rant**ee**d

ha**rass**
h**eig**ht (no *h* after *t*)
her**oes**
her**oi**ne/her**oi**n
hin**dra**nce (no *e* after *d*)
hospit**a**lization
hug**e**
hum**o**rist
hum**orous**
hypocri**s**y
hypocrit**e**

igno**rant**
im**a**gine
i**mm**ediately
i**mm**ense

importance
incidentally
independence
indispensable
individually
industrious
initiative
intellect
intelligence
interrupt
irrelevant
irresistible
irritable
its/it's

jealousy
judgment (no *e* after g)

know/no/now

laboratory
laborer
laboriously
laid
leisurely
library
license
lieutenant
lightning (no *e*)
likelihood
literature
liveliest
livelihood
liveliness
loneliness
lonely
loose/lose
losing (no *e*)
loss
luxury

magazine
maintenance
maneuver
marriage
material
maybe/may be
meant
medieval
melancholy
millennium
miniature
minuscule (not *i*)
mischief
mischievous (no *i* after *v*)
moral/morale
morally
mysterious

narrative
necessary
ninety
noticeable
noticing (no *e*)
numerous

occasion
occurred
off/of
omit
opportunity
opponent
opposite
optimism

paid
pamphlets
parallel
parliament
paralyzed
passed/past
perceive

S

persist**ent**ly
perso**nal**/perso**nnel**
**ph**ase/**fa**ze
phenom**e**non
p**ie**ce
plau**si**ble
pl**eas**ant
politi**cian**
po**ss**e**ss**ion
pre**ce**de
prefe**rr**ed
pre**j**udice (no *d* before
   or after *j*)
pre**s**ence
prest**i**ge
preva**l**ent
proc**e**dure
pro**ceed**
profession (one *f*)
**prof**essor (one *f*)
pron**ou**nce
pron**u**nciation (no *o* after *n*)
prophe**cy**/prophe**sy**
**psycho**analysis
**psych**ology
**psycho**somatic

qu**ie**t/qu**i**te

rece**i**ve
re**cog**nize
reco**mm**end
refe**rr**ing
rel**ie**ve
remem**br**ance
remini**sce**
res**ou**rces
rhythm
r**i**dicule
roo**mm**ate

s**ce**ne
**sch**edule
s**ei**ze
sen**t**ence
sep**a**rate
s**er**g**ea**nt
shep**h**erd
signifi**cance**
soph**o**more
stabi**li**zation
stren**gth**
stud**y**ing
substan**t**ial
sub**t**le
subtl**y** (no *e*)
suc**ceed**
su**cc**e**ss**ion
su**ffi**cient
su**mm**ary
su**pp**ress
su**r**prise
su**s**ceptible
suspen**s**e
symbo**l**
syno**n**y**m**

te**chn**i**que**
tend**ency**
th**a**n/th**e**n
th**eir**/th**ere**/th**ey're**
themsel**ves**
therefor**e**
th**orough**/th**rough**
though**t**
to/t**oo**/t**wo**
transfe**rr**ed
tremend**ous**
tr**ie**d
tr**ie**s
tyra**nn**y

S

undoubtedly
unnecessary
unusually
useful
useless
using

vacuum
valuable
varies
various
vengeance

warrant
weather/whether
weird
where/were
whose/who's
woman/women
write
writing

yield
your/you're

## Catching Spelling Errors by Proofreading

Proofread carefully each of the following paragraphs. There are five spelling errors in the first and seven in the second. See if you can find and correct them all.

1. In order to achieve one's academic goals, one must lead a disciplined life as a student. The arrangment of one's time is of first importance. The student should set aside regular hours for studing: so many hours per week for reading, so many for writing papers, so many for gainful employment, and so on. It helps if the same hours are set aside for each activitie, for the mind is best trained by regularity. Nor should liesure time be neglected; a balanced life is best for any kind of achievement. Discipline also requires that the student appear promptly for confferences with instructors and that he, in fact, be mature enough to ask that instructors meet with him. Reaching one's academic goals thus requires discipline *and* maturity.

2. Most of us, when we see on the calender that Christmas is approaching, are paniced if we haven't completed our shoping. To avoid that sinking feelling in the pit of your stomach, take a few tips from me. (1) Inteligent gift givers will feel that old urge at the first sign of a nip in the air; begining with the first fall frost, start buying. (2) Paralell with an early start should go a slow start: buy one gift at a time, leaving that long list at home and crossing off names as you go. If you will heed these two simple rules, you

S

will save money — prices are usually lower *before* the season starts — and the anxiety of the Christmas rush. Instead, you'll have given yourself the gift of peace.

# Study and Examination-taking Skills

To acquire and retain study skills, you should be aware that studying requires some of the same virtues the rest of this book has been urging on you, that is, the virtues of organization, clarity, concreteness, logic, and concentration. In this entry, we will try to show you how to apply and develop these virtues as they affect your study and examination-taking skills.

## Preparation

The physical items and ideas necessary to get ready to study are the following:

**1** The proper materials: all the texts and notes you need, together with paper, highlighting magic markers, and the like.

**2** An appropriate place for studying: a quiet room, a section of a study hall — a place where you can concentrate.

**3** Concentration. If you have trouble concentrating for a reasonable period of time, you need to rid your mind of anxiety-laden distractions that prevent concentration or learn how to increase your concentration. Try this method of increasing concentration: Sit down on a Monday at 2 o'clock (or some other convenient hour) and concentrate by reading for as long as you can before you feel you must give up. Note how long you lasted. Perhaps it was five minutes. On Tuesday, extend the time to seven minutes; on Wednesday, to nine minutes. Continue the pattern until you are able to go on for a half hour (or some other length of time that strikes you as productive). You musn't be afraid of taking little breaks, though; they help your overall concentration by releasing tension.

**4** Proper goals. During a study session, you should aim to master a manageable concept — the concept of I.Q., for example, rather than half of your psychology text — and should not dwell on long-term goals, such as getting an A in the course.

**5**  A schedule. Divide your week, all 168 hours, into periods when you sleep, eat, rest, work — and have fun (drudgery is not the answer). A schedule helps by enabling you to absorb your experience in manageable segments and allowing you the time you need for each of your activities.

**6**  An understanding that the mind can only process limited bits of information at any one time.

**7**  An understanding that you must associate what you learn in one course with whatever else you learn, either in another course or outside your classes. This type of learning will help you to retain what you learn.

**8**  The determination to engage in periodic review or reinforcement of what you've been learning. Protect your investment in study time. Don't let your hard-won knowledge slip away.

**9**  A determination to avoid cramming. Cramming is simply an inefficient way to get the job done. At best — when it works — it affords you a short-term grasp of information, which lasts just long enough for one exam.

## Reading

Everything we learn, we learn by analogy. *Something* is there to assist us: a model, a fragment of similar information, an idea. When you read a college text, it is important to do so in an organized way so that you can begin with a model or an analog, however fragmentary. You should not begin by plunging into a text with a close reading.

First, *skim* the chapter or section. Examine the boldface or italicized subheads. Get into your mind the general area of study; prepare yourself with a model or analogy onto which you can hook those numerous concrete details. The goal in skimming is to gain a *general* idea of the author's organization and major ideas. You might, in skimming, go through a process like the following:

**1**  What does the chapter title mean? Can you relate the subject to anything else you know?

**2**    Read the first few paragraphs and then the last few: Frequently, these summarize the major ideas. What are they, roughly? Say them aloud to yourself, in your own words.

**3**    Skim the chapter from heading to heading, subhead to subhead. Can you feel what the author's getting at? how he's proceeding?

**4**    Look a little more carefully at any maps, diagrams, charts, graphs, tables, pictures, or schematics. Do these add anything to your first grasp?

**5**    Pause and think over what you've learned so far. See if you can tell yourself in your own words what the major idea or ideas are.

As soon after your skimming as possible, read carefully through the chapter or section with a view toward grasping the ideas or groups of related ideas and understanding the concrete details out of which these ideas arose. Follow a procedure something like the following:

**1**    As you read, try to distinguish the main ideas from the supporting evidence or ideas. To help you, stop after a paragraph or a group of related paragraphs to be sure you've understood them and have been alerted to any special terms the author uses or highlights in a special typeface or color. Remember that every discipline proceeds by *naming* its concepts. If you want to master psychoanalysis, for example, you must master terms like *unconscious, transference,* and *Oedipus complex.* The special language of a subject *is*, in a sense, the subject.

**2**    Examine the structure of the chapter as if it were a graphic guide to the author's ideas. Notice what happens as the author goes through explanatory steps, pauses for diagrams, or shifts his focus through extended analogies. Every once in a while, skip to the summary at the end or the introductory paragraphs at the beginning: How are you doing in understanding the ideas related there? If you are lost, go back and read a bit more carefully the section or sections you don't quite grasp.

**3**    After reading a section or sections, start annotating in the margins and highlighting with magic marker. Take the section or sections under your review and see if you can repeat the main and supporting ideas in your own words. Relate what you've learned to anything else you know. Integrate.

When you have done this, after a short period of time has intervened, do a quick review for reinforcement's sake. Check your underlinings and annotations, the special terms, the graphic material. Whatever seems foreign or unfamiliar needs rereading. Make a rough reading outline, a set of notes in outline form. Practice from head to hand is another form of reinforcement.

## Taking Notes and Using Them

Going into a lecture or class discussion *cold* — without having done the assigned reading for that class — is an inefficient mistake. It robs you of that model we spoke about a moment ago and thus hampers you in grasping the material to be had from the class hour.

The aim in taking class notes is (1) to reinforce what you have learned in your own reading and (2) to integrate your instructor's view of the material with your own. You *can* listen (and/or make a classroom contribution yourself) and take notes at the same time — *if* you're prepared. If not, you'll waste time writing down every word spoken, when in fact what you want is to take down main and subordinate ideas in such a way that they appear so in your notes. Thus you should block out the main ideas in larger script, the subordinate ones in smaller. Underline special terms. Above all, do not try to write down everything. First, it can't be done; second, it's unnecessary. If you do miss something, leave a space in your notebook that you can fill in later. Later, you can consult a fellow student to fill in the gaps or even ask the instructor. If you've read the material of the lecture or class, you should have even less trouble filling in. Within hours of taking notes, go over them for a quick skimming review, taking time to highlight important points with a special marker.

The acquisition of a "great" set of notes is useless unless they are profitably employed. Notes should be periodically reviewed; short study sessions should be set aside solely for this purpose. There are few better ways to reinforce what you know *and,* not incidentally, slowly and carefully prepare yourself for examinations. If you don't want your notes to seem as foreign to you as a brand-new subject would be, keep up a process of periodic review and revision.

S

## TEST YOURSELF ON
## Improving Study Skills

Get together with two other students in one of your classes. Let the three of you read a chapter of the text, each in his or her own study session. Then get together again. Taking turns, each of you should present his or her version of the chapter's main and supporting ideas along with a definition of key terms. See which of you came nearest the mark in mastering the chapter's materials. Do the others have a way of reading that can help you? After discussing the chapter's contents, discuss study methods.

## Taking Examinations

Taking an essay examination involves some of the same skills we have been seeking to acquire in pursuit of effective writing. That is, your instructor will expect you to use standard English, organize your ideas properly, and support them with effective examples or details. Although it is obvious that you cannot be as careful when you are under the pressure of time in an in-class examination as you can be when you've taken an assignment home, you can nevertheless follow the same procedures as when writing any other essay — with a few modifications.

### Before the Examination

You will need to do three things before the examination:

**1**   Organize your notes and other materials. Reread everything. Recite out loud to yourself main ideas and supporting details. Pick out a couple of supporting details that strike you as particularly effective.

**2**   Review the material in a coherent way. Look at your materials in the way the instructor presented them. Then look at them in different contexts: cause and effect, advantage and disadvantage, analysis, synthesis, and so forth.

**3**   Test yourself. Make up test questions in several different subject areas. Actually write out the answers and check them against your notes and your text. Ask yourself to analyze, define terms, compare, and contrast. For math courses, do a series of tough calculations. Students of history will obviously have to know causes and effects. The kind of course will suggest the kind of testing.

### During the Examination

Regardless of how much time is allotted for the examination, you should proceed in an orderly manner. That is, you should work as if you were at home preparing an assignment: Plan, write, rewrite, proofread.

**1**   But first, read the examination question or questions carefully. If you are asked to write more than one essay, be sure to leave the most time for the question worth the most in examination points. Be sure you understand what the question asks you to do: summarize? analyze? synthesize? compare? *Important note:* Be prepared to answer the question precisely. It won't do to use the question as an opportunity to blurt out everything you know. Instructors who ask you to write essays on examinations want you to do something precise.

**2**   Next, begin to plan. Jot down on scratch paper or the back of the exam answer booklet the general outline of the subject area covered by the essay question. Bend the material to fit the essay question. Try to pluck out one of those contexts you worked with as you prepared for the exam. Jot down several good supporting ideas or other kinds of detail. Work up a thesis statement — it will help you to write cleanly and directly on the question and it will please the instructor who reads it: He'll be impressed by your control.

**3**   Leave enough time to look over your essay. That is, read it carefully to insert missing words, to make your writing more legible, to correct misspellings or grammatical mistakes, to insert a sharper example where you can.

S

## TEST YOURSELF ON
## Taking Examinations

**A**   Evaluate an examination you have previously taken. Note in the margins where you went wrong. Notice your strengths and weaknesses as an examination writer. Now go back to your notes and reanswer questions that were poorly dealt with until you feel certain that your new examination would receive a better grade than the old one.

**B**   Give your notes to a student who is unfamiliar with the course. Ask him to create an examination for you. Take it with watch in hand. Ask the student to grade it. If you receive a poor grade, go over the examination as suggested in A above.

---

# Subjects for Essays: Choosing and Limiting a Topic

---

## Choosing a Topic

The only time selecting a subject may become a problem for you is when you are asked to select one. (If you are assigned a subject, the problem doesn't come up.) Your best course of action then is to choose a subject that interests you, one that captures your imagination and that you either know or want to learn more about.

The place to begin is in your personal experience — in the things that have happened to you, the things you have done, the beliefs you hold, the skills and special interests you have nurtured.

Student writers who think they have nothing to say are much mistaken. *Everybody has something to say.* In fact, we might define being human as the state of having something to say. The trouble is that we are not always aware of what we have to say until we've begun to look for it. That is why you should begin with experience; there is the great repository of writing materials, and questions are the entrée to this great storehouse.

What do I like and dislike? Whom have I known that would be of interest to others? What interesting places have I seen? What books and articles have I read that have provoked me? What movies and television shows have impressed me — one way or another? What do I do in my spare time? About what aspects of life in my community, town, or country am I passionately concerned? Are there wrongs that I think should be righted? social inequities that stick in my craw?

Questions like these will generate subject matter for essays, and if you generate the concrete details that make these subjects come alive, the essays will be interesting.

Sometimes these questions, this examination of the range of your personal experience, will lead you directly to a usable specific subject. But often the result will be a wide generalization. For example, the answer to one of the questions above ("What do I like?") might be "television comedy." Television comedy is simply too wide a generalization on which to base a 300- to 500-word essay. In any case, you would have to give specific examples of television comedy in your essay in order for it to be an effective piece of writing. Your task, then, when your experience suggests a widely general topic, is to narrow it down to a manageable specific one. Instead of "television comedy," you would have to come up with an essay topic like "The Humor of Bill Cosby in 'The Bill Cosby Show.' "

## TEST YOURSELF ON
## Generating Subject Matter

**A**  Examine your taste in television fare. Are there specific types of shows you like and watch consistently? Make a list of them. Now see if they are related. Make a list of five essay titles — possible writing assignments — suggested by the list. Examples might be such titles as "The Basic Plot of the Situation Comedy," "Will Anybody Shoot J. R. Again?" and "The Appeal in Watching Game Shows."

**B**  Make a list of places or buildings you've seen and been impressed by recently — or even during the past few years. Ask yourself what features of these natural or man-made environments appeal to you most or interest you most. Now make a list of five essay titles, possible writing assignments, suggested by those places. Examples might be such titles as "A Barn with a Gambrel Roof " or "A Campsite in Glacier National Park."

## Limiting a Topic

Subjects should "fit" the size of the paper or essay for which they are intended. If you were assigned to write a three-volume book, you might very well choose "The Life of George Washington" as your subject. Since you are unlikely to be given such an assignment, better forgo that subject. In fact, for the size of the assignment you are likely to be given — say a paper 300 to 500 words — better forgo all subjects on that massive scale. You can't possibly do a creditable job in 500 words of writing on topics such as "The Causes of the Civil War" or "The Drug Culture in America." Short papers on subjects such as these can only wind up being filled with windy judgments and vague generalities.

To limit yourself, it is necessary continually to pare down a topic until it is manageable. It is not enough to go from "The Drug Culture in America" to "Marijuana Use in Chicago" — you must go further, for "Marijuana Use in Chicago" is quite as unmanageable in 500 words as is "The Drug Culture in America." Another problem with large topics like these is that they probably go beyond your own experience and would require considerable research before you could plausibly do a good job on them.

The process of limiting a topic involves successive narrowings from a general topic to a usable subject for a short theme.

Suppose you have chosen the general topic of "Sports Cars." Since you probably have no knowledge of the history of sports cars — and therefore wouldn't be able to talk about Bugattis and Reos — your first narrowing would take you to "Contemporary American Sports Cars." This may strike you as exactly right until you realize that it would be folly to try to talk about the dizzying number of makes and models available from American manufacturers nowadays.

Then you get a brainstorm: You decide to talk about your own sports car. This is a shrewd decision, but you realize further that "My Sports Car" is a subject that would certainly require more than the assigned 500 words, because of the complexity of the piece of machinery you own. Try talking about a 1968 Thunderbird — about its basic specifications, size, equipment, road-handling characteristics, and so forth, all in 500 words. Not possible. At this point, you see that *one* of the aspects of your own car would really do nicely, and you finally (and correctly) decide on "Acceleration and Deceleration in My Thunderbird."

This subject is not only the right size, it is also well within the bounds of your experience — so far within, in fact, that you are a great authority on the subject, probably the *only* authority.

You may find that your method of narrowing down a general topic requires less deliberation than the process above. Perhaps you will be able to proceed more quickly. Whatever the case, limiting a topic requires a disciplined effort to proceed toward the specific and manageable from the wide generalization.

## Limiting a Topic

**A**  Below are listed five general topics and the manageable subjects derived from each. Provide the intermediate steps between them. Use the previous analysis as a model in arriving at each stage.

1. *Clothing fashions:* The Role of Designer Blue Jeans on Campus
2. *Education:* My Troubles at the Beginning of Biology [or some other subject] 101
3. *Television:* What Archie Bunker Hates Most
4. *Student self-government:* The Duties of the Student Senator at My School
5. *Urban decay:* Why My Family Left the City (the South Side of Chicago)

**B**  Write specific, manageable titles for five of the topics listed below.

1. Political parties
2. The United Nations
3. Basketball
4. Vacations
5. Water pollution
6. Kurt Vonnegut
7. Racial prejudice in the United States
8. The energy crisis
9. Television commercials
10. Farm-price supports

# Subject-Verb Agreement

In English, the problem of subject-verb agreement arises mainly in the present tense. To understand what it means, consider the verb *to play* and the forms of *play* in the present tense:

| Subject | Verb | Subject | Verb |
|---------|------|---------|------|
| I | play | we | play |
| you | play | you | play |
| he, she, it | plays | they | play |

The subjects in the left-hand column are all *singular;* the subjects in the right-hand column are all *plural.* All the verb forms are the same — except the third one in the left-hand column. It is a

S

feature of the English language that whenever the subject is *he, she,* or *it,* in the present tense, indicative mood, the verb form that goes with it must end in *-s.*

> He *considers* me his friend.
>
> She *tells* me when to pick her up.
>
> It *seems* like a nice day.

Most of us have no trouble when the subject is *he, she,* or *it.* The trouble starts when the subject gets more complicated.

> My Aunt Vicky *plays* basketball on Friday nights.
>
> My Uncle Joe and my cousin Lewis *think* she's a good player.

In these cases, once you have decided whether the subject is singular or plural, you can make the right choice. In the first sentence, you can think of Aunt Vicky as *she;* in the second, there is what we call a compound (and therefore plural) subject. Therefore, the first sentence requires a verb with an *-s* at the end, and the second does not. In the first sentence, there is a singular subject and a singular verb in the third person. In the second sentence, there is a plural (compound) subject and a plural verb form.

For some, the subject-verb agreement problem arises from a common confusion; that is, they know that *plural* nouns end in *-s,* so they make the analogy that words ending in *-s,* even verbs that end in *-s,* are all plural. But of course this is not the case. The number of the verb ending in *-s* is always singular. When the subject agrees with the verb in *number* (singular subject/singular verb; plural subject/plural verb), there is no subject-verb agreement problem.

## TEST YOURSELF ON
## Subject-Verb Agreement

**A**  Change each of the sentences below by following the procedure of the example.

*Example:* Joanna's best *feature is* her eyes.
   Her *eyes are* Joanna's best feature.

1. His main interest is guns.
2. Rock and roll records are my only hobby.
3. Our greatest need is dollars.

4. Many days of nonstop studying were the cause of his breakdown.
5. Too many drinks on an empty stomach were the cause of his
drunkenness.

**B** Change each of the sentences below by following the procedure of the example.

*Example:* They let me know when they want to take a break.
She lets me know when she wants to take a break.

1. They amuse themselves when they have no toys to play with.

He _____

2. This turns me off.

These _____

3. It seems to like being fed by the children.

They _____

4. That forces the argument in another direction.

Those _____

5. They happen a lot more often than you think.

It _____

6. She frightens me when she talks like that.

They _____

7. She seems to profit from the time she spends in the biology lab.

They _____

S

## The Subject: Singular or Plural

You can begin to clear up the problem of subject-verb agreement by
gaining an understanding of what number (singular or plural) to
assign to certain subjects.

### Compound Subjects

A compound subject consists of more than one noun or pronoun connected by *and* and therefore requires a plural verb.

> *Rocco, Vito,* and *Danny* are brothers.
>
> My *sister* Lucia and *I* are starting a rock band.

The use of *neither . . . nor* or *either . . . or* with a compound subject produces a singular subject when both individual subjects are singular.

> Neither my father nor my mother *is* a Democrat.
>
> Either biology or astronomy *is* required.

When one of the subjects is plural, use the verb that agrees with the closest one.

> Neither my uncle nor my *aunts play* pool.
>
> Either fruits or *cereal is* all right for breakfast.

When a compound subject consists of two items that are considered one unit, the subject can be thought of as singular.

> *Ham and eggs is* my favorite dish.
>
> *Stormin' Norman and Suzy is* my favorite rock group.

## TEST YOURSELF ON
## Subject-Verb Agreement with Compound Subjects and *either/or, neither/nor* Subjects

In some of the sentences below, the subject and verb agree. Next to these, write C. For the others, underline the complete subject and the verb and decide whether these are singular or plural. Correct the lack of agreement between subject and verb by changing one or the other.

1. _____ Either your father or your mother are responsible for

the financial aid repayment.

2. _____ Charlie and Dick open their new bookstore next

month.

3. _____ The professional and the rich man decides their own

fates in the labor market.

4. _____ Coffee and donuts is fine for breakfast.

5. _____ Was the sofa and chair on sale?

6. _____ Either lung cancer or heart disease is the chief killer

in the United States.

7. _____ Public transportation and welfare is the items need-

ing reform in American cities.

8. _____ Neither Margaret nor Maureen think their kid brother

is a failure.

9. _____ Air, water, the earth, and people are all being pol-

luted.

10. _____ Neither George nor the Joneses plays bridge.

### Collective Nouns as Subjects

Such collective nouns as *army, audience, class, faculty, committee, team,* and *public* indicate a number of people, but they usually take singular verbs because they are thought of as units.

> The *team is* in first place. (the team as one whole; not the separate players)
>
> The *crowd was* on *its* feet.

Collective nouns like *cattle, clergy, folks* (in the colloquial sense), *peasantry, gentry,* and *vermin* usually take plural verbs.

> The clergy *are* not used to being treated with disrespect. (Clearly, it is a number of *individuals* who are unaccustomed to such treatment.)

Other collective nouns such as *plurality, minority, mass,* and *majority* may take either singular or plural verbs, depending on how you use them.

S

A minority of students *are* Greek majors. (The minority consists of separate Greek majors — a plural number.)

A minority of students *is* a force to be reckoned with. (The minority is a political unit — a singular number.)

## TEST YOURSELF ON
## Subject-Verb Agreement with Collective Nouns as Subjects

In each of the following sentences, determine whether the collective noun subject refers to a single unit or a plural number of individuals. Then cross out the incorrect verb in parentheses.

1. In this course, the class (decide, decides) whether to have a final exam.
2. The jury (render, renders) a verdict of *not guilty.*
3. The majority of my stamp collection (is, are) valuable.
4. The majority of my stamps (is, are) valuable.
5. The Congress (vote, votes) into law a thousand bills every year.
6. A plurality of Democrats (vote, votes) for liberal candidates.
7. The Appointments Committee (settle, settles) the fate of the faculty.
8. The staff (organize, organizes) the summer program.
9. The mass of men (leads, lead) lives of quiet desperation.
10. The audience (applaud, applauds) the performance vigorously.

### Subjects Modified by Phrases and Clauses

Sometimes the full subject of a verb is a whole string of words, consisting of the simple subject and its modifiers; these modifiers are frequently phrases, clauses, or both. But regardless of how many or what kinds of words intervene between the simple subject and the verb, the basic rule still holds: the verb must agree with the simple subject.

#### Subject Modified by a Phrase

*Living alone in college dormitories* seems to encourage students' maturity.

The full subject is the italicized portion of the example. But the headword, *living,* is the simple subject; it is singular and agrees with the singular verb *seems.*

### Subject Modified by a Clause

*Students who butter up their professors* earn better grades than those who don't.

The full subject is the italicized portion of the example, but the headword, *students,* is the simple subject; it is plural and agrees with the plural verb *earn.*

We could take either of these examples and make the full subject longer and longer by adding more and more phrases and clauses, but the fact is that these long strings of words accompanying the simple subject are *modifiers;* and the verb never agrees with a word or words in the modifier — only with the simple subject.

The *music is* beautiful. (*Music* is singular; therefore the verb, *is,* is also singular.)

The *music* of the *strings is* beautiful. (*Strings* is plural but *strings* is part of the modifying phrase *of the strings;* the verb remains singular because singular *music* is still the subject.)

## TEST YOURSELF ON
## Choosing the Correct Verb for Subjects Modified by Phrases and Clauses

Underline the simple subject of each of the following sentences. Then cross out the phrase or clause that modifies it and read the sentence to determine which of the verbs in parentheses agrees with that subject. Cross out the incorrect verb.

*Example:* <u>Actors</u> (hate, hates) to be reminded of the fact.

1. The passenger with a cowboy hat and boots in the aisle seat (look, looks) like my brother.

2. The patrons who are waiting in line behind the ropes (want, wants) desperately to be seated.

3. The purpose of the rules (is, are) to assure order.

4. The catch-22 in the examinations given by the Biology Department (lie, lies) in the large number of choices you are given.

5. The guard who stands at the doors of the museum (punch, punches) the tickets.

6. The difference between you and your cousins (appear, appears) to be that you are more comfortable away from home.

7. The smell of those fresh pastries (make, makes) my mouth water.

8. The progress of Jim's achievements in college (please, pleases) his parents.

9. Classes that meet late in the day (is, are) poorly attended.

10. Ed's affection for politics (distract, distracts) him from his real work.

### Special Cases

**1**   Pronouns as subjects. All of the following are singular and take singular verbs:

| | | | |
|---|---|---|---|
| anybody | each | everyone | nobody |
| anything | either | everything | none |
| anyone | everybody | neither | no one |
| somebody | someone | something | one |

*Everyone* with an interest in ecology *opposes* offshore oil drilling.
*Each writes* well.
*Neither writes* brilliantly.

**2**   Words ending in *-ics* as subjects. Words like *mathematics, economics, politics,* and *dialectics* are singular when you are speaking of the subject as a whole — as *one* thing.

*Mathematics offers* us a way of looking at the world.
*Economics has* no solution to the problem of inflation.

Where these terms refer to a number or collection of ideas rather than a singular, academic subject, they take a plural verb.

Marx's *economics do* not apply in all societies.

Since 1968, my *politics have* changed considerably.

**3**   *One of those which / who.* Where you find this structure, the first verb you use must be plural, the second singular.

> *One* of those *who sing* in the choir *is* my brother. (*Sing* agrees with the subject of the relative clause *who*—which agrees with *those* [plural]—and *is* agrees with *one*, the main subject.)

**4**   *There is, there are. There* is not usually a subject. That's the trouble. Whether you use *is* or *are* depends on what follows the word *there*.

> There is something I want to discuss with you. (The subject here is *something*, which agrees with the singular *is*.)

> There are reasons that I can't see you tonight. (*Reasons* is the plural subject here—agreeing with the plural verb *are*.)

**5**   *A number of, the number of. The number of* always takes a singular verb; *a number of* always takes a plural verb.

> *A number of dogs are* playing in the garden.

> *The number of dogs* playing in the garden *is* small.

**6**   *Part* and *portion*. These words, though they indicate a quantity, always take a singular verb, because each signifies a single unit or fraction.

> *Part* of my time *is* spent loafing.

> *Part* of my work *is* boring.

> A *portion* of my salary *goes* into savings bonds.

> A *portion* of cherries *is* fine for dessert.

**7**   Expressions such as *together with, as well as, in addition to, including.* A parenthetical expression introduced by phrases such as these does not affect the agreement of the subject and the verb.

> The *truck cab* and the *trailer are* barreling down the highway. (The compound subject—*track cab and trailer*—requires the plural verb *are*.)

> The *truck cab*, together with the trailer, is barreling down the highway. (The subject is now *truck cab*—the parenthetical expression introduced by *together with* doesn't count—and the verb is therefore the singular *is*.)

S

TEST YOURSELF ON
## Subject-Verb Agreement in Special Cases

For each of the sentences below, cross out the verb in the parentheses that does not agree with the italicized subject.

1. *Billiards* (is, are) a difficult game to learn.
2. *Economics* (involve, involves) a lot of statistics.
3. Joanna noticed that Bill's *trousers* (was, were) dirty.
4. *Gymnastics* (require, requires) a high degree of agility.
5. The *news* these days (depress, depresses) me.
6. Now that I have graduated, a *part* of my life's tasks (is, are) over.
7. A *portion* of these marbles (is, are) yours.
8. A *portion* of blueberry pancakes (is, are) served with butter and syrup.

TEST YOURSELF ON
## Proofreading to Catch Subject-Verb Agreement Errors

Each of the following paragraphs contains five errors in subject-verb agreement. See if, by careful proofreading, you can catch them all.

1. Paris is a city that has something for everyone. There is gardens, the Louvre, restaurants, and — ah, yes! — cafés. These are the very center of outdoor life in this beautiful city. Rising up from the tables at cafés are talk of politics, art, love, the very stuff of sophisticated European life. One of those who sings the praises of Paris most loudly is my brother Lazare. Neither Lazare nor I are stinting in our praise, but he is a fanatic. Although I never fail to be charmed by a visit to the Louvre or a walk along the beautiful Seine, I manage a quiet joy. Lazare, on the other hand, think that Paris not only has something for everyone but that all these "somethings" are for him.

2. Either my mother or my father are always pestering me about progress in my schoolwork. Their attitude is that I need to report improvement every semester. I tell them that living alone in dormitories have deepened my maturity and that I don't need their pressure. But neither of them will listen. The music of my

grade reports are beautiful to them, and they never forget to ask for those reports. Economics, my major, are a difficult subject for me, but even though I'm running a B+ in eco, you should hear my parents bellow when I report a B in advanced statistics. Neither my father nor my mother and her sisters (who also get into the act) understands that sometimes progress isn't measurable by grades alone and that I need to be left alone to make more progress as a human being.

# Subjunctive Mood

See **Verbs** and Part 1, Verbs.

# Subordination

Subordination is the technique of indicating that one idea is not as important as another. Consider these two ideas.

1. The rate of inflation in the United States is growing at a rapid pace.
2. Prices and wages are in an upward spiral.

Both ideas are interesting, but though we can be sure the two are related, there is nothing to indicate their *relative* importance. In a piece of writing whose thesis was that sentence 1 was more important than 2, we should rewrite the sentences like this:

> Because prices and wages are in an upward spiral, the rate of inflation in the United States is growing at a rapid pace.

Of course, your thesis might be that the reverse is true and that sentence 2 is more important than 1. Then the two ideas would be expressed like this:

> Because the rate of inflation in the United States is growing at a rapid pace, prices and wages are in an upward spiral.

In either case, however, it is important that you learn the technique of subordination and then go on to use it habitually in your writing.

S

Subordinate ideas may be expressed, as above, by putting them in the form of a dependent (subordinate) clause. They may also be put in the form of phrases or even single words.

> Included in my wardrobe is a summer suit, *which is made of cotton*. (subordinate idea cast in the form of a dependent, subordinate clause)
>
> Included in my wardrobe is a summer suit *made of cotton*. (subordinate idea cast in the form of a participial phrase)
>
> Included in my wardrobe is a *cotton* summer suit. (subordinate idea made into an adjective)

Probably the most important technique of subordination is casting subordinate ideas into the form of subordinate clauses. Otherwise your prose can sound like the following childish and monotonous passage:

> I went to the movies. I ran into my friend Charlie. The movie ran two hours. I hated it. Charlie wanted to sit up front. I wanted to smoke in the balcony. We sat in the third row.

Because these seven ideas are presented as seven separate sentences, they appear to be of equal importance. But of course they are not. Nor would it be much help to string them together with *and* or *but* or other coordinating conjunctions. In fact, you should avoid such strings at all costs. What is needed is subordination — reducing the less important ideas and highlighting the more important ones. One possible way of revising the passage is this:

> I went to the movies, where I ran into my friend Charlie. The movie, which I hated, ran for two hours. Although I wanted to smoke in the balcony, Charlie wanted to sit up front and we sat in the third row.

You might disagree over whether this is the best way to revise the passage, but you would surely agree that this change is for the better.

In practicing subordination, you should be wary of two errors that are likely to crop up.

**1**   Don't subordinate the more important idea. Where you have two ideas and want to subordinate one of them, do not haphazardly make your choice. That is, do not subordinate one of the ideas without thinking through the problem and deciding what you want to stress. What you want to stress will, of course, go into the main clause.

> Ali won the fight.
> Ali was tiring at the end.
> Although Ali won the fight, he was tiring at the end. (Are you just subordinating the first of the two ideas because it is the first one your eye fell on, or do you really want to stress the fact that Ali was tiring rather than that he won the fight?)
>
> I break out in hives.
> I eat strawberries.
> Whenever I break out in hives, I eat strawberries. (In this case, subordinating the first of the two ideas because your eye fell on it first results in an absurdity.)
> Whenever I eat strawberries, I break out in hives. (Of course, this is in keeping with the more probable sequence of events.)

**2** Don't use the wrong subordinating conjunctions. Be sure to use the correct subordinating conjunction whenever you *do* subordinate.

> ***Poor*** *While* my English professor is not Woody Allen, he does have a good sense of humor.
> ***Better*** *Although* my English professor is not Woody Allen, he does have a good sense of humor.
>
> ***Poor*** I read in the paper *where* the Bee-Gees are making a comeback.
> ***Better*** I read in the paper *that* the Bee-Gees are making a comeback.
>
> ***Poor*** My final exams, *what* I have to take next week, have me scared.
> ***Better*** My final exams, *which* I have to take next week, have me scared.

## TEST YOURSELF ON
# Subordination

**A** Combine each of the following groups of sentences into one or two effective ones by using the techniques of subordination.

*Examples:* 1. I ran into the water.
It was cold.

When I ran into the water, it was cold.

2. James Joyce was an Irish novelist.
   He did all his writing in exile in Europe.
   He wrote five books.
   *Dubliners* was a book he wrote.

   James Joyce, an Irish novelist who did all his writing in exile in Europe, wrote five books, including *Dubliners*.

*Note:* Not every student will combine the groups in exactly the same way. Several ways are possible.

1. Marylea has a lovely blue shirt.
   The shirt is cotton.
   She likes to take it to the beach.
   She likes to walk around with it.
2. My television set is broken again.
   I paid four hundred dollars for it.
   It happens.
   I get furious.
3. Air pollution is a problem.
   The problem affects us all.
   The problem affects us if we live in the country.
   The problem affects us if we live in the city.
4. We left Cleveland.
   It was raining there.
   We arrived in Chicago.
   Chicago surprised us with its sunlit beauty.
5. My friend's name is Chris.
   He is English.
   He loves the United States.
   He occasionally longs to return to London.
6. Some crimes are against the person.
   These crimes are increasing.
   These crimes must be dealt with.
   These crimes must be dealt with firmly.
7. It was early.
   It was a Sunday.
   It was morning.
   The streets were deadly quiet.
8. Promises are made.
   These promises are sincere.

Promises can be broken.
The breaking is easy.
9. It rains.
My roof leaks.
The roof tiles are loose.
They were never repaired by the former owner.
10. Paul Klee was a painter.
He was a Swiss.
His paintings look like drawings.
The drawings are made by children.

**B** Revise the following sentences through the effective use of subordination.

1. My hair is drying. I'll read a book.
2. I eat too much pastry and I gain a lot of weight.
3. A whole set of encyclopedias came in the mail and I didn't order it.
4. You see a rainbow across the meadow and you know there's been a recent rainstorm.
5. Jerry was unpacking but Noella was cooking supper.
6. She was frightened of air travel and she got on the plane for Paris.
7. Her exams were over, so she could afford to relax.
8. She had enough money and she had enough time and she needed a change of scenery, so she went out to California to visit Craig.
9. The car is a symbol of his virility, so he spends a lot of time polishing it to a high luster.
10. He likes working in the darkroom, so he does his own printing.

# Thesis Statement

*Thesis statement* is the name given to a central idea when it is written out as a sentence. A thesis, or theme, is simply the stand you take on an issue or the main point you want to make about a subject.

*The Decline of American Cities*, for example, is not a thesis statement but a title. In fact, it isn't a sentence, and a thesis statement must be a complete sentence. "My subject is the decline of

T-Z

American cities" is not a thesis statement, either, but an announcement to the reader of what your subject will be — a job done better by a title. (Notice that it is not an improvement to write "My *thesis* is the decline of American cities.") "The decline of American cities is deplorable" is also not a thesis statement, because it needs no essay to support it; it is a fairly obvious statement of fact. A reader would be as interested in reading an essay about it as he would be in reading one that supports the statement "Hank Aaron holds the major league home run record."

You need an effective thesis statement in order to control your writing. A poorly worded thesis statement guarantees a poorly constructed, badly focused, and uninteresting piece of writing. In order to be sure that you have a thesis statement that will help control your writing, you should pay attention to the following criteria of a good thesis statement:

**1**   An effective thesis statement is limited or narrowed down from a larger statement. The idea is to give yourself a manageable, *limited* piece of territory to cover. "College teachers go too fast for the average college student" is a very broad statement that would take you into too large a territory. For example, you would have to talk about more than one college teacher and would also have to deal with whatever is an "average college student." The territory can be scaled down considerably if this topic is changed to "Professor Lucia John goes too fast for her math students." You can see how this limits the territory to one professor in just one class and how it provides real material in the form of actual students. Here are two more examples of large and narrower statements:

> *Large*   Our tax burdens are too great.
> *Narrower*   Federal tax rates penalize people for being single.
>
> *Large*   Baseball is fun.
> *Narrower*   Nothing matches the excitement of a low-scoring baseball game between evenly matched teams.

**2**   An effective thesis statement is singular. More than one major idea in an essay is too many. If you have too many major ideas, you will write diffusely, your essay will wander all over the territory, and the reader will lose track of what he or she is supposed to be following. "The United Nations has not fulfilled its original purpose of keeping world peace; it's used for narrow political purposes instead, and many countries neglect to pay their share of its upkeep — which is quite expensive." This is a mouthful — enough for at least two and probably three essays. Better would be either "The United Nations has not fulfilled its original peace-keeping purpose" or "The United Nations is used for narrow political purposes." Here are two more examples:

> ***Multiple*** The social life of a freshman at this college is very limited; the place is so big that you can get lost looking for a classroom, and besides, the professors are an unfriendly bunch.
> ***Singular*** A freshman at this college has a number of difficult adjustments to make.
> The social life of a freshman at this college is very limited.
> The professors at this college are an unfriendly bunch.

> ***Multiple*** Contributions to our mounting ecological problems will be made by the energy crisis, rapid increases in world population, and the plans for modern industrial development by the third-world countries.
> ***Singular*** The energy crisis is contributing to our mounting ecological problems.
> Plans for industrial development by third-world countries will contribute to our ecological problems.
> Rapid increases in world population will contribute to our ecological problems.

**3** An effective thesis statement is concrete. A thesis statement that is limited and singular must also be concrete. An abstract or vague expression can ruin it.

> ***Vague*** The Pittsburgh Steelers are a great football team. (What does *great* mean?)
> ***Concrete*** The Pittsburgh Steelers are solid at every position. (that is, at quarterback, tackle, end, etc.)

> ***Vague*** Those who stop smoking care about their health. (What *aspect* of health?)
> ***Concrete*** Giving up smoking reduces the smoker's chances of contracting lung cancer. (Lung cancer is a concrete item to work with.)

## TEST YOURSELF ON
## Recognizing an Appropriate Thesis Statement

Place a check next to any of the following sentences that seem to be strong and effective thesis statements. Rework the others.

1. Diabetes is a leading killer of Americans.
2. American movies are hung up on nostalgia for the fifties.

3. My Aunt Rose is a stylish dresser.
4. Punk rock is for punks.
5. Mathematics is an engineering student's most useful basic subject.
6. The difference between newspaper coverage and television coverage of the fire on 29th Street illustrates an important media principle.
7. *Hamlet* is a better play than *Macbeth*.
8. The rules for getting a candidate on the ballot for mayor in this town are unfair to those without funds.
9. Utilities in this country make a fortune in profit.
10. The life of a pro athlete is a poor model for youth.
11. Science and art have nothing to say to one another.
12. A person's hobby is the key to that person's character.

# Topic Sentence

See **Unity.**

# Transitions

Transition is the relating of one idea to the next as your essay proceeds from start to finish. Smooth transition contributes to the coherence of sentences, paragraphs, and essays. A tight organizational pattern is usually the best guarantee that you will achieve coherence. (For more on **Coherence,** see that entry.)

The necessity for coherence is based on your readers' need to be led from point to point in the writing by some familiar principle of order. In other words, readers need a solid bridge to get from sentence to sentence, paragraph to paragraph, idea to idea. When such bridges are absent, readers lose confidence in the writing and distractedly wander away from what they are reading.

Thus unless the organizational pattern is so powerful that the writing has exceptionally smooth flow from part to part, it is a good idea to use what are called *transitional devices* to establish points of reference, bridges for the readers' eyes and minds. These devices are also useful because they establish the exact relationship between succeeding parts. In that sense they are useful in *saying* more, and saying is the essential function of expository writing.

The major transitional devices, sometimes used in combination, are the following.

## Repetition

Repeating a word or a phrase is a most common device. Sometimes a pronoun, referring back to a subject, will also do the trick, as will repeating a reference to an idea.

## Whole Sentence or Brief Paragraph

A sentence can be used as a transition between different ideas following and preceding it. A brief paragraph can also serve as a transition between two longer paragraphs.

## Transitional Words or Phrases

Standard transitional words and phrases are good bridges, and most are also useful in indicating relationships. A few of the large number available are listed below:

| | |
|---|---|
| soon | likewise |
| later | in the same way |
| at the same time | on the other hand |
| afterward | however |
| meanwhile | but |
| simultaneously | nevertheless |
| in a little while | still |
| subsequently | yet |
| nearby | by contrast |
| close by | moreover |
| there | furthermore |
| here | finally |
| at the other end | also |
| therefore | in addition |
| thus | indeed |
| hence | in fact |
| consequently | in other words |
| similarly | |

## TEST YOURSELF ON
## Making Effective Transitions

Each of the groups of sentences below could be made more coherent by the use of one or more transitional devices. Use either repetition (which will require a little rewriting) or standard transitional words and phrases.

1. She had given Tom a handsome wedding gift. She had offered him a well-paying job with the firm.
2. He stood in a small ravine. There was a running brook.
3. The country is running out of oil. Our coal supply is low. Research and development for new energy sources are at a standstill.
4. She received a receipt for her tuition. She was able to register.
5. She wanted to go to the seashore. He preferred the mountains.
6. Reading stimulated his taste for mulling over in his mind the writer's great ideas. The notions gave him a sense of participating in some great enterprise. He was always reading.
7. Among his possessions were a sports car, a motorcycle, a boat, and a bicycle. He had no need to use public transportation.
8. Sam made his way through his classes by impressing on his teacher what a bright, personable young man he was. He made contacts with girls and impressed them, too.
9. After walking around downtown for an hour, she stopped and had dinner. She went to the movies.
10. He was graduated *summa cum laude.* he was able to pick and choose from a number of high-paying jobs.
11. She treated him shabbily, never letting him know from one minute to the next how she felt about him, breaking appointments, speaking rudely to him in public. He could find things about her to love.
12. She said she had known him in Chicago. He had never been to Chicago.

U

# Underlining

See **Italics**

# Unity

Effective paragraphs possess a quality called *unity*. All the sentences in a unified paragraph are directed toward a single purpose: they supply specific details to illustrate, explain, or define a single generalization made somewhere in, but usually at the beginning of, that paragraph. This generalization is called the *topic sentence,* and it states what the paragraph is *about.*

Thus every unified paragraph is about one thing and pursues the one thing by organizing itself about its topic sentence. The three ways of placing the topic sentence are illustrated by the following sample paragraphs.

**1**   The topic sentence can be the opening sentence of the paragraph. Such a paragraph follows the deductive method of stating the generalization and then adding illustrative or supporting details.

In the folklore of the country, numerous superstitions relate to winter weather. Back-country farmers examine their corn husks — the thicker the husk, the colder the winter. They watch the acorn crop — the more acorns, the more severe the season. They observe where white-faced hornets place their paper nests — the higher they are, the deeper will be the snow. They examine the size and shape and color of the spleens of butchered hogs for clues to the severity of the season. They keep track of the blooming of dogwood in the spring — the more abundant the blooms, the more bitter the cold in January. When chipmunks carry their tails high and squirrels have heavier fur and mice come into country houses early in the fall, the superstitious gird themselves for a long, hard winter. Without any scientific basis, a wider-than-usual black band on a woolly-bear caterpillar is accepted as a sign that winter will arrive early and stay late. Even the way a cat sits beside the stove carries its message to the credulous. According to a belief once widely held in the Ozarks, a cat sitting with its tail to the fire indicates very cold weather is on the way.
Edwin Way Teale, *Wandering Through Winter*

Observations indicate that the different clusters of galaxies are constantly moving apart from each other. To illustrate by a homely analogy, think of a raisin cake baking in an oven. Suppose the cake swells uniformly as it cooks, but the raisins themselves

**U**

remain of the same size. Let each raisin represent a cluster of galaxies, and imagine yourself inside one of them. As the cake swells, you will observe that all the other raisins move away from you. Moreover, the further away the raisin, the faster it will seem to move. When the cake has swollen to twice its initial dimensions, the distance between all the raisins will have doubled itself—two raisins that were initially an inch apart will now be two inches apart; two raisins that were a foot apart will have moved two feet apart. Since the entire action takes place within the same time interval, obviously the more distant raisins must move apart faster than those close at hand. So it happens with the clusters of galaxies.
Fred Hoyle, "When Time Began"

**2**　The topic sentence can be the final sentence of the paragraph. Such a paragraph follows the inductive method by giving details first and allowing these details to lead up to the concluding general statement.

Television sells cars as if they were sex objects. It tells one-hour stories that wind up with all the pieces in the right places, the heroines and heroes clearly marked. It pictures the news only in pictures—as if there were nothing else newsworthy. It relegates "educational" programs to a special channel—as if educational material did not belong with the other material. And it's right to do so, because commercial television does everything it can to sell us illusions.

The sports pages have columns telling us how to hit a tennis ball and how to flog a golf ball. The slick magazines give us expert advice on how to sew, build furniture, repair cars, use tools, and redecorate our houses. Stirring books are printed every day with titles bearing the words "How To . . ." and television talk shows consistently feature people who are *experts,* people who have *accomplished* something. Thus it is easy to see that Americans value nothing so much as competence.

**3**　The topic sentence can be unstated but implied. This is a frequent tactic of narrative and descriptive paragraphs. In the example given below, the implied topic is *a description of the plant life at the edge of a concrete highway.*

The concrete highway was edged with a mat of tangled, broken, dry grass, and the grass heads were heavy with oat beards to catch on a dog's coat, and foxtails to tangle in a horse's fetlocks, and clover burrs to fasten in sheep's wool; sleeping life waiting to

be spread and dispersed, every seed armed with an appliance of dispersal, twisting darts and parachutes for the wind, little spears and balls of tiny thorns, and all waiting for animals and for the wind, for a man's trouser cuff or the hem of a woman's skirt, all passive but armed with appliances of activity, still, but each possessed of the anlage of movement.
John Steinbeck, *The Grapes of Wrath**

## TEST YOURSELF ON
## Identifying Topic Sentences

What are the topic sentences in the paragraphs below? If you cannot find one expressed directly, consider the possibility that it may be implied.

1. While the relationship between loving and being loved is an intimate one, this is not to say that love is automatically reciprocated. Indeed, it may lead to feelings of revulsion if the individual's self-image is already irretrievably low: "Anyone who says he loves *me* must be either a fool or a fraud." Still a person is relatively likely to love someone who loves him. Indirect support for this generalization comes from a number of experiments in which persons are falsely informed that they are liked (or disliked) by other members of their group. This misinformation is enough to elicit congruent feelings in most of the deceived subjects. A similar kind of feedback often operates in the elaborate American game of dating. The young woman, for any of several reasons, may pretend to like her escort more than is actually the case. The man, hungry for precisely this kind of response, responds favorably and in kind. And the woman, gratified by this expression of affection, now feels the fondness she had formerly feigned. Falling in love may be regarded, in cases such as these, as a snowball with a hollow core.
Lawrence Casler, "The Thing Called Love Is Pathological"

2. The gallows stood in a small yard, separate from the main grounds of the prison, and overgrown with tall prickly weeds. It was a brick erection like three sides of a shed, with planking on top, and above that two beams and a crossbar with the rope dangling. The hangman, a greyhaired convict in the white uni-

form of the prison, was waiting beside his machine. He greeted us with a servile crouch as we entered. At a word from Francis the two warders, gripping the prisoner more closely than ever, half led, half pushed him to the gallows and helped him clumsily up the ladder. Then the hangman climbed up and fixed the rope round the prisoner's neck.

George Orwell, "A Hanging," from *Shooting an Elephant*

3. Money in England is august. What a fine, scrolled document an English banknote is, and how carefully one thinks before one parts with it. How noble and weighty is the English penny, compared with the equivalent American coin, which is a mere scrap of metal. Try and get hold of an English penny; weigh it in your hand; savor its medallion-like quality, and think how painful it is to spend it on a mere bus ticket or a visit to the lavatory. And then think of the flimsiness of American cash, and how glad one is, really, to get rid of it. It doesn't confer status on a man, the way cash does in England. Indeed, one discerns a strange sense of abasement in American financial quarters. The last thing an American banker would like you to think of him is that he might *deal* in cash. He deals in bonds, and he finances things, but he doesn't touch money.

Malcolm Bradbury, "Can We Bring Back the Old Fashioned Bank Robber?"

4. Anyone who has worked on a committee preparing a document to be signed by all fellowwriters knows some of the difficulties. Disagreements of opinion and emphasis can produce a voice that is hardly a voice at all. Constant qualification makes for weakness. The various writers, all too aware of their audience as real people, may try to anticipate hopelessly conflicting prejudices and objections. Everybody has a point he wants included, but what is worse, no one feels any personal responsibility for the tone of the whole. Nobody cares, really. Contrast the situation of the single writer alone at his desk, who can establish a single speaking voice and an ideal assumed reader to listen to it. Yet a great deal of modern prose is written, or at any rate rewritten, not at a lonely desk but around a table where everybody talks at once. The loss of personality almost inevitable under such circumstances should cause us anguish whenever, as so often happens, we have to read or write the prose of organization life. When we speak of official prose as *stuffy,* we are referring, I think, directly to this loss of personality. (Not that you need a committee to produce stuffiness. . . .) Stuffiness may

imply, by way of the stuffed shirt, that the speaker has no insides, no humanity. It is scarecrow prose. Other familiar metaphors also seem to recognize an emptiness within; thus we speak of the "inflated" language of officialese, the speaker in that case being filled with gas, or hot air.
Walker Gibson, *Tough, Sweet, and Stuffy*

5. Hackers are the mutant offspring of the eggheads who once prowled through engineering buildings with slide rules attached to their belts. The computer's power has made the hackers a subculture to be reckoned with. Their fellow students may consider them creepy, but among themselves they are risk takers, explorers, artists. They communicate with one another by intricate computer networks, speak in their own jargon and qualify for lucrative jobs in which they will create the complex programs essential for the everyday functioning of our nation, our world. They have the potential to be supercriminals, to use digital skeleton keys to electronic vaults holding money, confidential personal data and national security secrets. But the power is not without a price: an addiction to computing, a compulsion to program. And they think it's fun.
Stephen Levy, "Hackers in Paradise"

## TEST YOURSELF ON
## Achieving Unity in Paragraphs

Each of the three topic sentences printed below is accompanied by a set of statements. Each topic sentence together with its accompanying statements could be made into an effective paragraph were it not for one problem: Some of the statements in each set are irrelevant to the topic sentence. In each set, eliminate the potential hurdles to unity and organize the rest into an effective paragraph. Slight alterations in the statements are permissible.

**A**  Basketball is the game requiring great physical skills and coordination.

1. Basketball players must be able to run backward as well as forward.
2. They must have good peripheral vision in order to see their teammates and their opponents.

3. In order to leap for the ball off the backboard, players must have excellent timing.
4. Timing is also important in passing and shooting — the exact moment counts in basketball.
5. In football, such skills and coordination are not necessary; there you need brute strength.
6. Basketball can be played anywhere.
7. The speed at which the game is played seems to be the factor that requires these skills.

**B**  Your chances of getting a summer job are best if you make a systematic search and present yourself as a useful worker.

1. Explore all the relevant sources for jobs: want ads, school placement agency, friends and relatives, and signs hanging in the windows of businesses in your hometown.
2. Begin your campaign early.
3. If you get the right summer job, you can earn as much as $2,500 over the summer.
4. If you are applying to a large corporation, show your professionalism by presenting a résumé.
5. The résumé should not be modest; it should list all the skills you possess.
6. Then decide on what kind of job you want and go after it.
7. In appearing for an interview, be on time and present a neat and businesslike appearance.
8. The vigorous job seeker will appear vigorous to an employer.
9. A summer job is not so tiring that you will not be able to have fun and work at the same time.

**C**  There are a number of reasons why it is difficult for most high school seniors to adjust to college life.

1. For one thing, they usually come to a large campus from a much smaller high school setting, and this change alone is unsettling.
2. College administrators should be forced to go to freshman registration and see what's involved.
3. Not only a big school but big classes contribute to the freshman's unease.
4. Crowded together in a large lecture hall with hundreds of students, they miss the intimacy they enjoyed in high school.
5. Where they were once friendly with a small number of

U

"teachers," they are now subject to the alienating presence of the "professor."

6. Moreover, going to college often involves a change of residence — from home with the family to a college dorm in another town — and this factor requires some adjustment.

7. Colleges should try to make this transition easier.

# Verbs

A verb is a part of speech that expresses either action or some state of existence or condition of being.

> Dr. J. *sank* a jumper.
> The Rolling Stones *played* a concert.
> My Uncle Gene *eats* like a whole platoon of Marines.
> The typewriter *sits* waiting.

> After a while, I *felt* better.
> Eddie *seemed* depressed today.
> She *is* a princess.
> They *were* startled.

The verbs italicized in the second set of examples above are called *linking verbs*. (See Part 1, Verbs, for more information about them.) The verbs italicized in the first set of examples above denote some kind of action. (See Part 1, Verbs, under the headings *transitive* and *intransitive* for information about them.)

What all these verbs have in common is the fact that each one not only carries a meaning but also indicates *time*.

1. I *begin* work at eight o'clock. (present tense)
2. I *am beginning* work at eight o'clock. (continuous or progressive present tense)
3. I *was beginning* work at eight o'clock. (continuous past tense)
4. Yesterday, I *began* work at nine o'clock. (past tense)
5. Every day this week, I *have begun* work before ten o'clock. (perfect tense)
6. Before that, I *had begun* work at eleven o'clock. (past perfect tense)
7. Tomorrow, I *will begin* work at twelve o'clock. (future tense)
8. I *will have begun* work by twelve noon. (future perfect tense)

**V**

Sentence 1 indicates action taking place in the present or action that is typical and ongoing (something like "I *always* begin work at eight o'clock—I have done so and I will do so in the future"). Sentence 2 says much the same, perhaps with a bit more urgency—the statement could be read as a kind of warning, that is, "You'd better say what you have to say to me now because I'll be too busy after eight: I am beginning work at eight o'clock." Sentence 3 might answer the question "What time were you beginning work last week?" Sentence 4, the simple past tense, indicates that the action took place in the past and was completed then. Sentence 5 suggests that the action was begun in the past and has continued on up to the present. Sentence 6 tells us that the action specified took place and was completed *prior* to some other time in the past, perhaps prior to the week spoken of in sentence 5. Sentence 7 indicates future time, and sentence 8 indicates an action that *will be* completed at or by some specific time in the future.

There are other important things to notice about these examples. First, you should notice that a verb can consist of more than one word. Second, you should notice that in all the examples there appear only four forms of the verb *begin:*

> begin (stem, or present tense form)
> began (past tense)
> begun (past participle)
> beginning (present participle)

These are called the *principal parts* of the verb. Knowing the principal parts of a verb and knowing the forms of the auxiliary (helping) verbs *be* and *have* will enable you to form any tense or form of that verb.

## Conjugation of *Be* and *Have*

The *conjugation* of a verb is a listing of its forms.

| **Be** | | **Have** | |
|---|---|---|---|
| *present tense* | | *present tense* | |
| I am | we are | I have | we have |
| you are | you are | you have | you have |
| he, she, it is | they are | he, she, it has | they have |
| *past tense* | | *past tense* | |
| I was | we were | I had | we had |
| you were | you were | you had | you had |
| he, she, it was | they were | he, she, it had | they had |

V

*perfect tense:* have been
*past perfect tense:* had been
*future tense:* will be
*future perfect tense:* will
have been

*perfect tense:* have had
*past perfect tense:* had had
*future tense:* will have
*future perfect tense:* will
have had

## Regular and Irregular Verbs: Principal Parts

Notice these principal parts:

| Present (stem) | Past | Present Participle | Past Participle |
|---|---|---|---|
| talk | talked | talking | talked |
| play | played | playing | played |
| freeze | froze | freezing | frozen |
| catch | caught | catching | caught |

Notice that in the case of the first two verbs, the past and the past participle simply add *-ed* (the two forms are the same). These are called regular verbs. The last two are *irregular.*

Irregular verbs in English do not form the past and past participle with *-ed.* The irregularities of these verbs must be studied and memorized; here is a list of some of the main irregular verbs, together with their principal parts.

| Present (stem) | Past | Present Participle | Past Participle |
|---|---|---|---|
| arise | arose | arising | arisen |
| bear | bore | bearing | borne |
| begin | began | beginning | begun |
| bind | bound | binding | bound |
| blow | blew | blowing | blown |
| break | broke | breaking | broken |
| bring | brought | bringing | brought |
| buy | bought | buying | bought |
| catch | caught | catching | caught |
| choose | chose | choosing | chosen |
| come | came | coming | come |
| creep | crept | creeping | crept |
| deal | dealt | dealing | dealt |
| do | did | doing | done |
| draw | drew | drawing | drawn |
| drink | drank | drinking | drunk |
| drive | drove | driving | driven |

V

| Present (stem) | Past | Present Participle | Past Participle |
| --- | --- | --- | --- |
| eat | ate | eating | eaten |
| fall | fell | falling | fallen |
| flee | fled | fleeing | fled |
| fly | flew | flying | flown |
| forbid | forbade | forbidding | forbidden |
| forget | forgot | forgetting | forgotten |
| freeze | froze | freezing | frozen |
| get | got | getting | gotten |
| give | gave | giving | given |
| go | went | going | gone |
| grind | ground | grinding | ground |
| grow | grew | growing | grown |
| hang | hung* | hanging | hung* |
| hold | held | holding | held |
| hurt | hurt | hurting | hurt |
| know | knew | knowing | known |
| lay | laid | laying | laid |
| lead | led | leading | led |
| lend | lent | lending | lent |
| lie | lay | lying | lain |
| lose | lost | losing | lost |
| mean | meant | meaning | meant |
| mistake | mistook | mistaking | mistaken |
| ride | rode | riding | ridden |
| ring | rang | ringing | rung |
| rise | rose | rising | risen |
| run | run | running | run |
| see | saw | seeing | seen |
| seek | sought | seeking | sought |
| send | sent | sending | sent |
| shake | shook | shaking | shaken |
| shine | shone/shined | shining | shone/shined |
| sing | sang | singing | sung |
| sleep | slept | sleeping | slept |
| slide | slid | sliding | slid |
| speak | spoke | speaking | spoken |

* The past and past participle forms are *hanged* when the word is used in the sense of *executed*.

| Present (stem) | Past | Present Participle | Past Participle |
| --- | --- | --- | --- |
| spin | spun | spinning | spun |
| spill | spilt/spilled | spilling | spilled |
| spit | spat | spitting | spat |
| spread | spread | spreading | spread |
| spring | sprang | springing | sprung |
| steal | stole | stealing | stolen |
| sting | stung | stinging | stung |
| stink | stank | stinking | stunk |
| strike | struck | striking | stricken/ struck |
| swear | swore | swearing | sworn |
| swim | swam | swimming | swum |
| swing | swung | swinging | swung |
| take | took | taking | taken |
| teach | taught | teaching | taught |
| tear | tore | tearing | torn |
| thrive | throve/thrived | thriving | thrived/thriven |
| throw | threw | throwing | thrown |
| wear | wore | wearing | worn |
| weep | wept | weeping | wept |
| win | won | winning | won |
| write | wrote | writing | written |

## TEST YOURSELF ON
## Forming the Tenses of Irregular Verbs

**A**   Construct five sentences using the perfect tense of the following irregular verbs: *blow, drink, forbid, hang* (what is done to a picture on the wall), and *strike.*

**B**   Fill in the blanks in the following sentences with the correct form of the verb that is given in parentheses:

1. For almost twenty years, he had (arise) _____

   _____ early every Sunday because he had

   (sing) _____ in the church choir.

2. Every  day  he  (drink) _____ coffee  for

**V**

breakfast, but on Saturday, out of deference to his wife, he (choose) _____ tea and then (lie) _____ around reading his paper before doing the grocery shopping.

3. On some of her birthdays, her children (bring) _____ _____ her the same gifts she had (bring) _____ them on their birthdays. It was a family joke and whenever it happened she was always (shake) _____ with laughter and tears.

4. She (lay) _____ the package down on the table and, after she had (take) _____ off her hat, she (lend) _____ Susan a hand with her packages.

5. Every night after supper, Grandpa (spin) _____ _____ a yarn about the old days in Colorado while the children's faces (shine) _____ _____ with pleasure.

6. Suddenly, the dog (spring) _____ at him, but he (freeze) _____ for just a moment and the animal (flee) _____ through the bushes.

7. He had always (sleep) _____ on his side, but now with his leg injury he was (drive) _____ _____ to flip over onto his back.

8. He had (teach) _____ for a number of

years, but the whole experience had just about (grind)

_____ him down and now he wanted to be

(bear) _____ away into retirement.

9. The stories the newspapers had (write) _____

_____ about their marriage and divorce

were (forget) _____ but the whole un-

pleasant experience still (sting) _____

him.

10. He had (seek) _____ peace by buying a

little cottage on the lake, but there new and vexing problems

had (arise) _____ .

## TEST YOURSELF ON
## Forming Principal Parts

In the boxes below, some principal parts are given; others are not.
Fill in the blank spaces with the appropriate principal part. Find the
part you need by looking at the forms already filled in.

| | **Stem** | **Past** | **Present Participle** | **Past Participle** |
|---|---|---|---|---|
| 1 | | kept | | kept |
| 2 | lose | | | |
| 3 | | played | | |
| 4 | tell | | | told |
| 5 | pursue | | | |
| 6 | love | loved | | |
| 7 | | | growing | grown |

**V**

|    | Stem | Past | Present Participle | Past Participle |
|----|------|------|--------------------|-----------------|
| 8  | answer |     |                    |                 |
| 9  |      | dreamt/dreamed | dreaming |                 |
| 10 |      | tried | trying |                          |
| 11 |      |      | asking | asked                       |
| 12 |      | wanted |      |                          |
| 13 | shave |     | shaving |                        |
| 14 | walk | walked |      |                         |
| 15 |      | sewed |      |                          |
| 16 |      |      | smoking |                        |
| 17 |      | went |      |                           |
| 18 |      | hit  |      |                           |
| 19 |      |      | having |                         |
| 20 | build |     |      |                           |
| 21 |      |      | breaking |                       |
| 22 |      |      |      | seen                      |
| 23 |      |      |      | become                    |
| 24 |      | rode |      |                           |
| 25 | prove |     |      |                           |

**V**

## TEST YOURSELF ON
## Forming Tenses

Circle the form or forms appropriate to complete each of the phrases given.

*Example:* I will have *went,* ⟨*played,*⟩ *doing,* ⟨*grown,*⟩ *build*

    *I will have played* and *I will have grown* are correct.

1. I will have    *went, played, doing, grown, build*

2. She was    *giving, lose, wrote, prepared, saw*

3. They could have    *became, run, saw, operated, driven*

4. We had    *travel, happened, dreaming, walk, wish*

5. They will    *going, believed, decided, grown, punish*

6. We are not    *became, laughed, dance, jumping, buying*

7. They could be    *want, follow, requested, teach, guess*

8. This property might have been    *change, appraise, divide, rent, sold*

9. Complications could not have been    *rule, testing, know, avoided, saw*

10. Many men should have    *telephone, speaking, singing, talked, known*

11. The ordinary problem is    *say, use, suggested, going, called*

12. My son John might have been    *named, charge, singing, swearing, known*

## Using Verb Tenses Correctly

### Present Tense

The present tense indicates action taking place at the present moment:

    I *suggest* you go later.

    He *suggests** we take a walk.

    They *suggest* dinner and a movie.

---

* Note the *-s* ending on this verb. See **Subject-Verb Agreement** for information about this ending.

**V**

The present tense is also used to indicate an action that is habitual or ongoing:

This dog *bites* people.

My mother *hates* bananas.

Lucia *loves* beautiful plates.

Another form of the present tense is called the progressive present tense. Used with forms of the verb *to be*, it denotes action that is *continuing:*

I *am suggesting Reading, Writing, and Rhetoric* for my freshman students.

He *is draining* the water out of the boat.

*Note:* Substitute *suggest* for the first verb and *drains* for the second in these sentences. Can you see what is gained or lost by the changes?

### Past Tense

The past tense consists of a single form — the simple past:

I *suggested* the book.

I *wrote* my paper.

You should be careful to use the proper form of the past. This is not a problem with regular verbs (which end in *-ed* in both the past and the past participle) but it *is* a problem with irregular verbs:

**Wrong** I *rung* the bell.
**Right** I *rang* the bell.

**Wrong** He *torn* his pants.
**Right** He *tore* his pants.

### Perfect Tense

The perfect tense uses the past participle with a form of the auxiliary verb *have*. This tense denotes action begun some time in the past and continuing up to and including the present moment:

I *have written* a letter.

He *has played* basketball every day this week.

The problem in using this tense is that writers frequently use the auxiliary with the *past tense* instead of the auxiliary with the *past participle.* Again, there is no problem when the verb involved is a regular verb; there *is* a problem where the verb is irregular:

> **Wrong**  She *has wrote* her term paper.
> **Right**  She *has written* her term paper.
>
> **Wrong**  He *has rode* horses since he was a boy.
> **Right**  He *has ridden* horses since he was a boy.

### Past Perfect Tense

The past perfect tense is used to denote the earlier of two actions, both of which have taken place in the past:

> Dana *discovered* [simple past tense] that he *had taken* the wrong road. (past perfect tense for earlier action)
>
> Bill *saw* that Joanna *had rearranged* the furniture. (The *seeing* is later than the *rearranging*.)

### Future Tense

Few problems are presented by the future tense. It is formed by using the words *will* or *shall* with the present stem of the main verb:

> I *will go* tomorrow.
>
> We *shall begin* Wednesday.

*Note:* In the formal English, *shall* in the first person and *will* in the second and third person are used to express simple future:

> I shall go to the library tomorrow.
>
> Mary will go with me.

For more on this verb, see the "Glossary of Usage," **shall, will, should, would.**

### Future Perfect Tense

The future perfect tense is used to express the *earlier* of two actions, both of which will be completed in the future:

> By the time I *arrive* in Oneonta, she *will have risen.* (*Arrive* here is used to denote the *future; will have risen* denotes the earlier of the two actions.)
>
> Before I *leave* for the airport, he *will have packed* my bag. (The *leaving* must take place *after* the *packing.*)

V

## the Correct Use of Tenses

Underline the verbs in parentheses that make the sentences correct.

1. The tournament will end soon and our team (will lose, will have lost) its chance for the championship.

2. By the time the police get here, the burglar (will be, will have been) gone for half an hour.

3. When Jean (entered, had entered) the room, she saw that George (rearranged, had rearranged) the furniture.

4. I (learned, have learned) quite a lot about Shakespeare this year, and I am hoping to learn even more next year.

5. Fred was terrified that his dog (bit, had bitten) the policeman.

6. By my next birthday, I (will live, will have lived) for half a century.

7. Once I (finished, had finished) writing Volume 1, I (began, had begun) to worry about Volume 2.

8. The people we saw in the restaurant (acted, had acted) like clowns.

9. Lasagna (was, had been) my favorite pasta before I discovered macaroni.

10. When the game (ended, had ended), the stadium (closed, had closed).

11. The chairman (left, had left) the meeting before it (adjourned, had adjourned).

V

12. He (was brought up, had been brought up) on charges after we

(discovered, had discovered) his misconduct.

## Some Problems with Verbs

### 1   Final *-d* or *-ed*

Some writers make the error of omitting a final *-d* or *-ed* from past tense or past participle verb forms. It is especially important that you beware of the problem in one-syllable words, where the *-ed* ending is not likely to be sounded (as in *blamed, dreamed, missed,* and so forth). The *-ed* ending is not so frequently forgotten in words of more than one syllable, such as *completed* or *departed,* but the error is occasionally made in two-syllable words. *Supposed* and *used* (as in *I used to go to church regularly* and *I was supposed to see my analyst today*) are especially likely to be pronounced or written incorrectly.

## TEST YOURSELF ON
## the Final *-d* Sound

**A**   Pronounce the following italicized words so that the sound of the final *-d* is clearly heard by other students in the room:

1. I am *tired.*
2. He is *prejudiced.*
3. After he *arrived.*
4. The store he *owned.*
5. The lesson she *learned.*
6. He *blamed* me.
7. The meat is *weighed.*
8. Vegetables are *preferred.*
9. The defendant is *judged.*
10. Students are *graded.*
11. The army *surrendered.*
12. My song was *played.*
13. The crowd *cheered.*
14. Drowning man *saved.*
15. My pay *increased.*
16. Food is *provided.*
17. Choice is *offered.*
18. Package is *received.*
19. My heart was *deceived.*
20. I am *relieved.*

**B**   In the passage below, some words have had *-d* endings removed and some are spelled correctly. Read the passage aloud and notice how the fact that you pronounce some endings (the ones that are there) influences your pronunciation of others (ones that are *not* there). Write in endings wherever they are needed.

**V**

Something was needed to cheer me up. I was tire and hadn't been to bed in two days. I thought I would never be rescue and I was worried that even my best friends would not have notice me gone. My foot hurt a lot from when I had slip down the side of the gully and I would have given anything for a little sip of water.

A bird start to chirp. I wish I was as happy as he was. I wish I had his wings!

The accident must have happen because I wasn't as young as I use to be. Still, I was only 23! Are people suppose to lose all their agility after the age of 19? It all weighed on my heart. Suddenly, I notice that the sky was getting very dark. If anybody look for me now, they would have a hard time seeing me. I try to move a little, to see if I could climb to the crest of the hill and make myself more visible. But it was no use. I wish I had climbed up there earlier, when I had more strength.

---

### 2   Sequence of Tenses

If you are using two or more verbs in a sequence, either within a single sentence or in sentences that follow each other, it is important that you indicate precise time to the reader.

**A**   *Finite verbs* (forms expressing tense, person, number, and mood):

When the Judge *banged* his gavel, the courtroom *grew* silent.
(Both verbs in the past — both actions took place at the same time in the past.)

Although I *have complained*, I *have received* no satisfaction.
(Two perfect tenses — the actions started in the past and are continuing up to the present, in both cases.)

**V**

He *said* that he *was* a Martian. (Indirect discourse; both tenses should match—here, the past.)

By the time I *hand in* my papers, I *will have finished* the term's work. (Correct sequence for use of future perfect.)

**B** *Infinitives* (*to* forms): Use the present infinitive to indicate action that happens at the same time as or later than the main verb, and use the present perfect infinitive (*to* + *have* + past participle) for action prior to that of the main verb.

Bill *needed* [past tense] *to forget* [present infinitive]. Bill *needs* [present tense] *to forget* [present infinitive].

He *would love to have charged* his purchase. (Present perfect infinitive used for time prior to main verb.)

**C** *Participles:* To denote action happening at the same time as the action of the main verb, use the present participle. To denote action that happened prior to that of the main verb, use the present perfect participle (present participle of *have* + past participle of verb).

*Jogging* along the main road, he *noticed* many other joggers. (The *noticing* and the *jogging* take place at the same time.)

*Having mastered* geometry, he *knew* he could tackle calculus. (First came the *mastering,* then the *knowing; having mastered* is the present perfect participle.)

## TEST YOURSELF ON
## Sequence of Tenses

Underline the correct verb form in the parentheses for the sequence of tenses in each of the sentences below.

1. Because the patient's heart has begun beating, the doctors believe that the danger to his life (diminished, has diminished).

2. (Having finished, Finishing) the painting, Edward walked away from the easel.

3. They had not expected (to go, to have gone) to California last summer.

**V**

4. Pamela plans (to publish, to have published) her novel next year.

5. Arthur thought William missed the point, that he (neglected, had neglected) important issues.

6. (Having been taught, Being taught) good manners by my parents, I did not yawn when he began to speak.

7. (Reaching, Having reached) Chicago, she knew she could drive to Montana.

8. When they (visited, have visited) Italy, they never ate a poor meal.

9. Allan regretted (being born, having been born) handsome instead of rich.

10. Beth wanted (to read, to have read) the books in sequence.

11. Dan insisted that he (once saw, had once seen) a drunken Irishman.

12. (Teaching English, Having taught English), she thought she knew grammar.

---

**3   Could of, being that, would have**

Never use the expression *could of*. It is an approximation of what some writers hear when they say *could have* or *could've*.

> **Wrong**   He *could of* gone with me to the movies.
> **Right**   He *could have* gone with me to the movies.

The same holds true for the forms *would of* and *should of* and any other *of*.

Never use the expression *being that* for *since* or *because*.

> **Wrong**   *Being that* he was just a kid, I helped him across the street.
> **Right**   *Because* he was just a kid, I helped him across the street.

**V**

Never use the expression *would have* in place of *had*.

**Wrong**  If he *would have* done well on his GRE's, he would have been admitted to graduate school.
**Right**  If he *had* done well on his GRE's, he would have been admitted to graduate school.

## 4   The Subjunctive Mood

The subjunctive mood expresses actions or states of being that are contrary to fact, wishful, imaginary, or not yet actualities. Current English usage has found substitute expressions for virtually all uses of the subjunctive:

| | |
|---|---|
| If he *were* to leave | If he *leaves* |
| I imagine he *be* young. | I imagine he *is* young. |
| I wish I *were* finished. | I wish I *was* finished. |

Nevertheless, there are a few circumstances in which the subjunctive is required usage.

**A**   In contrary-to-fact propositions:

He was eating the pizza as if there *were* nothing else on his mind.
I wish you *were* here.

**B**   Where clarity is urgently needed:

I insist that the barn *be* painted red. (Substituting *is* for *be* makes the sentence say something entirely different, i.e., that the speaker insists the color of the barn *is already* red.)

**C**   In certain *that* clauses:

He moved that the meeting *be* adjourned.
The student asked that he *be* given an oral examination.
Is it right that a woman *suffer* just because she is a woman?
It is necessary that justice *be* done.

The subjunctive also persists in certain idiomatic expressions:

Peace *be* with you.
*Be* that as it may.
*Be* it ever so humble, there's no place like home.

V

## TEST YOURSELF ON
# the Correct Use of Verb Forms

**A** In each of the sentences below, some form of *could, should, would,* or *being* is misused. Correct the errors.

1. If he would have gone earlier, he would have seen the pregame show.

2. Being that it had the best psychology program she could find, she went to Jefferson College.

3. I could of been a star.

4. She wasn't as alert as she should of been.

5. If he had gone earlier, he would of seen the pregame show.

**B** For each italicized verb form in the sentences that follow, supply the correct subjunctive form.

1. It is necessary that justice *is* done.

2. He was eating as if there *was* no tomorrow.

3. He suggested that their lunch date *is* postponed until the following week.

4. Is it right that a man *suffers* for someone else's crime?

5. My brother asked that he *is* given the car tomorrow.

# Voice

Most verbs can be used in either the active or the passive voice.

> ***Active Voice*** John *saw* his son yesterday.
> ***Passive Voice*** John *was seen* by his son yesterday.

The subject of both sentences is *John*. In the first (active voice) sentence, *John* is performing the action; in the second sentence, *John* is undergoing the action.

In English, the active voice is more vigorous and more emphatic than the passive voice. Beginning writers frequently find their sentences slipping into the passive voice because they are not quite sure what they want to emphasize.

> **Passive**   These fancy jeans *were bought* by me at the Clothes Barn.

> **Active**   I *bought* these fancy jeans at the Clothes Barn.

These sentences convey the same information, but each emphasizes a different thing. The passive emphasizes the *fancy jeans* (because *jeans* is in the subject position in the sentence) and the active emphasizes *I*. The passive sentence also requires two more words to say the same thing that the active sentence says. The passive sentence is also made awkward because of the *by me* phrase.

We emphasize that the active voice is the stronger and therefore the preferred choice because beginning writers, as well as more experienced ones, are frequently evasive in their use of the passive voice. The use of the active voice corrects this tendency.

### Evasion by a Beginning Writer
Tutoring help in algebra *is needed* by Al. (The sentence reads as if the writer were a little reluctant to mention Al's name, so he has delayed saying that name as long as possible.)

### Evasiveness Corrected by Using the Active Voice
Al *needs* tutoring in algebra.

### Evasion by a More Experienced Writer
It *has been decided* that your application *will not be considered* at this time. (The evasion here is that no decision maker is named.)

### Evasiveness Corrected by Using the Active Voice
We *have decided* not to consider your application.

Of course, there are circumstances where the use of the passive voice is appropriate.

**1**   Use of the passive voice when the doer of the action is not known.

> The making of bronze *was begun* in Southwest Asia around 2500 B.C.

> A fire *was set* in an abandoned warehouse on Pier 88 this morning.

**V**

It is easy to see why the specific doer in the first of these examples — the person who began to make bronze — is not known. In the second, the opening sentence of a newspaper story, it is clear that the person who set the fire is unknown. Nor would this sentence be improved if the author had written something like "Somebody set a fire . . ." or "A person or persons unknown set a fire. . . ."

**2**   Use the passive voice when it is more important to emphasize the receiver than the doer of the action.

> The vote on the Equal Rights Amendment *was* not *taken* until midnight.

> My vegetable garden *was ruined* by the heavy rainstorm in April, but it *was replanted* in time to give us enough vegetables to last the summer.

In the first sentence, the vote on the amendment is much more important than those who voted. In the second, the rainstorm is unimportant compared to the garden (in the first clause), and the people who replanted it less important than the garden itself (referred to by the pronoun *it* in the second clause).

*Nevertheless,* you should beware of using weakly or evasively passive sentences in a consistent pattern in your work. Sentences such as "This class *was taken* by me last semester" and "My car *was smashed into* by a truck" can only make your writing weak and uninteresting.

## TEST YOURSELF ON
## the Appropriate Use of the Active Voice

**A**   Change each of the following passive sentences into an active one.

1. I was bored by the book.
2. Dr. Waldhorn is respected by his patients.
3. Everyone on my block is annoyed by Joe's dog.
4. The rich and the famous are admired by most people.
5. The police are angered by disrespect.
6. Financial aid is hoped for by all students.
7. Milk cows are given special care by dairy farmers.

8. Paying bills in an inflationary economy is disliked by every-body.
9. Help is urgently needed by the earthquake victims.
10. Subway riders are exhausted by rush hour traffic.

**B** Some of the sentences below use the passive voice appropriately. Next to these, write C. Where the passive voice is either weak or evasive, recast the sentence into the active voice.

1. _____ It is thought by my mother that I'm too young to drive.

2. _____ The Montreal Canadiens were badly beaten by the Boston Bruins at the Montreal Forum last night.

3. _____ Freedom was given to us by God.

4. _____ The ring was given to me for Christmas by my brother.

5. _____ Television is watched by more and more people in this country.

6. _____ Crime is feared more by people in the cities than by people in the country.

7. _____ The labels on canned foods are not read by shoppers in supermarkets.

8. _____ While the kids were being filled with Cokes at the fountain, the car was being filled with gas.

9. _____ It is forbidden to feed the animals.

10. _____ The victims of the two-car crash were taken to the hospital by ambulance.

11. _____ The fuse was ignited.

12. _____ Hot cereal was eaten for breakfast by Jake.

**V**

# Wordiness

Direct expression is best. Wordiness, the use of more words than necessary, defeats directness. A good rule is to use as few words as possible but as many as necessary to say what you mean. Below are listed some of the writing faults that cause wordiness; discussed under each heading are ways of making your writing more economical.

## Redundancy: The Elimination of Deadwood

*Redundancy* means "needless repetition." Examine your writing carefully to make sure you are not being redundant.

**1**    Transform your clauses into phrases and your phrases into single words wherever possible. What you eliminate is called *deadwood.*

> **Unnecessary Clause**    The professor, *who teaches mathematics,* was angry.
> **Revised**    The professor *of mathematics* was angry.
> **Revised**    The *mathematics* professor was angry.
>
> **Unnecessary Phrase**    She was lovely *in appearance.*
> **Revised**    She was lovely.
>
> **Deadwood**    After the concert had come to a close, we went to dinner.
> **Revised**    After the concert, we went to dinner.
>
> **Deadwood**    I am learning the skill of how to do the work of the job.
> **Revised**    I am learning how to do the job.
>
> **Deadwood**    The driver of the truck was angry.
> **Revised**    The truck driver was angry.

**2**    Eliminate "twofers" from your writing. A *twofer* is the use of two words that mean virtually the same imprecise thing where a single more accurate word, or one of the pair, will do.

> **Twofer**    He was a *real* and *true* friend.
> **Revised**    He was a *genuine* friend.
>
> **Twofer**    The *light* and the *brightness* were dazzling.
> **Revised**    The *sun* was dazzling.

**W**

***Twofer***   I had a lot of *love* and *regard* for her.
***Revised***   I *cared* for her very much.

***Twofer***   She gave me a *warm* and *friendly* smile.
***Revised***   She gave me a *friendly* smile.

**3**   Eliminate words that needlessly repeat what you have already said. *He made revised changes in his book* has a needless repetition. The sentence should read either *He made changes in his book* or *He revised his book.*

***Repetitious***   A hermit is someone who is isolated by himself.
***Revised***   A hermit is someone who is isolated.

***Repetitious***   The animals' roars were audible to the ear.
***Revised***   The animals' roars were audible.

***Repetitious***   Her shawl was a deep red in color.
***Revised***   Her shawl was deep red.

***Repetitious***   The assignments he gave were several in number.
***Revised***   He gave several assignments.

**4**   Do not use several words where one will do. Eliminate from your writing any long-winded expressions you have acquired.

***Long-winded***   *In this day and age* [or, *in this modern world*], people have increased expectations of prosperity.
***Better***   *Today,* people have increased expectations of prosperity.

***Long-winded***   *It should be noticed* that few cocktail party conversations manage to avoid the subject of computers.
***Better***   *Notice* that few cocktail party conversations manage to avoid the subject of the computer.

***Long-winded***   *As far as* Harry *is concerned,* he drinks too much.
***Better***   Harry drinks too much.

## TEST YOURSELF ON
## Eliminating Redundancies

The following sentences all contain some kind of redundancy. Correct each one by eliminating the redundancy.

1. John is an expert in the field of urban government.
2. Professor Buckley referred back to the Civil War.
3. The snow which fell yesterday is melting into water today.
4. At 9 a.m. in the morning, the driver started to drive toward Cincinnati.

**W**

5. As soon as he started to look for a job, he connected up with a large corporation.
6. I'm going to repeat again what I said a moment ago.
7. As far as reading is concerned, I would say that it is a difficult thing for me to do.
8. Most students spend the majority of the hours in each school day attending classes for which they are registered.
9. Although he seemed to be a warm and friendly man, I didn't care for him or like him for some reason.
10. It was not exactly a meaningful or worthwhile experience.

## Awkward Repetition

Effective repetition of words can make for emphasis. Awkward repetition is merely wordy: It makes for dullness.

> ***Awkward***   The *driver drove* steadily; his *driving* made us feel safe.
> ***Revised***   The driver was steady; his skill made us feel safe.
>
> ***Awkward***   My *membership* application was accepted by the club and I was made a *member.*
> ***Revised***   The club accepted my membership application.
>
> ***Awkward***   If *one examines* the *case, one can* see that it is *one* of the *cases* that *cannot* stand close *examination.*
> ***Revised***   The case cannot stand close examination.
>
> ***Effective Repetition***   The average politician has a *sinister* past, a *sinister* attitude, and a *sinister* plan for the future.
> ***Effective Repetition***   *New* mouthwash, *new* deodorant, *new* toothpaste, *new* teeth — television sells them all with equal enthusiasm.

## Wordy Formulas

Eliminate from your writing phrases such as *to be, there is, it is, the type of, the fact that, the use of.* These can just as well be left out of most sentences.

> ***Wordy***   She seems *to be* sad this morning. (Read the sentence without the italicized portion and notice that nothing is lost.)
> ***Wordy***   Higher mathematics appears *to be* difficult.
> ***Wordy***   The cowboy was considered *to be* a hero.
>
> ***Wordy***   *There is* something I have to say.
> ***Revised***   I have something to say.

**W**

> **Wordy**  *It is* the truth that is important.
> **Revised**  The truth is important.
>
> **Wordy**  I got *the type* of job I wanted.
> **Revised**  I got the job I wanted.
>
> **Wordy**  Because of *the fact that* it was raining, we couldn't play the game.
> **Revised**  Because it was raining, we couldn't play the game.
>
> **Wordy**  His *use of* English is bad.
> **Revised**  His English is bad.

## Passive Voice

By using the active instead of the passive voice, you can eliminate words and create a more vigorous style.

> **Passive**  Anxiety about examinations *is felt* by some students.
> **Active**  Some students *feel* anxious about examinations.
>
> **Passive**  The holiday *was enjoyed* by everybody.
> **Active**  Everybody *enjoyed* the holiday.

## Complicated Diction

Eliminate complicated diction from your writing. Invariably, the fancy way to say something requires more words than the plain way and is not more effective.

> **Fancy**  It is my intention to make a careful scrutiny of the record.
> **Plain**  I plan to look closely at the record.
>
> **Fancy**  I observed that his behavior was somewhat less than intelligent.
> **Plain**  I saw that he was acting foolish.

## TEST YOURSELF ON
## Eliminating Wordiness

Each of the following sentences contains awkward repetitions, wordy formulas, wordy passive voice constructions, or complicated diction. Correct each by using straightforward, active language.

1. The important subject of my speech will be a subject important to students, educators, and others to whom the subject is of professional interest.

**W**

2. It should be made clear to everyone that utmost silence is necessary while working in the library.
3. Whenever he's in trouble, he makes use of rationalization.
4. There is a special beach I'd like to take you to.
5. It is a terrible thing to be chronically sick.
6. That point was made by Darwin.
7. He is the type of person unaware of the fact that people in this modern day and age are unhappy.
8. Because of the fact that we used logic, we solved the problem and came up with the solution.
9. George is known to be moody.
10. Some of the best times we had were when we were on vacation.

## PART 3

The Research Paper

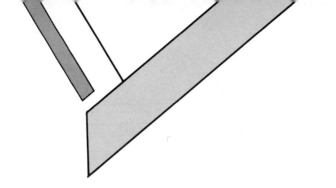

# The Nature of the Research Paper

If you were assigned to write a paper on your life, you would simply reach into your memory for the necessary information. If an assignment asked you to describe the physical landscape of your town or neighborhood, again you would have no difficulty: You'd simply wake up your perceptions, take a good long look, and start making notes. In both these writing assignments, you would of course be asked to come to some conclusion, to develop a point of view about your information. Essays not under the control of a central idea or thesis statement — facts without a conclusion — are dull stuff.

The research paper differs from these assignments in that you are asked to gather the information you need not from your own perceptions or memory but — by means of an active and systematic search — either from library resources or through a direct investigation of some aspect of experience. The research paper is similar to the others in that here, too, you are asked to come to a conclusion about your facts — to develop a thesis statement.

You'll be able to do this because after completing your research you should be something of an expert in your field — more of one than your instructor or anyone in your class.

# Finding and Narrowing a Topic

If your instructor hands you a ready-made topic, you may skip this section. In general, however, instructors are likely to ask you to participate in the search for one. It's an invigorating exercise, for one thing; but more important is that your participation will lead you to a topic that excites your interest and that will produce a more interesting paper.

## Limiting the Range of Topics

To begin the search, you should understand the limitations that govern the selection of a topic.

**1** Certain subjective topics are not good choices. For example, it is futile to look for facts that will determine whether Michael Jackson is a better musician than Elton John, or Walt Whitman a better poet than T. S. Eliot. Such judgments depend not on research but on taste.

**2** Topics that are too recent should be avoided. It takes time to develop the good evidence and careful thought that produce useful writing on a subject. If your topic is too recent, you won't find too much on it in the library.

**3** Topics that rely on a single source should be eliminated. You can gather all you need to know about photosynthesis or steel manufacturing from a single source. Therefore, these are not good topics because one object of the research paper is to offer the writer practice in using and synthesizing many sources.

**4** Topics that call for the direct investigation of some private aspect of your experience are also poor choices. To interview all your relatives for their impressions of you at various stages in your development so that you can research how your character was formed — that may be fun, but its appeal to a reader is doubtful.

**5** The length of the usual college research paper — 1,500 to 2,000 words — will also limit your choice of a topic. You cannot, for example, fit a biography of Ronald Reagan into a paper of that length. Nor can you do an adequate job in that space on the conflicts causing so much turmoil in the Middle East. The size of your topic must be appropriate to the space limits set by your instructor.

**6** You will also be limited by your choice of a purpose. That is, do you wish to write a paper that is informative, analytic, or argumentative? Although a paper on Abraham Lincoln's military service would have a point of view or thesis statement, it would argue nothing — only inform. A paper on the slang used by teenagers in your hometown or neighborhood would naturally analyze — that is, it would dissect the meanings of words and come to some conclusions about patterns of speech and dialect. Finally, an argumentative research paper might undertake to show that its position was correct — for example, that capital punishment does not deter potential murders.

Informative purposes also generate papers that qualify as market research, that is, those papers that, relying on questionnaires, interviews, sampling, and testing, develop information useful for the production of new consumer products. Allied to market research are technical studies that produce information for industry and business — for example, a study that gives information on traffic flow in and around two adjacent towns for the purpose of deciding where a shopping mall might be best situated. A computer-generated research paper also qualifies as informative. It asks you to generate and organize data in the most useful ways for a variety of purposes.

## Exploring Your Interests

Now that you understand these limitations, how to proceed? There are two ways, both based on exploring your own interests.

**1**   If you have a question about something — Why are they fighting in Northern Ireland? Why did President Truman drop the atomic bomb instead of first demonstrating its power? — you are very far along toward a topic *and* a thesis statement. The answers to those questions will be thesis statements for the paper; simply research the answers.

**2**   If you have an interest in a large subject area, such as John F. Kennedy or China or language, you're not quite so far along but are at least ready to start narrowing your subject down.

## Narrowing the Topic

Here are some ways that subjects might get narrowed down:

*China* — education in China — grammar school education in China — the kindergarten curriculum in China — kindergarten reading texts in China — the content of kindergarten reading texts in China — *the political content of kindergarten reading texts in China*

*John F. Kennedy* — the presidency of John F. Kennedy — foreign policy during the presidency of John F. Kennedy — foreign policy toward Communist countries during the presidency of John F. Kennedy—*President Kennedy's decision in the Cuban missile crisis of 1962*

*Language*—the English language—the English language in the United States—the language of Boston, Mass.—the language of Cambridge in Boston—the language of teenagers in Cambridge—the vocabulary of teenagers living on Lancaster Street in Cambridge—*the slang vocabulary of teenagers living on Lancaster Street in Cambridge*

The last (italicized) strings of words in each example are suitable topics. But how do we get there? Is it as easy as it looks? Not quite. But the following suggestions may make the job easier.

**1** Notice that each successive term in an example *qualifies* the preceding term, makes it more precise, focuses it. Try doing free-writing on your subject with the aim of adding qualifications to the successive terms, as in the examples.

**2** Consult somebody you think is an expert in the field. Ask that person about narrower topics within the subject area you're thinking of. For example, if you're interested in art, ask an artist or an art teacher what you can learn about the subject through research.

**3** Do some preliminary reading in your broad subject area. See what details you find that stir your interest in some specific corner of the subject or that suggest specific questions whose answers you'd like to know.

**4** Ask yourself some questions about the subject area. Any sort of question will do; it's not easy to get to *the* question, the one your paper will answer, but even odd questions will keep your mind running toward possible pay dirt.

**5** Do this preliminary work with a pencil or pen in hand. Simply sitting in a chair thinking is not conducive to bringing together ideas that will set off sparks. Writing things down *is*.

The topic-selection stage does not necessarily go smoothly, so persistence here is crucial. This stage more or less comes to a close when you have finally whittled your large subject area down to a manageable one and can formulate a good research question for yourself.

## Formulating a Research Question

A good research question for the paper on China might be, How do the Chinese begin to indoctrinate their citizens into their political system? The Kennedy paper might answer the question, What major considerations went into Kennedy's decision to institute the Cuban missile blockade? The primary research undertaken for the language paper would probably answer a question such as, What linguistic operations and dialectical considerations govern the kinds of slang used by teenagers on Lancaster Street in Cambridge?

## Additional Sources for Ideas

If after exploring your interest in a large subject area and trying the narrowing process, you are still not satisfied that you've found a topic, you must work harder at the search. You need to be continually *active* in your search by making such inquiries as these:

**1** Go over notes for other courses. What issues, people, or events puzzle you or excite your interest? Are there problems in anthropology, history, sociology that stick in your memory?

**2** Look at your neighborhood or community: What aspects of these places are you curious about? Is there a problem on the streets or on the farm or in the town that you notice and care about?

**3** Read a newspaper from cover to cover every day for as long as it takes you to uncover some group, person, or event that excites or interests you. Begin to work with one of these.

**4** Ask for an appointment with one of your instructors. Explain your problem and see if the instructor can suggest a broad area of interest.

Finally, let us repeat, only your *active* search can land you a topic — and the sooner the better.

## TEST YOURSELF ON
## Identifying or Narrowing Down to a Suitable Topic

Listed below are a number of possible topics. If you think one is suitable, mark it with a check. If not, mark it with an X. In either case, be prepared to explain your judgment. Decide which unsuitable topics could be successfully narrowed down to make good ones. Do some preliminary reading on the topics; consult both your instructor and the list of texts on pages 308–316 for reading suggestions. Then narrow down the broad subjects until they are appropriate research paper topics.

1. How bees make honey.
2. The energy crisis in the United States.
3. Abraham Lincoln's military service.
4. The kinds of food ordered by the lunch crowd at MacDonald's between 1 and 2 P.M.
5. The voting habits of the people in your neighborhood or community.
6. Norman Lear's situation comedies: what they have in common.
7. Mohammed and Jesus.
8. The Mormon settlement of Salt Lack City.
9. How Geraldine Ferraro was chosen to run with Walter Mondale in 1984.
10. Symbolism in dreams.
11. Gas rationing during World War II.
12. The significance of agribusiness to American farming.
13. The bombing of the American Embassy in Beirut, Lebanon, 1984.
14. The job market in America for graduates of the class of 1986.
15. Computer-generated statistical profile of rural New Mexico family with mean state income (from U.S. Census).

# Research Tools

## Direct Investigations

Some instructors will permit you to do direct research on some aspect of experience.* A variety of interesting papers can be written reporting on the results of research into such features of the public landscape as advertising (both television and print); television programming; the opinions, values, ideas, politics, and future plans of various campus groups — professors, administrators, art majors, or pre-med students — or off-campus populations.

* In a course like this, you will probably not be permitted to do scientific research.

The principal research instruments used in projects like these are the *interview,* the *questionnaire,* and the *survey.*

### The Interview

The advantage of the interview is that you can ask follow-up questions. The difficulty is that you must think on your feet and be ready to respond to what your subject says. So a careful plan is necessary: You must prepare a good set of questions keyed to what you want to know, along with several follow-up questions based on anticipated responses. For interviews, it is best to use a tape recorder, but ask permission first. For neat record keeping, identify the interview by name of subject and date of interview.

### The Survey

A survey is a measurement, and you can make measurements with various kinds of rulers. For example, you can survey the kind and quality of television programming on a particular station or during specific viewing hours. You could also survey ads that appear in the print media. By analyzing a specific number of, say, full-page ads from a single source, you could measure the kinds of appeals that are being made to sell particular items to particular age groups. The survey can be presented in tabular form; the research paper can first justify the procedure of the survey and then go on to explain the results depicted in the table.

### The Questionnaire

The advantages of the questionnaire are that (1) it permits anonymity for the subject and perhaps therefore a greater willingness to respond, and (2) it accommodates the kind of answer that can be treated numerically; a number of questionnaires can be handed out and the results tabulated. A questionnaire is a kind of interview; the possibilities for answers are limited, but some researchers think materials from questionnaires are easier to obtain and work with than materials from interviews. Using shrewdly worded questionnaires, you could do projects to analyze the plans, opinions, tastes, and professional objectives of the members of various groups on campus or elsewhere.

## Primary and Secondary Sources

Materials such as interviews, questionnaire answers, and survey results are called *primary sources.* Also falling into this category are plays, novels, and poems; letters, diaries, journals, and speeches; eyewitness accounts; certain official documents; scientific findings, market research, and other kinds of informational research. Primary sources are the first-hand documents of experience.

*Secondary sources* are those which comment upon and analyze primary sources. Secondary sources include books, magazine and newspaper articles, encyclopedia entries, and any other works that inquire into, analyze, or argue about your topic.

Whenever possible, you should use a primary source. The use of primary sources enlivens and enriches your paper by bringing the reader closer to the experience you're writing about; secondary sources are one step removed from that experience.

## Preliminary Reading: A List of General Reference Works

Below are listed a number of works in which you may begin your preliminary reading. By reading general material about your topic, you gain a broad acquaintance with your field, get some help with narrowing the topic, and acquire suggestions for further reading.

If you can't find a title in these lists that fits your needs, ask your librarian for help, or consult the standard work in the field, Eugene P. Sheehy's *Guide to Reference Books*, 9th edition. (Many of the annotations are based on details given in Sheehy.)

### Agriculture

*Cyclopedia of American Agriculture.* 4 vols. A popular survey of agriculture in the United States and Canada, covering such topics as crops, livestock, machinery, statistics on productivity.

### Arts (Architecture, Dance, Drama, Film, and Music)

*Art Dictionary.* A compendium of terms used in painting, sculpture, architecture, heraldry, and so on. Many of the definitions are accompanied by illustrations.

*Dance Encyclopedia.* Revised and enlarged edition. Numerous articles on all phases of the dance, from the so-called primitive to the most sophisticated modern and ballet.

*Dictionary of Architecture and Building: Biographical, Historical and Descriptive.* 3 vols. Many specialists write on all aspects of these subjects; covers the United States and foreign countries; profusely illustrated.

*Dictionary of Films.* Lists casts, plots, production information, and critical status of more than 1,300 important American and foreign films.

*Dictionary of Filmmakers.* Biographical sketches and filmographies of important film artists (actors, directors, producers, cameramen) from the beginnings of the art to 1971.

*Encyclopedia of Folk, Country and Western Music.* Covers the development and aesthetics of these branches of popular music.

*Encyclopedia of Jazz.* Biographies of over 2,000 jazz performers from the beginnings through 1959; history of jazz on records; discography and bibliography.

*Encyclopedia of Painting: Painters and Painting of the World from Prehistoric Times to the Present Day.* Illustrated one-volume encyclopedia of art, artists, styles, and so forth.

*Grove's Dictionary of Music and Musicians.* 5th ed. 10 vols. Articles on music, forms, styles, instruments — and musicians of all periods.

*New York Times Film Reviews.* Collects all this newspaper's film reviews from 1913 to 1970; contains index of titles, names of people associated with films, and awards.

*Oxford Companion to the Theatre.* Complete coverage of all aspects of theater in all countries of the world — plays, theaters, actors, scenery, etc.

### Biography

*Chambers's Biographical Dictionary.* Gives brief biographies of the more famous people who have ever lived in the world — includes kings, queens, princes.

*Current Biography.* 37 vols. and supplements. Valuable source of biographical data on people who have recently made some achievement.

*Dictionary of American Biography.* 20 vols. and supplements. Biographies of noted Americans no longer living.

*Dictionary of National Biography.* 22 vols. and supplements. The British equivalent of the preceding work.

*Who's Who in America.* Appears biennially. The companion is *Who Was Who in America.*

### Computers and Computer Technology

*Computer Dictionary and Handbook.* Gives 22,000 definitions and explanations of concepts as well as data on programming, model building, flowcharts, logic, and much else.

*Computer Filing of Index, Bibliographic and Catalog Entries.* On the processing of data for storage and management.

*Computer Literature Bibliography, 1946–1967.* 2 vols. in 1. Lists literature on computers and computer technology for the years indicated.

*Computer Programming Handbook.* Strong on the techniques and languages of programming, especially FORTRAN.

*Computer-Readable Bibliographic Data Bases: A Directory and Sourcebook.* Basic and complete information on some 300 data bases available to computer users.

*Computer Yearbook.* An annual that gives updated basic information on such elementary matters as state of the art, new programming and applications, financial health of the industry, employment opportunities and personnel in the world of computers, and more.

*Condensed Computer Encyclopedia.* Alphabetically arranged definitions of computer terms and concepts, with a bibliography, intended for the nonspecialist.

*Encyclopedia of Computer Science and Technology.* 14 vols. With an *Index* published separately, this is the exhaustive work on every aspect of computers.

*A Guide to Computer Literature.* 2nd ed. This is an authoritative list of works up to 1972 on all phases of the subject.

*Microcomputer Dictionary and Guide.* Thorough coverage of its special subject, the small or family or home or work-station computer.

*On-Line Database Search Services Directory.* Printed in two parts in 1983 and 1984. The two volumes list the essential data for more than 1,200 databases.

### Current Events

*Britannica Book of the Year.* Alphabetically arranged review of the past year. Contains detailed articles on a cross section of topics, written by specialists; many charts, tables, photographs.

*Facts on File.* A weekly digest of world news, with annual index;

useful compendium of events in politics, science, sports, education, and so on.

*Statesman's Yearbook.* Gives current information — including statistics and some historical data — about all the countries of the
world.

*Statistical Abstract of the United States.* Statistics of every imagin-
able kind on the status and activities of United States citizens.

*World Almanac and Book of Facts.* A one-volume work that reports
international statistical information. Also contains short essays
on various topics and biographical sketches of important people.
Arranged by subject.

## Ecology

*The Ecology Action Guide.* Discusses man's influence on nature and
the accretion of pollutants and suggests courses of action.

*The Environment Index.* An annual published since 1971; gives
references to the literature.

*Environmental Conservation.* 3rd ed. Discussions of natural resources and the principles involved in their conservation.

*A Guide to the Study of Terrestrial Ecology.* Articles on the environment and experimental work in ecosystems.

*Man's Impact on Terrestrial and Oceanic Ecosystems.* Articles on
various aspects of these subjects; includes bibliographies.

*Wildlife in Danger.* Contains short, detailed articles about endan-
gered species and some on the verge of extinction. Discusses
natural habitats, physical characteristics, ecological status of the
animals; includes many photographs and illustrations.

## Education

*Dictionary of Education.* Gives definitions of technical and professional terms. It defines common foreign terms; cross-refer-
enced.

*Encyclopedia of Education.* 10 vols. More than 1,000 signed articles dealing with various aspects of education: history, institutions, theory, philosophy, and so on.

*Encyclopedia of Educational Research.* Contains articles by educators on the latest developments in the field of education.

*World Survey of Education.* 4 vols. A publication of UNESCO:
covers all levels of education, arranged by countries of the
world.

### Ethnic Studies

*Black Studies: A Bibliography.* A guide to the literature.

*Directory of Afro-American Resources.* Gives a list of primary sources — documents, diaries, papers, narratives — available through organizations and institutions in the United States.

*Ethnic Studies in Higher Education: State of the Art and Bibliography.* Gives general information, sources, research issues on blacks, Chicanos, Asian-Americans, Native Americans, Puerto Rican and other Spanish-speaking peoples, and various white ethnic groups.

*Mexican Americans: A Research Bibliography.* 2 vols. A computer-assisted bibliography that covers the whole subject by theme and topic.

*Minority Studies: A Selective Annotated Bibliography.* Gives select materials available through 1974 on a rich selection of American minorities, including Hawaiians, Filipinos, Japanese, Chinese, blacks, Spanish-Americans, and Native Americans.

*The Puerto Ricans: An Annotated Bibliography.* Arranged by topic, covers history, geography, current status.

*Reference Encyclopedia of the American Indian.* 2nd ed. 2 vols. A guide to sources of information about Native Americans. Includes a who's who and bibliographies.

### History

*Cambridge Ancient History.* 12 vols. Immensely detailed history of the Western world from the beginnings through the middle of the 4th century A.D.

*Cambridge Medieval History.* 8 vols. The same for the Medieval period, to the beginning of the Renaissance.

*Chronology of the Modern World, 1763 to the Present Time.* This and a companion volume, *Chronology of the Expanding World, 1492–1762,* cover the history of all areas from Columbus onward.

*Dictionary of American History.* 7 vols. plus supplement. Consists of short articles on all aspects of American history.

*An Encyclopedia of World History.* 5th ed., rev. and enl. A one-volume treatment of world events.

*Harvard Guide to American History.* rev. ed. 2 vols. A guide to research; methods and resources; contains valuable bibliographies arranged by periods.

*New Cambridge Modern History.* 14 vols. A detailed history from the Renaissance onward.

### Literature and Mythology

*Cambridge History of American Literature.* 4 vols. From the Colonial through the modern period, ending in the 1930s.

*Cambridge History of English Literature.* 15 vols. From the Anglo-Saxon beginnings through the modern period, ending in the 1930s.

*Columbia Dictionary of Modern European Literature.* Begins at the end of the nineteenth century and gives critical commentary on many works of the modern period.

*Everyman's Dictionary of Non-Classical Mythology.* Emphasizes non-Western mythology.

*Funk & Wagnall's Standard Dictionary of Folklore, Mythology and Legend.* 2 vols. Covers the mythologies of the world. (1972 ed. is 1 vol.; it is a reissue of the 1949–50 ed. with minor corrections.)

*The Golden Bough.* 12 vols. (Also available in one-volume edition.) An exhaustive study of mythology.

*Mythology of all Races.* 13 vols. Mythologies in very great detail.

*New Larousse Encyclopedia of Mythology.* Essays on world mythologies.

*Oxford Classical Dictionary.* 2nd ed. Good brief articles on classical subjects.

### Philosophy

*Encyclopedia of Philosophy.* 8 vols. Contains entries on both Western and Eastern philosophers and philosophies.

*History of Western Philosophy.* An excellent overview by a noted philosopher, Bertrand Russell.

*How to Find Out in Philosophy and Psychology.* A guide, for undergraduates, to research methods in these fields.

### Political Science

*Cyclopedia of American Government.* 3 vols. Brief articles on all aspects of government in the United States from the founding to the early twentieth century.

*Dictionary of American Politics.* A one-volume compendium of aspects and figures of American politics.

*International Encyclopedia of the Social Sciences.* 17 vols. Longer articles on political movements and ideas — as well as on comprehensive subjects in the social sciences.

*Palgrave's Dictionary of Political Economy.* 3 vols. Reprints of classic articles on economics as it relates to politics.

### Religion

*Book of Saints.* 5th ed. A dictionary of canonized saints, together with a calendar of their days and brief biographies.

*A Dictionary of Angels, Including the Fallen Angels.* Information about all the angels and angelology.

*Dictionary of the Bible.* Entries on people and places mentioned in the Bible.

*Encyclopedia of the Jewish Religion.* A compendium of information on theology and history of Jewish religion.

*Encyclopaedia of Religion and Ethics.* 13 vols. Very detailed articles on all aspects.

*History of Religions.* 2 vols. Detailed accounts of the rise of religions in Europe, Asia, and the Near East.

*New Catholic Encyclopedia.* 15 vols. Treats every aspect of Catholicism in great detail.

*Scared Books of the East.* 50 vols. Contains translations of the major works of the seven non-Christian religions that have influenced Asian culture. The *Concise Dictionary of Eastern Religion* is an index to these volumes.

### Science

*Britannica Yearbook of Science and the Future.* Annual; gives the latest scientific developments — with illustrations.

*The Dictionary of the Biological Sciences* and *Encyclopedia of the Biological Sciences.* 2nd ed. Together, these cover all aspects of the field.

*Famous First Facts.* 3rd ed. A record of discoveries and inventions in the United States, with dates and descriptions.

*History of Magic and Experimental Science.* 8 vols. Details the history and development of the experimental sciences and ideas of magic which at one time or another served a scientific function.

*McGraw-Hill Encyclopedia of Science and Technology: An International Reference Work.* 15 vols. Supplemented by the *McGraw-*

*Hill Yearbook of Comprehensive Science and Technology.* Contains general and specific essays dealing with every branch of science and technology. Biographical and historical material is not included. Psychology and medicine are treated only in their preprofessional aspects.

*Van Nostrand's Scientific Encyclopedia.* 5th ed. A one-volume compendium of inclusive scientific knowledge.

### Social Sciences

*Anthropology Today: An Encyclopedic Inventory.* Extensive bibliographies of work in this field up to 1952; gives the range and extent of the whole field.

*Dictionary of Psychology.* rev. ed. Defines terms and gives foreign equivalents.

*Handbook for Social Research in Urban Areas.* A guide to research on urban sociological themes; bibliographies.

*History of Psychiatry; An Evaluation of Psychiatric Thought and Practice from Prehistoric Times to the Present.* A comprehensive review of ideas and developments in the field.

*International Encyclopedia of the Social Sciences.* 17 vols. A comprehensive set of articles on all aspects of the social sciences.

### Women's Studies

*American Women: The Official Who's Who Among the Women of the Nation.* 3 vols. Published from 1935–1940. A valuable source of biographies of accomplished women of the period.

*The Book of Women's Achievements.* A list of these achievements and notes on the achievers, arranged by area of work.

*Female Studies.* 6 vols. College syllabi for study; reading lists; a review of women's studies.

*Index to Women of the World from Ancient to Modern Times.* A list; brief biographies, bibliographies.

*Research Guide in Women's Studies.* A valuable guide to writing research papers in this field.

*Women and Society: A Critical Review of the Literature with a Selected Annotated Bibliography.* The title is accurate.

*Women and Sport.* Bibliography of research involving female subjects.

*Women's Rights Almanac.* State-by-state lists giving information sources and other resources of interest to women; discussions of legal issues important to women.

*The World Who's Who of Women*. Published from time to time; gives brief biographies of prominent women of the world.

## Other General Reference Works

Two other types of general reference works should be mentioned here.

### General Encyclopedias

For preliminary reading as well as for bibliographic references, the most useful general encyclopedias are the *Encyclopaedia Britannica* and the *Encyclopedia Americana*. Good one-volume works are the *Columbia Encyclopedia* and the *Random House Encyclopedia*.

### Dictionaries

Dictionaries rarely contain bibliographies, but the student working in the field of language should know about these useful sources:

*A Dictionary of American English on Historical Principles*. 4 vols.

*The Oxford English Dictionary*. 12 vols. and supplement. Also issued in a two-volume *Compact Edition*, complete but photographically reduced.

*Webster's Third New International Dictionary*.

*Dictionary of Afro-American Slang*.

*Dictionary of Word and Phrase Origins*.

*Oxford Dictionary of English Etymology*.

*Dictionary of Slang and Unconventional English*. 7th ed.

*Dictionary of American Slang*. 2nd ed.

## TEST YOURSELF ON
## Using Reference Works

In order to gain practice in using general reference works in the library, find at least five general reference works in which you can find information on one of the following:

1. Your research paper topic
2. A sample topic assigned by your instructor

3. One of these topics: (a) the development of computers; (b) Napoleon Bonaparte (1769 – 1821); (c) the Iroquois Indians; (d) gas rationing in the United States; (e) the drug *laetrile;* (f) the origins of the Democratic party in the United States; (g) dolphins

# Preparing a Bibliography

The *working bibliography* is a list of books, articles, pamphlets, and other reference materials that you are using for your research. It is kept on a series of index cards according to a system explained below. As you go along, you might add some items or drop some, so that the list you actually use for your paper — the list of *works cited*, or your *final bibliography* — may not be identical with your working list.

## Sources

The following are the principal sources for your working bibliography.

### The Card Catalog

Probably your most important source will be your library's card catalog. Some libraries have boxes of 3″ X 5″ index cards which list alphabetically every piece of printed or recorded material the library owns. Others have done away with actual cards; their listings are given on microfiche cards, pieces of positive film that are used with a mechanical reader. In either case, for each book there are usually three cards, author, title, and subject (see p. 318 for samples of each). The author card is the basic one; the others are duplicates of it with title or subject heading typed across the top.

The different kinds of cards are there to help you in your research. You may, for example, remember that a particular author writes well on a subject that interests you. Finding that author's name in the catalog will lead you to the books you want. Or you may remember a title but not the author; the title card will be most useful to you in that case. Finally, if you know neither author nor title but have only a subject in mind, the card catalog lists books under numerous subject headings.

It is useful to read the explanatory key printed with the sample cards below, because knowing what the card symbols mean can help you to select books on your topic that are especially valuable rather than just general. For example, a card may offer

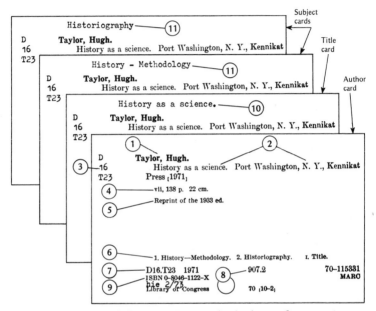

1. Author's name; following name, author's dates often are given.
2. Title of book, place of publication, name of publisher, edition, date of publication or copyright (brackets around year indicate that date is not printed on title page).
3. Call number in the library.
4. Number of pages (roman numerals indicate pages of introductory matter); illustrations, if present; height of book in centimeters. (As this book is a little under 9″ high, it would normally be found in its regular shelf place; large books often are shelved on a separate large-size shelf.)
5. Explanatory notes; description of special features, if present
6. Other places in the card catalog where cards for this book are filed. (These other cards are shown here.)
7. Call number under the Library of Congress System.
8. Call number under the Dewey Decimal System.
9. International Standard Book Number.
10. Title.
11. Subject.

information on the book's contents — whether or not it contains a bibliography (and if so, how long), illustrations, maps, graphs, and so on. When you can quickly assimilate this information, you can make a much shrewder choice of books to add to your working bibliography than a researcher who cannot. Take another example: Paying attention to dates of publication and information on the edition of the book (how many times it has been revised and reissued) can also be useful. As a researcher, you may be making a good choice by consulting a recently published work on your topic, but you should also consult a book whose first edition was published, say, ten years ago but whose latest edition is marked "4th ed." This information would suggest that the book may be on its way to achieving status close to that of a standard in its field — by virtue of its having been reissued so often over so short a period of time.

### Lists of Periodicals

Researchers who want to locate a periodical should consult one of the following:

*Ayer Directory of Publications.* A standard source of information about newspapers and magazines published in the United States, Canada, Bermuda, Panama, and the Philippines.
*Ulrich's International Periodicals Directory.* Periodicals of the whole world, arranged by subject.
*Union List of Serials in Libraries of the United States and Canada.*

### Indexes to Periodical Literature

Articles in newspapers and magazines are an important source for research material, but they are not listed in the library's card catalog and must be sought in the various indexes to periodical literature. The major index for articles on a wide variety of subjects published in nonspecialized magazines is the *Readers' Guide to Periodical Literature.* This is published twice a month and then cumulated in annual volumes. Articles are indexed by subject and author and by titles of certain creative works (including films). Here is a sample of entries from the *Readers' Guide.**

---

* *Readers' Guide to Periodical Literature.* Copyright © 1977. Material reproduced by permission of The H. W. Wilson Company, publisher.

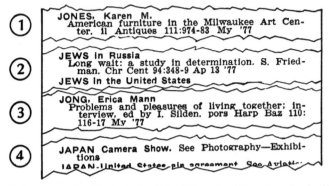

1. Author entry for illustrated article, "American Furniture in the Milwaukee Art Center," in *Antiques*, volume 111, pages 974–983, May 1977 issue.

2. Subject entry for article by S. Friedman in *Christian Century*, volume 94, pages 348–349, issue of April 13, 1977.

3. Another subject entry, but this subject is a person: the writer Erica Jong. The entry refers to an interview with her, illustrated with several portraits, in *Harper's Bazaar*, volume 110, pages 116–117, May 1977 issue.

4. Cross-reference entry that refers to the Photography section of the *Guide*.

Very useful for topics of current interest as well as for topics that require day-by-day information dating back to 1851 is *The New York Times Index*. The *Index* refers you to articles in the *Times*, giving date of issue and page number. Here is a set of sample entries.*

**BEARS. See** Hunting F 21, 2d Ag 8 par
Wounded black bear sighted, Letchworth, NY; Rockland County areas alerted, Ja 26,39:1
R Murphy article on polar bears, threat of extinction and US move to preserve them; illus, Mr 28, VI,p38; depletion in Arctic area linked to high prices of skins at Vancouver fur auction, Je 6, 117:4; scientists from US, USSR, Canada, Norway and Denmark to conf, Anchorage, Alaska; more polar bears reptd being killed in Alaska by airborne hunters; illus, Jl 11,52:3
Bears claw 2, Gt Smoky Mts Natl Pk, Je 1,31:3
Drs F C and J J Craighead rev 7-yr experiment in which they drugged grizzlies in Yellowstone Natl Pk and attached devices to study their behavior; details; Natl Geographic Soc and Natl Science Foundation sponsors, D 19,58:1

①
②
③
④
⑤

**BEARSTED, Lord (Marcus Richard Samuel). See** Hill, Samuel & Co
**BEASLEY, (Asst Sec) D Otis.** To retire, D 11,31:5
**BEATLES, The (George Harrison, John Lennon, Paul McCartney, Ringo Starr). See** Motion Pictures—Revs, Hard Day's Night; Help!.Music—Gen F 13,19, My 19, Ag 11 par. Music—Tours, Foreign. Recordings Je 10, Ag 9, N 9, D 14,17. TV—Programs, Beatles

R Starr weds M Cox, London, F 12,19:1

Queen Elizabeth names Beatles members of Brit Empire Order, Je 12,1:8; Brit reaction, Je 13,3:2; MP H Dupuis (Canada) to return his medal in protest, Je 15,15:1

2 Brit war heroes protest award of Brit Empire Order, Je 16,13:1; Lt Col Wagg returns all 12 of his medals to Queen in protest, Je 17,3:3; comment on dispute; group of Labor MPs signs motion welcoming award, Je 20,IV,5:3

Investiture ceremony, Buckingham Palace; illus, O 27,49:8
**BEATON, Cecil.** Diaries, 1939–44, revd, N 7,VII, p90

Notes on the "BEATLES" entry:

1. Paragraph 1 compresses much information in a group of cross-references to full entries elsewhere: (1) Reviews and other news items about the Beatles' movies *A Hard Day's Night* and *Help!* can be located by looking up the titles under the index heading Motion Pictures—Reviews. (2) News items relating to the Beatles' music printed on February 13 and 19, May 19, and August 11 (paragraph) are described and further identified under the index heading Music—General, where the entries are arranged in order of dates of news items. (3) News items about the Beatles' tours can be found under Music—Tours, Foreign, alphabetically under "Beatles." (4) Items about the Beatles' recordings printed on June 10, August 9, November 9, December 14 and 17 are described and further identified under the index heading Recordings, where the entries are in order of dates. (5) Items about the Beatles' TV programs can be found under Television—Programs, alphabetically under "Beatles." Following are a number of actual entries describing and locating general news items:

2. Paragraph 2 refers to a news story about Ringo's marriage to M. Cox in London; the article appears in the February 12 *Times* on page 19, column 1.

3, 4, 5. These paragraphs concern the award of the Order of the British Empire to the Beatles and the uproar this caused among certain British citizens. At the end of paragraph 4, the roman number "IV" refers to section 4 of the paper. At the end of paragraph 5, the abbreviation "illus" means that the article is accompanied by one or more photographs.

### Specialized Indexes

In addition to the periodical indexes, you can consult a large number of specialized indexes, by subject area. The following is only a partial list:

*Agricultural Index*
*Applied Science and Technology Index*
*Bibliographic Index*
*Book Review Index*
*Business Periodicals Index*
*Engineering Index*
*Essay and General Literature Index*
*Index of Economic Journals*
*Index to Legal Periodicals*
*Music Index*
*Public Affairs Information Service Bulletin*
*Social Sciences and Humanities Index*

In addition to these, numerous other, even more specialized, indexes are available and listed in the card catalog. Look for the cards that follow a subject or author entry that have printed across the top in red the word *BIBLIOGRAPHY* or *INDEX*.

*Note:* All indexes, including the *Readers' Guide* and *The New York Times Index,* supply the reader with keys to their abbreviations. These "key" pages usually appear at the front of the volume. Looking over these pages before you begin to search the volume can usually save you a great deal of time and confusion.

### Indexes to Current Issues

*The Magazine Index,* published since 1976, indexes some 400 magazines and is especially useful for current topics. A companion is *Hot Topics,* a loose-leaf bound monthly list of such current topics of interest as abortion, ecology, illegal immigration, and the like.

### Government Documents

The federal government publishes an enormous amount of material on numerous subjects. Guides to this literature are the *Monthly Catalog of United States Government Publications* and the *Monthly Checklist of State Publications.*

### Computer Databases

With the help of your librarian, you may be able to add to your working bibliography by instituting a search of database computer files. If your library offers such a service, then it has a computer capable of logging onto a national network of research files via telephone hookup. The librarian will ask you to cooperate by providing such information as the probable finished title of your paper, at least three key words that the computer can use in the search, and whether you would wish to limit the search narrowly and in what specific ways. At the end of the search, you might be rewarded with citations of various printed materials appropriate to your topic along with summaries of their contents. The service is not available in all libraries, however, and where it is, it is not inexpensive. Nor is it always appropriate to spend the money for a particular research project. The librarian you consult will be able to help you with the decision.

## TEST YOURSELF ON
## Sources of Information

Using your research paper topic or a sample topic assigned to the whole class, make a list of subject headings under which you might find sources of information. Take the list to the library and look up each subject heading in the following three sources:

1. The *Readers' Guide*
2. *The New York Times Index*
3. The card catalog

Add to your list of subject headings as you discover new ones. Which source was best for your particular topic? Why?

## Setting Up the Working Bibliography

The mechanics of setting up your working bibliography are simple though they may appear to you excessively tedious. But if you establish good work habits at this stage, your life while working on this paper will be free of stress. Skipping past the meticulousness required here will surely cause you grief later. The experience of millions of researchers attests to that.

PS
3537
T4753
Z6216
  ①

② ⑦

Burney, William. ③
Wallace Stevens. Twayne
United States Authors
Series. New York:
Twayne Publishers, 1968

④ Has bibliography of secondary
sources.

---

AP2.1A
①

② ⑧

McPhee, John. ③
"Coming into the Country III."
The New Yorker 4 July 1977:
33-65. ⑤

⑥ 3rd part of four-part article.
Has data on legal status of
Alaskan gold miners.

---

1. The call number of the book or magazine volume; once you've noted it here, you need not return to the card catalog every time you want the book or article.
2. Your own item number. In your rough first draft of the paper, you can use this number instead of formal documentation. You also use this number on your note cards.
3. Name of author, exact title, facts of publication. Being exact here can save you trouble: you can use this card for your final list of works cited.
4. An important note reminding yourself of an especially useful feature of the source.
5. Exact page numbers of the article.
6. Note reminding yourself that this article is one of a series and that it contains data of special interest to you.

For this work you should acquire 3″ × 5″ lined index cards. Use one card for each book or article or pamphlet. Never put more than one entry on a single card. On page 325 are sample cards for a book and a magazine article. Note carefully the reasons given for including each bit of information.

Also following is a series of sample bibliographical entries for various kinds of materials. You may use these entries as models for your own bibliography. Note carefully the order in which the information is presented and exact punctuation used to separate the items.

## Bibliographic Form: Sample Entries

### Book

Waldhorn, Arthur. A Reader's Guide to Ernest Hemingway. New York: Farrar, 1972.

*Note:* It is acceptable to abbreviate the names of publishers. See pages 349–350.

### Book by More Than One Author

Lynn, Naomi B., Ann B. Matasar, and Marie Barovic Rosenberg. Research Guide in Women's Studies. Morristown, N.J.: General Learning, 1974.

*Note:* Only the first author's name is inverted.

### Book in Several Volumes

Jaeger, Werner. Paideia: The Ideals of Greek Culture. Trans. Gilbert Highet. 3 vols. New York: Oxford UP, 1943.

### Later or Revised Edition

French, Robert Dudley. A Chaucer Handbook. 2nd ed. New York: Appleton, 1956.

### Article from an Edited Collection

Rovit, Earl H. "Ralph Ellison and the American Comic Tradition." Ralph Ellison: A Collection of Critical Essays. Ed. John Hersey. Englewood Cliffs, N.J.: Prentice, 1974, pp. 78–90.

### Article from a General Reference Work

"Fleming, Sir Alexander." Chambers's Biographical Dictionary. New Edition. 1972.

*Note:* For a well-known general reference work, you need give only the title of the work and the edition.

### Article from a Weekly or Monthly Magazine
Otten, Jane. "Living in Syntax." Newsweek, 30 Dec. 1974:9.

Mattingly, Ignatius C. "Some Cultural Aspects of Serial Cartoons, or Get a Load of Those Funnies." Harper's, Dec. 1955:34–39.

*Note:* Observe that all months except May, June, and July are abbreviated. Where you have an unsigned article, simply begin with the title.

### Article from a Learned Journal
Erikson, Erik H. "The Problem of Ego Identity." Journal of the American Psychoanalytic Association 4 (1956):56–121.

### Newspaper Article
Ferretti, Fred. "The Pre-Marathon Menu: Almost Anything." New York Times, 24 Oct. 1984, late ed.: A1+.

*Note:* Observe that October is abbreviated, that the edition is given, and that the notation "A1+" means the story appears on page 1 of section A and is continued elsewhere (+ = another page). If the article is unsigned, simply begin with the title.

### Public Document
United States. Cong. Senate. Committee on the Judiciary. Hearings before the Subcommittee to Investigate Juvenile Delinquency. 86th Cong. 2nd sess. Washington: GPO, 1954.

### Interview — Personal
Beatty, Warren. Personal interview. 28 Mar. 1986.

### Interview — Printed
Jackson, Michael. Interview. Rolling Stone, 17 Jan. 1985: 13–17.

### Movie or Television Program
Tess. Dir. Roman Polanski. Prod. Charles Berri. With Nastassia Kinski. Columbia Pictures, 1981.

Americans in Love. Narr. Sam Rovit. Writ. and prod. Abigail McKenzie. PBS News Special. WGBH, Boston. 19 Oct. 1984.

*Note:* If you are concentrating on the contribution of a particular individual, begin with that person's name instead of the title.

### Recording

Bear, Lisa, lead singer. Long House. <u>Long House in Concert at Carnegie Hall.</u> Rec. 5 September 1985. Prestige, P-44115, 1986.

### Computer Software

<u>Ms. Pacman.</u> Computer software. Atari, Inc., 1983.

## Setting Up a List of Works Cited

In order to document quotations, summaries, or paraphrases of the works of others, you will need a page in your research paper called "Works Cited." On this page, you will need to give full information on every source that you use in your paper. To do this job, simply take those working bibliography cards you actually used in preparing your paper and put them in alphabetical order according to authors' last names. For unsigned material, alphabetize the first word of the title that is not *the* or *a.* Then simply type the cards into a list that looks exactly like the Works Cited page of the sample research paper (p. 381). Be sure to follow the same spacing and indentation that the sample uses: Each entry begins flush with the left-hand margin, subsequent lines are indented five spaces, and the whole page is double spaced. Be careful to follow the punctuation of the sample and notice that none of the items is numbered.

How you refer to these Works Cited in the body of your text will be considered under Documentation (pp. 340–350).

## TEST YOURSELF ON
## Bibliography Form

Using the forms just discussed, set up working bibliography cards for each of the following items.

1. A book by Claude Lévi-Strauss called Structural Anthropology, translated by Claire Jacobson and Brooke G. Scoepf and published in New York City in 1963 by Basic Books, Inc.
2. An article by Donald Kaplan called On Preaching Old Virtues While Practicing Old Vices: A Psychoanalytic Perspective on Morality. It was published in the Bulletin of the Menninger Clinic, volume 39, number 2, in March 1975, on pages 113–130.
3. A book in two volumes by Vernon L. Parrington called Main

Currents in American Thought, published in New York by Harcourt, Brace & World, Inc., in 1954.
4. A newspaper article by Christopher S. Wren called Soviet Sharpens Criticism of U.S. Plans for Missile, published on page 1 of the New York Times for July 4, 1977, and continued on page 2.
5. A book edited by Mary Jane Moffat and Charlotte Painter called Revelations: Diaries of Women. It was published in 1974 by Random House in New York.

# Reading and Taking Notes

You are now ready to begin a period of intensive reading of the material in your working bibliography. How do you go about it and how do you take notes on what you read?

First, avoid crashing. That is, avoid all emergency schedules — such as all-night sessions or forty-eight hour squeezes. Instead, plan on a reading period of two weeks, during which you read in the library or your room for two to three hours every working day.

Second, read the whole of the articles on your list but not the books. When using books, you should learn to look carefully at the indexes and tables of contents so that you can select chapters or shorter passages that relate directly to your topic. If you're working with the ecology of redwoods, you may not need to read the whole of *Trees of California,* only the thirty pages or so devoted to redwoods. It's important that you learn to pick your way selectively through the jungle of data to find precisely what you need.

Note-taking requires good mechanical habits. You must use index cards and keep them well-organized. Random notes on scraps of paper are sure to get lost, and notes in a notebook are hard to keep organized in a useful way. A lined 5″ × 8″ index card is just the ticket for this job. The lines will encourage neat writing (you're the one who'll have to decipher these notes); the 5″ × 8″ size will provide room for a good deal of information and also distinguish these cards from your bibliography cards. Use one card for each note you make. If you've followed the system recommended earlier in this section, all you need for identification is a number in the upper right-hand corner (referring back to the bibliography card) and a page number for exact location of the note. (See samples on p. 324.)

Two things will now guide your note-taking. One will be a rough outline. You will object at this point that you can hardly have any kind of outline since you have not yet begun to read. However, at this time, you *will* have a research question, and most research questions lead to a very rough outline:

TOPIC: Mandatory retirement
QUESTION: Should it be abolished?
ROUGH OUTLINE:
  **I. Advantages of retirement at ages 65–70**
    A. Advantages to individual
    B. Advantages to society
  **II. Disadvantages of retirement at a prescribed age**
    A. Disadvantages to individual
    B. Disadvantages to society

As you can see, your note-taking should aim to fill in these divisions.

Your good instincts will also guide you in note-taking. They will help you to decide what needs noting. These instincts, sharpened by general reading and some acquaintance with your field, will also enable you to write the *personal observation note*—a potentially important contributor to your paper. Here is a sample of such a note:

> Why is everybody so hard on these illegal immigrants? They may be a problem but this treatment smacks of scapegoating.

As you can see, the note does not cite facts or quotations or ideas from the source. Rather, it makes a tentative evaluation of the field of research and nudges the researcher's mind along toward his or her eventual thesis statement.

In addition to the personal observation note, it is possible to make three other kinds of notes: the *summary,* the *paraphrase* and the *direct quotation.*

The summary can condense information or a narrative. In summarizing, you give the essential details in your own concise words. You must be careful not to distort the meaning of the original. You may, however, omit a certain level of unimportant detail. Such omissions are not distortions.

### Original

The one woman doctor to receive recognition from the Union government, Mary Walker, applied for a post when the war broke out in 1861. The Union refused to grant her a commission until 1864. Her application approved, she was sent to the front at Chattanooga, Tennessee. Shortly thereafter, she became a prisoner of war and was quite a curiosity to her captors. After being exchanged for a Confederate physician, Walker went on to supervise the Female Military Prison in Louisville. She was honorably discharged and awarded a medal by President Andrew Johnson. Her talent and willingness to serve were not extraordinary, but the recognition she received proved exceptional. (Catherine Clinton, *The Other Civil War: American Women in the Nineteenth Century,* New York: Hill & Wang, 1984: p. 83.)

### Poor Summary

The only woman doctor noticed by the Union in the Civil War, Mary Walker, attempted to join up in 1861 but had to wait three years before she was accepted. After that she saw action in Tennessee, but became a prisoner of war. Later she was exchanged for a Confederate doctor. After that she was assigned as commander of a female military prison in Louisville. After being discharged, President Andrew Johnson gave her a medal.

### Better Summary

Mary Walker, the only woman doctor whose service was acknowledged by the Union, applied for a commission in 1861 but had to wait three years to get it. After seeing action in Tennessee, she was captured, causing a stir among her jailors. She was later supervisor of a woman's military prison in Louisville. For these services, she was given a medal, though her performance seemed unexceptional.

The poor summary is wordy and, in fact, frequently chooses very poor words, for example, "noticed by the Union." The poor summary also includes the unessential fact that Dr. Walker had been exchanged, an inference easily made since she was on active service after she was a prisoner. An important omission is Catherine

Clinton's crucial last sentence, which the better summary doesn't overlook.

The *paraphrase* is also a condensation, but of an idea or an opinion or a train of reasoning, rather than of information or of a story. The paraphrase tries to stay close to the gist of the original but uses the language of the note-taker.

### Original

Third, a related but perhaps even more profound development flows from the growing numbers of illegal immigrants. Because political representation and the disbursement of substantial amounts of federal funds is based upon population, the 1980 census made major efforts to include illegal immigrants. To the extent that illegal immigrants increase the population of any particular state, their relative political representation is increased, as is their receipt of federal dollars. This suggests a skewed system in which there might be little incentive for states to work *against* the inclusion of illegal immigrants or *for* the reform of immigration statutes, if by the presence of large numbers of illegal immigrants they gain in tax revenues and political clout. (Georges Fauriol, "U.S. Immigration Policy and the National Interest," *Humanist,* May/June 1984:9)

### Poor Paraphrase

Political representation and the disbursement of substantial funds from the federal government is based on population size; so the 1980 census started to include illegal immigrants. When a state has a large or increasing population of illegals, it has a large or increasing population that is counted in its representation in the federal government and it gets more federal disbursements. It gains in tax revenues and political clout. If this is the case, then a state with a large or increasing number of illegals would have no interest in working against illegal immigration or for the reform of the immigration statutes.

### Better Paraphrase

The federal funds that states are entitled to depends on population size, a factor that also governs how many representatives they send to Congress. Since it is in the interest of state governments to gain greater representation and receive more federal funds, they are not likely to oppose illegal immigration or reformed immigration laws if they have large numbers of these immigrants within their borders.

The better paraphrase avoids the language of the original wherever possible, while the poor paraphrase does not. Notice "disbursements," "tax revenues," and "political clout." Moreover, the poor paraphrase is not much of a condensation. As you can see, it is wordy. The better paraphrase is brief and to the point.

In direct quotation, the note-taker must be careful to quote exactly. However, judgment can be used in omitting parts of the original as long as you do not distort the original by the way in which you've made your cuts.

### Original
The issue of women's rights was not taken up after the Civil War because the North was preoccupied with the task of Southern Reconstruction.

### Distorted Quotation
The issue of women's rights was not taken up after the Civil War because the North was preoccupied . . . (The three dots signal a cut has been made, but this cut is distorting because it omits an essential point made in the original — that is, *why* the North was preoccupied.)

### Acceptable Quotation
The issue of women's rights was not taken up after the Civil War because . . . of Southern Reconstruction.

In general, a reader will be looking at what you have written in order to find out what *you* have to say. If what you've written consists of a series of quotations from sources, the reader is likely to be put off. Therefore, it is usually better to be sparing in your use of quotations.

Direct quotation should be used only when (1) you need to prove something, and only the actual words you have read will do that job; (2) you intend to be critical of the actual words an author has used; or (3) the words are so appropriate, dramatic, emphatic, or witty that no paraphrase can do them justice. For example, suppose you are reading about an event that took place in the 1950s, a hearing on the use of air power by the United States Air Force. The then commander of our Strategic Air Forces, General Curtis LeMay, Jr., you read, suggested to a congressional committee that we "bomb them back into the Stone Age." You want to record General LeMay's attitude. Do you paraphrase, noting "LeMay favored total destruction of the enemy by air power," or do you quote him directly? No difficulty there.

Naturally, there are harder problems than this example. But as you read and take notes, you will become more expert at making these decisions. You can always go back — after gaining some experience — and check to see what you can do to improve your notes.

After each reading session, you are likely to have a pile of cards — perhaps ten or more. Whatever the number, you must now perform an important task. Read each card carefully and see what its essence is; that is, see if you can summarize each card in one or two words. Take a large felt-tip marker and write this term across the top. After your two-week reading period, you will have a large number of cards, ready to be organized by the subject headings you've written across the top of each. These subject headings should correspond — or with slight revision can correspond — to the rough outline you had in mind before you started the period of intensive reading. In any case, they are needed for the next step: preparing an outline.

## Preparing an Outline

An outline is an instrument for controlling the writing of a paper. It details the order in which you present your material. A *topic outline* is useful for the preliminary stages of a research paper, because it assists you in ordering your reading and your notes. Here is a typical — and simple — topic outline for a paper on the energy crisis in America:

I. **The energy situation in the U.S. before 1973**
II. **Action by oil-exporting countries in 1973**
III. **Situation in U.S. between 1974 and 1977**

This is an efficient way to order a chronological set of materials. But notice that while this kind of outline orders the material, it *says* nothing about that which it orders; it expresses no point of view, so that we have no idea of the writer's viewpoint on the material. A point of view can be provided by a *sentence outline.*

I. **The energy situation in the U.S. before 1973 was already critical but little noticed.**
II. **The action by the oil-exporting countries in 1973 made the situation much worse.**
III. **The situation in the U.S. between 1974 and 1977 has been one of frantically and inefficiently scrambling after "a solution."**

What makes this outline more useful than the topic outline is the fact that each of the roman numerals precedes a sentence — a statement that *says* something, that articulates a point of view, and that gives direction to the writer who must use it in writing the paper.

So important is it to develop the sentence outline that many instructors will not permit a student writer to begin composing a paper until this job is done. And at this stage, ready or not, the writer must take the plunge and begin to do the job.

What is most essential for the sentence outline is a thesis — a controlling, central point of view, the conclusion you have come to after all your reading and thinking about your topic. The thesis can emerge in one of two ways. (1) You have been, as you were engaged in intensive reading and note-taking, an avid reader of your own note cards; each day, after you finished, you thought about the notes you had taken, the subject headings you had written across them, and the implications of all this. Now you read your notes one last time and suddenly your thesis appears full-blown in your mind. (2) You work on your cards in an organized way until your thesis emerges from your subject headings.

## Organizing the Note Cards

Let us suppose that you have been researching an aspect of the energy crisis that developed in the United States after 1973. You have narrowed your topic to "The Relative Merits of Nuclear and Solar Power: Making a Rational Choice." You intend in your paper to answer two questions: (1) Which form of power is the more advantageous to fulfill our needs? (2) What are the prospects for America's adopting the one that seems more advantageous? You have done your reading and now have a batch of note cards under each of the following subject headings:

    A. development of nuclear reactors for power needs
    B. ancient devices for using the sun
    C. nuclear accidents
    D. nuclear waste disposal
    E. advantages of solar power
    F. advantages of nuclear power
    G. absence of solar power technology
    H. no portable systems for solar power
    I. high nuclear costs
    J. high solar start-up costs

K. solar storage: a problem
L. costs of dismantling nuclear plants
M. industry's attitudes toward solar power
N. industry's attitudes toward nuclear power
O. government's sponsorship of nuclear power
P. government's failure to sponsor solar power

It seems easy enough to impose a preliminary order on these batches of cards. For example, A and B obviously go together in an introduction. M, N, O, and P belong at the end, where you would discuss the prospects for adopting the better choice (either nuclear or solar power). The remaining batches of cards belong in the central part of your paper, but they need to be put together under new subject headings. Logically, batches C through K fall into four separate categories under these headings:

1. advantages of nuclear power
2. disadvantages of nuclear power
3. advantages of solar power
4. disadvantages of solar power

To accompany these four, we should combine M, N, O, and P into two:

5. government and industry's attitude toward nuclear power
6. government and industry's attitude toward solar power

When you have done this, you are ready for an important task. You must *turn these six subject headings into sentences* that accurately express what *you* think is said by the totality of the cards you've arranged under these new subject headings. To do this, you must read each pack of cards carefully and, from the mass of details they contain, extract a generalization (a sentence) that accurately covers what the cards contain. Your sentence for any one pack need not contain *everything* on the cards; at this stage you may ignore some cards, deciding that some of the information is irrelevant to your sentence. But you do need a sentence for each subject heading.

Let us suppose now that you've done the job and the sentences come out like this:

1. The advantages of nuclear power are few.
2. The disadvantages of nuclear power are considerable.
3. The advantages of solar power are considerable.

4. The disadvantages of solar power are the same as those for any other newly developing technology.
5. The government has sponsored nuclear research, and industry is inclined to follow the path of nuclear development.
6. The government has given little aid to solar power research, and industry is reluctant to pay the costs of solar power development.

## Writing the Thesis Statement

The reader who examines these sentences carefully will see that it is possible to find embedded in them a plausible thesis. What is required now are the *words* to express that thesis. As an exercise, before you read any further, try writing a rather longish sentence, using the materials in 1 through 6 above, that you think would do for a thesis.

Compare what you have written with the following:

> The advantages that solar power has over nuclear power make it seem more suitable for America's energy needs, but government and industry are not inclined to press for its wide-scale adoption.

For more information on thesis statements, see the entry in Part 2.

## Writing the Outline

Now that you have a thesis, you are ready to "divide" it into an outline.

I. **Introduction: Solar energy has been used successfully for thousands of years; nuclear energy is a recent development dating from 1945, when it was first used in the atomic bomb.**
II. **The advantages of nuclear energy are far outweighed by its disadvantages.**
    A. The advantages of nuclear energy are few.
        1. There is a relatively stable supply of fuel.
        2. There is an available and developing technology.
        3. There is a body of engineers and workers trained in nuclear technology.
    B. The disadvantages of nuclear energy are considerable.
        1. It is thermodynamically inefficient.
        2. It needs extraordinary handling because of its deadly

character, and its waste products remain deadly for centuries.

  3. It can give rise to catastrophic accidents.

  4. Its recycled products can be made into dangerous weapons.

III. **The advantages of solar power far outweigh its disadvantages.**

 A. The advantages of solar power are considerable.

  1. Its fuel, the sun, is in endless supply at no cost.

  2. It is thermodynamically efficient.

  3. It results in no deadly waste products.

  4. It cannot give rise to catastrophic accidents.

 B. The disadvantages of solar power are virtually the same as those of any other newly developing technology.

  1. It will be fairly expensive to integrate solar power with current systems.

  2. It is not yet efficient to store solar power.

  3. It is not yet efficient to use solar power for transportation.

IV. **Since government and industry are not enthusiastic about making the effort solar power will require and since both have heavy investments in nuclear technology, it seems unlikely that solar power will be adopted on a large scale in America in the near future.**

Note the following important points about the outline:

**1** The introduction rephrases into a sentence the materials on the original note cards, batches A and B (see p. 334).

**2** Roman numerals II, III, and IV literally divide up the thesis statement on page 336. As we go from the A's and B's to arabic numerals, the dividing and specifying process continues.

**3** Sentences II and III are parallel in form. In addition, the parallelism extends to the A's and B's, and the numerical entries under these are also parallel.

**4** The specific points made in the statements marked by arabic numerals come from the note cards.

Of course, a different set of note cards for a different paper will present different problems, but the process is essentially the same: Consider your material until it yields more and more inclusive generalizations, from subject headings to sentences and from these sentences to a thesis. From the thesis to the outline is a matter of proper division and adding details from the cards.

The following few rules may be useful if you want to check your outline against some standard before submitting it to the instructor.

**1** No outline should be written unless you are sure the thesis is a satisfactory one. Here is an example of an unsatisfactory thesis for the outline we have just discussed:

> There are many advantages and disadvantages to using nuclear power and solar power.

This is unsatisfactory because it is too vague — and would remain so even if it named some of the advantages and disadvantages it speaks of. It is also a failure in not saying specifically what the writer thinks *after* doing the research; a statement like this one could have been made *before* reading about the subject. Compare it to the thesis statement on page 336.

**2** The outline should always divide its material logically. For example, consider this piece of outline:

**II. By hard work, Woodward and Bernstein tracked down their important sources.**
    A. They tracked down a secretary at CREEP.
    B. They found an important source in the F.B.I.
**III. They located a "leak" in the White House itself.**

Notice that roman numeral III should be capital C. It clearly refers back to roman numeral II and is in parallel form with A and B.

**3** The outline should present its material in logical order. Consider this preliminary outline:

   **I. Modern methods of early diagnosis cut down on heart disease fatalities.**
   **II. Treatment of heart disease was hampered before 1950 by inadequate diagnostic understanding.**
  **III. Treatment of heart disease cases used to consist of rest and only rest.**
  **IV. Modern treatment of heart attack is based on the theory of prevention by physical and psychological conditioning.**

Can you rearrange these into a more logical order? If you changed I to III, kept IV, and changed II and III to I and II, respectively, you have a good eye for logical order.

# Writing the Paper

If you have done your work efficiently to this point, you now have an outline in hand and batches of note cards in the same order as the divisions in that outline — and you are ready to write.

## The Mechanics

You should be prepared to write at least two drafts. It is not inappropriate to suggest, in fact, that you write as many drafts as you need to write; it is hard to imagine extra attention spoiling your work. Depending on your preference in work habits, you may either write your drafts in longhand or type them; either way, be sure to keep careful track of your notes and documentation from draft to draft. (See Documentation, below, for detailed information.)

When you are ready for a final draft, it should be typed on good white bond, $8\frac{1}{2}'' \times 11''$, on one side of the page only, with footnotes at the foot of the page or all together at the end, as your instructor requests. You should supply a title page (see Sample Research Paper) and a final bibliography. All of these should be proofread carefully.

Finally, you should know that there are a variety of words and phrases available to use in introducing quoted material. It is useful rhetorical strategy, for example, to introduce a quote with an expression like "as the noted astronomer and cosmologist Carl Sagan has observed. . . . " In this way, you let the reader know that an authority's words are about to be spoken, and the reader might be properly impressed. In any case, there are many ways to introduce quotes and you should think about the values inherent in each. For your convenience, here is a small list (there are many others):

| | |
|---|---|
| As Prof. X *declared* | Edward Heath *asserted that* |
| Dr. Falk *notes* | Nixon *summarized it as* |
| Winston Churchill *observed* | In Kennedy's *analysis* |
| As Pablo Picasso *put it* | By Freud's *definition* |
| Nietzsche *has written that* | |

## The Rhetoric

Everything you know about writing should, of course, be applied to the writing of the research paper. But this paper presents a special problem that you have not encountered before: the necessity to weave into your paper materials taken from a number of sources. The way to deal with this problem is to take the approach that these materials are *not* in and of themselves the heart of your paper; the heart of your paper is *your* purpose in writing, the thesis that you have set out to present. Once you have made the decision to take this approach, the materials you have been collecting will fall into their proper place. That is, you will see that they are to be used for your purposes, *woven* into the texture of your paper to support and illustrate your thesis and *not* haphazardly strung together like numerous odd beads because they are all you have to show.

# Documentation

## What to Document

In a research paper, you must tell the reader where you found your material. The telling is known as documentation. It takes the form of a parenthetical reference* in the body of your text to the source of any of the following:

1. A direct quotation, the actual words someone has used.
2. Statistics, including graphs, tables, charts, maps, or diagrams taken from someone else's work.
3. A summary or condensation of someone else's narrative or array of facts.
4. Your paraphrase of someone else's ideas or opinions.

You need not document details you did not know before you began work on the paper *provided those details are considered common knowledge in the field of your topic*. For example, if you're writing on some aspect of the history of the United States from 1960 through 1963, you need not document that Robert Kennedy was the Attorney General at the time. It is considered common knowledge in the history of that period.

---

\* It may also take the form of a superscript number referring a reader to an endnote. The superscript system, often called the footnote system, is discussed on pp. 347 – 349.

## Ethics

In working with other people's material — an invariable part of writing a research paper — you may be faced with two ethical considerations. The first is the necessity to acknowledge the debt you owe to a source for words, ideas, or facts. The failure to make such acknowledgments is a serious breach of ethics known as plagiarism. For plagiarism, published writers are subject to court action and student writers to disciplinary action by the schools they attend. The second consideration is the duty you have to present with absolute fairness the essential meaning of what you are quoting. Failure to make such a presentation is at best carelessness and at worst deception.

To ensure that you are not guilty of plagiarism, you should be scrupulous in acknowledging the source of whatever you quote — whether you paraphrase it or quote it directly. Moreover, you should transcribe quoted material exactly as you find it in your source, being sure to include every punctuation mark, because even a misplaced comma can alter the meaning of a passage.

To avoid deceiving a reader, you should quote a passage without distorting its essential meaning. For example, suppose you had on one of your note cards a quoted passage such as this one:

> The American parent seems solidly behind his teenage child, though numerous research studies and cultural articles like novels and television shows indicate that he is greatly troubled by his child's participation in the drug culture or his early involvement with sex. He is proud of his teenager's accomplishments and is likely to support teenage pursuits in sports, hobbies, or socializing, but he admits to little awareness of how to provide discipline or vocational guidance.

Since you have at your disposal ellipsis points, three spaced periods (. . .), to indicate an omission, you might quote in your paper a version of the above that goes like this:

> The American parent seems solidly behind his teenage child. . . . He is proud of his accomplishments and is likely to support teenage pursuits. . . .

But this would be a deceptive distortion, since the original passage clearly shows the parent to be much more uncertain than the abbreviated quotation would suggest.

To be sure that your work follows the highest ethical standard, the best guidelines are these: quote with accuracy, convey the essential meaning of what you are quoting, and acknowledge the source of the quotation. To acknowledge the source, use either a parenthetical reference to a list of works cited or a superscript numeral referring to an end note.

## Parenthetical References

The list of works cited at the end of your paper will be one part of your documentation of sources. The other part will be a brief parenthetical reference in the body of your text giving the last name of the author or shortened title of a book or article together with a page number.

The following samples of various kinds of parenthetical references have been adapted from Joseph Gibaldi and Walter S. Achtert, *MLA Handbook for Writers of Research Papers,* 2nd ed. (New York: MLA, 1984). Take careful note of the placement of the various punctuation marks in each example.

### References to Authors

#### *Parenthetical Reference to Author and Page Number*

To a dedicated jogger, the pain of shin splints is not so much an adequate reason to stop running as it is a joyous signal that he is doing his duty by his body (Rovit 319).

*Note:* In the parenthetical reference there is no comma after *Rovit* and neither *p.* nor *page* before the number.

To find the full details on this source, the reader looks under *R* in Works Cited.

#### *Entry in Works Cited*

Rovit, Earl H. Fitness and the Music of Pain. Boston: Little, 1985.

If the author's name appears within the text itself, only the page number is needed in parentheses.

#### *Author's Name in the Text*

Rovit insists that to a dedicated jogger the pain of shin splints is not so much an adequate reason to stop running as it is a joyous signal that he is doing his duty by his body (319).

Rovit (319) insists that to a dedicated jogger the pain of shin splints is not so much an adequate reason to stop running as it is a joyous signal that he is doing his duty by his body.

*Note:* The placement of the parentheses should interfere as little as possible with the reader's concentration on the flow of your words. Therefore, parentheses should go where there is a natural pause in the sentence, that is, before a comma, or at the end, before a period. Of course, they should go as near as possible to the borrowed material. By this rule, then, the placement of *(319)* after *Rovit* in the preceding example is permissible — but not wise. However, a circumstance *could* arise where you would place page numbers on parentheses after authors' names:

### *Two Authors' Names in the Text*

Rovit (234) and Sherwin (10) come to exactly opposite conclusions.

The overriding concern of the writer should be clarity. The writer should supply information in the parentheses in such a way that the reader has no difficulty finding the source or determining whose ideas are being expressed. Two authors of a single book would, of course, be treated differently.

### *Dual Authors' Names in the Text*

Brooks and Warren regard poetry as a kind of sovereign speech (23–24).

### *Dual Authors' Names in the Reference*

They regard poetry as a kind of sovereign speech (Brooks and Warren 23–24).

If several authors are listed in Works Cited as "et al.," they are referred to that way in the text.

### *Multiple Authors' Names in the Reference*

Their approaches to elementary education are based on Piaget's ideas of development (Wolpert et al.).

### *Entry in Works Cited*

Wolpert, Gloria, et al., eds. Teaching the Handicapped in Grades K-6. New York: Harper & Row, 1986.

## References to Books and Articles

### Reference to a Work in More Than One Volume

Jaeger underscores the educational value to Hellenic Greeks of all the Homeric Texts (2:13).

*Note:* The "2" in parenthesis refers to the second of three volumes. The "13" is the page number.

### Reference to a Work Listed by Title

Burglaries in New York are said to be frightening store owners into moving out of the city entirely ("Holdups").

In Works Cited, the entry, an unsigned newspaper article; would be found under *H*.

### Entry in Works Cited

"Holdups Frighten Manhattan Merchants." New York Times 14 Oct. 1984, late ed.: B17.

### Reference When There Are Two or More Works by a Single Author

Lustig writes that "students of modern physics have no trouble eating math for breakfast, lunch and dinner" (Scientists 29).

In Works Cited, Lustig is listed as the author of two books, *Problems in Higher Education* and *Educating Modern Scientists*. The parenthetical reference *Scientists* obviously refers to the latter. Note that in this example, the parentheses come after the quotation marks and before the period.

### Two or More Works in a Single Reference

Prominent musicians report that from an early age they could distinguish sharply between conflicting sounds (Copeland 379; Thomson 244).

Two references in parentheses should be a limit. More than that tends to disrupt the reader's concentration and should be left for a content note. (See pp. 346 – 347.)

### Reference at the End of a Long, Indented Quotation

The explanation of what is 'modern' in the drama deserves to be quoted in full:

> When Aristotle declared the drama to be the 'imitation' of an action, he confounded dramatic criticism, theory and practice for nearly 2,300 years. With Aristotle's dictum was born the notion that drama can only be mimetic. And with it was born the low estate of the drama. To become modern and raise itself up to a proper esthetic height, the drama had to overthrow this idea. Jarry's Ubu Roi imitated nothing. It did not depend on the audience's prior experience. It was a spectacle to be seen for itself, a set of scathing poetic images that had immediate impact. The play reminded the audience of nothing it had seen before and they could abstract nothing from it — form no idea of the "imitated." Audiences are not easily taken along this path, but the modernity of drama continues to be measured by this standard — whether the play is the imitation of an action or not. Using this standard, for example, we discover that Sam Shepard is modern, Lanford Wilson is not (Alexander 215a).

### Reference to Indirect Source

Fisher said he always suspected that Capablanca was a "timid player" at heart (qtd. in Bell 57).

The *qtd. in* stands for *quoted in*. Whenever you can, you should use first-hand sources, but there are occasions when this is impossible — either because someone like Bell (above) is the *only* source or because the first-hand source is impossible to get to, being available only in manuscript or other documentary form.

### *Referring to an Entire Work in General Terms*

<u>Literature and Psychology</u> covers the field thoroughly (Kauvar).

or, better:

Kauvar covers the field thoroughly.

In comments like this one, where you refer to a book as an entity, you can do so *without* the use of a parenthetical reference since you need not refer a reader to a specific location.

## Content Notes

Along with parenthetical documentation, it is sometimes useful to offer a reader information that cannot be included in the body of your text. Such information would include explanations of methods (interviewing, surveying, and the like), conflicts in the evidence you've been dealing with, and multiple citations that seem too long to include in a single parenthetical reference.

Place the content note reference numeral in your text about a half space above the line of text. The notes should be placed on a separate page, labeled "Notes," at the back of your text before Works Cited. Here is a sample piece of text followed by a sample content note:

### *Text*

Victims of abusive husbands are in many cases the middle child in the family and, when growing up, were subjected to certain additional stresses that weakened their potential resistance to being abused by violent males.[4]

### *Content Note*

[4] For a complete review of the suggestive evidence on the family position of abuse victims and the childhood stresses that would make them vulnerable, see Baker 23-26, Charles 127-129, and Eamon 345-348.

The purpose of this content note is to refer a reader to research materials. Other purposes of such notes would be to explain conflicts in evidence you are presenting, to explain research methods and tools, or to provide certain supporting materials that would impede the reader's progress if they were included in the text.

## Endnotes or Footnotes

Another form of documentation consists of a superscript numeral in the body of the text to mark the passage to be documented and a corresponding note identifying the source. At one time, these notes always appeared at the foot of the page; hence the name *footnote*. But unless your instructor advises you to keep them at the foot of the page, place your notes at the end of your paper.

Number this page in sequence after the last page of your text. Call it "Notes" in a title centered and an inch or so from the top. To begin your notes, indent five spaces from the left-hand margin, type the number of the note without punctuation, skip half a space down and begin to write the information on your reference. Continue to double space throughout. If more than one line is needed for the reference, the second and any subsequent lines should proceed from the left-hand margin. (See "Notes" at the end of the Sample Research Paper.)

When using this system, your instructor may or may not require a bibliography. If a bibliography is required, follow instructions for setting up a list of works cited (p. 327).

Observe the differences between a bibliographic entry and a footnote or endnote citation:

### Bibliography or Works Cited Entry

Waldhorn, Arthur. A Reader's Guide to Ernest Hemingway. New York: Farrar, 1972.

### Footnote/Endnote First Citation

[1] Arthur Waldhorn, A Reader's Guide to Ernest Hemingway (New York: Farrar, 1972) 112.

As you can see, the bibliography entry has the author's name inverted and ends each section of information (author's name, title, publication information) with a period. The footnote or endnote entry does not invert the author's name, separates it from the title with a comma, and then gives the publication information in parentheses. The parentheses are followed by the page number with no "p." and no word "page."

After the first citation, references to the same book are shortened.

### Subsequent Reference
[13] Waldhorn 37.

But if there is more than one book by the same author on your list, the name of the book is also needed.

### Subsequent Reference to Author of More Than One Book
[13] Waldhorn, Hemingway 37.

Notice the details of punctuation and spacing in the following sample first footnote/endnote citations.

### Reference to a Book with More Than One Author
[2] Naomi B. Lynn, Ann B. Matasar, and Marie Barovic Rosenberg. Research Guide in Women's Studies (Morristown, N.J.: General Learning, 1974) 156.

### Reference to a Book in Several Volumes
[3] Werner Jaeger, Paideia: The Ideals of Greek Culture, trans. Gilbert Highet, 3 vols. (New York: Oxford UP, 1943) 2:34–37.

### Reference to a Later or Revised Edition
[4] Robert Dudley French, A Chaucer Handbook, 2nd ed. (New York: Appleton, 1956) 27.

### Reference to an Article in an Edited Collection
[5] Earl H. Rovit, "Ralph Ellison and the American Comic Tradition," Ralph Ellison: A Collection of Critical Essays, ed. John Hersey (Englewood Cliffs, N.J.: Prentice, 1974) 78–90.

### Reference to an Article from a General Reference Work
[6] "Fleming, Sir Alexander," Chambers's Biographical Dictionary, new edition, 1972.

### Reference to an Article from a Weekly or Monthly Magazine
[7] Jane Otten, "Living in Syntax," Newsweek 30 Dec. 1974:9.

[8] Ignatius C. Mattingly, "Some Cultural Aspects of Serial Cartoons, or Get a Load of Those Funnies," Harper's Dec. 1955: 34–39.

### Reference to an Article from a Learned Journal
[9] Erik H. Erikson, "The Problem of Ego Identity," Journal of the American Psychoanalytical Association 4 (1956):56–121.

### Reference to a Newspaper Article
[10] Fred Ferretti, "The Pre-Marathon Menu: Almost Anything," New York Times 24 Oct. 1984, late ed.: A1+.

### Reference to a Public Document
[11] United States Congress, Senate, Committee on the Judiciary, Hearings before the Subcommittee to Investigate Juvenile Delinquency, 86th Cong., 2nd sess. (Washington: GPO, 1954).

### Reference to Interviews
[12] Warren Beatty, personal interview, 28 Mar. 1986.

[13] Michael Jackson, interview, Rolling Stone 17 Jan. 1985:13–17.

### Reference to a Movie or Television Program
[14] Tess, dir. Roman Polanski, prod. Charles Berri, with Nastassia Kinski, Columbia Pictures, 1981.

[15] Americans in Love, narr. Sam Rovit, writ. and prod. Abigail McKenzie, PBS News Special, WGBH, Boston, 19 Oct. 1984.

### Reference to a Recording
[16] Lisa Bear, lead singer, Long House, Long House in Concert at Carnegie Hall, rec. 5 September 1985, Prestige, P-44115, 1986.

### Reference to Computer Software
[17] Ms. Pacman, computer software, Atari, Inc., 1983.

Subsequent references to these are shortened forms — usually, as in parenthetical references, the author's last name followed by a page number (see p. 348). If you are using two or more books by the same author, use a shortened form of the title. Use these shortened forms even when two consecutive numbers refer to the same work.

## Abbreviations

### Abbreviations of Publishers' Names
It is acceptable to use shortened forms of publishers' names in your documentation. Usually, a single word in the publisher's full name is enough — as in *Bobbs* for *The Bobbs-Merrill Co. Inc.* or

*Holt* for *Holt, Rinehart and Winston.* For various university presses, simply use *UP* for *University Press* along with the name of the university, as in *Princeton UP.* Initials are permissible for such entities as The New American Library (NAL), The National Council of English Teachers (NCTE), The National Education Association (NEA) and the Modern Language Association of America (MLA). The important thing is to make sure that whatever abbreviation you use your reader can easily identify the publisher's name.

### Other Abbreviations

The following abbreviations may also be useful in your documentation:

| | |
|---|---|
| anon. | anonymous |
| c., ca. *(circa)* | about (c. 1485) |
| cf. *(confer)* | compare |
| ch., chs., chap., chaps. | chapter(s) |
| diss. | dissertation |
| ed., eds. | edited by, edition, editor(s) |
| e.g. *(exempli gratia)* | for example |
| et al. *(et alii)* | and others |
| f., ff. | and the following page(s) |
| ibid. *(ibidem)* | in the same place |
| i.e. *(id est)* | that is |
| intro. | introduction |
| l., ll. | line(s) |
| loc. cit. *(loco citato)* | in the place cited |
| MS., ms., MSS., mss. | manuscript(s) |
| n. | note |
| n.d. | no date (of publication) |
| n.p. | no place (of publication) |
| numb. | numbered |
| op. cit. *(opere citato)* | in the work cited |
| p., pp. | page(s) |
| passim | here and there; throughout |
| rev. | revised |
| tr., trans. | translated by, translator |
| v. *(vide)* | see, consult |
| vol., vols. | volume(s) |

# Sample Research Paper

The sample research paper that follows is shown in final typed form. Commentary on the text appears facing each page.

Illegal Immigrants: Are We Seeing Them Clearly?

by

Judith Solomon

English 110C

Prof. J. Baumel

November 20, 1984

Judith's instructor, Prof. Baumel, required that this outline and thesis statement accompany the draft she submitted.

THESIS STATEMENT: The passage of large numbers of illegal immigrants across our borders is seen by many Americans as a lawless act, solely the fault of the immigrants, that threatens our way of life and drains our resources, but this view needs to be modified.

I. The passage of illegal immigrants to the United States is large and growing.
   A. The numbers coming across the border every year are very large.
   B. The numbers already settled here over the past ten years are very large.

II. These people are seen as a threat in many ways, but some of these views are irrational and others overstatements.
   A. They are seen as a threat because they are dark-skinned Hispanics, but this view is irrational.
   B. They are seen as a threat because they are more fertile than we are and will increase our population, but this view, too, is irrational.
   C. They are seen as threatening to take many jobs from American workers, but most Americans don't want the jobs they fill.
   D. They are seen as threatening because they use our resources, especially our social services, but in fact they use little of these.

III. Although the illegal immigrants have broken the law in sneaking across our borders, their action is more a sociological phenomenon than a criminal one.
   A. They have been pushed across the border in large

numbers by intolerable conditions of poverty in
Mexico and in other third-world countries.

B. They have been pulled here by employers eager to
exploit them.

C. They are given institutional sanction in being
employed even by U.S. officials.

1 Judith's opening, the first three paragraphs, catches the reader's attention by its quiet narrative tone. Notice, however, that Judith has included certain details that pique the reader's curiosity: buying the house "for cash"; "they don't even use the public schools."

1

Juan Gomez came to the United States from his
native Mexico eight years ago. After two years, he sent
for his wife Esmerelda and his sons Luis and Esteban. A
daughter Hilda was born here. The family lives in a
small, white frame house in a working-class section of
the borough of Queens in New York City. Juan bought this
house, for cash, four years after the family arrived, but
the name on the deed is Hilda Gomez. Juan is an
excellent mechanic and managed to get the house
cheaply and make it livable by the sweat of his own labor.
When he first came, he bought an old wreck of a car very
cheaply and repaired it well enough to run it fourteen
hours a day as a gypsy, or unlicensed, taxicab. Business
was so good that he was later able to do the same with
three more old cars and then begin to hire others to
operate his little fleet.

A creator of jobs, Juan Gomez and his family also
pay taxes: the sales tax on the gasoline for his cabs, real
estate taxes on his house, and sales taxes on the things
the family buys.

Being prosperous, they have no need of such
municipal services as health care or welfare or of such
federal and state assistance programs as food stamps or
unemployment benefits. They don't even use the public
schools. The Gomez children all attend the local Catholic
parochial school. And they are grateful to have little
contact with public officials. They think there is only one
"real" American in their family--Hilda, because she was
born here--and that's why their house is in her name. Yet
it saddens the others that they are not quite citizens, for

2 The superscript number 1 corresponds to a content note at the end of the paper just before the Works Cited page. The note discusses what name to give to illegal immigrants and why Judith has chosen as she has. The issue is important but does not belong in her text.

3 The superscript number 2 also refers the reader to a content note. This one explains that the interview with Juan Gomez has been transcribed and that page numbers will refer to that transcription.

4 The introduction of Judith's thesis statement at this point in the paper has impact since its content goes contrary to what we have supposed after reading of the Gomez' good behavior.

5 The parenthetical reference to Stoddard tells the reader that Judith learned from him the fact that the border is not rigorously patrolled. The other information in the parentheses saves a content note.

2

they consider Queens their home, think of themselves as Americans in some large sense, and wouldn't consider leaving here. But they also live in fear that they will be found out some day and shipped back to Mexico. The fear is so strong that they have insisted this paper call them "Gomez," which is not their real name. For they are undocumented workers,[1] illegal immigrants in this country, and, though they seem to have made a good life for themselves here, they feel that their hold on it is precarious (Gomez 1 – 12).[2]

There are millions like the Gomez family who have migrated here illegally. Although few have been as successful as the Gomezes, all are having an impact on this country as we are having an impact on them. This mutual interaction has become part of American life. Nevertheless, the passage of such large numbers of illegal immigrants across our borders is seen by many Americans as a lawless act, solely the fault of the immigrants, that threatens our way of life and drains our resources, but this view needs to be modified.

People have always slipped illegally across borders. Legal access to the United States is limited and cannot accommodate those wishing to come here. But since we are not a police state, easy access to our 2,000 mile long border with Mexico, for example, is available with very little risk of detection by the relatively small number of agents of the Immigration and Naturalization Service (hereafter referred to as the INS; Stoddard 168). Estimates vary, but one writer suggests that 650,000 slip across our borders every year (Fauriol 5), while others

6 Judith needs to refer to more than one source in her parentheses. Notice that she uses a semicolon to separate the two.

7 Notice here that since Judith has used Hewlett's name in her text, she doesn't use the name in the parenthetical reference — only the page number.

8 Judith uses <u>Marielitos,</u> underlined because it is a foreign word (meaning "those from Mariel"), instead of a whole phrase, a piece of economic writing that suggests her familiarity with the Spanish language.

3

6

7

contend that the figure is only half a million (Hewlett 369; Chaze 47). A refinement on these numbers comes from Hewlett, who maintains that more than two and a half million come across--but that only half a million stay (365). Estimates of the total number who have settled here in the past ten years range from 4 to 15 million, but nobody is sure for the obvious reason that getting exact figures on clandestine activity is difficult (Church 16). To make the point that the number is large, however, and that the problem is growing, experts cite the number of people arrested trying the illegal crossing over the past twenty years (Fauriol 8; "Illegal Immigrants" 26). In 1964, 40,000 were arrested; by 1970, the figure had risen beyond 260,000; and by the end of 1983 it was in excess of 1.3 million. And it is easy to see that for every person apprehended, two or three escaped.

Perhaps the sheer numbers involved have provoked such terms as an "alien invasion" (Stoddard 157). Perhaps some of the extremes of American reactions have also been provoked by recent experience with the inflow of Haitians, Vietnamese boat people, and those who came from Mariel in Cuba in 1980. These refugees-- to be distinguished from illegal immigrants in that their entry into the country is legal--have not assimilated without difficulty. In particular, we now know that the

8

mayhem caused by many of the Marielitos was attribut- able to the criminals and mental patients included among the other Cubans (Fauriol 7) in a deliberate act of Cuban foreign policy. So threatening do they seem,

9 Judith smoothly introduces a long, indented quotation by integrating it into the preceding sentence. With a view toward accuracy of citation, Judith has used "Qtd." (for *quoted*) in her parenthetical reference.

---

JV6507. C73 1983                    Crewdson, The Tarnished Door, 16

### HISPANIC STATISTICS

The United States is now the fifth largest Hispanic country in the world. First four: Mexico, Spain, Argentina and Columbia. But only six percent of Mexicans have come to the U.S. legally or illegally. 7% of Cubans and Haitians; 8% of Dominicans; 12% of Trinidadians; 18% of Barbadians and 22% of Jamaicans.

---

10 The Crewdson card is a summary of statistics. Notice that Judith has the call number in the upper left hand corner so that she can, at the last minute, check the accuracy of what's on the card. Note, too, that the card has an appropriate heading written with a felt-tip marker. The Fauriol card is part paraphrase and part direct quotation. Note carefully what's used in the text from both cards and what's omitted.

4

moreover, that Zero Population Growth, an organization dedicated to humane conservation, has said of the illegal immigrants that they

> depress wages, displace low-skilled American
> workers, drive unemployed workers to seek
> assistance from social service programs. Further-
> more, they have a negative effect on our balance of
> payments, inasmuch as they typically remit funds
> to family members in the home country. They
> certainly do nothing to enhance environmental
> quality because they increase crowding and add to
> the burden on water, energy and sanitation
> facilities (Qtd. in Halsell 5).

Perhaps the most significant way in which the illegal immigrant is seen as an undesirable and a threat is in the emphasis placed on his ethnic identity. Although illegal immigrants come from more than sixty nations, the fact that 50 percent are estimated to come from Mexico causes even objective reporters to register fear in the subtle idiom of racism (Morris and Mayio 12). For example, Crewdson notes that the United States, because of this immigration, is now the fifth largest Hispanic country in the world (16; one wonders if, in the event it were the case, Crewdson would report "the fifth largest Anglo-Saxon country in the world"); and that while only 6 percent of Mexico's population has migrated here, the percentages are higher for other countries. He gives an alarmingly upwardly scaled series in such a way that the reader imagines the last of the series: 100 percent of the population of some nation has emptied its entire popula-tion on our shores. Hewlett notices, in this connection, that Los Angeles, now 40 percent Hispanic, will soon be 75 percent (360). Of course, a necessary corollary to the

Humanist, May/June 1984      Fauriol, "U.S. Immigration Policy and the National Interest," 6-9.

## LANGUAGE BARRIERS

Illegal immigrants stick together more cohesively than earlier groups <u>because</u> they're illegal and seek each other's protection. Therefore, they speak only their own languages and develop only language related political interests or social interests, such as bilingual education. Nevertheless, economically, these foreign language groups will be disadvantaged. We're seeing, in fact, "the creation of enclaves of often second-class citizens, speaking only their native tongue."

11   Judith is here confronting Fauriol's views with her own, not with any she has taken from a source. Her instructor did not require a citation for Judith's knowledge about immigration patterns in the United States. It is fairly common knowledge in the area she's writing about.

5

idea that we are being overrun by foreigners is the
often-mentioned fact that the immigrants have higher
fertility rates than we do (Stoddard 159; Hewlett 370).

Examining immigration policy, Fauriol takes the
foreignness of immigrants to be a permanent drawback
because, he suggests, the language of the foreigner is a
barrier to assimilation. Not only is the Hispanic push for
bilingual education putting a costly strain on our resources, but illegal immigration has the effect of the
"creation of enclaves of often second-class citizens,
speaking only their native tongue" (6, 8–9). He sees
these enclaves as politically and socially divisive.

It is hard to address the fears of those who predict
the future size of Hispanically populated cities in the
United States, but Fauriol's points need to be confronted.
In the first place, waves of immigration, legal or illegal,
always produce "enclaves." Immigrants who do not
speak the language of their new country naturally
gravitate to those who do speak their language. Moreover, the American experience with waves of immigrating
Germans, Jews, and Italians contradicts Fauriol's
assertions: None of these groups has had trouble achieving full participation in American social and political life
and learning the language well enough to use it. Why
then should the Hispanic waves be thought any different?
Joshua A. Fishman has shown, in a recent study, that
the ethnic mother tongue school in the United States--
where the children of immigrants learn foreign lan-
guages--is really a place where particularly American
values are fostered, values like pride in an original

11

12 This one sentence paragraph makes a good transition to her next subject, that is, to the motives of illegal immigrants.

13 The quotation Judith uses from p. 159 of Stoddard is well integrated into the sentence. She has used ellipsis (three spaced points) to indicate that she's omitted part of what Stoddard had written and she has used square brackets for the notation that the italics were Stoddard's.

6

ethnicity, values "rich in faith, in feeling, in emotion" (237).

12    Foreign though these immigrants be, their motives for coming here are anything but strange.

Some of the illegal immigrants here have not come undocumented across our borders, but have entered legally and overstayed the terms of their permits. It is relatively easy to do this, especially if, like these so-called visa abusers, one can speak passable English or has an employable skill (Crewdson 104 – 105; Stoddard 165 – 170). These people come to improve their lot; the medical students among them seek better hospital facilities, the engineers more advanced technical training. Although these immigrants constitute a brain drain on their native lands and in some cases are causing a strain in relations with these countries, some writers think skilled immigrants are the only ones we should admit (Cafferty et al 150).

Although immigrants have always come here for a better life, the overwhelming majority of those who come now are not here to achieve anything better; rather they are here to achieve survival in the face of a "slow, sure death" in the poverty of their own countries (Halsell 124). Crewdson, analyzing rural Mexico, whence come large numbers of immigrants, notes that the alternative to work is starvation but that there is no work there (4). Stoddard puts it well when he says that those who come

13    are "unemployed and desperately seeking work [his italics], any work, not . . . a better income" (159). This is a considerable change from the motive of those who

14 This interesting observation is Judith's own, and is based on what would be common knowledge in the field of migration to the United States, that is, on what she says about the relative wealth of the earlier migrants.

15 Details like these from the interview with Juan Gomez tend to enliven Judith's paper. Primary sources always have that effect and should be used wherever possible.

16 Judith achieves sympathy for the illegal immigrants by a skillful excursion into this material on the exploitation of such workers.

7

came to our country in the early waves of migration,
when improvement was the goal, or those who came earlier, when the country was founded; the Puritans, in fact,
were fairly well off. The fact that the present immigrants
are penniless and destitute may have something to do
with their being scapegoated by the better off Americans
already here.

Juan Gomez's urban experience confirms this state
of affairs. He is vague when asked how he managed to
stay alive in the shantytown barrio on the outskirts of
Mexico City--one suspects that there are wounds of
shame silencing him on this point--but he insists that he
and his family were always on the verge of starvation,
barely managing by some form of scavenging on the
garbage mounds adjacent to his cardboard hovel (Gomez
5). The death of Juan's father and the sale of the father's
ring, which turned out to be more valuable than the older
man had ever hinted, was the stroke of luck that permitted Juan to buy his way across the border. Juan's
experience illustrates that at least one cause of the
immigrant's movement is dire necessity.

Now from the moment he tries to get here, the
illegal immigrant enters a system that exploits and
intimidates him. First, if he is coming from Mexico, he is
lost without a "coyote" (or guide), since he is only a pollo
(a chicken, because he travels with a flock of others as
defenseless as he). The coyote charges him anywhere
from $200 to $400 to provide passage across the border
and to introduce him to an employer on the other side.
Very frequently, if the crossing is successful, the coyote

17 Notice that Judith expresses skepticism about Juan's tale of extreme exploitation at the hands of the factory owner.

8

collects from the employer in California or Texas a fee for
providing pliable, low-cost help (Stoddard 161).

Workers on ranches in the borderlands are poorly
treated because they have no legal recourse--even
against beatings or other forms of physical maltreatment.
Besides, the worker is pathetically eager to please, rather
than be sent back where he came from and starve or
endure the shame of letting down the family that's
counting on his support. So he endures such treatment,
as well as the harsh working conditions and the substandard living quarters. And even if he is paid less than the
minimum wage of $3.55 per hour, his pay is bound to be
a lot more than the 55 cents an hour that is standard at
home--in Mexico, for example--when such work is
available (Stoddard 165 – 166).

Once established here, the illegal immigrant--unless
he is as talented and lucky as Juan Gomez--remains
caught in a web of exploitation and sometimes deception.
Without English or legal documents, he is afraid to
venture far or utter an outcry over conditions. More
often than not, then, he hears through friends of jobs in
factories or sweatshops or farms and takes them or
others of the most menial kind. Juan Gomez worked in a
furniture factory in the Bronx before buying his first taxi.
Among the indignities he recalls was a raid by the INS on
a Thursday--the day before what promised to be a
lucrative payday. Juan managed to escape over a roof
but never went back for his pay. He insists that the
factory owner himself called the Immigration Service in
order to save the money. Whether such a story is true or

17

not, it would take a huge effort to improve the working conditions of the illegal immigrant--even if he were here legally. Like any foreigner in any country, he would need to adapt to local customs, speak the local language, and learn the skills in local demand if he were to hope for better work. But the average illegal border crosser cannot acquire any of these necessities.

With employment here acting as a carrot and poverty at home acting as a stick, the immigrant is pushed and pulled to break the law. And it is this economic motive that touches the nerve ends of the American worker and his union officials. The latter are opposed to the illegal immigrant because he makes it difficult for the unions to maintain effective boycotts or strikes. Moreover, union officials see the illegal immigrant much as their members see him, that is, as someone who takes away their jobs (Stoddard 174).

"My biggest objection is that they come over here and get the jobs we can't get. Then they live on practically nothing"--this is the attitude of an unemployed worker in Detroit (Qtd. in Chaze 48). "They'll do any kind of work," says an official of the International Ladies' Garment Workers' Union (Qtd. in Chaze 49). These attitudes suggest that the immigrants will do anything to earn money but that they have some kind of magical power to exist on very little money.

The truth is, however, that they have no such powers and are like any other workers. When their spending habits are studied, it is found that immigrants are like anybody else--they'll spend very little as long as

10

they earn very little and spend more when they earn more (Morrison 352).

Moreover, while workers and union officials think that illegal aliens are able to live on practically nothing while taking the food out of American workers' mouths, there is evidence to suggest that Americans really don't want the jobs held by illegal immigrants.

For example, a study was made of 13 firms in the Los Angeles area whose illegal immigrant employees were arrested by the INS and deported. Eventually, it was found, four-fifths of these employees made their way back to these firms and got their old jobs back. While they were gone, Americans would not replace them (Church 17). In another case, 340 undocumented workers were found in various menial jobs in the San Diego area. They were duly arrested and deported. At the end of a ninety-day recruiting period, during which the jobs were offered only to Americans, all the jobs in question had to be filled by commutes, Mexican citizens who enter the U.S. legally for the sole purpose of working and then return home (Schmidt 19).

While it is doubtless true that some immigrants replace some Americans, other studies could be cited to show that the results of the San Diego and Los Angeles studies are the more usual patterns. But despite this evidence, we are gripped by extreme, emotional opinions like that of former central intelligence director William E. Colby, who calls illegal immigrants "a greater threat to the future of the United States than the Soviet Union" (Qtd. in Crewdson 17).

18  Judith has not photocopied the table but simply retyped it.

19  Judith is here relying on common knowledge, that is, that third-world countries are likely to be poor. The suggestion that the reader think of Mexico as an extreme example of a third-world country is a fair one.

Aurora Schmidt, on the other hand, has shown that[11] in the view of some economists, illegal immigrants appear to have a positive economic effect on the country and do not drain away our resources or take away jobs (17–21). She presents a table from the study by David North and Marion Huston that shows this graphically:

18  TABLE

| PROGRAM ACTIVITY | PERCENTAGE OF RESPONDENT PARTICIPATION |
|---|---|
| Input | |
| Social Security taxes withheld | 77.3 |
| Federal income taxes withheld | 73.2 |
| Hospitalization payments withheld | 44.0 |
| Filed U.S. Income tax returns | 31.5 |
| Output | |
| Used hospitals or clinics | 27.4 |
| Collected one or more weeks of unemployment insurance | 3.9 |
| Have children in U.S. schools | 3.7 |
| Participated in U.S. funded job training programs | 1.4 |
| Secured food stamps | 1.3 |
| Secured welfare payments | 0.5 |
| (Schmidt 19) | |

To modify further the harsh picture of the illegal immigrant that is prevalent today, we must look, finally, at two conditions influencing him to come across the border.

19      First is the economic situation in his country. The situation in Mexico may be taken as an extreme model of what things are like in other third-world countries supplying us with illegal immigrants. Despite its great oil

reserves and its other natural resources, Mexico is an economic disaster area. It has a population of 74,000,000 that is growing by leaps and bounds. Half of the population is under fifteen years of age; thus half are unskilled, hungry, and getting ready for a tomorrow when they will be reproducing and demanding employment. There is a 50-percent unemployment rate, a killing 30-percent inflation rate, and not enough money for significant public assistance programs (Halsell 9–10). That 6 percent of Mexico's population is on the move north every year is a blessing to the Mexican government--so much so, in fact, that when the recent Simpson-Mazzoli Immigration Act was about to pass the United States Congress and inaugurate controls on this migration north, Mexico made its position known to our leaders, and, perhaps for that reason, the bill failed to pass (Crewdson 330).

The second factor that influences illegal crossings is, of course, the interest of large agribusiness, principally, but also those of various manufacturing enterprises, especially the sweatshop faction of the garment industry. If these enterprises were not ready to employ illegal immigrants, the immigrants would have weaker motives to come here. But it is much to the interest of such industries to have compliant, vulnerable workers whose productivity and pay they can control completely (Stoddard 174–176). Crewdson describes the lobbying against Simpson-Mazzoli by the organized interests of these industries, for Simpson-Mazzoli would have mandated significant penalties for anyone employing undocumented workers (318–332). Added to these

13

factors is another that illuminates attitudes: Stoddard has shown that in the borderlands adjacent to Mexico many middle-class Americans, including officials of the INS, are happy to employ illegal immigrants as house-maids, gardeners, cooks, chauffeurs, and the like (Stoddard 176). Thus the institutional forces at work seem to suggest that we are not dealing so much with lawless acts of criminality on the part of individuals as we are with a mass movement, a sociological phenomenon.

That we must modify our harsh view of these immigrants should be evident when we consider the matter from this angle: to have come here at all, even illegally, requires of immigrants courage, determination, energy, a capacity to endure hardship, a strong taste for hard work, and a concern for one's family. But this list describes what is best about Americans. Is it not ironic that Americans should be looking blindly past the appearance of these traits in others?

## 14

## Notes

[1] Many names are used for these people, some derogatory, like "illegal aliens." <u>Undocumented workers</u> is a neutral term preferred by many, but it omits their status as migrants. Therefore, I have used <u>illegal immigrants</u> throughout.

[2] I used a tape recorder for the interview with Juan Gomez, known to me through his son, Esteban, who is my friend. The interview has been transcribed and now exists as a thirty-page typescript. I shall refer to these pages.

[3] So large is the whole issue of migration today that it is widely studied. There are two scholarly journals, <u>Migration Today</u> and the <u>International Migration Review,</u> and a Center for Migration Studies located in New York. A whole network of social agencies, too large to list here, has also sprung up to study and aid these people.

20 Note that "Works Cited" is centered. Each entry is typed double-spaced. The first line of each entry is flush with the left margin, and subsequent lines are indented five spaces. This makes it easy for a reader to look up a reference.

20

15

Works Cited

Cafferty, Pastora San Juan; Barry R. Chiswick; Andrew
M. Greeley; Teresa A. Sullivan. The Dilemma of
American Immigration: Beyond the Golden Door.
New Brunswick, N.J.: Transaction Books, 1983.

Chaze, William L. "Will U.S. Shut Door on Immigrants?"
U.S. News & World Report 12 Apr. 1982: 47–50.

Church, George J. "'We Are Overwhelmed.'" Time 25
June 1984: 16–17.

Crewdson, John. The Tarnished Door: The New Immigrants and the Transformation of America. New
York: Times Books, 1983.

Fauriol, Georges. "U.S. Immigration Policy and the
National Interest." The Humanist 44:3 (May/June
1984):5–14.

Fishman, Joshua A. "Ethnic Community Mother Tongue
Schools in the USA: Dynamics and Distribution."
International Migration Review 14:2 (Summer
1980):235–258.

Fragomen, Austin T., and Lydio F. Tomasi, eds. In
Defense of the Alien. New York: Center for Migration
Studies, 1979.

Gomez, Juan. Personal Interview, 3 September 1984.

Halsell, Grace. The Illegals. New York: Stein and Day, 1978.

Hewlett, Sally Ann. "Coping with Illegal Immigration."
Foreign Affairs 60 (Winter 1981/82):358–378.

"Illegal Immigrants: The U.S. May Gain More Than It
Loses." Business Week, 14 May 1984:26–27.

Morris, Milton D. and Albert Mayio. Curbing Illegal Immigration: A Staff Paper. Abridged by Alice M. Carroll. Washington: The Brookings Institution, 1982.

Morrison, R. J. "A Wild Motley Throng: Immigration Expenditures and the 'American' Standard of Living." International Immigration Review 14:3 (Fall 1980):343–355.

Schmidt, Aurora. "Refugees and Immigrants: In Conflict with the American Poor?" Migration Today 9:4–5 (1981):17–21.

Stoddard, Ellwyn R. "A Conceptual Analysis of the 'Alien Invasion': Institutionalized Support of Illegal Mexican Aliens in the U.S." International Migration Review 10:2 (Summer 1976):157–186.

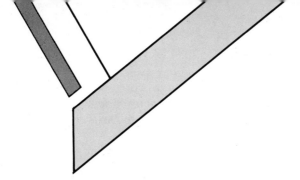

# Glossary of Usage

Each of the entries in this section discusses words or phrases that are frequently usage problems for student writers — as well as for more experienced ones. Suggestions for correct usage given in the entries describe current usage among educated writers and are based on the best dictionaries and recent studies in usage. Naturally, not every problem is treated here. Elsewhere in the book, you will find a brief list of troublesome idiomatic combinations (pp. 108–109) and a list of homophones (pp. 228–232). However, if you are unable to find the word, expression, or rule you are interested in, you should consult either a good dictionary or your instructor.

The following labels are used in the glossary:

*Formal:* Words or expressions of standard educated usage; appropriate to a high level of serious writing. Students are expected to produce this kind of writing in most colleges and in most courses.

*Informal:* The language of the everyday world. Informal words and expressions occur widely, but are also widely avoided in formal writing.

*Colloquial:* The language used in conversation, mainly informal; used by writers and speakers both educated and uneducated; but should, in most cases, be avoided in all but the most informal writing.

*Standard:* The language used in most printed matter; includes formal and informal, but is understood to stand closer to formal.

**383**

*Nonstandard:* Applies to words or expressions that good dictionaries label as *illiterate, nonstandard, obsolete, slang, dialect,* or *substandard.* These are to be avoided in all kinds of writing.

*Illiterate:* A species of the nonstandard occurring only in the most uneducated writing and speaking; of course, items so labeled are to be avoided.

*Slang:* Also a species of nonstandard writing. Slang aims to be fresh, funny, and forceful. Often, slang develops into a kind of shorthand language and quickly becomes overused. Exercise care in using slang; it belongs only in informal writing and should be used there sparingly.

**A, an**   Use *a* before a word beginning with a consonant *sound*— even when the word begins with a letter classified as a vowel, as in *a university.* Use *an* before a word beginning with a vowel (*an egg, an orange*) or a word with a silent *h* (*an hour, an honor*).

**Absolutely**   Overworked when used as an intensifier: "It was *absolutely* the greatest experience of my life."

**Accept, except**   *Accept* is a verb, meaning "to receive" or "to agree to," and *except* is a preposition, meaning "other than" or "but."

> I *accept* your invitation.
> I have invited everyone *except* Charlie.

**Actually**   Overworked as an intensifier — like *absolutely* and *really.* Instead of "They were *actually* happy" use "They were very happy" or "They were happy."

**Ad**   An abbreviated form of *advertisement,* not appropriate to formal writing. Similarly shortened forms are *auto, exam, photo, math,* and *phone.*

**Adapt, adopt**   To *adapt* is to be able to adjust to a situation or set of circumstances; to *adopt* is to take in or to agree to a course of action.

> Fred was not able to *adapt* to college life.
> We would like to *adopt* a child.

**Advice, advise**   *Advice* is the noun, *advise* the verb.

> I can give you good *advice.*
> Let me *advise* you.

**Affect, effect**   Usually, *affect* is a verb, meaning "to influence." The verb *effect* means "to bring about or achieve"; the noun *effect* means "the result."

> The music *affected* me deeply.
> We can, through political action, *effect* a change in government.
> The *effect* of a shave is to open little cuts on the face.

**Aggravate**   Means "to make worse" or "to intensify." Used colloquially to mean "annoy" or "provoke."

> ***Formal***   The argument *aggravated* my headache.
> ***Colloquial***   I was *aggravated* by his attitude.

**Agree to, agree with**   To *agree to* is to consent; to *agree with* is to concur.

> I *agree to* the contract, but I do not *agree with* his estimate of how much money I will make under its terms.

**Ain't**   Contraction of *am not*. Extended frequently to *is not, are not, has not,* and *have not*. Not only nonstandard, but also strongly disapproved by most educated speakers and writers.

**All, all of**   Use *all of* before proper nouns or pronouns, as in *all of Africa, all of these*. The *of* may be omitted to make expression more concise in constructions like *all of his energy* (better: *all his energy*) or *all of her strength* (better: *all her strength*).

**All ready, already**   *Already:* "before" or "by a certain time"; *all ready:* "completely prepared."

> When I arrived, she was *already* in the shower.
> The Cosmos are *all ready* for the big game.

**All right, alright**   Most dictionaries say *alright* is nonstandard for *all right*.

**All that**   Colloquial when used in constructions like "I didn't like the course *all that* much." How much is *all that*?

**All together, altogether**   *All together* means "in a group." *Altogether* means "entirely" or "thoroughly."

> We were *all together* in our decision.
> Smoking is an *altogether* unhealthy vice.

**Allusion**   See **illusion, allusion.**

**Almost**   See **most, almost.**

**Alot**   Should be two words: *a lot.*

**Among, between**   *Among* is usually reserved for more than two persons or things. *Between* is commonly used only for two. However, it is possible to use *between* for three or more items when they are regarded as having a reciprocal relationship or to express the relationship of one to the others.

> *Among* those at the meeting, there wasn't a single Democrat.
> The choice *between* ice cream and pie is easy to make.
> There's much competition *between* the three major car companies.
> We sailed directly *between* the three big rocks.

**Amount, number**   *Amount* refers to quantities, like water and air, that cannot be counted individually; *number* refers to things, like trees, that can be counted individually.

The *amount of traffic* on the road is staggering.
The *number of cars* going through the tunnel is staggering.

**An, a**   See **a, an.**

**Analyzation**   Illiterate for *analysis*.

**And etc.**   A redundancy, since *etc.* means "and so forth"; together the words would mean "and and so forth."

**And/or**   A construction found in legal documents. Some find it objectionable in formal writing.

**And which, and who**   See part 2, **Parallel Construction.**

**Ante, anti**   *Ante* means "before" (as in *antedate*); *anti* means "against" (as in *anti-American*). Use the hyphen after *anti* when it precedes capital letters and when it precedes a word beginning with *i*—as in *anti-intellectual*.

**Anyone, any one**   Not interchangeable. *Anyone* means "any person at all"; *any one* refers to a specific individual or thing in a group.

*Anyone* can learn to drive a car.
*Any one* of those drivers can teach you to drive a car.

*Note:* This distinction also applies to *everyone* and *someone*.

**Anyways**   Nonstandard for *anyway*.

**Apt, likely, liable**   *Apt* refers to a habitual tendency or a natural talent; *likely* means "probable" or "to be expected"; and *liable* means "legally responsible" or "susceptible to."

**Correct**   She is *apt* at solving equations.
**Correct**   She is not *likely* to go to college this fall.
**Correct**   He is *liable* to prosecution for grand larceny.

Informal usage sometimes confuses these meanings.

**Informal**   She is *apt* to go to college this fall.
**Informal**   She is *liable* to go to college this fall.

**Around**   Colloquial for "about" or "near."

**Formal**   It was *about* four o'clock.

**As, as if, like**   See **like, as, as if.**

**At**   Nonstandard after *where,* as in the following:

Where is he *at*?
I know where he's *at*.

**Auto**   See **ad.**

**Awful**   See **real.**

**Awfully**   Commonly used in speech to mean "exceedingly," but not preferred in writing.

> ***Formal***   She was *very* late.
> ***Colloquial***   She was *awfully* late.
> The play was *awfully* good.

**Bad**   Sometimes confused with the adverb *badly*. But *bad* is an adjective.

> She felt *bad* about breaking up with her boyfriend.
> She was hurt *badly* in the accident.

**Beauty**   See **real.**

**Being that, being as how**   Illiterate. Use the correct subordinating conjunctions *as, since, because.*

**Beside, besides**   Writers should be careful to distinguish between *beside* meaning "at the side of" and *besides* meaning "in addition to" or "also."

> He was *beside* me as we entered the room.
> *Besides,* I'm tired.

**Be sure and, try and**   Colloquial for *be sure to, try to.*

**Between**   See **among, between.**

**Breakdown**   Standard when used to mean "collapse," but colloquial when used instead of "itemization" or "analysis."

> ***Standard***   She suffered a nervous *breakdown.*
> ***Colloquial***   He made a *breakdown* of our receipts from the dance.

**Bunch**   Colloquial when used to mean a *group* or a *gathering* of people, as in a *bunch of people*, but standard when appropriately applied to, for example, *grapes*, as in a *bunch of grapes*.

**Burst, bursted, bust, busted**   *Burst* is the standard past tense and past participle form of *burst*. *Bursted* is no longer standard. *Bust* and *busted* are slang.

> ***Standard***   The water main *burst* last night.
> ***Nonstandard***   The water main *bursted* last night.
> ***Slang***   The water main *busted* last night.

**But, hardly, scarcely**   Each alone is negative; thus they should not be used with other negatives. See Part 2, **Double Negative.**

**But that, but what**   Wordy substitutes for plain *that,* used as either relative pronoun or conjunction.

I wasn't sure *that* you were sick.

**Can, may**   In informal usage, *can* is used to signify both ability (I *can* play basketball) and permission (*Can* I get you a drink?). In formal writing, many reserve *may* for permission (*May* I get you a drink?). *May* also expresses possibility (I *may* not vote this year.).

**Case, in the case of**   Cases of wordiness. See that entry in Part 2.

**Center about, center around**   Some think it more logical to *center on.*

**Commence**   Pretentious. Use *begin* or *start.*

**Compare with, compare to**   Similar items are compared *with* one another; dissimilar ones are compared *to* each other.

*Compared with* Florence, New York is ugly.
*Compared to* an airplane, a bird is a model of flight efficiency.

**Compliment, complement**   A *compliment* is an expression of praise; a *complement* is something that makes up or completes something else.

The remark was a *compliment.*
The remarks were a *complement* to the previous speaker's.

**Contact**   There is some feeling against the use of *contact* as a verb meaning "to meet with" or "to talk to," but it is in wide use just the same. The trouble with the word is that it is too general, and it is better replaced in writing by more specific terms such as *meet, consult, talk to.*

**Continual, continuous**   That which is *continuous* proceeds without interruption in time or space; the *continual* proceeds with some interruption.

The Alaska pipeline provides a *continuous* flow of oil.
We had a *continual* debate over the energy crisis.

**Could of**   Nonstandard. Use *could have.*

**Couple**   Should be followed by *of,* whether used to mean *a few* (in colloquial use) or *two* (in formal use).

**Cute lovely**   Very much overworked to indicate general approval.

**Data, phenomena**   Plural forms of *datum,* "a fact used to draw a conclusion," and *phenomenon,* "a fact or event perceptible to the senses." Informally, *data* is used as a collective noun and agrees with a singular verb.

> **Formal** These *data are* invaluable.
> **Informal** This *data is* invaluable.

**Deal** Colloquial, but bordering on slang when used to mean "transaction" (a good deal on a car), "secret contract" (a deal with the D. A.), or "treatment" (bad deal from the teacher).

**Definite, definitely** Vague intensifiers, used colloquially, as in "He has a *definite* talent," or "I will *definitely* come tonight."

**Different from, different than** *Different from* is idiomatic. *Different than* is becoming widely used, but should be restricted to introducing a clause.

> Rubgy is *different from* football.
> Rome was *different than* I had expected.

See also Idioms under **Diction,** Part 2.

**Differ from, differ with** To differ *from* someone or something is to be unlike that person or thing; to differ *with* someone is to have a dispute with that person or hold an opposite opinion.

**Disinterested, uninterested** *Disinterested* means "without bias"; *uninterested* means "without interest." These words are often used interchangeably to mean "without interest," but the distinction is worth preserving.

**Don't** The contraction of *do not*—not of *does not.*

> He *doesn't* (not he *don't*) have much money.

**Dose, does** A *dose* is a specified quantity of medication; *does* is the third person singular present tense form of the verb *to do.*

**Due to** Opinion is divided on this. Some authorities criticize the construction used in the sense of *owing to* or *because of.* The criticism objects to its use as a preposition at the head of an adverbial phrase, but this use is becoming widespread and can be used in all but the most formal circumstances.

> **Formal** Our picnic was canceled *because of* rain.
> **Informal** Our picnic was canceled *due to* rain.

**Each and every** Redundant for either *each* or *every.*

**Each other, one another** *Each other* refers to two people, *one another* to more than two people.

Tom and Jerry congratulated *each other*.
The Yankees congratulated *one another* after the victory.

**Effect** See **affect, effect.**

**Eminent, imminent, immanent** *Eminent* means "distinguished"; *imminent* means "about to happen"; *immanent* means "within a realm of reality or discourse."

Colin is an *eminent* sociologist.
Marvin's arrival is *imminent.*
David's book is on history as *immanent.*

**Enthuse, enthused** An informal construction. Recast the sentence and use *enthusiastic* instead.

**Equally as good** Omit the *as.*

**Etc.** Latin abbreviation for *and so forth.* Use it in formal writing only when its meaning is perfectly clear. Since etc. already includes *and,* never write *and etc.* See **Abbreviations** in Part 2.

**Ever so often** Colloquial for *frequently.*

**Everyone** See **anyone, any one.**

**Every so often** Colloquial for *occasionally.*

**Every which way** Colloquial for *in every way, in every direction,* or *in great disorder.*

**Exam** See **ad.**

**Except** See **accept, except.**

**Expect** "I *expect* he'll be here soon" or "I *expect* I should be going now" are colloquial. Use *suppose* and *believe* instead.

**Fact, the fact that** A wordy way to say *that.* See **Wordiness,** Part 2.

> ***Wordy*** Are you aware of *the fact that* she's leaving?
> ***Better*** Are you aware *that* she's leaving?

**Fantastic, fabulous** Avoid these terms of exaggerated astonishment.

**Farther, further** *Farther* is the correct word to express physical distance; *further,* the correct term for all other distance.

His house is *farther* down the road than mine.
In politics, he is *further* to the left than I am.

In informal usage, *further* is widely used in both senses.

**Fewer, less** *Fewer* is used when countable units are discussed; *less* is proper when an uncountable amount is discussed.

There are *fewer* calories in diet soda than in regular.
If the pollution stories are true, we'll soon have *less* water to drink.

**Field**  Much overworked, frequently unnecessary.

> ***Wordy***  He was an expert in *the field* of computers.
> ***Better***  He was an expert in computers.

See **Wordiness,** Part 2.

**Fine**  Vague when used as a general term of approval (as in "We had a *fine* meal") and colloquial when substituted for *well* in a construction like "The car works *fine*."

**Fix**  Colloquial for *predicament.*

**Flunk**  Colloquial for *fail.*

**Folks**  Colloquial when used to refer to members of one's family or relatives as in the sentence "The *folks* all thought I looked well." Standard when it refers to people in general or a specific group: *young folks.*

**Foot, feet**  As units of measurement, standard usage requires "a man six feet tall" or "a four-foot plank." "A man six foot tall" is nonstandard.

**Former, latter**  *Former* is applied to the first of two items, *latter* to the second. Use *first* and *last* when there are more than two items.

**Funny**  Colloquial for *odd, queer,* or *strange.*

**Gentleman**  See **lady, gentleman.**

**Get**  There are many colloquial and slang expressions of which the verb *get* is part. These are not appropriate in formal writing. Among them are the following: *get with it, get smart, get wise, get lost, get going.*

**Good**  A good adjective that should not be used as an adverb.

> ***Good***  The weather is *good* today.
> ***Not Good***  She dances *good.* (Should be *well.*)

**Good and**  Colloquial when used in phrases like "*good and* hungry."

**Great**  See **real.**

**Guess**  In a construction like "I *guess* you'll be happy with your motorbike," formal usage would prefer *think* or *suppose* to *guess.*

**Guy**  Colloquial for *man, boy,* or *fellow.*

**Had better, had best, better**  Legitimate idioms for *ought to* and *should,* which are somewhat more formal; *better* without the auxiliary is colloquial.

You *had better* [or *had best*] go now.
You *ought to* [or *should*] go now.
You *better* go now.

**Had ought to**  Illiterate for *ought to.*

> *Illiterate*  He *had ought to* change his oil.
> *Standard*  He *ought to* change his oil.

**Half a**  *Half a* and *a half* are good usage; *a half a* should be avoided.

*Half a* loaf is better than none.
I have *a half* hour to spare.

**Hanged, hung**  In formal writing, use *hanged* to refer to executed people, *hung* to refer to pictures or other objects.

**Hardly**  See **but, hardly, scarcely.**

**He or she**  This is a construction used to compensate for the allegedly sexist use of *he* to refer to both males and females. The construction is clumsy and logically leads to equally clumsy compromises such as *his or hers* and *him or her.*

> *Clumsy*  When a student is well motivated, *he or she* earns good grades.
> *Better*  When a student is well motivated, *he* earns good grades.

It is possible, of course, and often desirable to avoid the use of *he* to mean both sexes. This is done by rephrasing in some appropriate way:

> *Rephrased*  When students are well motivated, they earn good grades.
> *Rephrased*  A student who is well motivated earns good grades.

**Hisself**  Nonstandard for *himself.*

**Hopefully**  Used to mean "It is to be hoped" or "Let us hope," as in the sentence, "Hopefully, it won't rain while we're on vacation," *hopefully* is strongly disapproved by most educated speakers and writers. Nevertheless, it is widely used in those senses. Used as an adverb meaning "in a hopeful manner," it is correct.

The teacher entered the classroom *hopefully.*

**Idea** Often an imprecise substitute for *intention, plan,* or *purpose.*

> My *plan* [not *idea*] is to eat out tonight.
> The *purpose* [not the *idea*] of the course is to acquaint you with the elements of geometry.

**If, whether** Either *if* or *whether* may be used after such words as *say, ask, doubt, know, wonder,* or *understand.*

> She asked if [whether] she could join us.
> I wonder if [whether] you have a pencil to lend me.

In standard usage, choose *whether* when your sentence expresses alternatives.

> I don't understand *whether* you're going or not.

**Ignorant, stupid** An *ignorant* person has not been taught very much; a *stupid* one is not capable of learning.

**Illusion, allusion** *Illusion* means a "false image or impression"; *allusion* means an "indirect reference to" something or someone.

> It is an *illusion* to think you'll get a job this summer.
> She made an *allusion* to the fact that she needed the money.

**Immanent, imminent** See **eminent, imminent, immanent.**
**Imply** See **infer, imply.**
**In, into, in to** *In* denotes "within the confines of" or "inside." *Into* is the better word to mean "toward, to the inside of," but *in* is widely used in both senses. *In to* are separate words.

> My shirt is *in* the closet.
> Go back *into* the room and get it.
> You may go *in to* see her now.

**In back of, in behind, in between** Wordy formulas for *back of, behind, between.*

**Infer, imply** *Infer* means "to draw conclusions from evidence"; *imply* means "to suggest obliquely without actually saying" something.

> He *implied* he wouldn't go on the trip with us.
> Therefore, we *inferred* that he didn't like the people who were going.

**Ingenious, ingenuous**   The former means "clever," the latter "naive."

**In regard to**   See **Regarding, in regard to, with regard to, relating to, relative to, with respect to, respecting.**

**In regards to**   Nonstandard when substituted for *as regards* or *in regard to*.

**Inside of, outside of**   Mainly, the word *of* in these constructions is unnecessary. *Outside of* is also informal for *except* or *besides*.

> **Informal**   She'll be here *inside of* an hour.
> **Formal**   She'll be here *inside* [or *within*] an hour.

> **Informal**   *Outside of* me, nobody can operate the tractor.
> **Formal**   *Except me*, nobody can operate the tractor.

**In terms of**   A vague and wordy expression; to be avoided.

> **Wordy**   *In terms of* power, Aaron can hit home runs.
> **Better**   Aaron has the power to hit home runs.

**In the case of**   A vague and wordy expression; to be avoided.

> **Wordy**   *In the case of* my Shakespeare class, it's boring.
> **Better**   My Shakespeare class is boring.

**Irregardless**   Nonstandard. Use plain old *regardless*.

**Is because**   See **reason is because.**

**Is when, is where**   Clumsy and illogical expressions when *where* and *when* are used to introduce noun clauses as the complement of *is*.

> **Clumsy**   Capitalism *is where* there is private ownership of capital.
> **Better**   Capitalism is a form of economic development with private ownership of capital.

> **Clumsy**   A neurosis *is when* there is a disturbance of ego function.
> **Better**   A neurosis is a disturbance of ego function.

**It is me, it is I**   The latter is very (almost too) formal; the former is widely used informally. See **Case** in Part 2.

**It's, its**   *It's* is the contraction of *it is*. *Its* is a possessive pronoun.

**-ize, -wise**   The former suffix is frequently used to make a verb out of a noun or an adjective *(revolutionize, ionize)*, the latter to make an adverb out of a noun or an adjective *(clockwise, otherwise, likewise)*, but both are overworked, especially in bureaucratic jargon. Avoid their use except in established words.

Not "The agreement was *finalized*," but "The agreement was *made final*."
Not, "*Moneywise*, it was a good decision," but "From a *financial* viewpoint, it was a good decision."

**Kind of a** Leave out the *a*.

**Know, no, now** *Know* is "understand"; *no* is the negative particle; *now* means "at present."

**Lack, need, want** As nouns, a *lack* is a shortage; a *need* is a condition brought on by a *lack;* and a *want* is a lack of things that are necessary combined with an awareness of that lack.

New York City has a *lack* of funds.
He had a *need* for friendship and affection.
The people feel a *want* of responsiveness to their problems.

**Lady, gentleman** *Man* and *woman* are plainer and therefore preferred to the pompous *lady* and *gentleman*—unless you are using the terms to make real distinctions in refinement. *Ladies and Gentlemen* is a conventional phrase used in addressing various gatherings.

**Latter** See **former, latter.**

**Lay, lie** This pair of verbs continues to give trouble. *To lie* is to "rest in or place oneself into a horizontal position." *To lay* something is "to set it or place it somewhere." The only way to correct the trouble is to memorize the forms of this pair.

| *Infinitive* | *Past Tense* | *Past Participle* | *Present Participle* |
|---|---|---|---|
| to lie | lay | lain | lying |
| to lay | laid | laid | laying |

Here are correct examples of the use of each form:

*Lie*
I want to *lie* down.
After I *lay* there awhile, I had an idea.
After I *had lain* there for an hour, I made my decision.
After *lying* down past lunch hour, I got up and made myself a snack.

*Lay*
Please *lay* the package on the table.
He *laid* the package on the table.

She *had laid* the package on the table.
I *was laying* the package on the table.

*Note: Lay,* unlike *lie,* has a passive voice:

The package *had been laid* neatly inside the drawer.
The body *has been laid* to rest.

**Leave, let**  *Leave* means "to depart from"; let means "to permit." Nevertheless, "*leave* [or *let*] me alone" is a standard idiom. The trouble comes when you use *leave* for *let*.

> ***Nonstandard***  I won't *leave* you go with me.
> ***Standard***  I won't *let* you go with me.

**Less**  see **fewer, less.**

**Let's us**  Redundant, since *let us* already means *let us.*
**Liable, likely**  See **apt, likely, liable.**
**Lie**  see **lay, lie.**
**Like, as, as if**  In formal use, *like* is a preposition; *as* and *as if* are conjunctions. *Like* is much used in conversation as a conjunction, but in writing this usage should be avoided.

> ***Correct***  My daughter looks *like* me. (preposition)
> ***Avoid***  My daughter speaks *like* I do. (conjunction)
> ***Correct***  My daughter speaks *as* I do. (conjunction)
>
> ***Avoid***  He spends money *like* he's rich. (conjunction)
> ***Correct***  He spends money *as if* he were rich. (conjunction)

**Likely, liable**  See **apt, likely, liable.**
**Lose, loose**  *Lose* means "misplace; no longer having," or in better terminology, the opposite of *win. Loose* is an adjective meaning "free or unattached."

> If I don't make an A average, I'll *lose* my scholarship.
> My notes are on some *loose* sheets of paper.

**Lovely**  See **cute, lovely.**

**Mad**  Colloquial for "angry."
**Marvelous**  Avoid this overworked term of insincere approval.
**Math**  See **ad.**
**may**  see **can, may.**
**Maybe, may be**  *Maybe* means "perhaps"; *may be* is a two-part verb form.

It *may be* necessary to take Vitamin C in large amounts.
*Maybe* he hasn't got the money.

**Mighty**   Informal for "very" or "exceedingly." *Mighty* means "powerful."

*Informal*   This is *mighty* good coffee.
*Formal*   Hank Aaron was a *mighty* home run hitter.

**Moral, morale**   *Moral* as a noun is "a lesson" or "a conclusion to be drawn from a story"; the adjective *moral* means "pertaining to right or ethical conduct." *Morale*, a noun, refers to "the enthusiastic state of mind of an individual or a group."

Does this story have a *moral*?
His action was considered to be *moral* behavior.
The *morale* among the workers was high.

**Most, almost**   *Most* is an informal substitute for *almost*.

*Informal*   *Most* every time I see you, you're well dressed.
*Formal*   *Almost* every time I see you, you're well dressed.

**Mr.**   Never spell out *mister* except for special emphasis. In America, a period follows the abbreviation (unlike the custom in Britain, where it is omitted).

**Ms.**   A recently adopted abbreviation to identify women, married or unmarried. It answers the needs of those who believe it unfair that women — but not men — should have their marital status made public in the usual way (that is, *Mrs.* or *Miss*). Ms. is in widespread use. It can be used when you are uncertain of a woman's marital status. In other cases, the individual's preference should be respected.

**Must of**   Illiterate for *must have.*

**Myself (himself, etc.)**   Do not use *myself* where you would normally use *I* or *me*. *Myself* is used (1) reflexively, (2) for emphasis, (3) in absolute constructions, or (4) to indicate the normal, healthy state of the self. All other uses should be regarded as informal.

1. I'm going to buy *myself* a new car.
2. I *myself* will go to the station.
3. *Myself* a professor, I nevertheless avoided other professors.
4. I'm not *myself* today.

*Informal*   Joana and *myself* went to visit her parents. (Formal: *I.*)
*Informal*   The property was left to my sister and *myself*.
(Formal: *me.*)

**Need**   See **lack, need, want.**
**No, now**   See **know, no, now.**
**Nohow**   Nonstandard for *not at all.*
**Nothing like, nowhere near**   Colloquial for, respectively, *not like* and *not nearly.*

He was *not like* ([not *nothing like*] my brother.
She was *not nearly* [not *nowhere near*] as tall as her mother.

**Nowheres**   Nonstandard for *nowhere.*
**Number**   See **amount, number.**

**Off of**   No need for the *of.*
**Okay**   This or abbreviations like O.K. or OK are all okay — standard — but use a more specific word in formal writing.
**One and the same**   Stale and wordy for *the same.*
**One another**   See **each other, one another.**
**Ought to of**   Illiterate for *ought to have.*
**Outside of**   See **inside of, outside of.**
**Over with**   Colloquial for *over* and *ended.*

*Colloquial*   I'm glad the game is *over with.*
*Formal*   I'm glad the game is *over.*

**Per**   Appropriate only in business or technical writing *(per diem, per capita, feet per second)* but stuffy in formal writing where *a* and *an* are preferable ($6 *an* hour, four miles *a* day).
**Percent, percentage**   Both mean "rate per hundred"; *percent* may be written as two words or as one, but *percentage* is always written as one. In formal writing, use *percent* to follow a numeral *(75 percent)*. Do not use either word when you simply mean *part.*

*Formal*   A small *part* of my home is used as an office.
*Formal*   A small *percentage* of the team lacks spirit.
*Informal*   A small *percent* of government officials are corrupt.

**Phenomena**   See **data, phenomena.**
**Phone**   See **ad.**

**Photo** See **ad.**

**Plan on** In formal writing the correct idiom is *plan to. Plan on* is colloquial.

**Plenty** Informal when used to mean "very."

**Plus** As a preposition, means "increased by." It is informal when used in place of *and.*

> *Informal* Irv had a high fever *plus* he was breaking out in red spots.

**Pretty** Overworked when used as an intensifier to mean "somewhat," e.g., *pretty* good, *pretty* happy.

**Principal, principle** *Principal,* a noun meaning "person in controlling authority" or an adjective meaning "main" or "chief," should be distinguished from *principle,* a noun meaning "fundamental law" or "concept."

> The *principal* idea was to begin our vacation in January instead of June.
> The *principal* of the high school came to dinner.
> With him, it was a matter of *principle.*

**Prior to** Overblown usage for *before;* avoid it.

**Provided, provided that, providing** All three are now considered correct conjunctions.

> I will go on the trip *provided that* you take your camera.
> He will invite you to lunch *providing* you apologize.

**Quite a few, quite a bit, quite a little** Colloquial and wordy when used to substitute for *many, a substantial amount,* or *more than a little.*

**Raise, rise** Two different verbs. *Raise (raised, raised, raising)* is a transitive verb meaning "to cause or help to rise to a standing position." *Rise (rose, risen, rising)* is an intransitive verb meaning "to assume an upright position" or "to wake up from sleep."

> He had *risen* at five and gone straight to work.
> She *raises* chickens and sells egs.

**Rap** Informal for "talk" or "chat," but slang when used to mean "punishment" or "blame."

**Real, swell, great, terrific, beauty, awful**   However you may use these, they are becoming — or have become — vague and tired. Try for more specific words.

**Reason is because**   *Because* in this construction should be replaced by *that.*

> ***Informal***   The *reason* he can't see you tonight *is because* he has to make up a chem lab.
> ***Formal***   The *reason* he can't see you tonight *is that* he has to make up a chem lab.
>
> He can't see you tonight *because* he has to make up a chem lab.

**Reason why**   The *why* is usually superfluous.

> The *reason* she lost him is obvious.

**Regarding, in regard to, with regard to, relating to, relative to, with respect to, respecting**   High-blown substitutes for *on, about,* or *concerning.*

> The Chancellor spoke on [not *with regard to*] the future mission of the university.

**Relating to**   See **regarding, in regard to, with regard to, relating to, relative to, with respect to, respecting.**

**Relative to**   See **regarding, in regard to, with regard to, relating to, relative to, with respect to, respecting.**

**Respecting**   See **regarding, in regard to, with regard to, relating to, relative to, with respect to, respecting.**

**Rhetorical question**   When you ask a real question (e.g., *What time is it?*), you expect an answer. When you pose a rhetorical question *(Is anyone more beautiful than my wife?),* you are simply making a point.

**Right**   Dialect or colloquial form of *very* as in *right pleased* or *right new. Right away* is colloquial for *immediately.*

**Said**   Adapted from legal language *(said* party, *said* action), it should be avoided in ordinary writing.

**Scarcely**   See **but, hardly, scarcely.**

**Seeing as how, seeing that**   Colloquial for *since* or *because.*

**Set, sit**   Frequently confused pair. *Sit (sat, sat, sitting)* means "be seated." *Set (set, set, setting)* means "place" something somewhere.

The dog was *sitting* at my feet.
She *set* the dog down at my feet.
The package *was set* down beside me.

*Note: Set* has a passive voice; *sit* does not.

**Shall, will, should, would**   *Will* is now generally accepted for all persons *(I will, you will, he will)* except for questions in the first person requesting an opinion or consent (*Shall I* order dinner? *Shall* we dance?) or in formal contexts (I *shall* hope to see you on Thursday in my chambers). Ordinary questions about the future still employ *will* (When *will* I see you again?). *Should* expresses obligation or condition for all three persons (*I should* go swimming; *you should* take a nap; *Manny should* write a letter). *Would* is used for all three persons for a wish or a hypothetical or a customary action (*Would* that he had taken the job! *You would* do it if you could. Every morning, *they would* take coffee on the verandah.).

**Shape up**   Colloquial for "proceeding or developing in a satisfactory manner."

My vacation plans are *shaping up*.

**Should**   See **shall, will, should, would.**

**Show up**   Colloquial when used to mean "apear" or "prove."

***Formal***   John did not *appear* at the dance.
***Colloquial***   John did not *show up* at the dance.

***Formal***   Charles *proved* superior to Frank.
***Colloquial***   Charles *showed up* better than Frank.

**Situation**   Unnecessary addition in such phrases as "a *crisis* situation" (a *crisis* will do) and "The *situation* is that we need money" (where the last three words will do).

**So**   In clauses describing purposes, *so* used in place of *so that* is colloquial.

***Formal***   We met in a hotel room *so that* we could discuss our plans in private.
***Colloquial***   We met in a hotel room *so* we could discuss our plans in private.

*So* used instead of *very* is colloquial and overworked.

> **Formal**   She seems *very* sad.
> **Colloquial**   She seems *so* sad.

**Some**   Colloquial when used as an adverb substituting for "somewhat" and as an adjective substituting for "remarkable, exciting, unusual." (We'll have to hurry *somewhat* [not *some*] to get there on time. This is *a remarkable* [not *some*] photograph.)

**Someone**   See **anyone, any one.**

**Sometime, some time**   The former is used when an occasion or time not specified is meant and the latter when a period of time (of unspecified duration) is meant.

> *Sometime* I must visit the Empire State Building.
> I must spend *some time* walking up Fifth Avenue.

**Sort**   See **these kind.**

**Stationary, stationery**   *Stationary* means "at rest" or "in a fixed posture or position." *Stationery* is "paper, envelopes," and other such materials.

**Stupid**   See **ignorant, stupid.**

**Such**   Colloquial when used as an intensifier.

> **Formal**   He owned a *very* handsome dog.
> **Colloquial**   He owned *such* a handsome dog.

**Supposed to, used to**   Don't forget the final *-d* in the words *supposed* and *used.*

**Sure**   Colloquial for *surely* or *certainly.*

**Swell**   Slang when used to mean "excellent" or "very good." See **real.**

**Take and**   Nonstandard usually. "He *drove* the car away," not "He *took and* drove the car away."

**Terrific**   See **real.**

**Than, then**   Two different words. *Than* is a conjunction; *then* is an adverb or adverbial conjunction.

> His grades are better *than* mine.
> He had a long, cool drink; *then* he plunged into a cold shower.

**That**   Colloquial when used as an adverb instead of *so* or *very* (as in "She was *that* poor, she was often hungry" and "I didn't like him *that* much").

**That, which**   *That* always introduces restrictive clauses; *which* can introduce both restrictive and nonrestrictive clauses, but in formal speech and writing some prefer to limit *which* to introducing nonrestrictive clauses.

> **Restrictive**   The fruit *that I bought yesterday* is delicious.
> **Nonrestrictive**   The fruit, *which I bought yesterday,* is delicious.

**Their, there, they're**   Frequently confused. *Their* is the possessive pronoun; *there* is an adverb or expletive; *they're* is a contraction of *they are.*

> *Their* eyes stared straight at the flag.
> *There* is no reason to be afraid.
> *They're* going off on a holiday in July.

**Theirself, theirselves**   Nonstandard. Use *themselves.*

**These kind**   Should be *this kind* (or *that kind*) or *these kinds* (or *those kinds*). Same holds true for *sort.*

**Thing**   Too often used for everything. Where possible, a more specific word should be used.

**This here, that there, these here, them there**   Nonstandard all. Just use the first word of each pair.

**Through**   Informal when used instead of *finished.*

> **Formal**   He is *finished* studying.
> **Informal**   He is *through* studying.

**To, too, two**   Distinguish between the preposition *to,* the adverb *too,* and the number *two.*

> If it isn't *too* much trouble, I'd like *two* pounds of candy to give *to* my mother.

**Transpire**   Although the word means "to become known," it is widely used to mean "come to pass," "happen," or "occur," as in "It *transpired* that my scholarship check was late this month." Some authorities disapprove of this usage.

**Try and**   See **be sure and, try and.**

**Type**   Colloquial for *type of.*

> **Formal**   This *type of* air conditioner eats energy.
> **Colloquial**   This *type* air conditioner eats energy.

**Uninterested**   See **disinterested, uninterested.**

**Used to**   See **supposed to, used to.**

**Wait on**   Means to "serve" or "attend" and not, as in colloquial use, to "wait for."

> ***Correct:***   We *waited for* the counter girl to *wait on* us.

**Want**   See **lack, need, want.**

**Ways**   When referring to distance, *ways* is informal, *way* formal.

> ***Informal***   Davenport is a long *ways* from here.
> ***Formal***   Davenport is a long *way* from here.

**Where, were**   Pronounced differently, these are two different words. *Were* is the plural verb; *where* is an adverb, a conjunction, and a noun. Do not substitute *where* for *that.*

> ***Informal***   He could see *where* she was getting ready to leave.
> ***Formal***   He could see *that* she was getting ready to leave.

**Whether, if**   See **if, whether.**

**Which, who, that**   Use *who* or *that* to refer to persons, *which* or *that* to refer to all other things. See **that, which.**

**Who, whom**   See **case** in Glossary of Grammatical Terms or **Case** in Part 2.

**Will**   See **shall, will, should, would.**

**-wise**   Characteristic of governmental, business, or advertising jargon is the practice of converting a noun to an adverb by tacking on *-wise.* In formal writing, this is a vulgar practice.

> ***Jargon***   *Moneywise,* it's not a good deal.
> ***Better***   *Financially,* it's not a good deal.

> ***Jargon***   *Defensewise,* we need an early warning system.
> ***Better***   *For defense purposes,* we need an early warning system.

**With regard to**   See **regarding, in regard to, with regard to, relating to, relative to, with respect to, respecting.**

**With respect to**   See **regarding, in regard to, with regard to, relating to, relative to, with respect to, respecting.**

**Worst way**   Use *very much,* the formal way of saying *in the worst way.*

> ***Informal***   He wanted to go to the movies *in the worst way.*
> ***Formal***   He wanted *very much* to go to the movies.

**Would**   See **shall, will, should, would.**

**Would of**   Illiterate for *would have.* Based on sound perception by users who hear *of* instead of *have.*

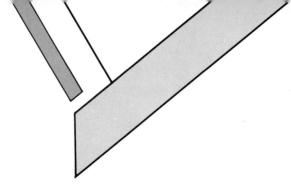

# Answer Key to Exercise Questions

Answers to the first five questions of each exercise, except those that ask you to write sentences or paragraphs, are given here.

## Part 1   A Basic Grammar

**Test Yourself on Identifying Nouns (p. 5)**
1. elephant   2. notebook   3. light   4. cheese, Wisconsin
5. Trail Blazers, team.

**Test Yourself on Identifying Verbs (p. 7)**
1. plays   2. earns   3. is jumping   4. waited   5. trusted

**Test Yourself on Identifying Verbs by Changing Tenses (p. 7)**
1. plays; *played*   2. will pass; *passes*   3. are; *were*
4. has made; *makes*   5. seems; *seemed.*

**Test Yourself on Identifying Types of Verbs (p. 9)**
1. feel—L   2. smokes—I   3. is riding—T
4. plays—T   5. exploded—I

**Test Yourself on Identifying Auxiliaries (p. 11)**
1. will, can, may, must, should, ought to, etc.   2. will, do, etc.   3. is, was, should be, must be, ought to be, etc.
4. are, were, have been, should have been, etc.   5. did, will, etc.

**Test Yourself on Identifying Adjectives (p. 13)**
1. better   2. courageous   3. kind   4. happier   5. childish, greedy

## Test Yourself on Identifying Adverbs (p. 15)
1. quickly; slowly   2. up; in   3. out; up   4. there; here   5. sourly; sweetly

## Test Yourself on Using Prepositions (p. 17)
1. on the farm   2. behind the apple   3. about the newspaper   4. against the automobile   5. away from the ferry

## Test Yourself on Using Pronouns (p. 23)
B.
1. She needs false teeth.
2. My old grandmother needs something.
3. Everybody complained to me.
4. He is funny.
5. All are politicians.
C.
1. his   2. mine   3. everybody, something   4. you, yourself   5. my, him, everyone

## Test Yourself on Locating Subjects of Sentences (p. 26)
A.
1. whiskey   2. she   3. father   4. hot dogs   5. parents
B.
1. *the charming English teacher* (teacher)
2. *the man in the blue suit* (man)
3. *the beautiful old woman* (woman)
4. *sensible young people* (people)
5. *my mother's old college roommate* (roommate)

## Test Yourself on Identifying Basic Sentence Parts: Subjects, Predicates, Predicate Nouns, Predicate Adjectives, Direct Objects, Indirect Objects, Object Complements, Nouns, and Adjectives (p. 28)
A. & B.

1. My mother is a good cook. (VL / PN)
2. We elected Jim our spokesman. (VT / DO / OCN)
3. He had an idea. (VT / DO)
4. Everybody likes ice cream. (VT / DO)
5. Some do not. (VI)

**Test Yourself on Clauses (p. 31)**

C.

1. What I want for supper — N
2. Until you come home — ADV
3. that pleases me most — ADJ
4. whatever you do — N
5. whom I pointed out — ADJ

D.

1. (I) The man was Judy's father; (D) that was here yesterday.
2. (I) I can write pretty well. (D) Although I never went past the tenth grade.
3. (I) You're in danger. (D) Whenever you cross the yellow line at the center of the road.
4. (D) Whoever asks (I) the whole sentence.
5. (D) What you're thinking (I) the whole sentence.

**Test Yourself on Phrases (p. 35)**

A.

1. in the afternoons — ADV
2. carried in stock — ADJ
3. after a few minutes — ADV; over the trees — ADV
4. Known for his pure tenor voice — ADJ; in the park — ADV
5. To love deeply — N; in life — ADJ

B.

1. The man *walking fast* looked sinister.
2. Charley traveled *in an old car.*
3. *Swimming today* should be a pleasure.
4. She looked like a lady *needing sympathy.*
5. He talked *for a long time.*

## Part 2    An Index to Usage and the Principles of Effective Writing

**Test Yourself on Abbreviations (p. 44)**

1. Mr. Tuten; 8 a.m.; 55 mph
2. 100 cc
3. C
4. South America
5. second sentence: Officials of CRUMBY set their goal at $3,000,000 and said they hoped to reach it by St. Patrick's Day.

**Test Yourself on Changing from One Form of Possession to the Other (p. 48)**
1. the game's outcome   2. Lenny's tirade   3. the Mayor's argument   4. the boy's future   5. my father's impatience

**Test Yourself on the Correct Use of the Apostrophe (p. 50)**
1. women's; its
2. '50s; wouldn't; theirs
3. Charley's; races
4. Attorney General's; crimes
5. 90's; 100's

**Test Yourself on Appositives (p. 53)**
1. , an old piece of canvas with a dozen holes in it
2. , Thomas Jones,
3. , a pickpocket and a burglar
4. , Rebecca Rose,
5. , a book by someone named Tolstoy

**Test Yourself on Capitalization (p. 56)**
1. Friday; Venus   2. Congress; Senator   3. C   4. I; College   5. Arabian

**Test Yourself on Using the Correct Case of Pronouns (p. 62)**
1. me   2. his   3. I   4. he   5. me

**Test Yourself on Revising Incoherent Sentences (p. 67)**
1. The basket is where I put the apples.
2. Cheating the consumer is so widespread that we need a permanent Department of Consumer affairs.
3. After the heat, the crowds, and the excitement, Jack fainted.
4. Because he suspected a kidney problem and wanted to be sure, the doctor wanted a urine sample.
5. The invitation said I was to reply only if I couldn't make it.

**Test Yourself on Making Coherent Paragraphs (p. 69)**
A. Ralph Ellison, the distinguished American novelist, was born in Oklahoma in 1914. While attending school in Oklahoma City, he had a decisive experience when he heard Lester Young play the saxophone. Hearing the great jazz player prompted him to go to Tuskegee Institute, in 1933, with the intention of studying music. Probably the whole experience helped orient him toward art in general. For afterwards, he became interested in sculpture and finally, of course, in writing. Ellison

started publishing in 1937, but it wasn't until 1945, after service in the Merchant Marine in World War II, that he began his famous *Invisible Man.* Since 1952, he has also published a collection of essays, *Shadow and Act;* from 1958 onwards, he has taught literature at various colleges. In 1965, *Invisible Man* was voted the most distinguished novel to have been published in the previous twenty years.

B.

1. Order of sentences: 1, 5, 4, 3, 6, 2, 7.
2. Order of sentences: 1, 7, 4, 3, 2, 6, 5.

## Test Yourself on Revising Incoherent Paragraphs (p. 72)

1. My parents always argue with me about my wanting a moped. They say the machines are dangerous, but I believe they are not, because mopeds go only twenty miles an hour. Besides, they run cheaply and have no license or insurance requirements. Moreover, the initial purchase price is relatively cheap, too.

2. Cooking is both easy and fun if you observe certain basic rules. First, you should have the right utensils. As the saying goes, "a cook is only as good as his pots." You should buy and use only fresh ingredients. Moreover, you should learn how much heat to apply to particular foods, and, finally, you should save good recipes.

3. A professor I know who is older than I am says that rock and roll is terrible music. But I say it's just a form of what he used to think was popular music when he was young. He says that rock lyrics can't be heard because the music is too loud and that the lyrics are foolish anyway. It may be true that the lyrics are foolish but they are not more foolish than the ones that go with his pop music. Besides, the degree of loudness is a matter of taste.

## Test Yourself on the Use of the Colon (p. 75)

1. It is now 2:45 p.m.
2. Whatever he wanted from Sarah, he got the following: love, affection, kindness, money, or food.
3. The things that need repairing around the house are the following: the rain gutters, the front steps, the upstairs storm windows, and the leaks in the attic.
4. What do I spend my money on? I spend my money on the following: food, clothing, shelter, movies, medicine, skateboards, lobsters — a lot of things!
5. You need only one thing for a perfect golf swing: control.

## Test Yourself on the Use of the Comma (p. 82)

B.

1. Placement of these commas depends on where *all* the boys are sitting. If they are all in the back of the room then the phrase is nonrestrictive and needs to be enclosed in commas; if the boys are

scattered throughout, then the phrase is restrictive and does not require commas.
2. eliminate the comma
3. summer,
4. all,
5. no comma if *pretty* is construed as an adverb modifying *slim;* comma after *pretty* if it's construed as an adjective.

## Test Yourself on Recognizing and Correcting Dangling Modifiers (p. 88)

1. Before leaving for California, we must make hotel reservations.
2. Being an American, he had limited knowledge of Italy.
3. Arriving in Chicago, he discovered that his suitcase was in California.
4. To understand one's spouse, one should establish good communications with him or her.
5. C

## Test Yourself on the Use of the Dash (p. 90)

1. thing — loyalty
2. we — who have paid our rent — will be evicted, etc.
3. — Catholicism's holy city
4. — a crying shame
5. life — divorce, separation from his children, the loss of his job, the attack of pneumonia — these, etc.

## Test Yourself on Diagramming Sentences (p. 97)

A.

1.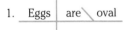

2.

| Fordham | defeated | Columbia |

3.

| John | loves | Mary |

4.

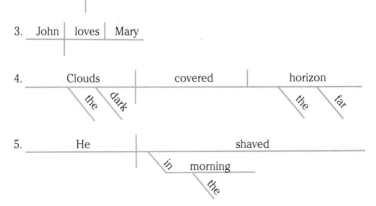

B.

1.

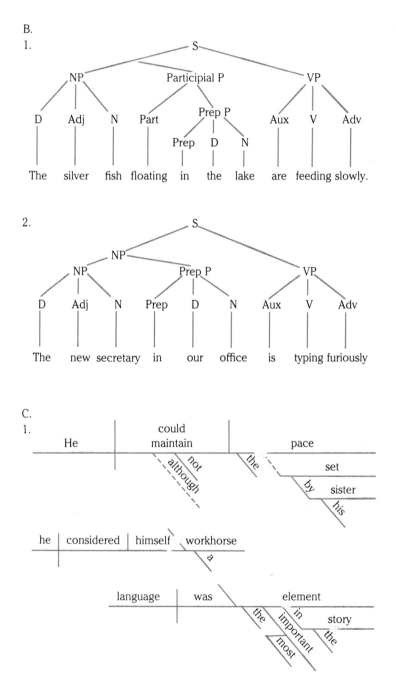

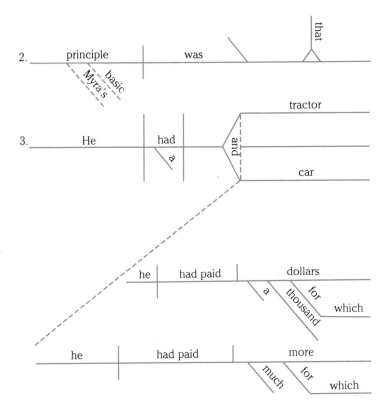

## Test Yourself on Identifying Slang and Colloquial Language (p. 105)

Labels are those applied by *The New World Dictionary of the American Language*, 1980 edition.

1. slang   2. slang   3. slang   4. slang, when it means "to embellish" as in "don't jazz up the story"   5. slang

## Test Yourself on Selecting the Proper Level of Usage for a Specific Piece of Writing (p. 105)

1. formal
2. informal — slang
3. informal
4. somewhat more formal
5. formal

## Test Yourself on Using Exact Expressions (p. 107)

1. revealed   2. executed   3. understood   4. scarce   5. factor

### Test Yourself on Using Correct Idiomatic Expressions (p. 110)
1. to   2. to tell   3. on   4. about   5. to; from

### Test Yourself on Identifying Clichés (p. 112)
1. financially embarrassed; fatter than a pig; do justice to; the bigger the better; eating like there was no tomorrow; last but not least; topped the whole thing off; the last straw; eaten myself sick; believe it or not; sadder but wiser
2. in this day and age; the American way of life; get on the ball; well-rounded personality; straight from the shoulder; hitting the books; get what you pay for; pass the acid test; beyond a shadow of a doubt; if you want to get more out of life, you have to put more into it

### Test Yourself on Using Specific, Concrete Language (p. 114)
A.
1. napped; dozed   2. wolfed; gobbled   3. admit; confess   4. cried; screamed   5. reveal; display

### Test Yourself on Eliminating Unacceptable Double or Triple Negatives (p. 116)
1. I don't want anything to do with you.
2. There was never anybody like him.
3. He never had a reason to give anybody a present.
4. He had hardly any friends.
5. There was scarcely a soul in the library when I was there on Saturday night.

### Test Yourself on Using the Exclamation Point Appropriately (p. 118)
1. eliminate   2. C   3. eliminate   4. C   5. C

### Test Yourself on Correcting Sentence Fragments (p. 121)
1. . . . basketball court because she wasn't wearing sneakers.
2. I'm worried about my final exams, which come in about three weeks.
3. Professor Urban took me out for an expensive dinner, although he had mentioned to me that he was short of money.
4. Unless I'm given the salary I want, I won't take the job.
5. Whenever he hears the Beatles sing "Yesterday," he's reminded of the sixties.

### Test Yourself on Recognizing and Correcting Sentence Fragments (p. 122)
A. Cross out:
1. until   2. although   3. whenever   4. unless   5. because

C.
1. Horses racing together through the surf make a beautiful sight.
2. C
3. convert the period after *wish* to a colon; small *t* in *to*
4. eliminate the period after *dinner;* make the next letter small
5. change the period to a comma and make the *w* in *which* small

## Test Yourself on Correcting Fragments by Proofreading (p. 124)

My father was a farmer, (1) although he'd gone to college where he studied engineering. Life on the farm was hard, but my father was ingenious, probably because of his training as an engineer, and he took delight in solving mechanical problems, (2) problems that would come up with the tractors or the milking machines or even the plumbing in the house. He never had time for long vacations, (3) which doesn't mean he ever in any way felt "burnt out," (4) the way so many of us feel today when we work long hours without appropriate rest. My father's secrets were two: he was a champion at resting whenever rest periods came, at night, for example, (5) when he'd settle down with the weekly paper by the fire after a good supper. The other secret was the real sense of joy he took in his work. No aspect of the work on the land or with the livestock ever seemed to bore him, (6) although some of the tasks required constant repetition. In fact, whenever he needed to leave the farm to be present at ceremonious occasions, a wedding, a funeral, a party, (7) he'd be nervous and irritable for all the time he was away. It would be fine if all of us could live a work life like my father's, (8) loving the labor we performed.

## Test Yourself on the Appropriate Use of the Hyphen (p. 129)

1. well-trained; well-paid
2. re-sort
3. C
4. do-it-yourself
5. C

## Test Yourself on the Use of Italics (p. 132)

1. no italics for nostalgia
2. *freaked out*
3. *Daily News*
4. *Moby-Dick; Anna Karenina*
5. C

## Test Yourself on Judging the Fairness of Generalizations (p. 134)

1. *Argumentum ad verecundiam.* The prestige of the great book is being used instead of an argument.

2. Pure prejudice. The speaker obviously doesn't like rock music.
3. Pure prejudice, fueled by the malice of envy.
4. Again, pure prejudice — a prejudgment not based upon evidence.
5. *Argumentum ad hominem* and begs the question, too.

### Test Yourself on Recognizing Biased, Insufficient, and Statistically Unreliable Evidence (p. 137)

1. Statistically unreliable. The 12 percent cannot be applied to any subgroup of a whole population.
2. Insufficient evidence. "Everybody" the speaker knows may not be a sufficient number on which to base the conclusion.
3. Insufficient evidence. Some Alaskans shiver all the time.
4. Biased evidence. Those interested in ecology in Oregon might be the whole population of the state — minus the number of lumberjacks.
5. Insufficient evidence. The sister is just one woman.

### Test Yourself on Applying Induction and Deduction (p. 142)
A.
1. A reasonable conclusion. The facts seem to hold up. By analogy we can be reasonably sure that Richard's military experience will fit him for the business job.
2. Not reasonable because the cases are not so typical as they might first seem to be. For example, we went to war in 1898 with a Republican in the White House, as we did in 1861.
3. A poor conclusion because it is based on too few facts — one marriage is not a convincing case upon which to base the conclusion.
4. What the speaker "heard" is a weak fact upon which to base a course of action. Besides, if he *did* study, he'd be more likely to be prepared, even for a "springer" like Brody.
5. Reasonable. Many temperature readings over many years have gone into making the average. It seems reliable.

B.
1.

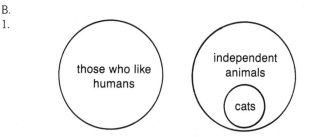

Valid but not true.

2.

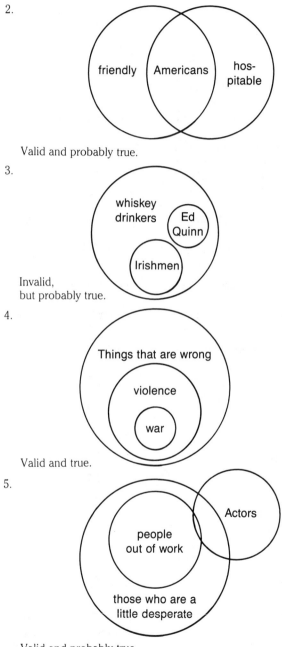

Valid and probably true.

3.

Invalid,
but probably true.

4.

Valid and true.

5.

Valid and probably true.

### Test Yourself on Recognizing Logical Fallacies (p. 146)
1. post hoc
2. begs the question
3. begs the question
4. faulty analogy
5. hasty generalization

### Test Yourself on Revising Misplaced and Squinting Modifiers (p. 148)
1. With this calculator, I can show you in twenty seconds how to make a million dollars.
2. Happily, the sick patient wanted to live.
3. The sunset that we loved stunned us completely.
4. C if the plans were to *depart* either on Friday, Saturday, or Sunday; not correct if the plans to leave — on an unspecified date — were formulated over the weekend.
5. Professors who teach get rich rarely.

### Test Yourself on Recognizing Modifiers: Adjectivals and Adverbials (p. 151)
1. adjectival   2. adverbial   3. adverbial   4. adverbial   5. adjectival

### Test Yourself on Using Numerals Correctly (p. 153)
1. Two thousand years ago, an important event took place in Palestine.
2. $5,638
3. 908 President Street; 3E
4. thirty-six
5. forty; thirty-seven; twelve

### Test Yourself on the Principles of Outlining (p. 161)
TOPIC:
  I. Frayed and ragged jeans
    A. For prestige
    B. To signal authenticity
  II. Nondescript, everyday jeans
    A. Worn to be in line
    B. Wearers not especially conscious
  III. High-style jeans
    A. On dates
    B. In public
SENTENCE:
  I. Frayed and ragged jeans are worn on all occasions consistently by the same wearers.

A. These are worn as a badge of prestige.

B. They are also worn to signal the wearer's authentic self — one that will not yield to convention.

II. Nondescript or everyday jeans are worn as a badge of belonging — on everyday occasions.

A. Wearers want to be in line with ordinary custom in blue-jeans wear.

B. Wearers are more or less unconscious of any other meanings attached to this choice.

III. High-style jeans are worn on special occasions.

A. On dates they are worn to show off the wearer's body and impress others with his up-to-the-minute sense of fashion.

B. On special public occasions, they are worn to intimidate the less well-dressed.

Paragraph:

1. Frayed, ragged, and hopelessly worn-out jeans are worn on campus with or without patches on all occasions by the same wearers; this practice suggests that the wearer has been "hip" for a long time (long enough for the jeans to have gotten that look) and the fact that he wears these jeans to class or on dates suggests that he makes no distinction between occasions; he is himself, authentic, at all times.

2. Nondescript or everyday jeans are worn on everyday occasions, more or less regularly, by a majority of students; these wearers want to be in line with what their contemporaries wear, and they seem to be unaware of the conformity in what they are doing.

3. High-style jeans are worn on special occasions by those stylish characters who are keenly aware of the high-fashion significance of trendy length, cuff widths, accessories, etc. On dates, these are worn to emphasize the body and impress others with the wearer's devotion to style; on special occasions, these jeans are meant to intimidate the dowdy — which they invariably do.

### Test Yourself on Developing Fragmentary Paragraphs (p. 162)

1. The more money you make, the more money you spend. When your income is low, you yearn for more — but learn to be restrained. Your low income will only go so far, and you know it. You make a budget and strive to live within the limits set for each category. You are careful to see to it that you do not overspend because you realize that there are limits to what you may spend. As soon as your salary rises, however, you begin to give in to your desires. You imagine that if your salary has risen once, it can rise again. Therefore, the idea of limits no longer has validity for you and you begin to spend more.

2. Television tends to make us passive. The reason for this is that we have nothing to *do* as television viewers. It's all done for us. Heroes chase and capture villains; family troubles are quickly solved; games

are won and lost. Television shows never ask us to think — which is a form of action even if it is internal. Television shows are simple-minded; therefore, they can't ask us to think. All they can do, finally, is ask us to be manipulated. We give in and become passive.

3. Woodworking is not as difficult as it appears. The first thing you need is a reliable set of tools. Once you have the tools, you need to learn the precise action of each tool on the particular type of wood you wish to work with. Knowing the characteristics of the various kinds of wood is also essential. And, of course, a good deal of practice is essential before mastery comes. There are many good manuals that show the best methods of joining wood and there are equally good manuals on wood finishing. Woodworking is not difficult; it merely requires the correct and patient approach.

### Test Yourself on Understanding Methods of Paragraph Development (p. 173)

A.
1. Comparison and contrast. There is an argumentative purpose here and the writer intends to argue against the parents' position by making marijuana appear less harmful than alcohol.
2. Spatial development for this description of a place.
3. Illustrative details and examples.
4. Causal analysis. The writer intends to pursue the reasons why the commercials are dedicated to selling.
5. Definition.

### Test Yourself on Filling in the Other Side of *and, but, or* Constructions (p. 175)

1. tiger's milk
2. whose father came from Albania
3. that hasn't been heard from
4. who dresses like a derelict
5. tall

### Test Yourself on Making Constructions Parallel (p. 175)

1. eliminate the words *so that we can*
2. . . . math, biology, and term-paper writing (*or* term-paper technique).
3. neat, patient, and proud.
4. falling in love and writing poetry.
5. C

### Test Yourself on Using Parentheses Correctly (p. 178)

1. C
2. C

3. C
4. C
5. The author (authors?) of Genesis spoke the stories with reverence.


## Test Yourself on Pronoun Agreement (p. 185)

1. Anybody who knows *his* music would know the Rolling Stones.
2. The Committee did its work in private.
3. Neither the new professor nor the first-year students knew *their* way around the campus.
4. Anybody who likes *his* coffee cold is peculiar.
5. When the team scored a touchdown, the band raised *their* instruments to play.


## Test Yourself on Pronoun References (p. 188)

1. . . . on the Bruins' (or Canadians') home ice last night.
2. C
3. . . . the North and South struggled over the question of slavery.
4. . . . was one that Fred (or Eddie) had thought of some years earlier.
5. . . . It was a wonderful weekend.


## Test Yourself on Proofreading Technique (p. 190)

A. Line 2: period after "live"; capital "T."
   Line 3: "They're" for "their."
   Line 5: "unprocessed" (sp.); "foods."
   Line 6: "plague" (sp.); period after this word. Capital "all."
   Line 7: an extra letter in "smokeouts."
   Line 8: "effects" instead of "affects"; an extra letter in "ther."
B. Line 1: apostrophe "what's" or "what is."
   Line 2: extra letter in "therapy," period after the word; capital "It"; "it's" needs an apostrophy.
   Line 3: "toward" should be "to"; leave off the -s on the end of "associates."
   Line 7: "opposite" (sp.).
   Line 8: Here· "the pits" really is and must go.
   Lines 10: "associate" for "experience"; "his or her" for "their."
   Last line: good lesson in this business of "he or she" and "they."


## Test Yourself on the Use of the Question Mark (p. 192)

A.
1. Marshak ran the school?
2. Give you my pen?

3. Take off my coat?
4. George likes apples?
5. Fred likes parties?

B.

1. C
2. . . . ball game?"
3. . . . seriously? . . . paper? . . . . session? . . . fairly?
4. . . . correctly? —
5. . . . (?) . . . (?)

### Test Yourself on the Use of Quotation Marks (p. 197)

A.

1. The student said, "I consider you one of the best professors in the English Department."
2. Mark said that Judy's ceramics are elegant.
3. Matt said that in his opinion Donna is a talented actress.
4. Fred said, "The policeman asked me why I was speeding."
5. Marian said to Jean, "I want to see you over Easter."

B.

1. . . . "The Killers"
2. . . . "Sailing to Byzantium" . . . "The salmon-falls, the mackerel-crowded seas"?
3. . . . "wet" . . .
4. . . . "Elephants . . . cage."
5. That song "Silverbird" is a winner.

C.

1. "You made a fool of me," Margaret said, "and I won't forgive you for it. The name of my article is not 'Childhood Reams' but 'Childhood Dreams.'"
2. She had written: "I don't care for the climate in the tropics," but when I saw her in Chicago she said, "I'm looking forward to visiting Puerto Rico for the second time."
3. "Can you lend me a hundred dollars?" she asked timidly. Slapping his hand down hard on the table, he replied, "I think not, madam. I never saw you before in my life."
4. "Imagine," he said, "that you are in a strange environment and surrounded by alien creatures. What thoughts go through your mind as you try to integrate yourself into this scene?" he went on.
5. She said to me, "He smirked, 'you're a loser,' and I was startled, to say the least."

### Test Yourself on Linking Independent Clauses with a Coordinating Conjunction (p. 203)

1. . . . Committee, and he . . .
2. . . . . car, for there was . . .

3. . . . type, but the paper . . .
4. . . . issue, and the President knew . . .
5. . . . Boston, or he could . . .

### Test Yourself on Linking Independent Clauses with a Semicolon and a Conjunctive Adverb (p. 204)

1. . . . write; therefore, she sat down . . .
2. . . . mass; consequently, they paint pictures . . .
3. . . . heritage; moreover, we have a whole tradition . . .
4. . . . points; thus the car was . . .
5. . . . July 25; therefore, on August 1, he began . . .

### Test Yourself on Recognizing and Correcting Run-On Sentences (p. 205)

1. . . . swim; there is no better exercise.
2. . . . on the 18th; therefore . . .
3. C
4. . . . a base hit, but the Yankees . . .
5. C

### Test Yourself on Proofreading to Catch Run-On Sentences (p. 206)

Hospitals can really be depressing. It's depressing seeing all those sick people in beds. Of course, some of them get well and go home with their families, but it's depressing knowing that some of them will die in those beds. It doesn't matter. Hospitals are still depressing places.

The white walls are gloomy. The beds are small and narrow. Some nurses are snobbish and make your stay impossible with their aloofness, but some of them are so nice you hate to leave. But doctors are so busy that they have no time for you personally, and they treat you like an experiment most of the time. As for the food, it too is depressing. It's supposed to make you healthy but it really makes you sick just to look at it; even the way it's prepared, the way it looks, causes that depressed feeling.

Some people enter the hospital with a minor illness, but by the time they have been there a few days, they have a major problem. Remember the movie *Hospital?* They had it right.

Of course, if you think your stay in the hospital is depressing, you should wait until you leave and get your bill. That's really depressing!

### Test Yourself on the Correct Use of the Semicolon (p. 208)

1. . . . lazy; therefore,
2. . . . bad; consequently,
3. . . . hotel; . . . trains;

4. . . . up; nevertheless,
5. . . . away; however

**Test Yourself on Revising Sentences of Monotonous Length (p. 211)**

A.

1. Because TV commercials annoyingly insult the intelligence and waste one's time, they should be banned from the airways.
2. President Regan, an actor in California and former governor of that state, has brought many business leaders to Washington.
3. Because she wanted to be a doctor, she studied chemistry and biology, putting in long hours in order to get good grades. Then when her senior year arrived, she applied to medical school and was accepted.
4. When the doctor came, he took my temperature, checked my heart and blood pressure, and prescribed some medicine. Then he said I'd probably recover in a few days.
5. Since I needed a job, I looked at want ads, went to employment agencies, and even visited a number of factories and offices. I got very tired, but I finally landed a job.

B.

1. As the train entered the station, I got ready to board, but when I found I'd left my bag in the checkroom, I ran back inside the waiting room to get it.
2. *Star Wars* was a very successful movie and broke many box office records, showing that science fiction adventure movies appeal greatly to the American public.
3. There are more than seven million American college students, most of whom believe that they need this education to get better jobs, but the job market is not encouraging for the hopes of these students, some of whom might do better in vocational training.
4. Dedicated members of the volunteer fire company, who give much of their time in public service, are not appreciated enough and often feel bitter because of this.
5. Soccer is the fastest growing sport in America, having as many as 70,000 fans turn out for a single game, but if Pelé hadn't given the sport a boost, things might not have turned out so well for soccer.

**Test Yourself on Achieving Sentence Variety (p. 213)**

1. Because the car had broken down the night before, they had to take the bus to school.
2. Holding a fundraiser at the Holiday Inn, the Republican Party attracted a surprising number of young people.
3. Because his grades were poor and his scholarship money almost gone, he knew he had to do something.

4. Working all night at the site of the cave-in, the rescue team was unable to stop for dinner.
5. When readers with lively imaginations read *The Hobbit,* they project themselves into its adventurous moments.

### Test Yourself on Correcting Shifts (p. 218)

1. People need to be praised when *they* work hard and accomplish *their* goals.
2. . . . argued . . . asked . . .
3. . . . went . . . asked; or . . . goes . . . asks . . .
4. . . . himself (not themselves)
5. My wife said she was thirsty and asked me to please get her a glass of water.

### Test Yourself on *ie* and *e* (p. 222)

1. friend   2. conceive   3. belief   4. achievement   5. experience

### Test Yourself on Final Silent *e* (p. 223)

1. moving   2. proving   3. movement   4. peaceable   5. changeable

### Test Yourself on Final *Y* (p. 224)

1. occupying   2. loneliness   3. annoying   4. plies   5. turkeys

### Test Yourself on Spelling Rules 1–4 (p. 227)

1. occasionally   2. Sheik   3. sensible
commitment   4. proceed   5. perceived

### Test Yourself on Catching Spelling Errors by Proofreading (p. 237)

1. stud*y*ing, activit*y*, le*i*sure, con*f*erences
2. calend*a*r, panic*k*ed, shop*p*ing, fee*l*ing, inte*l*ligent, begi*n*ning, paral*l*el

### Test Yourself on Limiting a Topic (p. 247)

A.
1. Clothing fashions (volumes) — Clothing Fashions in the U.S. (volumes) — Clothing Fashions in Connecticut (volumes) — Informal Clothing Fashions in Connecticut (still volumes) — Informal Clothing Fashions on Campus (20 pp.) — The Role of Blue Jeans on Campus (750 words)
2. Education — Education in the U.S. — Higher Education in the U.S. — Higher Education in My State — Education on My Campus — My Education on Campus — My Education in Biology — My Troubles at the Beginning of Biology 101 (750 words)
3. Television — Prime-Time Television — Comedy Series on Prime-Time Television — *All in the Family* — The Character of Archie Bunker on *All in the Family* — What Archie Bunker Hates Most (750 words)

4. Student self-government — Student Self-Government in Colleges in the U.S. — Student Self-Government in My School — The Student Senate at My School — The Duties of the Student Senator at My School (750 words)

5. Urban decay — Urban Decay in Chicago — Urban Decay on the South Side of Chicago — Why My Family Left the City (the South Side of Chicago) (750 words)

B.

3. The Prospects of the Boston Celtics in NBA Basketball This Year

4. A Day on Vacation at Fort Lauderdale

5. Testing the Quality of Water from Your Kitchen Tap

8. Saving Energy with an Automatic Light Switch

9. Fizz, Fizz, Plop, Plop: How the Alka-Seltzer Commercial Makes Its Pitch

### Test Yourself on Subject-Verb Agreement (p. 248)

A.

1. Guns are his main interest.

2. My only hobby is rock and roll records.

3. Dollars are our greatest need.

4. The cause of his breakdown was many days of nonstop studying.

5. The cause of his drunkenness was too many drinks on an empty stomach.

B.

1. He amuses himself when he has no toys to play with.

2. These turn me off.

3. They seem to like being fed by the children.

4. Those force the argument in another direction.

5. It happens a lot more often than you think.

### Test Yourself on Subject-Verb Agreement with Compound Subjects and *either/or, neither/nor* Subjects (p. 250)

1. *father* or *mother* (singular); *are* (plural), should be changed to *is*.

2. C

3. *Professional* and *rich man* (plural subject); *decides* (singular verb) should be changed to *decide*.

4. *Coffee and donuts* (plural subject); *is* (singular verb) should be changed to *are*.

5. Were the sofa and chair on sale?

### Test Yourself on Subject-Verb Agreement with Collective Nouns as Subjects (p. 252)

Following are the correct verbs.

1. decides   2. renders   3. is   4. are   5. votes

**Test Yourself on Choosing the Correct Verb for Subjects Modified by Phrases and Clauses (p. 253)**
Following are the correct verbs.
1. looks   2. want   3. is   4. lies   5. punches

**Test Yourself on Subject-Verb Agreement in Special Cases (p. 256)**
1. is   2. involves   3. were   4. requires   5. depresses

**Test Yourself on Proofreading to Catch Subject-Verb Agreement Errors (p. 256)**
1. . . . There *are* . . . Rising up from the tables at cafes *is* . . . One of those who *sing* . . . Neither Lazare nor I *am* . . . Lazare *thinks*
2. . . . mother or my father is . . . living . . . *has* . . . music . . . *is* . . . economics . . . *is* . . . sisters *understand*

**Test Yourself on Subordination (p. 259)**
A.
1. Marylea has a lovely, blue cotton shirt which she likes to take to the beach and walk around in.
2. The television set I paid four hundred dollars for is broken again. Whenever it happens, I get furious.
3. Air pollution is a problem that affects us all, whether we live in the city or the country.
4. It was raining in Cleveland when we left, but when we arrived in Chicago, that city surprised us with its sunlit beauty.
5. My English friend's name is Chris. Although he loves the United States, he occasionally longs to return to London.
B.
1. While my hair is drying, I'll read a book.
2. When I eat too much pastry, I gain a lot of weight.
3. A whole set of encyclopedias came in the mail, although I didn't order them.
4. Whenever you see a rainbow across the meadow, you know there's been a recent rainstorm.
5. Although Jerry was unpacking, Noella was cooking supper.

**Test Yourself on Recognizing an Appropriate Thesis Statement (p. 263)**
1. Effective.
2. Effective.
3. This one might be effective, but the writer would need to launch immediately into a definition of "stylish" and follow up with very striking details of Aunt Rose's dress. The problem with the statement is the vagueness of the phrase "stylish dresser."

4. Not effective. Too general. Should be limited by making more precise the audience it describes as "punks."
5. Effective.

## Test Yourself on Making Effective Transitions (p. 266)

1. He had given Tom a handsome wedding gift; moreover, he had offered him a well-paying job with the firm.
2. He stood in a small ravine; close by was a running brook.
3. Although the country is running out of oil and our coal supply is low, research and development for new energy sources are at a standstill.
4. He received a receipt for his tuition; consequently, he was able to register.
5. She wanted to go to the seashore. On the other hand, he preferred the mountains.

## Test Yourself on Identifying Topic Sentences (p. 269)

1. The first sentence.
2. Implied: a description of preparing a prisoner to be hanged.
3. The first sentence.
4. The first sentence.
5. The first sentence.

## Test Yourself on Achieving Unity in Paragraphs (p. 271)

A. Basketball is a game requiring great physical skills and coordination. Players must be able to run backward as well as forward. They must have good peripheral vision in order to see their teammates and their opponents. In order to leap for the ball off the backboards, players must have excellent timing. Timing is also important in passing and shooting — the exact moment counts in basketball. The speed at which the game is played necessitates the players acquiring these skills.

## Test Yourself on Forming Tenses (p. 277)

1. arisen, to sing
2. drank, chose, lay
3. brought, brought, shaken
4. laid, taken, lent
5. spun, shone

## Test Yourself on Forming Principal Parts (p. 279)

1. keep, keeping
2. lost, losing, lost
3. play, playing, played
4. told, telling
5. pursued, pursuing, pursued

### Test Yourself on Forming Tenses (p. 280)
1. played, grown
2. giving, prepared
3. run, operated, driven
4. happened
5. punish

### Test Yourself on the Correct Use of Tenses (p. 284)
1. will lose
2. will have been
3. entered, had rearranged
4. have learned
5. had bitten

### Test Yourself on the Final -*d* Sound (p. 285)
B.

    Something was needed to cheer me up. I was tir<u>ed</u> and hadn't been to bed in two days. I thought I would never be rescu<u>ed</u> and I was worried that even my best friends would not have notic<u>ed</u> me gone. My foot hurt a lot from when I had slipped down the side of the gully, and I would have given anything for a little sip of water.

    A bird start<u>ed</u> to chirp. I wish<u>ed</u> I were as happy as he was. I wish<u>ed</u> I had his wings!

    The accident must have happen<u>ed</u> because I wasn't as young as I us<u>ed</u> to be. Still, I was only 23! Are people suppos<u>ed</u> to lose all their agility after the age of nineteen? It all weighed on my heart. Suddenly, I notic<u>ed</u> that the sky was getting very dark. If anybody look<u>ed</u> for me now, they would have a hard time seeing me. I tri<u>ed</u> to move a little, to see if I could climb to the crest of the hill and make myself more visible. But it was no use. I wish<u>ed</u> I had climbed up there earlier, when I had more strength.

### Test Yourself on Sequence of Tenses (p. 287)
1. has diminished
2. having finished
3. to go
4. to publish
5. had neglected

### Test Yourself on the Correct Use of Verb Forms (p. 290)

A.

1. If he had gone earlier, he would have seen the pregame show.
2. Because it had the best psychology program she could find, she went to Jefferson College.
3. I could have been a star.
4. She wasn't as alert as she should have been.
5. If he had gone earlier, he would have seen the pregame show.

B.

1. be  2. were  3. be  4. suffer  5. be


### Test Yourself on the Appropriate Use of the Active Voice (p. 292)

A.

1. The book bored me.
2. Dr. Waldhorn's patients respected him. *Or* His patients respected Dr. Waldhorn.
3. Joe's dog annoyed everyone on my block.
4. Most people admire the rich and the famous.
5. Disrespect angers the police.

B.

1. My mother thinks I'm too young to drive.
2. C — if the writer is focusing on the Canadians
3. God gave us freedom.
4. My brother gave me the ring for Christmas.
5. More and more people in this country watch television.


### Test Yourself on Eliminating Redundancies (p. 295)

1. John is an expert in urban government.
2. Professor Buckley referred to the Civil War.
3. Yesterday's snow is melting today.
4. At 9 a.m., the driver started toward Cincinnati.
5. As soon as he started to look for a job, he connected with a large corporation.


### Test Yourself on Eliminating Wordiness (p. 297)

1. My speech will interest students and professional educators.
2. Be quiet in the library.
3. Whenever he's in trouble, he rationalizes.
4. I'd like to take you to a special beach.
5. To be chronically sick is terrible.

**Test Yourself on Identifying or Narrowing a Suitable Topic (p. 305)**

1. This is not suitable because it can be written from a single source. Narrowing won't help much either.
2. Much too large for a student-sized research paper. Can be narrowed to something like "Effects of the Energy Crisis on Enid, Oklahoma." Or, alternately, "The Gasoline Shortage in Skokie, Illinois, 1976."
3. This is a suitable topic. Lincoln's military service was brief and a number of interesting sources can be consulted for details.
4. A good topic for direct investigation. Requires on-site research.
5. Another one like 4. Its suitability depends on the student's neighborhood not being central Chicago or east Los Angeles.

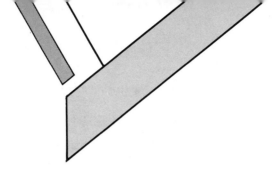

# Index